CompTIA® Network+® N10-009 Certification Guide

First Edition

Master networking fundamentals and pass the N10-009 exam the first time

Ian Neil

CompTIA® Network+® N10-009 Certification Guide
First Edition

Portfolio Director: Kartikey Pandey

Relationship Leads: Vijin Boricha and Deepak Kumar

Program Manager: Ankita Thakur

Project Manager: Gandhali Raut

Development Editor: Alex Mazonowicz

Technical Editor: Nithik Cheruvakodan

Copy Editor: Safis Editing

Indexer: Manju Arasan

Production Designer: Alishon Falcon

First published: October 2025

Production reference: 1081025

Published by Packt Publishing Ltd.

Grosvenor House

11 St Paul's Square

Birmingham

B3 1RB, UK.

ISBN 978-1-83664-927-4

www.packtpub.com

Contributors

About the author

Ian Neil is one of the world's top trainers of Network+. He is able to break down information into manageable chunks so that people with no background knowledge can gain the skills required to become certified. He has recently worked for the US Army in Europe and designed courses that catered to people from all backgrounds (not just IT professionals), with an extremely successful pass rate. He is an MCT, MCSE, A+, Network+, Security+, CASP, and RESILIA practitioner that has worked with high-end training providers over the past 24 years and was one of the first technical trainers to train Microsoft internal staff when they opened their Bucharest Office in 2006.

About the reviewer

Based in the West Country, UK, **Mark Nathan** is a CompTIA Certified Technical Trainer (CTT+), a Microsoft Certified Trainer (MCT), and a former Certified NetWare Instructor (CNI). He has more than 30 years of experience in IT administration, networking, and security. Mark has worked extensively with Microsoft Windows, from the early version 1.1, through NT 3 and 4, XP, and up to modern-day Windows 11 and Windows Server 2025. He also instructs on and supports Microsoft Azure.

Mark is the owner of MarkIT-Training delivering training in the above-mentioned areas. Outside of working, Mark enjoys cycling, walking coastal paths, and when relaxing, a glass of red wine.

Table of Contents

3

Summarize Cloud Concepts and Connectivity Options   45

4

Explain Common Networking Ports, Protocols, Services, and Traffic Types   57

8

Summarize Evolving Use Cases for Modern Network Environments 133

Domain 2 - Network Implementation

9

Explain Characteristics of Routing Technologies   159

10

Given a Scenario, Configure Switching Technologies and Features   177

11

Given a Scenario, Select and Configure Wireless Devices and Technologies   197

12

Domain 3 - Network Operations

13

14

15

Explain Disaster Recovery Concepts   277

16

Given a Scenario, Implement IPv4 and IPv6 Network Services   285

17

Compare and Contrast Network Access and Management Methods 311

Domain 4 - Network Security

18

Explain the Importance of Basic Network Security Concepts   325

19

Summarize Various Types of Attacks and Their Impact on the Network   355

20

Given a Scenario, Apply Network Security Features, Defense Techniques, and Solutions 369

Domain 5 - Network Troubleshooting

21

Explain the Troubleshooting Methodology 385

22

Given a Scenario, Troubleshoot Common Cabling and Physical Interface Issues 399

23

Given a Scenario, Troubleshoot Common Issues with Network Services 415

24

Given a Scenario, Troubleshoot Common Performance Issues   431

25

Given a Scenario, Use the Appropriate Tool or Protocol to Solve Networking Issues   445

Preface

The CompTIA Network+ (N10-009) certification validates the essential skills required to design, implement, manage, and troubleshoot wired and wireless networks in modern IT environments. This study guide is designed to equip networking professionals with the knowledge to establish reliable connectivity, configure and secure critical infrastructure, and support resilient operations across physical, virtual, and cloud-based networks. It addresses the application of core networking principles in enterprise and small-to-medium business contexts, while emphasizing the practical integration of routing, switching, wireless technologies, and network services. Throughout, the guide reinforces the importance of documentation, monitoring, troubleshooting methodologies, and security hardening techniques as foundational elements of network administration.

The CompTIA Network+ exam (N10-009) is an update to the previous N10-008 version, reflecting today's evolving networking landscape. The revised objectives place greater emphasis on cloud connectivity, virtualization, zero-trust architecture, and the expanding role of automation and security in modern infrastructures. The updated domain weighting for the exam is shown in the following table:

Domain	Percentage of examination
1.0 Networking Concepts	23%
2.0 Network Implementation	20%
3.0 Network Operations	19%
4.0 Network Security	14%
5.0 Network Troubleshooting	24%
Total	100%

This updated version of the CompTIA Network+ certification exam emphasizes evolving network environments, including software-defined networking, cloud connectivity, and zero-trust architectures, alongside traditional networking skills. It expands coverage of troubleshooting methodologies, modern network services, and security best practices for both physical and virtual infrastructures.

To help you best organize your study, this book has been structured to closely follow the CompTIA Network+ domains, objectives, and concepts. The book is divided into five sections—one for each domain—and each section is split into chapters that align with the official exam outline. Each chapter has been designed to follow the concepts in each objective, ensuring that your preparation maps directly to the skills assessed in the exam.

In addition, you will find multiple-choice practice questions and mock exams to help test your knowledge and get realistic preparation for taking the exam.

Who this book is for

This book is intended for early-career IT professionals preparing for the CompTIA Network+ (N10-009) certification, particularly those working as network administrators, help desk technicians, or junior systems engineers. It is especially valuable for those looking to validate their ability to design, implement, and troubleshoot wired and wireless networks, secure network infrastructures, and support modern cloud and virtualization environments.

Candidates are expected to have 9–12 months of hands-on networking experience and a solid understanding of basic IT concepts, though this guide could also be useful for students and career changers who want to build their foundational networking skills. This book will also benefit professionals preparing for further certifications, such as CompTIA Security+ or vendor-specific networking tracks.

What this book covers

Chapter 1, Explain Concepts Related to the OSI Model, introduces the seven layers of the OSI model and explains how each supports network communication and troubleshooting.

Chapter 2, Compare and Contrast Networking Appliances, Applications, and Functions, covers the roles of routers, switches, firewalls, IDS/IPS, load balancers, proxies, and virtual appliances, along with VPNs, CDNs, and QoS.

Chapter 3, Summarize Cloud Concepts and Connectivity Options, explores service and deployment models, gateways, VPNs, and Direct Connect options for integrating the cloud securely and efficiently.

Chapter 4, Explain Common Networking Ports, Protocols, Services, and Traffic Types, reviews well-known ports, protocols such as TCP, UDP, ICMP, and IPSec, and traffic types including unicast, multicast, broadcast, and anycast.

Chapter 5, Compare and Contrast Transmission Media and Transceivers, examines copper and fiber cabling, wireless standards, connector types, and common transceiver form factors.

Chapter 6, Compare and Contrast Network Topologies, Architectures, and Types, describes mesh, star, spine-and-leaf, and three-tier designs, along with IPv4 addressing, subnetting, and private/public IP concepts.

Chapter 7, Given a Scenario, Use Appropriate IPv4 Addressing, explains subnetting, CIDR, VLSM, and address class usage to design and configure IPv4 networks.

Chapter 8, Summarize Evolving Use Cases for Modern Network Environments, introduces SDN, SD-WAN, VXLAN, zero-trust architecture, SASE, and IPv6 adoption in modern infrastructures.

Chapter 9, Explain Characteristics of Routing Technologies, covers static and dynamic routing protocols, route selection, NAT, PAT, subinterfaces, and redundancy protocols.

Chapter 10, Given a Scenario, Configure Switching Technologies and Features, explains VLANs, trunking, link aggregation, spanning tree, MTU configuration, and switch interface options.

Chapter 11, Given a Scenario, Select and Configure Wireless Devices and Technologies, explores SSIDs, channels, antenna types, authentication, encryption, guest networks, and AP deployment models.

Chapter 12, Explain Important Factors of Physical Installations, highlights IDF/MDF placement, rack design, cabling, power requirements, UPS, PDUs, and environmental considerations.

Chapter 13, Explain the Purpose of Organizational Processes and Procedures, introduces documentation, change management, configuration baselines, lifecycle management, and service-level agreements.

Chapter 14, Given a Scenario, Use Network Monitoring Technologies, reviews SNMP, flow data, packet captures, logs, SIEM, APIs, port mirroring, and monitoring solutions.

Chapter 15, Explain Disaster Recovery Concepts, covers RPO, RTO, MTTR, DR sites, high-availability designs, and testing approaches such as tabletop exercises.

Chapter 16, Given a Scenario, Implement IPv4 and IPv6 Network Services, explains DHCP, DNS, NTP, VPNs, and name resolution methods for both IPv4 and IPv6.

Chapter 17, Compare and Contrast Network Access and Management Methods, examines SSH, GUI, API, in-band/out-of-band management, and jumpbox configurations.

Chapter 18, Explain the Importance of Basic Network Security Concepts, introduces encryption, PKI, IAM, MFA, role-based access, compliance requirements, and segmentation.

Chapter 19, Summarize Various Types of Attacks and Their Impact, covers DoS/DDoS, VLAN hopping, ARP spoofing, DNS poisoning, rogue devices, evil twins, malware, and social engineering.

Chapter 20, Given a Scenario, Apply Network Security Features, Defense Techniques, and Solutions, explains device hardening, NAC, ACLs, filtering, and security zoning.

Chapter 21, Explain the Troubleshooting Methodology, presents a structured process for identifying problems, testing theories, implementing solutions, and documenting outcomes.

Chapter 22, Given a Scenario, Troubleshoot Common Cabling and Physical Interface Issues, covers incorrect cabling, termination errors, crosstalk, attenuation, TX/RX issues, and interface counters.

Chapter 23, Given a Scenario, Troubleshoot Common Issues with Network Services, addresses DHCP scope issues, DNS misconfigurations, incorrect gateways, and IP conflicts.

Chapter 24, Given a Scenario, Troubleshoot Common Performance Issues, explains bottlenecks, latency, jitter, packet loss, wireless interference, and roaming misconfiguration.

Chapter 25, Given a Scenario, Use the Appropriate Tool or Protocol to Solve Networking Issues, introduces analyzers, CLI tools, discovery protocols, speed testers, Wi-Fi analyzers, and show commands.

Online practice resources

With this book, you will unlock unlimited access to our online exam-prep platform (*Figure 0.1*). This is your place to practice everything you learn in the book.

How to access the resources

To learn how to access the online resources, refer to *Chapter 26, Accessing the Online Practice Resources*, at the end of this book.

To get the most out of this book

CompTIA® Network+® N10-009 Certification Guide covers all the domains, exam objective and concepts from the N10-009 exam in order. Each chapter mirrors the objectives set by CompTIA exactly. At the end of each chapter is a link to practice questions to test your knowledge and understanding. The online platform also provides mock exams for practice and preparation.

Color images for this book are available on the books GitHub repository: `https://packt.link/aLt82`

Conventions used

There are a number of text conventions used throughout this book.

`CodeInText`: Indicates code words in text, database table names, folder names, filenames, file extensions, pathnames, dummy URLs, user input, and X handles. For example: " The loopback address `127.0.0.1` is used for diagnostic testing and to verify that TCP/IP has been initialized."

A block of code is set as follows:

```bash
configure terminal

# Create a port-channel interface and assign ID
interface Port-channel1

# Specify the mode as active
channel-group 1 mode active

# Set the desired properties for the port-channel
switchport mode trunk
switchport trunk native vlan 10
```

Any command-line input or output is written as follows:

```
C:\Windows\System32>ping www.bbc.co.uk
Pinging bbc.map.fastly.net [146.75.116.81] with 32 bytes of data:
Reply from 146.75.116.81: bytes=32 time=89ms TTL=58
Reply from 146.75.116.81: bytes=32 time=89ms TTL=58
Reply from 146.75.116.81: bytes=32 time=89ms TTL=58
Reply from 146.75.116.81: bytes=32 time=89ms TTL=58
```

Bold: Indicates a new term, an important word, or words that you see on the screen. For instance, words in menus or dialog boxes appear in the text like this. For example: " To manage and automate the process of link aggregation, many systems engineers often use **Link Aggregation Control Protocol (LACP)**."

Warnings or important notes appear like this.

Tips and tricks appear like this.

Get in touch

Feedback from our readers is always welcome.

General feedback: If you have questions about any aspect of this book or have any general feedback, please email us at customercare@packt.com and mention the book's title in the subject of your message.

Errata: Although we have taken every care to ensure the accuracy of our content, mistakes do happen. If you have found a mistake in this book, we would be grateful if you reported this to us. Please visit http://www.packt.com/submit-errata, click **Submit Errata**, and fill in the form. We ensure that all valid errata are promptly updated in the GitHub repository at https://github.com/PacktPublishing/CompTIA-Network-N10-009-Certification-Guide.

Piracy: If you come across any illegal copies of our works in any form on the internet, we would be grateful if you would provide us with the location address or website name. Please contact us at copyright@packt.com with a link to the material.

If you are interested in becoming an author: If there is a topic that you have expertise in and you are interested in either writing or contributing to a book, please visit http://authors.packt.com/.

Share your thoughts

Once you've read *CompTIA® Network+® N10-009 Certification Guide*, we'd love to hear your thoughts! Scan the QR code below to go straight to the Amazon review page for this book and share your feedback.

https://packt.link/r/1836649274

Your review is important to us and the tech community and will help us make sure we're delivering excellent quality content.

Domain 1

Networking Concepts

This first part of the book establishes the foundational principles of networking. It covers the OSI model, common appliances and applications, cloud service models, ports and protocols, transmission media, network topologies, and IPv4 addressing. The domain also introduces modern use cases such as SDN, SD-WAN, zero-trust architectures, and IPv6 adoption, giving candidates the grounding to understand how networks are designed and how they function in both traditional and evolving environments.

This part of the book includes the following chapters:

- *Chapter 1, Explain Concepts Related to the Open Systems Interconnection (OSI) Reference Model*
- *Chapter 2, Compare and Contrast Networking Appliances, Applications, and Functions*
- *Chapter 3, Summarize Cloud Concepts and Connectivity Options*
- *Chapter 4, Explain Common Networking Ports, Protocols, Services, and Traffic Types*
- *Chapter 5, Compare and Contrast Transmission Media and Transceivers*
- *Chapter 6, Compare and Contrast Network Topologies, Architectures, and Types*
- *Chapter 7, Given a Scenario, Use Appropriate IPv4 Network Addressing*
- *Chapter 8, Summarize Evolving Use Cases for Modern Network Environments*

1

Explain Concepts Related to the Open System Interconnection (OSI) Reference Model

As of 2025, 5.56 billion people worldwide use the internet regularly, meaning that more than two-thirds of the global population is connected to a computer network in one way or another. In the information age, everything from phones to servers, lightbulbs to cameras, and laptops to cars is intertwined through cables and radio waves.

Although the growth of global communication has been largely organic, building a modern network that is stable, secure, and efficient requires careful planning, regular maintenance, and expert troubleshooting. Today's IT networks come in many forms and are constantly evolving. To be an effective network engineer, you need the skills and knowledge to analyze, manage, and operate an almost infinite variety of network setups.

The *CompTIA Network+* exam is designed to validate those skills and that knowledge. Earning this certification gives prospective clients and employers confidence that you can navigate the complexity of modern network engineering. It will also give you the confidence that you have the tools to progress in a vital, rewarding career.

This book covers everything you need to know to become *CompTIA Network+* certified. Over the following chapters, you will learn about the core concepts, implementation strategies, operational practices, security essentials, and troubleshooting methodologies necessary for success in the exam.

However, before diving into the details of network functions, components, risks, and solutions, it's important to first understand what a network actually is. The **Open Systems Interconnection (OSI)** reference model provides a conceptual framework for understanding and standardizing the functions of a network. Rather than focusing on cables and hardware, the OSI model takes an abstract, layered approach that applies to all networks, regardless of their internal structure or underlying technologies. Developed by the **International Organization for Standardization (ISO)**, the OSI model establishes a common language for describing and designing networks.

This chapter covers the first objective in *Domain 1: 1.1 Explain concepts related to the Open System Interconnection (OSI) reference model.*

> **Note**
>
> A full breakdown of objective 1.1 will be given at the end of the chapter.

What is the OSI model?

Modern IT networks can range from a small setup with just a few computers sharing a printer to vast infrastructures spanning multiple offices, continents, and cloud resources. No matter the size, architecture, or geographical spread, the job of the network engineer is to keep information flowing through that network reliably, efficiently, and securely. To do this, there is a range of physical and virtual appliances, protocols, techniques, and standards. The following chapters will cover these, but before doing so, it's worth looking at what a network is conceptually.

When you think of a network, you can break it down into its individual components, such as a router or a **virtual private network (VPN)**. You can also consider it in terms of different functions, such as data routing, user interaction, or a mobile device connecting wirelessly. Often, when troubleshooting a problem, you won't start by identifying which piece of equipment has failed but rather by understanding how something isn't working. A user is more likely to complain that they can't access certain resources than to say that a routing table needs to be updated.

So, what does thinking about a network in terms of functions mean? This is where the OSI model comes in. The OSI model divides the process of network communication into seven distinct layers, with layer 1 being the physical layer, and layer 7 being the application layer. Each layer is dependent on the layer beneath it and serves the layer above, and each has its own specific functions and protocols. These layers, from top to bottom, are shown in *Table 1.1*.

Layer	Title	Function	Protocol/Devices
7	Application	Provides user access to network services. Examples include web browsers and email clients.	HTTP, HTTPS, **Domain Name System (DNS)**, **Simple Mail Transfer Protocol (SMTP)**, **File Transfer Protocol (FTP)**, **Post Office Protocol version 3 (POP3)**, **Internet Message Access Protocol (IMAP)**, Telnet, **Secure Shell (SSH)**, **Secure Sockets Layer (SSL)/Transport Layer Security (TLS)**, **web application firewalls (WAFs)**, **intrusion prevention systems (IPSs)**, and sophisticated load balancers.
6	Presentation	Ensures that data is in a usable format and is where data encryption occurs.	ASCII, Unicode, SSL/TLS.
5	Session	Manages sessions between applications. Establishes, manages, and terminates connections between local and remote applications.	Logging in and creating a session, and logging out to terminate the session. Establishes connections.
4	Transport	End-to-end error communication, recovery, and flow control. Protocols such as TCP and UDP operate at this layer.	Datagrams: basic load balancers, transport layer firewall (also known as a Layer 4 firewall).
3	Network	Addressing and routing of data. Manages packet forwarding, including routing through intermediate routers.	Packets and IP addresses – routers, firewalls, packet filtering.

| 2 | Data Link | Manages the reliable transmission of data frames over a physical medium, ensuring error-free communication between directly connected devices. | Frames, **media access control (MAC)** addresses – switch and bridge. Defines the format of the data on the network. |
| 1 | Physical | Connects devices using cables, wireless communication, hubs, and repeaters. | Bits: hubs and repeaters

Cables: coax, Ethernet, fiber, Wi-Fi, and Bluetooth |

Table 1.1: The OSI layers, functions, protocols, and devices.

Table 1.1 gives an overview of what each of the layers does. Understanding the order and function of the layers is important for the exam. One way of learning the model is with the mnemonic shown in *Figure 1.1*.

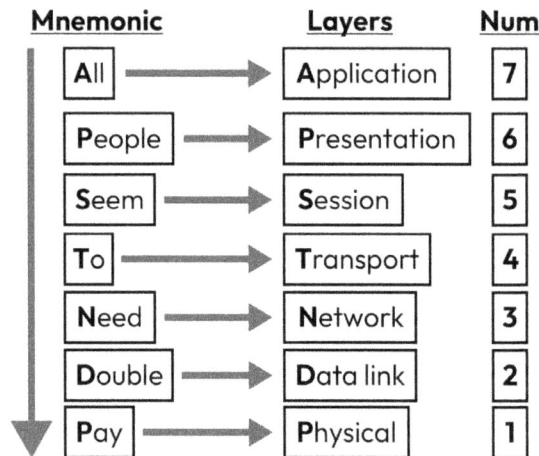

Mnemonic	Layers	Num
All	→ Application	7
People	→ Presentation	6
Seem	→ Session	5
To	→ Transport	4
Need	→ Network	3
Double	→ Data link	2
Pay	→ Physical	1

Figure 1.1: A mnemonic for the functions of the seven layers of the OSI model

Note

When you prepare for the exam, you must know the function and the order of the layers. The mnemonic in *Figure 1.1* can help you.

The following section will go into each layer in more detail.

Layer 1: Physical layer

The devices that operate at the **physical layer** are hubs, repeaters, and network cables. These cables can be Ethernet cables made out of copper, which transmit electrical signals, or fiber-optic cables, which transmit light pulses. The quality and type of cable determine how far and fast data can travel. Wireless also operates at this layer. Electronic devices that can connect to a **local area network (LAN)** using an Ethernet cable are known as **Ethernet devices**.

A **hub** is a basic networking device that connects multiple computers or other network devices together. When a hub receives data from one device, it broadcasts it to all other connected devices. However, hubs do not distinguish between different devices, as seen in *Figure 1.2*, meaning all data is sent to all devices, regardless of the intended recipient. This can cause network congestion and inefficiency.

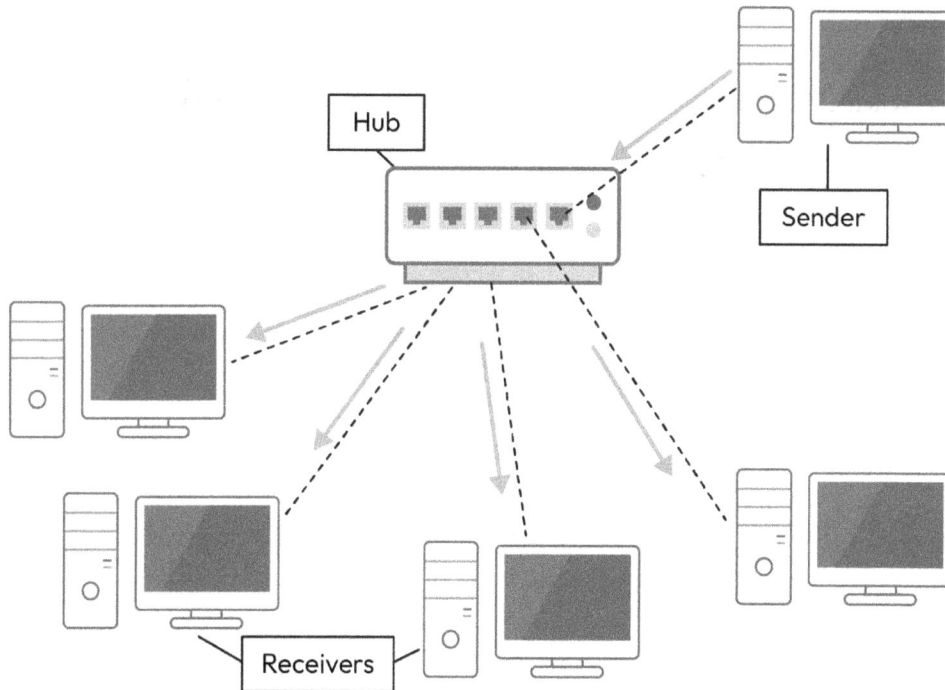

Figure 1.2: A hub transmitting data to all hosts

Repeaters are devices that extend the range of a network by amplifying the signal. As data travels through a cable, it can degrade over distance. A repeater takes the weak signal, regenerates it, and sends it out again, allowing the signal to travel further without losing integrity. This is shown in *Figure 1.3*.

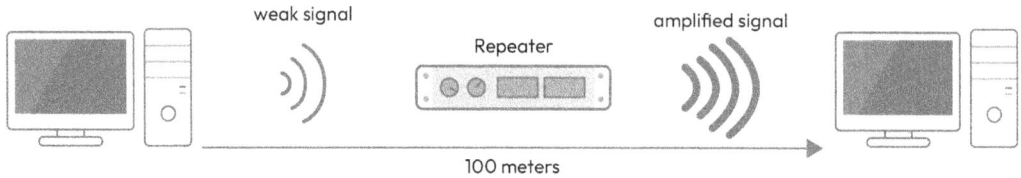

Figure 1.3: A weak signal being regenerated at full strength by a repeater

Layer 2: Data link layer

The **data link layer** is responsible for node-to-node data transfer and error detection. Devices that work at this layer are called switches and bridges; these are described shortly. Data is organized into frames, which include the MAC address of the source and destination, along with the data and an error-checking code, known as a **cyclic redundancy check (CRC)**.

A **switch** (as shown in Figure 1.4) is a more intelligent device than a hub. It connects multiple devices within a network and learns MAC addresses to determine the destination of each data frame. When a switch receives a frame, it reads the destination MAC address and forwards the frame only to the appropriate port, reducing unnecessary traffic on the network. This makes switches more efficient and secure than hubs.

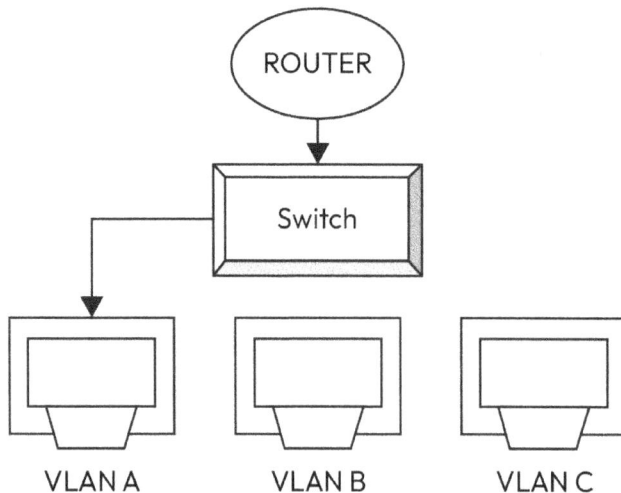

Figure 1.4: A switch sending a packet directly to one host rather than all hosts

Bridges connect two or more network segments, allowing them to function as a single network. Like switches, bridges operate using MAC addresses to filter and forward frames. They reduce traffic by dividing the network into segments, ensuring that data meant for one segment doesn't congest another.

Network interface cards (NICs) are hardware components installed in computers and other network devices. They provide physical connections to the network and convert data from the device into a format that can be transmitted over the network. NICs have a unique MAC address that identifies the device on the network. They handle both Layer 1 (physical) and Layer 2 (data link) operations by managing the physical sending and receiving of data and packaging it into frames.

Layer 3: Network layer

The **network layer** is responsible for routing data between different networks, and this is what a router does. It decides the best path to deliver the data from the source to the destination across multiple networks, such as the internet. At this layer, data is organized into packets that include the IP addresses (logical addresses) of both the source and destination, as well as other routing information. The network layer also handles IP addressing and dividing networks into smaller parts called **subnets**.

A **router** is a device that forwards these data packets between different networks by analyzing the destination IP address. It determines the most efficient route for the data to take by consulting **routing tables**, which contain information about possible paths. For instance, a router connects a home network to the internet, allowing devices at home to access online resources.

A Layer 3 switch is a device that combines the features of a regular network switch with the ability to perform routing. Like a regular switch, it connects devices within the same local network and forwards data based on MAC addresses, but it also has the ability to route data between different parts of the network, such as **virtual local area networks** (VLANs) or subnets, using IP addresses. Layer 3 switches are typically used in large networks where there's a need for both fast data switching within a local network and routing between different segments of that network, all in one device. They're ideal for managing internal traffic in big organizations or data centers.

Stateful firewalls also operate at Layer 3 and Layer 4, and they keep track of the state of active connections using a state table that logs IP addresses, ports, and **Transmission Control Protocol** (**TCP**) flags such as SYN (**synchronize**) and ACK (**acknowledgment**). In contrast, a Layer 7 firewall, such as a WAF, inspects traffic at the application level, analyzing the actual data in packets to detect threats such as malware, SQL injection, or blocked applications.

Layer 4: Transport layer

The **transport layer** handles error correction and data flow control, and can provide end-to-end communication. It ensures reliable data transfer between devices and uses TCP, which is connection-oriented, or **User Datagram Protocol** (UDP), which is connectionless. It divides data into smaller chunks called segments and ensures they are reassembled correctly at the destination. While not hardware-specific, transport layer functions are often handled by software in computers and networking devices such as firewalls. Data is organized into segments (TCP) or datagrams (UDP), which include port numbers for identifying specific applications and sequence numbers for ordering data.

TCP is one of the core protocols of the IP suite. It is designed to provide reliable, ordered, and error-checked delivery of data between applications running on hosts communicating over an IP network. TCP is called *connection-oriented* because it establishes a connection between the sender and receiver before any data is transmitted. This is often referred to as a **handshake**, or more specifically, a **three-way handshake**, where both sides agree to the connection parameters. This is shown in Figure 1.5.

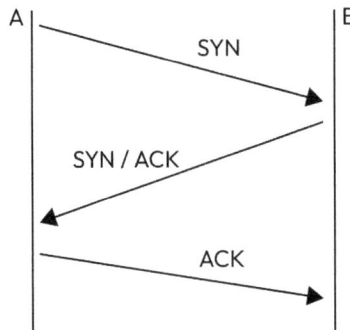

*Figure 1.5: A **TCP** three-way handshake*

TCP includes mechanisms to detect errors in data transmission. If errors are detected, the data is retransmitted. **TCP** also manages the rate of data transmission between sender and receiving devices to prevent overloading the network or the receiving device. It also adjusts the rate of data transmission based on network traffic to prevent congestion on the network.

UDP is a connectionless protocol. Unlike **TCP**, it does not establish a connection before sending data, and it does not guarantee reliable or ordered delivery. It simply sends packets called **datagrams** to the receiver, without checking whether they arrive or are in order. UDP is used for streaming video and gaming, where speed is of the essence. If you were to play *Call of Duty* using a **TCP** session, you would be dead before you could pull your gun out!

Firewalls are security devices that monitor and control incoming and outgoing network traffic based on the implemented rules. Operating at Layer 4, they examine data segments, using information such as IP addresses and port numbers to allow or block traffic. Firewalls can be hardware-based or software-based and are crucial for protecting networks from unauthorized access and various types of cyber threats. They can filter traffic at different layers, but they primarily operate at the transport layer when filtering by port numbers.

Layer 5: Session layer

The **session layer** is responsible for establishing, managing, and terminating sessions between two communicating devices. A **session** is essentially a connection for an ongoing exchange of data between two systems. Once a session is established between two devices, this layer maintains the session and ensures that it stays active for as long as needed and handles things such as synchronizing data streams and managing the exchange of information. It can also implement **checkpointing**, which allows the session to resume from a certain point if there is an interruption.

The **session layer** also deals with **session synchronization**, which involves keeping the **data exchange** in the correct order and ensuring that the data is consistent across both ends of the session. If part of the **data transmission** is interrupted or lost, the **session layer** can synchronize the **session** and resume transmission from a specific point. **Checkpoints** are used as part of this process, allowing the session to roll back to the last **checkpoint** if an error occurs.

When the communication is complete, the **session layer** gracefully terminates the **session**. This ensures that all data has been properly transmitted and that the resources allocated for the session are released. The termination process also involves closing any open **sessions**, logging the activity, and ensuring that no data is lost during the termination.

Several protocols operate at the **session layer**, each serving specific purposes in managing **sessions**. Some examples are as follows:

Network Basic Input/Output System (NetBIOS): This provides session layer services in networks using the **Server Message Block (SMB)** protocol.

Layer 6: Presentation layer

The **presentation layer** translates data between the application layer and the lower layers. It is responsible for **data encryption/decryption**, compression, and format translation, for example, converting data from a specific format, such as JPEG. It doesn't deal with packets directly but may modify the data within them, for example, in the process of encrypting and decrypting.

Layer 7: Application layer

The **application layer** is the closest layer to the end user. It relies on the other layers for packet delivery. As data travels down through the OSI layers, **headers** are added. When the data gets to its final destination, these headers are removed as it then moves up through the layers. The **application layer** handles protocols such as **HTTP**, **FTP**, and **SMTP**. Applications such as **stateful firewalls** and **IPSs** operate at this layer. **Layer 7** provides network services directly to applications such as web browsers, email clients, and file transfer programs.

WAFs also operate at this layer, protecting web applications by filtering and monitoring **HTTP/HTTPS requests**. They inspect the content of requests and responses to detect and block attacks such as **SQL injections, cross-site scripting (XSS)**, and other web-based threats. Unlike regular **firewalls** that focus on **ports** and **protocols**, **WAFs** analyze the data in web requests, looking for malicious patterns in the payloads themselves.

While **IPS** devices can operate at multiple layers, they often function at **Layer 7** to detect and block sophisticated attacks that may exploit vulnerabilities in applications. The **IPS** scans traffic in real time, analyzing packets for known attack signatures, anomalies, or policy violations, and can block or reject traffic that appears malicious.

Why do we use the OSI model?

The OSI model is used for several key reasons. By providing a standardized framework, the model allows different types of network hardware and software to communicate efficiently. This universal standard helps ensure interoperability between various systems and products from different manufacturers. It is a clear framework for designing and developing network protocols and hardware. It serves as a guideline for manufacturers and software developers to create compatible and efficient networking solutions.

The model's layered approach enables you to understand how each layer develops and functions independently. This modularity simplifies the troubleshooting and upgrading processes since changes in one layer do not necessarily affect the others.

Summary

This chapter reviewed the OSI reference model, which is a foundational element in the field of networking. The OSI reference model provides a clear, standardized framework that facilitates communication, development, and education in network systems. By segmenting the networking process into seven distinct layers, it enhances the interoperability, scalability, and manageability of networked systems.

The knowledge gained in this chapter will prepare you to answer questions relating to exam objective 1.1 in the *CompTIA Network+ (N10-009)* exam.

Exam objective 1.1

Explain concepts related to the Open System Interconnection (OSI) reference model

- **Layer 7**: Application layer
- **Layer 6**: Presentation layer

- **Layer 5**: Session layer
- **Layer 4**: Transport layer
- **Layer 3**: Network layer
- **Layer 2**: Data link layer
- **Layer 1**: Physical layer

Chapter review questions

Now that you've completed the chapter, you can check your knowledge using the practice questions provided in the online platform at `https://packt.link/N10-009ch1`. You can also use the QR code below.

> **Reminder**
>
> Before you can access the end of chapter questions, mock exams and acronym flashcards, you must first register your purchase of the book.
>
> This can be done with the following steps.
>
> 1. Open the link `https://packt.link/N10-009unlock`.
> 2. Log in to your Packt account or register a new Packt account.
> 3. Enter the unique unlock code, which can be found in Chapter 6 page 473.
> 4. You are now ready to use all the free resources can come with the CompTIA® Network+® N10-009 Certification Guide.
>
> For a more detailed description, visit Chapter 26 on page 471.

2

Compare and Contrast Networking Appliances, Applications, and Functions

In the first chapter, you learned how a network is logically divided into seven layers to aid in architecture design and troubleshooting. While the OSI model is incredibly useful, it is a theoretical framework. A real-world network consists of physical and virtual appliances, such as routers, cables, and firewalls; applications, such as **content delivery networks (CDNs)**; and functions, such as **quality of service (QoS)**. Understanding these components is essential to the daily responsibilities of a network engineer.

Appliances perform specific network-related tasks, so it is important to understand how different appliances handle functions such as routing, switching, and security. Knowing their capabilities allows for more efficient and secure network design. Network engineers must also assess how applications interact with the network, their bandwidth requirements, and their impact on performance. Additionally, functions such as load balancing and data transmission influence how networks are designed and managed. Understanding how these elements fit together—and how they differ—is critical to effective network management.

This chapter is divided into three sections. The first section explores physical and virtual appliances, including routers, switches, firewalls, **intrusion detection systems (IDSs)**, load balancers, proxies, storage, and wireless devices. The second section covers CDNs, and the final section discusses key functions, such as VPNs and **time to live (TTL)**.

The goal of this chapter is to provide an overview of appliances, applications, and functions. Many of these topics will be explored in greater detail in later chapters. A solid understanding of how these components work together is essential for optimizing network performance, ensuring security, and troubleshooting effectively.

This chapter covers the second objective in Domain 1: *1.2 Compare and contrast networking appliances, applications, and functions.*

> **Note**
>
> A full breakdown of *objective 1.2* will be given at the end of the chapter.

Physical and virtual appliances

There was a time when if a journal wanted to print a story about a politician, a reporter would make notes at the scene of the event, then rush to a telephone to call it through to an editor at head office. This editor would make written notes, then walk over to a typewriter and type them up. They would ask a junior member of staff to do some background research on the politician. The junior member would walk down three flights of stairs to a basement with a filing system where they could find microfiche that contained copies of old newspapers. They would then run back upstairs and give the information to their seniors. Once the story had been typed up and then corrected with pen and ink, it would then be sent to a typesetting team through a pneumatic tube system that would recreate the story on a plate ready for printing. These people, filing systems, buildings, typewriters, and telephone lines, in the widest terms, all formed a network.

These days, all this work is done digitally with much less walking around. A single computer can do all the jobs of recording and retrieving information, as well as typesetting the journal. But the mechanisms of a modern publishing company, or any other business larger than one person, are still complex. There are still different devices, resources, and people that need to be connected, and with modern security risks, they need to be protected, too.

This section will introduce the hardware (or physical appliances) and software (or virtual appliances) that underpin the network. They include routers, switches, firewalls, IDSs, **intrusion prevention systems (IPSs)**, load balancers, proxies, network-attached storage, and storage area networks. It will also cover wireless access points and controllers.

Physical and virtual appliances are critical in modern network infrastructure, providing the essential services and capabilities needed for connectivity, security, and data management. These functions can become complex when it comes to security or QoS, but to start, we will look at one of the simplest but still essential devices: the hub.

> **Note**
>
> You can revise layers by going to *Chapter 1, Explain Concepts Related to the Open Systems Interconnection (OSI) Reference Model.*

Hub

A **hub** is a basic networking device that connects internal Ethernet devices, operating at Layer 1 of the OSI model. Its primary role is to provide connectivity by acting as a central point for devices on a network. The traffic is half duplex, using the **Carrier Sense Multiple Access/Collision Detection (CSMA/CD)** protocol. **Half-duplex** means that signals are sent in only one direction at a time, as opposed to **full duplex**, which means signals are sent in both directions at the same time. Therefore, half duplex is slower than full duplex, as only one signal can be carried on the shared medium, the wire, at a time. With CSMA/CD, each device will first check whether a communication channel is free; if it is, it will send the data. While sending the data, it will monitor collisions with packets from other devices. If a collision occurs, it will stop sending the data and send a jam signal. It will then wait a random amount of time and send the signal again.

> **Note**
>
> Full and half duplex are covered in greater detail in *Chapter 10, Given a Scenario, Configure Switching Technologies and Features.*

Figure 2.1 shows a diagram of a typical hub connection.

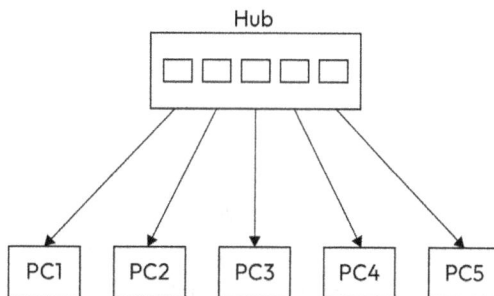

Figure 2.1: All traffic is sent to every node

As you can see in *Figure 2.1*, when a hub receives a data packet from one device, it broadcasts the packet to all other connected devices without filtering or managing traffic. This means all devices will send signals that have the potential to collide; in other words, they share the same **collision domain**. This high chance of data collisions impacts overall network performance and is inefficient.

There are three types of hubs: passive, active, and intelligent.

- **Passive hubs** are unpowered, so as the signal passes through, it simply goes to the connections unaltered, without amplification of the signal. Because of this, they are only suitable for short distances with a small number of connections. Despite limitations, they are cheap, easy to set up, and require minimal maintenance, so they are useful for small offices or joining a few devices in a close network.

- An **active hub**, on the other hand, is powered and can increase a signal. When data arrives at one of the ports on an active hub, the device regenerates and amplifies the signal before sending it out to all the other connected ports. This helps maintain the strength and quality of the signal across the network, especially in larger networks where signal degradation could occur over longer cable distances. They are useful for larger offices and **local area networks** (**LANs**).

- An **intelligent hub**, also known as a **managed hub**, goes beyond the basic signal amplification provided by an active hub by adding some management capabilities. They can monitor the data traffic passing through them and offer basic troubleshooting and network management features. This can help network administrators detect issues such as **network collisions** or connectivity problems.

In most modern environments, hubs have been replaced by switches and routers. Switches provide full duplex communication and work at Layer 2 and Layer 3 of the OSI model. They manage traffic more efficiently by sending data only to the intended recipient. Routers operate at Layer 3 and route data between different networks. Both technologies will be covered next.

Switch

A **switch** is an advanced networking device that operates mainly at Layer 2 and sometimes Layer 3 of the OSI model. Similar to a hub, they connect devices within a LAN, but unlike a hub, which broadcasts data to all connected devices, a switch directs data specifically to the device it is intended for. The main objective is to eliminate collisions by reducing the number of connections to which data is sent. This enhances overall network performance and makes switches a preferred choice for modern networking. A switch works in full duplex, sending traffic in both directions, which makes it much faster than a hub.

The functionality of a typical switch at Layer 2 relies heavily on its **media access control (MAC)** address table, also known as the **content addressable memory (CAM)** table. When a switch receives a data packet, it examines the source MAC address and records it in the CAM table, mapping the MAC address to the specific port where the device is connected. For each incoming data packet, the switch checks the destination MAC address against the CAM table. If the address is found, the switch forwards the packet directly to the correct port. If the destination MAC address is not in the table, the switch broadcasts the packet to all ports except the one it came from.

Figure 2.2 shows a simple switch connection.

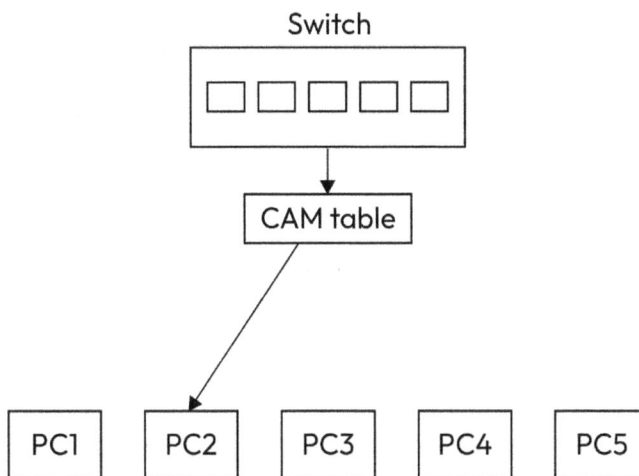

Figure 2.2: The switch checks the CAM table and sends data to one node

In *Figure 2.2*, the switch CAM table is essential for efficient data forwarding and is dynamically maintained by the switch. It continuously updates with new MAC addresses as devices send data, ensuring accurate mapping of devices to ports. Entries in the CAM table have an aging process, meaning that if a MAC address is not seen for a certain period, it is removed to keep the table current. This process ensures that the switch can quickly and accurately direct data to the intended recipient, optimizing network traffic management and reducing unnecessary data transmissions.

Switches have different characteristics, which are important when considering network architecture. These include unmanaged, managed, **Power over Ethernet (PoE), modular, fixed,** Layer 2, and Layer 3.

An **unmanaged switch** is a simple plug-and-play device that cannot be configured. You just plug it in, connect your devices, and it starts working. This is suitable for small home networks or **small office/home office (SOHO)** networks where you just need to connect a few devices. It has basic functionality, as described previously, so it only offers connectivity with the added efficiency of filtering for recipients. Its simplicity makes it useful for small networks.

- A **managed switch** offers more control over the network. It can authenticate users and devices by using the **802.1x network access protocol**, which means it can allow access to only authenticated users or devices, otherwise known as **port-based authentication**. To connect to a managed switch using 802.1x, an **endpoint** needs a certificate for authentication. For wireless authentication, the switch should use a **Remote Authentication Dial-In User Service (RADIUS)** server for enterprise networks. The managed switch also allows you to configure settings, manage traffic, and create VLANs. This makes it ideal for businesses and enterprises that need advanced network management. Administrators can adjust settings, monitor network performance, control who can access the network, and troubleshoot issues.

> **Note**
>
> Switching configurations, VLANs, and 802.1x will be covered in greater detail in *Chapter 10*.

- A **PoE switch** can provide both data connection and electrical power to devices through the same network cable. This is useful for powering devices such as IP cameras, **Voice over Internet Protocol (VoIP)** phones, and wireless access points without needing a separate power source. They can be unmanaged, smart, or managed with PoE functionality to power devices.
- If a switch is fixed, it means it has a set number of ports that cannot be expanded (i.e., you get what you buy). However, if a switch is modular, it can be expanded to include additional modules using plug-in cards for more ports, PoE capabilities, or other features.
- **Layer 2 switches** operate at the data link layer of the OSI model. They use MAC addresses to forward data between devices. Most basic switches are Layer 2. **Layer 3 switches** operate at both the data link (Layer 2) and network layer (Layer 3). Layer 2 switches are suitable for simple networks, while Layer 3 switches are used in more complex setups that require routing between different network segments, also known as subnets.

Having a switch performing simple routing operations can be useful when you need basic inter-VLAN routing or want to reduce network latency. However, in most cases, to handle complex routing tasks, provide firewall security, or manage traffic across different network types, a network will have an actual router, which we will cover next.

Router

A **router** operates at Layer 3 of the OSI model and typically connects multiple networks together, enabling communication across the internet. The router directs traffic between different networks by determining the best path for data packets based on destination IP addresses. To do this, routers use **routing tables,** which are lists of paths to various network destinations. Routers choose the best path to send packets based on these routes. SSH is used to remotely access the router and run commands securely; the same can also be done with switches. This will be covered in more detail in *Chapter 17, Compare and Contrast Network Access and Management Methods.*

Figure 2.3 shows a screenshot from a routing table on the Windows OS, followed by *Table 2.1,* which shows the same detail in tabular form.

```
IPv4 Route Table
===========================================================================
Active Routes:
Network Destination        Netmask          Gateway       Interface  Metric
          0.0.0.0          0.0.0.0      192.168.0.1    192.168.0.173     25
        127.0.0.0        255.0.0.0         On-link        127.0.0.1    331
        127.0.0.1  255.255.255.255         On-link        127.0.0.1    331
  127.255.255.255  255.255.255.255         On-link        127.0.0.1    331
      192.168.0.0    255.255.255.0         On-link    192.168.0.173    281
    192.168.0.173  255.255.255.255         On-link    192.168.0.173    281
    192.168.0.255  255.255.255.255         On-link    192.168.0.173    281
        224.0.0.0        240.0.0.0         On-link        127.0.0.1    331
        224.0.0.0        240.0.0.0         On-link    192.168.0.173    281
  255.255.255.255  255.255.255.255         On-link        127.0.0.1    331
  255.255.255.255  255.255.255.255         On-link    192.168.0.173    281
```

Figure 2.3: A Windows routing table

IPv4 Route Table					
Active routes					
	Network destination	**Netmask**	**Gateway**	**Interface**	**Metric**
1	0.0.0.0	0.0.0.0	192.168.0.1	192.168.9.173	25
2	127.0.0.0	255.0.0.0	On-link	127.0.0.1	331
3	127.0.0.1	255.255.255.255	On-link	127.0.0.1	331
4	127.255.255.255	255.255.255.255	On-link	127.0.0.1	331
5	192.168.0.0	255.255.255.0	On-link	192.168.0.173	281
6	192.168.0.173	255.255.255.255	On-link	192.168.0.173	281
7	192.168.0.255	255.255.255.255	On-link	192.168.0.173	281

8	224.0.0.0	240.0.0.0	On-link	127.0.0.1	331
9	224.0.0.0	240.0.0.0	On-link	192.168.0.173	281
10	255.255.255.255	255.255.255.255	On-link	127.0.0.1	331
11	255.255.255.255	255.255.255.255	On-link	192.168.0.173	281

Table 2.1: A routing table

Table 2.1 shows the current active routes on the router. For each entry, the router has the destination, netmask, gateway, interface, and metric. The numbers on the left have been added for the purpose of clarity and do not normally appear in routing tables.

The **network destination** is the destination IP address or network that the router can send packets to. Each entry specifies a network or a host address.

The **netmask** is used to define the size of the network for the corresponding destination. It tells the router which portion of the IP address is the network portion and which is the host portion. It determines whether the packet has a local or remote destination.

> **Note**
>
> Netmasks and network addresses are covered in greater detail in *Chapter 7*.

The **gateway** through which packets should be sent to reach the destination. The data will be sent to the gateway, typically another router for another network or subnet. **On-link** means that the destination is in the same local network or subnet and, therefore, directly reachable without needing to pass through a gateway.

An **interface** is a network connection on the router through which packets will be sent. 192.168.0.173 is the IP address of the local computer that is sending the packets.

Metric is a value that helps determine the priority of routes when there are multiple possible paths to the same destination. A lower metric value indicates a preferred route. The metric of 25 is the preferred route; it is also the default route. Metric is also sometimes called the **administrative distance**.

The routing table shows a **network** address of 192.168.0.0 and a **loopback** address of 127.0.0.1, which is the standard. When you ping 127.0.0.1, the router sends a network request to itself. If you receive a response, it indicates that the TCP/IP stack is operational on your machine, confirming that the network software is initialized and able to handle network communications internally.

An important entry is the default route, `0.0.0.0`, which is used by the router as a last resort. If the router does not know where to send the packet, it forwards it to the default route, which connects to either the network gateway or the **internet service provider (ISP)**.

There are two main types of routes: static routes, which are manually configured, and dynamic routes, which are automatically calculated by the router.

Static routes

Static routes are manually configured in the router by a network administrator. These routes don't change unless someone manually modifies them. Since the route is set manually, the path is always the same, which makes it very reliable, but it also means the route won't automatically adapt to changes in the network. Static routes do not consume router resources for calculating routes, as they are predefined and don't need constant updating like dynamic routes. They are mostly used in small networks or when there are specific needs for security and control.

For example, you have two networks, network A and network B:

- Network A has IP addresses in the range `192.168.1.0/24` (i.e., `192.168.1.1` to `192.168.1.254`)

- Network B has IP addresses in the range `192.168.2.0/24` (i.e., `192.168.2.1` to `192.168.2.254`)

Your router is connected to network A on the `eth0` interface and network B on the `eth1` interface. Now, you want to set up a static route so that any traffic destined for network B (`192.168.2.0/24`) will be sent through the router's `eth1` interface.

Here's how you might configure a static route in a command-line interface:

```
ip route add 192.168.2.0/24 via 192.168.1.1 dev eth0
```

This command tells the router that for any packet destined for the `192.168.2.0/24` network (network B), send it via the router's gateway at `192.168.1.1` through the `eth0` interface.

In this scenario, network A is considered the local network, and network B is a remote network.

The static route ensures that packets going to network B know how to get there by following the specific route set by the administrator.

Dynamic routes

Dynamic routes are automatically calculated by the router using routing protocols such as **Open Shortest Path First (OSPF)**, **Routing Information Protocol (RIP)**, or **Border Gateway Protocol**

(BGP). They adjust automatically based on changes in the network topology, such as when a link goes down or the network grows. These routes are generally used in larger networks because of their adaptability and efficiency, but come with more overhead and complexity.

If we look at *Figure 2.4*, we can see five different routers that connect networks between New York, Dublin, Paris, London, and Edinburgh.

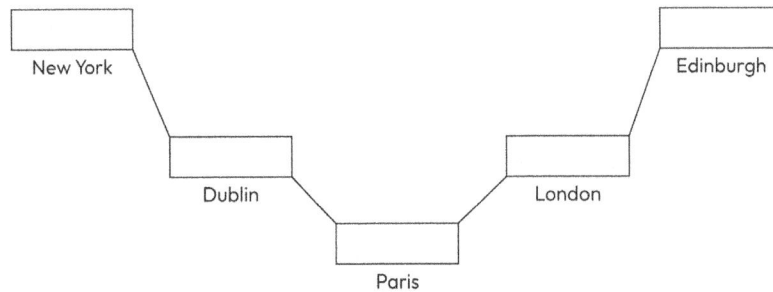

Figure 2.4: Routing packets

If we think of these routers as post offices delivering mail, it may make it easier to understand. If mail arrives at the Paris post office, the people working there have two sacks, one for Dublin and the other for London; they just need to know where to send the mail next. They cannot have sacks for every destination in the world; it is just not feasible.

Let's look at an example:

- If mail arrives at the Paris post office and is destined for Edinburgh, the post office staff know that they just need to put the mail in the London sack. Once the mail arrives in London, there will be two different sacks, one destined for Edinburgh and the other destined for Paris. The workers know to place the mail for Edinburgh in the Edinburgh sack.

- If mail arrives at the Paris post office and is destined for New York, they know to place it in the Dublin sack. Once the mail arrives in Dublin, it is placed in the New York sack.

Routing packets is no more difficult than moving mail around the world; the router has many routes in a routing table and knows the next hop for packet delivery. Several protocols are used in the management and control of IP packets going through the router.

Note

Metrics, static routes, and other routing concepts are covered in greater detail in *Chapter 9, Explain Characteristics of Routing Technologies*. TCP/IP will be covered in greater detail in *Chapter 4*.

A router will also have an **access control list (ACL)**, which is a security tool used to control traffic coming through the router. The ACL is a list of allow rules based on IP addresses, protocols, and port numbers, with the last rule being to deny all. If traffic that is not on the list arrives, then the last rule of denial will apply, which is known as **implicit deny**.

Routers are the main devices for controlling data traffic. Using routing tables, a router ensures the correct data packets go to the correct destinations within the network or subnet, or sends them on to the next point—often another router—where the data packet will then be directed again. These points are also known as **hops**. Using ACLs, routers provide a certain level of security by filtering traffic within the network, but the detailed regulation of traffic entering and leaving a network is typically handled by another device, the firewall, which is covered next.

Firewall

A **firewall** is a security tool designed to oversee and regulate network traffic entering and leaving a system, based on established security guidelines. Serving as a shield between a secure internal network and potentially risky external networks such as the internet, it blocks unauthorized access and safeguards against risks such as malware and cyber attackers. Network-based firewalls are the most common type, but there are also WAFs, **unified threat management (UTM)** firewalls, and **next-generation firewalls (NGFWs)**, each with specific features and functions. Firewalls can be **stateful**, often working at Layer 3 and Layer 4, where they track the state of connections, or **stateless**, which typically operate at the same layers but analyze each packet independently. Some firewalls, such as WAFs and certain NGFWs, operate at Layer 7 for deep packet inspection and application-specific rules.

Network-based firewalls

Network-based firewalls are security devices or software deployed at key points within a network to monitor and control incoming and outgoing traffic. Their primary function is to enforce security policies by filtering packets based on various criteria, such as IP addresses, ports, and protocols. They are commonly placed at the boundary between a trusted internal network and an external network (such as the internet) to protect internal systems from unauthorized access and potential threats.

WAFs

The purpose of a **WAF** is to protect your web server and the web-based applications running on your web server from attack. The WAF shields your web applications and websites from an onslaught of cyber threats, safeguarding them against attacks such as SQL injection, XSS attacks, and **distributed denial-of-service (DDoS)** assaults. The WAF operates at Layer 7.

UTM firewalls

UTM firewalls provide malware inspection, **data loss prevention** (DLP), content filtering, and URL filtering. UTM firewalls are also the go-to when you need an all-in-one security solution to simplify your defense strategy.

NGFWs

NGFWs combine traditional firewall capabilities with advanced, application-aware security and threat intelligence. They operate at **Layer 7** and have advanced protection across both on-premises and cloud environments, facilitate **TLS,** and have deep packet filtering and intrusion prevention capabilities. They use advanced behavioral analysis and user behavior monitoring to proactively ensure the early detection and mitigation of potential insider threats to protect sensitive data from compromise.

Network firewalls, **UTM firewalls,** and **NGFWs** all serve different purposes and functions within a network. **Network firewalls** will give general protection by controlling traffic based on **IP addresses**, **ports**, and **protocols**. They have limited to no visibility into application layer data, so they cannot prevent specific attacks such as **SQL injection**. **WAFs**, on the other hand, analyze data based on patterns and rules relating to web applications, so they will typically be placed in front of web servers to protect public-facing applications and **application programming interfaces (APIs)**.

A small office might only rely on a network-based interface, but if you are running a website on which users are inputting data, such as a web shop, it would be a good idea to ensure you are using a **WAF**.

A **UTM** might also be a good solution as it combines the functionality of network firewalls and **WAFs**, as well as adding other functionality such as content filtering and intrusion protection. This can be useful for small to medium-sized businesses as it avoids the setup and maintenance of multiple devices. However, it does create a single point of failure and can also mean that you lose some of the granular control you might have with a dedicated WAF.

NGFWs go further than UTMs in that they inspect data at a much deeper level. They can combine all the traits of WAFs and network firewalls, along with some of the other functions of UTMs, but allow for even greater granular control. They typically require a lot of support to get the most out of them, but they can be very useful in large enterprises. While more traditional firewalls will filter based on ports, protocols, and IP addresses, NGFWs can perform identity-based filtering, enforcing rules based on individuals, groups, or roles. NGFWs can also help to monitor hybrid cloud solutions. This can be useful in businesses susceptible to insider threats and other espionage.

Layer 4 firewalls

A **Layer 4 firewall** is the gatekeeper of network traffic, entrusted with the straightforward yet critical mission of basic packet filtering. It's primarily focused on determining whether incoming or outgoing packets should be permitted based on predefined rules. It ensures that the **TCP/IP three-way handshake** takes place and determines access based on the type of packets coming in. It is therefore known as a **packet filtering firewall**. It does not provide deep packet inspection.

Layer 7 firewalls

A **Layer 7 firewall**, or **application firewall**, examines network traffic at the application layer, allowing for detailed inspection of data packets. This enables it to identify, manage, and control specific applications, user actions, and content, thereby providing enhanced security and management capabilities in contemporary network environments.

Stateless firewall

A **stateless firewall** is a basic packet filtering firewall that looks at each packet's header, which contains information such as the **source address** (where it's coming from), **destination address** (where it's going), **protocol type**, and **port number**. Based on this information, the firewall decides whether the packet should be allowed to pass through or be blocked.

Stateful firewall

A **stateful firewall** operates at **Layer 3** and **Layer 4** and analyzes data deeply, making informed decisions, and thus it can prevent **DDoS attacks**. It is best suited when you need to inspect application traffic and permit or block based on application behavior. A stateful firewall knows the size and format of each type of **network packet**. It monitors the established session and prevents malicious sessions.

With **UTMs** and **NGFWs**, the difference between a traditional firewall and an **IDS** or **IPS** is becoming fuzzier. However, conceptually, there are differences. A firewall, in the strictest definition, will block all traffic except that which it is programmed to allow, whereas an **IDS/IPS** will actively monitor for anomalies, as you will see in the next section.

> **Note**
>
> Network devices such as routers, switches, printers and firewalls need to be configured with a static IP address. This will be covered in more detail in Chapter 7.

Intrusion detection system (IDS)/Intrusion prevention system (IPS)

If you imagine a firewall to be like a security guard on a door, only letting people into a building if they have an ID or are on a guest list, then an **IDS** is more like a guard monitoring **CCTV**, actively looking for suspicious activity and flagging up any potential threats. An **IPS** would be someone who then directly addressed the threat by preventing access to the building based on gathered intelligence.

The **IDS** analyzes patterns and anomalies in data traffic and alerts administrators to potential threats, while an **IPS** goes a step further by actively blocking or preventing identified threats from compromising the network, offering real-time protection against attacks.

An **IDS** monitors traffic for an entire network and uses user behavior analytics to determine normal traffic patterns and then detect deviations from these to determine malicious activities. The **IDS** also uses sensors and collectors to identify new traffic.

Traffic analysis is performed in real time, examining data packets for unusual patterns, signatures, or users' behaviors that may indicate a security threat. For example, a spike in traffic from a single IP address could signal a potential DDoS attack. If data packets have signatures associated with known malware, such as specific byte sequences or payload structures, this could indicate that a system is being targeted by a malicious program. A sudden transfer of sensitive data to an unfamiliar location might signal unauthorized data exfiltration.

When a potential threat is detected, **IDSs** generate **alerts or notifications**, informing the security teams who will take prompt action to respond to incidents promptly. They use sensors, collectors, and user behavioral analysis to gather information to raise the alert.

IDSs are passive in that they do not actively block or prevent attacks but rather serve as early warning systems, providing insights into potential security breaches. IPSs are proactive security measures in that they not only detect but also actively block or mitigate security threats within a network.

Similar to **IDSs**, **IPSs** continuously analyze network traffic but with the added ability to take immediate action rather than simply monitoring and generating alerts. An **IPS** can be used for **inline analysis**, meaning that it is placed in front of the incoming traffic to inspect the traffic as it passes through.

When an **IPS** identifies a threat, it can attempt to block or prevent malicious activity, such as dropping suspicious packets or blocking access to specific **IP addresses. IPSs** can enforce security policies and rules defined by administrators, ensuring that network traffic complies with security guidelines. Like **IDSs**, the **IPSs** also generate alerts and reports, giving administrators visibility into the security events occurring within the network.

Both systems use patterns or characteristics known as **IDS/IPS signatures**, which represent known threats, including malware, viruses, and attack methods. These signatures are stored in a database, which is used as a reference when analyzing patterns. When a match is found, an alarm is triggered, alerting security teams to a potential security breach. However, it is dependent on updates; if these are infrequent, it may not detect threats. The database is regularly updated to ensure that **IDS/IPS** solutions remain effective in detecting the latest threats, and organizations can create custom signatures tailored to their specific network and application environment.

IDS/IPS solutions also incorporate behavioral signatures, which focus on detecting deviations from expected network behavior. This approach helps identify novel threats that may not have a predefined signature.

Security is a key concern when managing network traffic, and a combination of firewall technologies and IDSs/IPSs helps mitigate many network risks. However, it's also essential to maintain an efficient network. With the large volumes of data traffic coming into and traveling across the network, bottlenecks can occur, which can degrade performance. One way to prevent this is by using a **load balancer**, which will be covered next.

Load balancer

A **load balancer** allocates incoming network traffic among several identical servers or resources to enhance resource efficiency, increase throughput, and maintain high availability and reliability of applications. The load balancer evenly distributes the workload, improves performance, and prevents any single server from being overwhelmed.

The web traffic, shown in *Figure 2.5*, arrives at the load balancer via the **virtual IP address (VIP)** on the frontend. The load balancer then forwards this traffic to one of the web servers in the server farm. This would be the least utilized host, which helps to balance each load and can mitigate DDoS attacks.

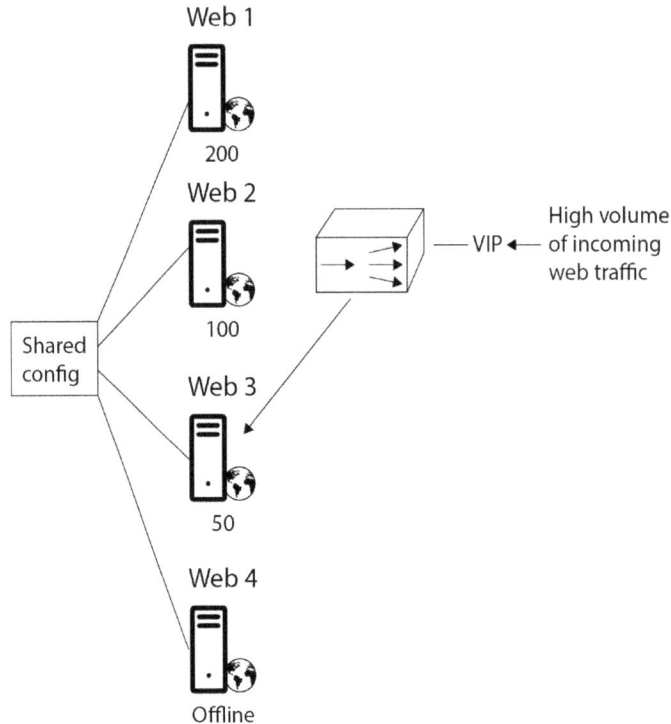

Figure 2.5: Load balancer

Load balancers can use various algorithms to distribute traffic, such as **round-robin, least connections, least response time**, and **IP hash. Round-robin algorithms** distribute requests sequentially across all available servers in a rotating order. With the **least connections algorithm,** the load balancer sends traffic to the server with the fewest active connections, helping balance uneven workloads. The **least response time algorithm** directs traffic to the server with the lowest average response time, ensuring faster processing. **IP hash algorithms** use a hash of the client's **IP address** to consistently route requests to the same server, which makes sessions more stable.

They will also usually perform health checks on servers to ensure they are capable of handling requests. If a server is down or not responding, the load balancer will redirect traffic to other available servers.

Load balancers can be hardware-based or software-based and can operate at different layers of the **OSI model**, such as **Layer 4** or **Layer 7**. Some load balancers provide **SSL** offloading, where they handle the encryption and decryption of **SSL traffic**, reducing the load on the web servers. They are commonly used in environments with multiple servers, such as **web applications, databases**, or **cloud services**, to maintain uptime and reliability.

While **load balancers** serve as a kind of traffic control, ensuring that incoming data does not overwhelm any individual server, it does so by distributing traffic evenly to servers. However, in the transferring of data, there is often the need for complex communications of requests and responses between clients and servers. This kind of data handling requires a more sophisticated go-between, such as a proxy server, which we will cover in the next section.

Proxy server

A **proxy server** acts as an intermediary between clients and servers, forwarding requests and responses while providing additional functionalities such as caching, filtering, and anonymity. It enhances security and performance by controlling access to resources and masking the identity of clients. A proxy server manages requests from clients seeking resources on the internet or an external network. Proxy servers can log both allowed and blocked requests, aiding in monitoring and compliance. Think of it as a go-between that makes requests on behalf of the client, ensuring that external entities do not know the details of the requesting host. The proxy server maintains a log file of every request, enabling tracking of a user's internet usage.

The flow of data in this context is from internal to external, and this is known as a **forward proxy**, as shown in *Figure 2.6*.

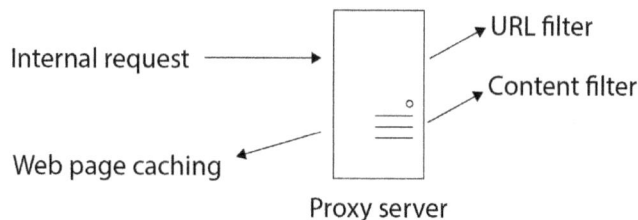

Figure 2.6: Proxy server

A proxy server has three main functions: URL filtering, content filtering, and web page caching:

- **URL filtering**: When a user visits a website, they type the URL, for example, `www.facebook.com`. Companies may not want their employees accessing social media sites such as Facebook or X (formerly known as Twitter) during working hours, so these websites are placed on a default block list. The URL filter checks this block list to see whether the requested website should be blocked. The employee visiting Facebook will receive a warning stating that the page is blocked, and the attempt is logged.

- **Content filtering**: This filter examines the content on the requested web page, and depending on the filters set up, the request may be blocked based on text, images, or other elements on the web page. For instance, if gambling sites are blocked, users attempting to visit poker or horse betting sites will be denied access, based on the content of the websites. Typically, content filters block gambling, inappropriate content, or other specified categories.

- **Web page caching**: Many companies within the same industry frequently visit specific websites related to their business. During lunch breaks, employees might check sports scores, for example. Each time they access the internet, a session is opened through the firewall, which can expose unsecured sessions and consume bandwidth. A proxy server can cache web pages to reduce bandwidth usage and speed up access by serving content from the local network. However, it's crucial to ensure that cached content is updated frequently enough to remain relevant. For instance, caching pages showing stock market data would not be feasible due to constant price fluctuations.

Caching can either be active or passive. **Active caching** would be if you set your proxy server up to cache web pages at specific times, such as caching www.nfl.com at 3 a.m. local time to ensure it has the latest results. With **passive caching**, when new web pages are requested, the pages are fetched and submitted to the requesting host, and a copy is placed in the cache. This allows subsequent requests for the same page to be served from the cache.

So far, most of the technologies discussed have focused on controlling the transmission of data, whether by directing it, balancing loads, or securing the network. However, data also needs to be stored, especially if it is to be readily accessible for future use, backups, or collaborative work. In the next two sections, we will explore solutions for data storage with **network-attached storage (NAS)** and the related **storage area network (SAN)**.

Network-attached storage (NAS)

A **NAS device** is a storage device connected to a network that allows multiple users and devices to store and access files centrally. Think of it as a shared storage space that everyone on the network can access, similar to a shared drive in an office, but often used at home or in small businesses as well. NAS devices make it easy to organize, back up, and share data with anyone who has permission to access it, whether they're using a computer, laptop, or even a mobile device.

NAS devices store data in one location, which can be accessed by all authorized users on the network. This central storage means that files no longer have to be kept on each individual computer, which can free up space and make it easier to manage files in one place. They are designed to be accessible by multiple users and are often used for file sharing, using **Server Message Block (SMB)** for Windows systems.

Once a NAS device is set up on a network, users can connect to it by mapping a network drive. This makes the NAS device appear as a local drive on your computer, making access easy and familiar.

> **Note**
>
> SMB for Windows systems will be covered in greater detail in *Chapter 4, Explain Common Networking Ports, Protocols, Services, and Traffic Types.*

Storage area network (SAN)

Because NAS devices are designed for use by multiple people and often hold large files, they are easy to set up and rely on standard network protocols; however, the data transfer can be relatively slow, making the system cumbersome for large numbers of queries to a database, for instance. Though NAS can handle less intensive tasks, often a more dedicated system is needed.

A SAN is a specialized high-speed network that connects servers to storage devices, providing fast and reliable access to large amounts of data. Unlike a **NAS** system, which provides file-level storage and can be accessed like a shared drive, a **SAN** provides block-level access, which means it allows data to be read and written in small units or blocks, often referred to as **logical unit numbers** (**LUNs**). This makes **SANs** highly suitable for applications that require quick access to large amounts of data, such as databases and virtualized environments.

SANs can be set up using two main protocols, **Fibre Channel Protocol** (**FCP**) and **Internet Small Computer Systems Interface** (**iSCSI**). Both technologies enable fast data transfer, but they work differently. **FCP** is a protocol that creates a dedicated and reliable connection between servers and storage devices within the **SAN**. It provides extremely high speeds of up to 128 Gbps in modern setups. It requires specialized hardware, including **fiber channel** (**FC**) **switches** and **host bus adapters** (**HBAs**) on servers. This can make **FC SANs** more expensive to set up but highly reliable. **FC SANs** are commonly used in large enterprises with high-performance and reliability needs, such as financial institutions and data centers.

iSCSI is a protocol that allows **SANs** to use standard **Ethernet networks** instead of **FC** hardware. It uses **TCP/IP** to send storage data over local or wide-area networks. While not as fast as **FCP**, **iSCSI** can still achieve high speeds, especially with modern **Ethernet standards**, such as 10 Gbps or 25 Gbps. It's a more cost-effective option, especially for small to medium-sized organizations. **iSCSI** is relatively easy to set up because it can use existing Ethernet infrastructure, eliminating the need for specialized **FC** equipment. Servers in an **iSCSI SAN** typically connect to storage using an **Ethernet connection** and an **iSCSI initiator**, which can be software or hardware. **iSCSI** is popular for organizations that need efficient storage solutions on a budget, especially for applications that don't require the ultra-high speeds provided by **FCP**.

SANs can easily grow by adding additional storage devices or increasing capacity, making them adaptable to an organization's needs. As mentioned, they provide fast data access for databases, transaction-heavy applications, or virtual machines, and they can also offer large-scale storage for data centers or cloud environments.

We've already looked at standard devices such as routers that enable wired connections. But these days, almost all networks have endpoint devices that are not plugged in through the Ethernet. In the last part of this section, we will look at two main wireless applications: access points and controls.

Wireless

A **wireless access point** (**AP**) is a wireless networking device that acts like a bridge connecting wireless devices such as laptops, smartphones, and tablets to a wired network using **Wi-Fi**. It acts as a bridge between wireless clients and the wired network infrastructure, providing wireless connectivity within a designated area (Wi-Fi hotspot). A **wireless controller** manages multiple **access points** (**APs**) within a wireless network. It centralizes the configuration, management, and monitoring of APs, ensuring seamless roaming, load balancing, and wireless network optimization. A thin controller is used in enterprise networks to update multiple APs, whereas a thick controller is more like a home wireless router that has all of its settings locally.

Applications

So far, you have seen how different appliances, both physical and virtual, help to manage traffic, enforce security policies, and perform routing or switching functions in a network. These devices operate at different OSI levels, directly manipulating data packets. However, there are other important parts of a network that help ensure efficient, safe, and reliable data transmission without directly interfering with the data. One key application enhancing web performance and user experience is the CDN, which will be described in the next section.

Content delivery network

Consider an e-commerce site based in the UK. With servers in London, anyone based in the UK and much of Europe will have a fast load time when visiting the website because they are close to the servers. However, users in Australia would experience great lag because the data has to cover a greater distance. A CDN solves this issue by storing caches of the website in different locations around the globe.

A **CDN** is a network of geographically distributed servers that deliver web content and multimedia efficiently to users based on their geographic location. They reduce latency, optimize bandwidth usage, and enhance website performance by having content closer to end users. They also provide high availability because of the multiple copies. So, for example, images for web pages can be stored in the local region and are then placed in web pages. **Software as a service (SaaS)** apps can also be hosted in different regions, providing fast performance even if the service provider is in a different global region, as shown in *Figure 2.7.*

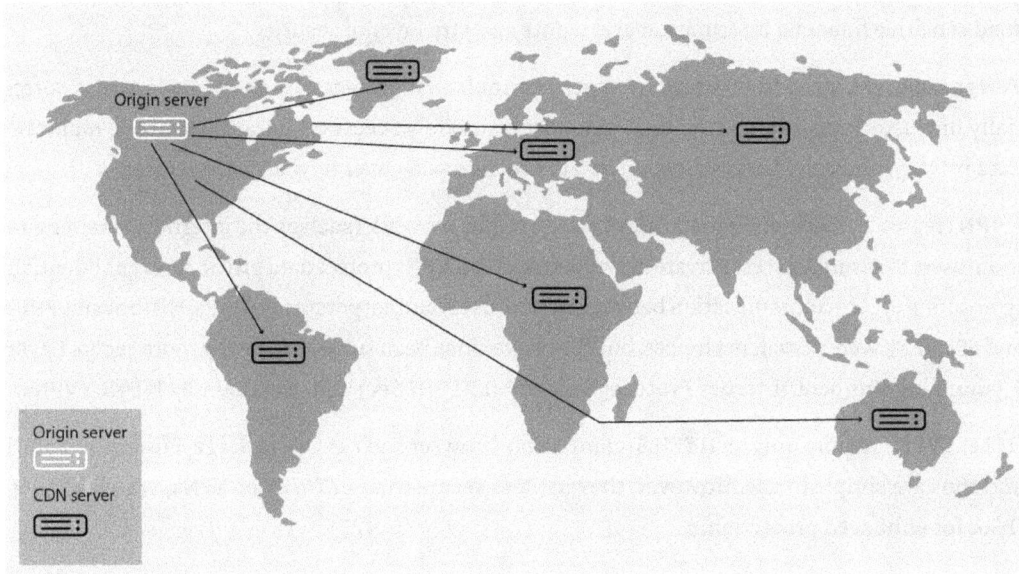

Figure 2.7: A CDN

CDNs are important for user experience, as slow loading times can lose customers and readers. Cloudflare, Amazon CloudFront, Microsoft Azure CDN, and Google CDN are popular services, some of which integrate with existing cloud-based infrastructure.

Functions

The final aspect of networking to discuss is functions. While appliances are devices that move and store data, and applications are services that create specific capabilities for a data network, functions are operations or protocols governing how data is transmitted. This section will look at three examples of functions: VPNs, QoS, and TTL.

Virtual private networks

Security is present throughout a network, with firewalls, switches, routers, and APs all controlling the data and agents that can travel through it. However, even with this protection, it is possible to intercept, spy upon, and otherwise maliciously attack data transmissions. There are numerous instances when two parties want to connect over a local or global network and ensure that only they are able to see that communication. A person needs remote access to an organization's file server from a public internet connection in an airport coffee shop, or perhaps someone needs to send sensitive financial information and wants an extra layer of security.

VPNs answer this need by creating encrypted **tunnels** that protect data as it travels across potentially untrusted networks, allowing remote users to safely access corporate resources, maintain data privacy, and communicate securely. This section will cover how a VPN operates.

A **VPN** creates a secure, encrypted tunnel over a public network (such as the internet), enabling remote users to securely access private network resources. VPNs protect data privacy and confidentiality, ensuring secure communication between remote users and corporate networks. Historically, PPTP and SSL VPNs were prevalent choices, but they have since been surpassed by the more secure **Layer 2 Tunneling Protocol/Internet Protocol Security** (**L2TP/IPSec**) and user-friendly HTML5 VPNs.

HTML5 VPNs require only an HTML5-compatible browser such as Opera, Edge, Firefox, or Safari, and thus are simple to use. However, they are less secure than L2TP/IPSec VPNs, which employ IPSec for enhanced protection.

Tunneling

Tunneling is a networking technique used to secure and encrypt data as it travels over potentially untrusted networks, ensuring the privacy, integrity, and safe passage of information. It uses network protocols to encrypt a secure tunnel through a public network. There are several protocols that can be used to perform this task, including the TLS and IPSec tunneling protocols, described here:

- TLS uses certificates for authentication, ensuring a firm handshake of security. Once the encrypted tunnel is created, the authentication credentials are sent to a RADIUS server. With the user authenticated and the connection solidified, the VPN gateway provides secure communication for the local network.

- IPSec can be used to create a secure session between a client computer and a server. An IPSec packet is formed of two different portions, the **authentication header** (**AH**) and the **encapsulated security payload** (**ESP**).

- The AH consists of either **SHA-1** or **MD5** hashing algorithms, which provide data integrity to ensure the packet has not been tampered with in transit.

- The ESP is the part of the IPSec packet in which the data is stored and encrypted using symmetric encryption via DES, 3DES, or AES. It comprises the following:

  - **Header:** ESP adds an additional header to the IP packet. The header contains information necessary for the proper processing of the packet during transmission and reception.

  - **Payload data:** This is the actual data that is being transmitted and can be any type of network traffic, such as email, web browsing, or file transfers.

Internet Key Exchange (IKE)

IKE is another essential part of tunneling. When an IPSec tunnel is created, the **Diffie-Hellman (DH)** key exchange protocol should be used in conjunction with VPN concentrators to establish a shared secret key between two parties—typically a remote client and the VPN concentrator. The IKE phase of the IPSec session uses DH over UDP port 500 to create what is known as **quick mode**. This creates a secure session so that the data can flow through it. In the second phase of IKE, the data is encrypted with DES, 3DES, or AES, which provides the most secure VPN session as it uses 128, 192, or 256 bits.

There are three different IPSec modes, as defined in *Table 2.2*.

IPSec modes	Description
Tunnel mode	This is the mode in which a user creates a VPN session from a remote location. During *tunnel* mode, the AH and ESP are both encrypted. Authentication methods include certificates, Kerberos authentication, and pre-shared keys.
Always-on mode	This mode is applied during the creation of a site-to-site VPN, the purpose of which is to build a point-to-point connection between two sites in possession of their own VPNs. The session is set to *Always-on* to ensure the connection is available all the time. While a site-to-site VPN is active, both the AH and the ESP are encrypted.
Transport mode	This mode is used during the creation of an IPSec tunnel with an internal network using client/server-to-server communication. During *transport* mode, only the ESP is encrypted.

Table 2.2: IPSec modes

IPSec Security Association

IPSec is a suite of security protocols that play a vital role in protecting data by establishing secure communication channels between devices. Though not part of the core TCP/IP suite, it is used alongside TCP/IP to secure IP traffic in, for example, VPNs.

Security is achieved by the two-phase process of creating IPSec **Security Associations (SAs)**, which define the security keys and parameters, including the length of the session for this secure channel. To get to this point, the two parties must agree on the encryption and authentication methods to use. They must also agree on which DH group to use.

A **DH** group defines the mathematical properties used in the key exchange process, ensuring that both peers can generate the same shared secret key securely. The **DH key exchange** is a method that allows two parties to generate a shared secret key over an insecure channel. Even if an eavesdropper intercepts the exchange, they won't be able to determine the shared key. The **DH group** determines the strength of the key exchange process. Higher **DH group** numbers generally indicate stronger cryptographic strength but may also require more processing power.

IPSec can be used to create a secure session between a client computer and a server. An IPSec packet is formed of two different portions, the **AH** and the **ESP**.

The **AH** is the first part of the data packet and provides data integrity to ensure the packet has not been tampered with in transit. It provides a hash that is made with either the **SHA-1** or **MD5** hashing algorithms, which the receiver can check.

The **ESP** is the part of the **IPSec** packet where the data is stored. It is encrypted using symmetric encryption via **DES**, **3DES**, or **AES**, and includes an additional header to the **IP packet**. This header contains information necessary for the proper processing of the packet during transmission and reception. The payload data is the name given to the actual data that is being transmitted and can be any type of network traffic, such as email, web browsing, or file transfers.

The next section will explain **phase 1** and **phase 2** of an **IPSec** SA in more detail, using a specific scenario to illustrate how these phases work together to create a secure and encrypted tunnel for data transfer between peer A and peer B.

> **Note**
>
> Encryption and hashing will be covered later in *Chapter 18, Explain the Importance of Basic Network Security Concepts.*

Phase 1: Establishing the secure channel

The main goal of phase 1 is to establish a secure and authenticated communication channel between two IPSec peers (e.g., two VPNs, routers, or firewalls). This phase ensures that both parties are who they say they are and that they can communicate securely. There are four steps, as follows:

1. **Negotiation:** Peer A and peer B agree on the encryption and authentication methods to use, such as AES-256 and SHA-256. They also agree on the DH group to use.

2. **DH key exchange:** The key exchange is carried out.

3. **Authentication:** Both peers verify that the other party is who they claim to be using PSKs, a digital certificate, or other methods.

4. **Establishing the IKE SA:** Once authentication is successful, an IKE is created using the IKE protocol, and the peers create an IKE SA, establishing **the parameters for further communication.**

Phase 2: Establishing the IPSec Tunnel

The next phase creates the IPSec tunnel for encrypting and decrypting data traffic. It consists of three steps, as follows:

1. **Negotiation:** Peers negotiate the IPSec SA within the secure channel from phase

2. **IPSec SA establishment:** The peers define parameters for protecting data traffic, including encryption and hashing algorithms.

3. **Data transfer:** Secure data transfer occurs through the IPSec tunnel.

Example scenario

Two peers, A and B, want to establish a site-to-site VPN. They will use DH group 14, which is a favored group due to a high level of cryptographic security, making communication robust against potential attacks. They will also use the AES-256 encryption algorithm and the SHA-256 hash function for integrity:

- **Peer A IP:** `1.1.1.1`
- **Peer B IP:** `2.2.2.2`
- **Authentication method:** Pre-shared key (a shared secret called `MySecretKey`)
- **DH group:** 14

Phase 1

Peer A and peer B use IKE to negotiate and authenticate using the `MySecretKey` pre-shared key.

They agree to use **DH group 14** for the key exchange, **AES-256** for encryption, and **SHA-256** for hashing to protect the IKE.

The **DH key exchange** is performed, and both peers derive the same shared secret key.

An **IKE SA is** established with the agreed-upon parameters, creating a secure channel for further negotiations.

Phase 2

Within the secure channel from phase 1, peer A and peer B negotiate the IPSec SA.

They agree on using AES for encryption and SHA for hashing for further communication.

An IPSec tunnel is established, and data can now be securely sent between `1.1.1.1` and `2.2.2.2`.

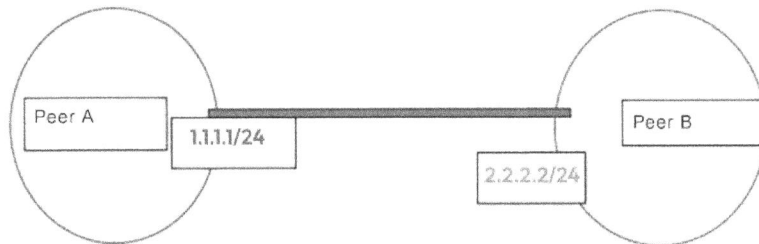

Phase 1

Peer IP   2.2.2.2

PSK: **MySecretKey**

Encryption: AES256

Phase 2

ESP

Encryption method AES256

Hashing method SHA256

Source IP 1.1.1.1/24

Destination IP 2.2.2.2/24

Phase 1

Peer IP   1.1.1.1

PSK: **MySecretKey**

Encryption: AES256

Phase 2

ESP

Encryption method AES256

Hashing method SHA256

Source IP 2.2.2.2/24

Destination IP 1.1.1.1/24

Figure 2.8: Creating an SA using IPSec

As seen in *Figure 2.8*, phase 1 establishes a secure and authenticated channel using IKE, including the DH key exchange to securely generate a shared secret key. This secure channel then allows for the setup of the IPSec tunnel in phase 2, which uses encryption and protects data traffic.

Quality of service (QoS)

You have already seen how **load balancers**, as well as some modern **routers** and **switches** with load-balancing functionality, can help network performance by ensuring traffic is distributed evenly between servers. This is a vital part of basic network management because it helps avoid bottlenecks and keeps data transfer smooth. However, load balancers on their own do not take into consideration different uses of the network, nor do they consider how data might travel across an entire network. There are many cases when one type of data or connection might need to be prioritized when it comes to speed and efficiency.

VoIP data, video conferencing, or minute-to-minute financial transactions for exchange all rely on data being received in a timely manner, while emails or static media transfer can take a little longer. For example, video conferencing requires a lot of data to move smoothly and consistently to prevent lagging, freezing, or audio cuts, while text-based communication, even if long, is by nature a smaller size and not as time-dependent.

This is where **QoS** comes in. It is a set of techniques and mechanisms used to prioritize and manage network traffic, ensuring reliable performance and meeting **service-level agreements** (SLAs) for critical applications. **QoS** mechanisms include traffic prioritization, bandwidth management, and congestion avoidance, which is done by configuring network devices (such as **routers** and **switches**) to recognize and prioritize specific types of traffic.

In the preceding example, without **QoS**, someone streaming a less-important video while on a break might cause your video conference to lag or lose quality. But with **QoS** enabled, the network knows the video conference is a priority and allocates enough bandwidth to it, reducing lag and making sure audio and video quality stay clear. So, even if someone else is downloading files, your video call won't be interrupted.

QoS operates across the entire network and affects the handling of traffic throughout all connected devices, influencing how traffic flows are managed across the network. It's designed to ensure end-to-end performance for high-priority applications. While network appliances will deal with standard traffic management tasks, **QoS** can help prioritize critical applications, reduce latency, and ensure sufficient bandwidth for essential services.

As you have seen, network appliances are constantly routing and rerouting data packets. This is a fundamental characteristic of IT networking, but it does raise the issue of what happens when this routing goes wrong. As covered in the *Physical and virtual appliances* section, routing tables are updated either manually or using a set of rules, and this runs the risk of creating a situation where a data packet might accidentally be sent around a network in a loop without ever reaching its destination. This can, in turn, cause congestion, slowing down the network. This deals with TTL, which is the final concept to be covered in this chapter.

Time to live

In networking, **TTL** is a field in an IP packet's header that controls how long a data packet can *live* on the network. It is essentially a countdown that prevents data packets from endlessly looping around a network due to routing errors, which could slow down the network and cause congestion. When a data packet is first created and sent from a device (such as a computer or smartphone), it's given a starting **TTL** value, normally 128. This number represents the maximum hops or routers the packet can travel through on its way to its destination. Each time the packet passes through a router, the **TTL** number is reduced by one.

For example, a packet has been traveling across networks until it arrives at *router Y* with a **TTL** value of 10. It is destined for *subnet X*, but somewhere along the way, one of the routers has an incorrect IP route for *subnet X*. The packet is then directed to a different router, which sends it back to *router Y*. Each hop decreases the **TTL** by 1, so the packet's **TTL** is now 8. The packet will continue to circulate four more times before its **TTL** reaches zero, at which point it will be dropped.

Misconfigurations are only one situation that can cause data packets to end up in loops. The data packet itself might be *undeliverable* if it were wrongly addressed, resulting in routers repeatedly forwarding it as they try to find a valid route.

Summary

In this chapter, you explored the key components of a network: **appliances**, **applications**, and **functions**. You saw how physical and virtual appliances such as **routers**, **switches**, **firewalls**, and **load balancers** manage network traffic and security. You also covered applications such as **CDNs**, which enhance performance and reliability, as well as essential functions such as **VPNs**, **QoS**, and TTL, which impact security, traffic prioritization, and packet management.

Understanding how these elements work together is crucial for designing, maintaining, and securing a network. As you continue preparing for the *CompTIA Network+* exam, keep in mind how these technologies interact to support efficient and secure communication. In the next chapter, you will build on this knowledge by looking at cloud concepts and connectivity options. The knowledge gained in this chapter will prepare you to answer questions relating to exam objective 1.3 in your *Comptia Network+ (N10-009)* exam.

Exam objective 1.2

Compare and contrast networking appliances, applications, and functions

Physical and virtual appliances:

- **Router:** Directs traffic between different networks based on IP addresses
- **Switch:** Connects devices within a network, forwarding data based on MAC addresses
- **Firewall:** Monitors and controls incoming/outgoing network traffic to enforce security policies
- **IDS/IPS:** IDS detects and IPS prevents network threats and intrusions in real time
- **Load balancer:** Distributes network traffic across multiple servers for optimal performance
- **Proxy:** Acts as an intermediary between clients and servers, enhancing security
- **NAS:** Centralized file storage and sharing over a network for easy access
- **SAN:** High-speed, block-level storage network for data-intensive applications
- **Wireless:**
    - **Wireless AP:** Connects wireless devices to a wired network infrastructure securely
    - **Controller:** Manages and optimizes multiple APs within a wireless network
- **Applications:**
    - **Content delivery network:** Delivers web content efficiently by caching data closer to end users
- **Functions:**
    - **VPN:** Securely connects remote users to a private network over the internet
    - **QoS:** Prioritizes and manages network traffic to ensure performance and reliability
    - **TTL:** Limits the lifespan of packets to prevent network congestion and loops

Chapter review questions

Now that you've completed the chapter, you can check your knowledge using the practice questions provided in the online platform at `https://packt.link/N10-009ch2`. You can also use the QR code below. Accessing these questions requires you to unlock the accompanying online content first. Head over to Chapter 26 for detailed instructions.

3

Summarize Cloud Concepts and Connectivity Options

Chapter 2 covered the main physical and virtual appliances that you will find in a standard on-premises network. However, organizations are increasingly turning to cloud-based services to fulfill some or all of their networking requirements. Like on-premises networks, cloud-based networks come in a variety of different formats depending on the needs of users, both in terms of size and functionality, and security and privacy.

As a network engineer, you will need to connect to and set up cloud-based networks, as well as advise on the best models and formats to use to meet business requirements.

This chapter covers essential concepts, including **network functions virtualization** (**NFV**) for virtualizing network services and **virtual private clouds** (**VPCs**) for creating secure environments. Key security tools, such as network security groups and network security lists, will also be discussed. You will then explore connectivity options such as **VPNs** and **Direct Connect** for secure data transfer, as well as gateways that facilitate internet and private cloud connections. Finally, you will examine deployment models such as public, private, and hybrid; service models, such as **software as a service** (**SaaS**), **infrastructure as a service** (**IaaS**), and **platform as a service** (**PaaS**); and important cloud features such as **scalability**, **elasticity**, and **multitenancy**.

This chapter covers the third objective in *Domain 1: 1.3 Summarize cloud concepts and connectivity options.*

> **Note**
>
> A full breakdown of objective 1.3 will be given at the end of the chapter.

Network functions virtualization

Imagine a company that streams virtual workshops. Its network has a physical server with all the content files, with a **firewall** for security. As the company becomes more successful, it adds a second physical **server**, with another **firewall** and a **load balancer**. Demand increases, and the company adds more servers, with more firewalls and load balancers. They offer additional services, all of which demand an ever-growing physical infrastructure. Although this is a viable solution, maintaining this physical infrastructure can be difficult, costly, and challenging for scalability.

One way to deal with these issues is to replace the physical servers, load balancers, and firewalls with software-based solutions. With **NFV**, you can use **virtual machines (VMs)**, **containers**, and **virtual appliances** to perform functions that traditionally required dedicated physical devices, all on shared hardware. These **virtual appliances** are covered in more detail in this section.

A **VM** is a software emulation of a computer running inside a real one. Just like a real computer, it has its own **operating system (OS)**, such as **Windows** or **Linux**, and it will run applications. A physical machine can run multiple **VMs**; however, even though they share the same physical resources, each one runs independently. You can replace physical servers with **VMs**, so they can be used for content delivery, firewalls, or anything else you would use a server for. They make scaling easier because new **VMs** can easily be set up on existing physical resources.

Containers are portable, self-sufficient units that package all the essential components of an application, including its code, libraries, dependencies, and configurations, and enable consistent and efficient deployment across various environments. They work independently from any OS and bring newfound agility to development and deployment, allowing software to move seamlessly between different environments, whether it's the developer's laptop, a staging server, or a cloud data center. The containers do not care which OS the applications are moved to.

They allow the isolation of applications, are not dependent on any OS, and allow developers to deploy apps across any **OS**. For example, media companies such as **Netflix** use containers to run different parts of the service, such as billing, streaming, or recommendations. Each function runs in a separate container, so updates and scaling happen without affecting the whole system.

Containers can be managed with software such as **Docker**, which is an open-source platform used to create, deploy, share, and manage containers. It can be used for sharing containers, is lightweight and efficient, and is ideal for running specific services without needing a separate **OS**.

A **virtual appliance** is prepackaged software designed to perform a specific network task, such as firewalling or load balancing. **Virtual appliances** act as software versions of physical network devices and can run inside a **VM** or a container. Many **virtual appliances** are built to meet industry standards such as **ETSI's NFV**, which helps them work across various networks.

> **Note**
>
> **ETSI ISG** stands for **European Telecommunications Standards Institute, Industry Specification Group**. It was founded in November 2012 by seven of the world's leading telecoms network operators. It is the home of NFV.

NFV frameworks are split into three parts: **virtual network functions (VNFs)**, **NFV infrastructure (NFVi)**, and orchestration and automation:

- A VNF is the actual network task (such as routing, firewalling, or load balancing) done by a virtual appliance, VM, or container.
- The NFVi includes the hardware (such as servers, storage, and network connections) that supports VMs and containers, allowing VNFs to run smoothly.
- **Orchestration** tools are used to coordinate how VNFs (whether in VMs or containers) are deployed, updated, and managed. This makes it easy to automate many parts of network management using scripting, which saves time and reduces errors.

For example, let's say a company needs to set up a firewall and a load balancer to handle its traffic. Instead of physical devices, the company could deploy these tasks as **VNFs** using virtual appliances that run in **VMs** or containers.

NFVi will host these **VNFs** on shared hardware. Orchestration tools use **automation** to deploy, monitor, and adjust these **VNFs** as demand changes. For example, if traffic spikes, the orchestrator can dynamically allocate more resources to the firewall and load balancer to ensure optimal performance, and scale them down when demand decreases, optimizing resource usage

NFV means you can have complex networks with relatively little hardware. In fact, if you want to cut down on hardware even more, you can host your VMs, containers, and virtual appliances on a VPC, which we will look at next.

Virtual private cloud

A **VPC** is a private section of a cloud provider's network that you control. Although the cloud provider might have multiple users, your **VPC** is isolated from others, making it secure and private so you can create and manage your own servers, databases, and other resources securely. Even though it's on a shared cloud, your **VPC** is isolated from others. The **VPC** is divided into smaller sections called **subnets**. Think of these subnets as different zones within your **VPC** for placing different resources depending on security needs. Subnets can either be public or private.

A **public subnet** is connected directly to the internet, which makes it ideal for resources that need to be accessible from outside your **VPC**. If you are hosting a public-facing website, you would place the **web servers** here to allow access. You can also place **load balancers** here to distribute traffic across multiple servers, helping with performance and reliability.

The public subnet is also where you place the **bastion host**, also known as **a jump box**. This is a secure server that lets administrators and authorized users access your private resources. Users connect to the bastion host, which then connects them to the private subnet resources.

A **private subnet** is isolated from the internet, which makes it more secure. Only other parts of the **VPC**, such as a **public subnet** or a **VPN**, can access this **subnet** directly. This is the place for any internal services that don't need public access, such as data processing or backup servers. **Databases** often store sensitive data, so they're placed in the private subnet for extra security. The servers that run the main business logic of your applications, known as **application servers**, are also placed in the **private subnet** if they only need to interact with your database or web servers and not with the public.

When users access the web servers in the public subnet, for example, by visiting a website, the web servers connect to the application servers or databases in the private subnet. Examples include fetching information such as airline tickets or storing data such as credit card numbers. Since the private subnet is not accessible from the internet, it adds a layer of security to sensitive resources.

Security can also be controlled using **network security groups** (**NSGs**) and **network security lists** (**NSLs**), which will be covered next.

Network security groups

NSGs act like a security guard for your cloud resources, controlling what type of traffic can come in (**inbound**) and go out (**outbound**) of specific parts of your network. They contain rules that allow or block traffic based on certain conditions, such as the type of connection, source or destination IP address, and port. These rules decide which kinds of data, also known as **traffic**, are allowed in or out. A rule could allow only specific IP addresses or types of traffic to reach a web server while blocking everything else. Think of **NSGs** as rules of entry and exit for your resources in the cloud, such as setting up entry/exit policies for a building.

For example, a web server will have an inbound rule in the **NSG** to allow traffic on port 80 (for **HTTP**) or 443 (for **HTTPS**) so people can access the website. They will also have an outbound rule to allow your server to send data to other servers, such as accessing an external API, while blocking everything else.

Network security lists

An **NSL** is a security feature used to create and manage lists of rules for network access. **NSLs** define what types of network traffic are considered secure and allowed to pass through. Similar to **NSGs**, **NSLs** specify rules that control secure access, often by identifying allowed IP addresses, protocols, and ports.

However, **NSLs** are typically more static than **NSGs** and can be applied broadly across segments of your cloud network to maintain consistency.

For example, you might create an **NSL** that allows access to a secure database only from specific **IP addresses** (e.g., your office network) while blocking all other traffic. This approach ensures that only trusted locations can connect to critical resources, enhancing the overall security posture.

Comparing NSGs and NSLs

NSGs are commonly used in **Microsoft Azure**, where they allow you to apply inbound and outbound security rules to virtual network interfaces, subnets, or both, enabling fine-grained control at multiple layers.

In contrast, **NSLs**, used in **Oracle Cloud Infrastructure** (**OCI**), are applied at the subnet level and control traffic based on source and destination IPs, ports, and protocols. For example, in Azure, an **NSG** can be applied directly to a VM's network interface to allow only SSH (port 22) from a specific **IP address**, while in **OCI**, an **NSL** might allow all web traffic (ports 80 and 443) into a subnet hosting web servers. **NSGs** tend to offer more flexibility due to their multiple attachment points, while **NSLs** provide simpler, subnet-wide controls.

Cloud gateways

In order to connect to cloud resources such as **VPCs**, there needs to be a secure, reliable method to bridge your on-premises network or other cloud environments to your cloud infrastructure. These methods are provided by **cloud gateways**, which facilitate this connectivity. **Cloud gateways** provide secure and controlled pathways for data traffic, allowing cloud environments to operate efficiently while protecting resources. The main types of **cloud gateways** are **internet gateways** and **network address translation (NAT) gateways**.

- **Internet gateways** enable users to connect directly and securely to cloud resources from the internet. They are essentially bridges between the public internet and the cloud resources, enabling secure access.

- **NAT gateways** allow private cloud resources to access the internet for updates while keeping them hidden from external users. For example, you have a private database in the cloud that needs to access the internet for things such as software updates but shouldn't be directly exposed to users on the internet. The **NAT gateway** allows this private database to connect to the internet to download updates while keeping it secure from outside access.

Cloud connectivity options

When a company wants its systems and data in the cloud to connect securely with systems and data on its own network, also referred to as **on-premises**, there are two main options: a **VPN** and **Direct Connect**. Each option offers different levels of security, speed, and reliability.

A **VPN** is a secure, **encrypted connection** that lets you link your on-premises network with your cloud network over the internet. Think of it like a secure tunnel that protects data as it travels across public networks. It uses encryption to protect data, meaning that even if someone intercepted the data, they wouldn't be able to read it. They are also usually cheaper than dedicated connections, because they run over the internet and are easy to set up, so they can work from any location with an internet connection.

For example, a company might need to give remote employees access to a database in the cloud. With a **VPN**, employees can securely access this database from anywhere as if they were directly connected to the company's network.

Direct Connect

Rather than using the public internet as in VPNs, **Direct Connect** is a dedicated private link between an on-premises network and a cloud provider such as AWS, Azure, or Google Cloud. It is faster, more reliable, and often more expensive than VPNs. Data travels more quickly and consistently, which is crucial for applications that require real-time data, such as video streaming or financial transactions, and it offers an extra level of security. If a company runs a lot of critical applications in the cloud that require consistent, fast access from its data center, it might choose

Direct Connect for smooth, uninterrupted performance. Direct Connect does not encrypt data by default, so organizations often implement encryption at higher network layers if needed. For companies running critical cloud applications that demand low-latency, high-throughput connections, Direct Connect can deliver smoother, uninterrupted performance—though usually at a higher cost than VPNs.

Cloud deployment models

Before a company moves to the cloud, it needs to select a reputable **cloud service provider (CSP)**, such as Microsoft Azure or **Amazon Web Services (AWS)**, that it is certain it can trust. The benefit of using a cloud service is that they are scalable and cost-effective, as you pay for the resources you need. There are four main cloud models: public, private, hybrid, and community. These are covered next.

Public cloud

A **public cloud** is the most common model, wherein the CSP hosts multiple tenants, sometimes on the same hardware. Public clouds are known as **multitenant**, which means that multiple customers share the same infrastructure and resources. This can increase security risks if proper protections are not in place, as one user's data could potentially be exposed to others. The risk in multitenancy cloud models is that, since multiple organizations are hosted on the same server, the actions of one tenant can impact the actions of another, and your organization could suffer a data breach.

Private cloud

With a **private cloud**, a company may purchase its hardware or have the CSP host it on separate servers from other companies. This model gives the company more control over its data and is generally more secure than other cloud models, as it is single-tenant, meaning that the company is the only one hosted on that particular server. For example, the U.S. military's IT infrastructure is now hosted in a private cloud because of the level of security it offers. In a private cloud, organizations prioritize security over cost by investing in dedicated infrastructure and resources, which allows for enhanced data protection and compliance with regulatory requirements, even though it may be more expensive than using shared resources in a public cloud. The U.S. military has its cloud with multiple vendors, such as AWS and Microsoft, for redundancy.

Note

For more information on how the U.S. military uses different vendors, visit `https://edition.cnn.com/2022/12/08/tech/pentagon-cloud-contract-big-tech/index.html`.

Hybrid cloud

Hybrid clouds are ideal for companies that decide not to host all of their organization in the cloud. A hybrid cloud is a mixture of both on-premises and cloud infrastructures. An example could be a manufacturing company that maintains a physical site to make products but has its mobile international salesforce hosted in the cloud. Their office is a car and a mobile phone.

Community cloud

With a **community cloud**, companies from the same industry collectively pay for a bespoke application to be written, and the cloud provider hosts it on a dedicated cloud infrastructure. They all share the cost between them and have their own separate copies of the application. It is a very cost-effective model if there are no off-the-shelf applications that fit the purpose.

Cloud service models

Depending on the needs of your business, there are different service models, including SaaS, IaaS, and PaaS. These models determine the level of control, management, and responsibility shared between the user and the service provider. Understanding the differences can help organizations choose the right approach for their specific requirements. They are covered next.

Software as a service (SaaS)

In SaaS, the CSP hosts a ready-to-use, predefined software application that you access through a web browser. They are subscription services and cannot be modified. These applications, such as Salesforce, Spotify, Microsoft 365, and Goldmine, are leased to users who simply pay for access, eliminating the need to manage or update the software themselves.

Infrastructure as a service (IaaS)

With IaaS, the CSP will provide network infrastructure, including desktops, servers, storage, firewalls, routers, and switches—the hardware devices for a network. When you purchase these devices, they have a default factory setting, and these settings need to be reconfigured to suit the needs of the organization. The customer needs to install the OS and configure and patch the devices. IaaS gives the customer more control but could come at a higher cost.

Platform as a service (PaaS)

PaaS offers developers the necessary environment to build applications seamlessly. Notable examples of PaaS include Microsoft Azure (specifically, App Service) and services such as MySQL. These platforms provide a comprehensive suite of tools and services that facilitate the development and deployment of applications across various platforms, including iOS, Android, and Windows devices.

Scalability

Scalability is the ability to increase or decrease resources (such as storage, processing power, or users) based on demand. However, the more resources you acquire, the more you have to pay for. For example, a company that sells concert tickets might need a standard amount of resources for regular days. However, when a big concert is announced, it needs more servers to handle the higher traffic. Once the demand drops, the resources can be reduced again to save costs.

Elasticity

Elasticity is like scalability but focuses on the automatic adjustment of resources. When demand increases, resources are automatically added, and when demand decreases, resources are automatically reduced without manual intervention. For example, an online store during a holiday sale will see a spike in visitors. The system automatically adds more computing power to handle the surge in visitors, and as soon as the sale ends, the system automatically reduces resources to save money.

Multitenancy

Multitenancy refers to multiple companies sharing the same cloud hardware while keeping their data separate and secure. While they all use the same physical servers and infrastructure, each company has its own isolated environment, ensuring that one company cannot access another company's data. It can include both internal and external tenants; each tenant has its data isolated from other tenants. It's like different businesses renting office spaces in the same building; each business has its own private space, but they all share the same building. This is used with a public cloud model.

Summary

This chapter covered essential cloud networking and infrastructure concepts, including NFV and VPCs. It explained how cloud environments are secured through network security groups and security lists and explored the use of cloud gateways such as internet gateways and NAT gateways. Connectivity options such as VPN and Direct Connect were also covered, offering insight into how organizations can securely connect to the cloud.

Additionally, the chapter outlined the different cloud deployment models—public, private, and hybrid—as well as service models such as SaaS, IaaS, and PaaS. It highlighted key characteristics of cloud computing, such as scalability, elasticity, and multitenancy, helping you understand how cloud services can dynamically adapt to changing demands while supporting multiple users and workloads efficiently.

The knowledge gained in this chapter will prepare you to answer questions relating to exam objective 1.3 in your *CompTIA Network+ (N10-009)* exam.

Exam objective 1.3

Summarize cloud concepts and connectivity options

Network functions virtualization (NFV): Virtualizes network services for cloud flexibility

Virtual private cloud (VPC): Creates secure, isolated cloud environments

Network security groups (NSGs): Control inbound and outbound cloud traffic

Network security lists (NSLs): Define rules for secure network access

Cloud gateways: Enable secure cloud internet connections

- **Internet gateway**: A popular and secure cloud gateway
- **NAT gateway**: Manages outbound internet traffic for private cloud resources

Cloud connectivity options:

- **VPN**: Secure, encrypted connection between cloud and on-premises
- **Direct Connect**: Dedicated private link for reliable cloud connectivity

Deployment models:

- **Public cloud**: Shared infrastructure, accessible to multiple users
- **Private cloud**: Dedicated, secure environment for one organization
- **Hybrid cloud**: Combines public and private cloud environments

Service models:

- **Software as a service (SaaS)**: Delivers applications via the cloud
- **Infrastructure as a service (IaaS)**: Provides virtualized computing resources
- **Platform as a service (PaaS)**: Supports the development and deployment of applications

Scalability: Ability to grow resources based on demand

Elasticity: Automatic adjustment of resources as needed

Multitenancy: Shared infrastructure with data isolation for multiple users

Chapter review questions

Now that you've completed the chapter, you can check your knowledge using the practice questions provided in the online platform at `https://packt.link/N10-009ch3`. You can also use the QR code below. Accessing these questions requires you to unlock the accompanying online content first. Head over to Chapter 26 for detailed instructions.

4

Explain Common Networking Ports, Protocols, Services, and Traffic Types

So far, you have seen the different layers of a network, the main applications and their functions, and the different ways a network is implemented in the cloud. However, the main point of a network is the information that is being passed between the different points. So, how does information travel throughout a network? How does it know where to go? And what are the rules for transferring this information?

In this chapter, you will see how modern networks use a system of ports, which are represented as numbers, to ensure communication goes to the correct application or service. Different ports are used for the different applications/protocols in a network; for example, port 80 is normally used for accessing HTTP websites, while port 22 is used for **SSH** connections. Traffic doesn't just need connections; it also needs rules for how to make those connections. In IT networks, these rules are called protocols. The rules dictate how information is shared, secured, and authenticated, and even how long a connection lasts. As a network engineer, you need to recognize ports and protocols so that you can analyze traffic within a network.

The last part of this chapter will cover different types of traffic, such as **one-to-one** connections and **one-to-many** connections.

This chapter covers the fourth objective in *Domain 1: 1.4, Explain common networking ports, protocols, services, and traffic types.*

Note

A full breakdown of objective 1.4 will be given at the end of the chapter.

Protocols and ports

While a protocol dictates the rules of how data is formatted and transmitted, a port acts as a virtual endpoint for communication between devices and applications over a network. A port is a designated channel through which data can be sent and received. Think of it like switching TV channels. If you want to watch sports, you tune to channel 1, and for the news, you switch to channel 2. Each channel is dedicated to a specific type of content. The same idea applies to computer ports. For example, port 80 (HTTP) is used to access websites. If you use the wrong port, you'll end up connecting to the wrong application or service. Ports are essential because they help identify the correct destination or service on a device, ensuring that data reaches its intended target accurately.

There are two different protocols for ports: the connection-oriented **Transmission Control Protocol** (**TCP**), which uses a three-way handshake, and the connectionless **UDP**. Both types will be covered later in the chapter; first, you will see some common ports and protocols.

Port numbers

Ports are categorized into different types based on their number ranges, and each type serves a specific purpose in network communication. Understanding these port types is essential to effectively manage and configure network services. *Table 4.1* shows the breakdown of these port types:

Port Types	Port number range	Purpose/service
Well-known ports	0–1023	Reserved for system services and applications. Examples include 80 (HTTP), 443 (HTTPS), and 25 (SMTP).
Registered ports	1024–49151	Registered for use by user processes or applications. Examples include 3389 (RDP) and 3306 (MySQL).
Dynamic or private ports	49152–65535	Typically used for ephemeral or temporary purposes. They are randomly assigned to client applications.

Table 4.1: Port numbers by type

Protocols

Protocols are standardized rules and conventions that govern how data is transmitted and received across a network. They ensure that different devices, applications, and systems can communicate with each other effectively, regardless of their underlying architecture. They define the **data format**, or how the data is structured and encoded for transmission, so that data can be understood by both parties. They define **addressing**, so network devices can be identified, **flow control** to avoid overloading, and **error checking**. They also define when data is sent or acknowledged. Each protocol has a specific purpose, defining how data should be formatted, transmitted, and handled, enabling reliable and structured communication over diverse networks. Depending on the needs of the transaction, different protocols prioritize different factors. For example, one file transfer protocol may have weak encryption but fast data transfer times, while another file transfer protocol might have stronger encryption, so it is more secure, but with slower transfer times.

Listed in *Table 4.2* are common protocols, functions, and ports that you need to know for the *CompTIA Network+* examination:

Protocol	Function	Port
FTP	Insecure file transfer	TCP port 20/21
Secure File Transfer Protocol (SFTP)	Secure file transfer	TCP port 22
SSH	Secure remote admin	TCP port 22
Telnet	Insecure remote admin	TCP port 23
Simple Mail Transfer Protocol (SMTP)	Mail transfer between mail servers	TCP port 25
Simple Mail Transfer Protocol Secure (SMTPS)	Secure email transmission between mail servers	TCP port 587
DNS	Hostname to IP address resolution	UDP port 53
DNS	Zone transfer: DNS servers updating each other	TCP port 53
Dynamic Host Configuration Protocol (DHCP)	Automatic IP address allocation	UDP port 67/68
Trivial File Transfer Protocol (TFTP)	Connectionless file transfer	UDP port 69
HTTP (which stands for **Hypertext Transfer Protocol**)	Insecure web traffic	TCP port 80
Network Time Protocol (NTP)	Synchronizes time	TCP port 123
Simple Network Management Protocol (SNMP)	Status and reports of network devices	UDP port 161/162

Protocol	Function	Port
Syslog	Centralizes logs	TCP port 514
Lightweight Directory Access Protocol (LDAP)	Insecure management of Active Directory	TCP port 389
Lightweight Directory Access Protocol Secure (LDAPS)	Secure management of Active Directory	TCP port 636
Hypertext Transfer Protocol Secure (HTTPS)	Secure web traffic	TCP port 443
Server Message Block (SMB)	File and print sharing	TCP port 445
TLS	Encrypted data in transit	TCP port 443
SQL	A language for managing and querying databases	TCP port 1433
Remote Desktop Protocol (RDP)	Remote administrator tool for Microsoft products	TCP port 3389
Session Initiation Protocol (SIP)	Enables voice, video calls over an internet-based network	TCP port 5060/5061
Spanning Tree Protocol (STP)	Prevents network loops in an Ethernet network. Bridge priority, default bridge	TCP port 32768

Table 4.2: Common protocols and their ports

Today, most networking occurs over the internet and intranets, making it important to understand **TCP/IP** in more depth. In the next section, we will explore different types of internet protocols in greater detail.

Internet protocol types

When discussing **Internet Protocol (IP)** types, it's essential to understand that different protocols serve specific purposes in the way data is transmitted and managed over networks. Each protocol is designed to handle a particular aspect of network communication, ensuring that data is delivered efficiently and securely across the internet. Some key IP types are **Internet Control Message Protocol (ICMP)**, which handles error reporting and diagnostics; **RDP**, which facilitates remote desktop connections; and IPsec, which secures IP communications by authenticating and encrypting each IP packet in a communication session. Understanding these protocols helps in managing and optimizing network traffic, ensuring reliable and secure data transmission.

Internet Control Message Protocol

ICMP is a network protocol used primarily for diagnostic and error-reporting purposes within IP networks. It operates at the network layer and is used by devices, such as routers, to send error messages and operational information, such as whether a service is available or a host is reachable. A common use of ICMP is in tools such as `ping` and `traceroute`, which help to test network connectivity and identify the path data takes through a network. Unlike TCP and UDP, ICMP is not typically used for transmitting user data but is essential for managing and troubleshooting network communication. The following code shows how `ping` is used.

```
C:\Windows\System32>ping www.bbc.co.uk
Pinging bbc.map.fastly.net [146.75.116.81] with 32 bytes of data:
Reply from 146.75.116.81: bytes=32 time=89ms TTL=58
Reply from 146.75.116.81: bytes=32 time=89ms TTL=58
Reply from 146.75.116.81: bytes=32 time=89ms TTL=58
Reply from 146.75.116.81: bytes=32 time=89ms TTL=58
Ping statistics for 146.75.116.81:
    Packets: Sent = 4, Received = 4, Lost = 0 (0% loss),
Approximate round trip time in milli-seconds:
    Minimum = 85ms, Maximum = 89ms, Average = 86ms
```

In the preceding example, you can see a ping packet testing the reachability of www.bbc.co.uk, specifically the IP address [146.75.116.81]. ICMP messages are responsible for sending the ping and getting a response from the target host. In this example, the connection is successful, with no data loss, and the average time taken for the ping to travel to bbc.co.uk and back is 86 ms.

> **Note**
>
> `ping` and `traceroute` are covered in more detail in Chapter 25, *Given a scenario, use the appropriate tool or protocol to solve networking issues*.

Transmission Control Protocol

TCP is **connection-oriented**, meaning it establishes a reliable connection between two devices before any data is transmitted. To initiate a connection for reliable delivery of data, TCP uses a process called the **three-way handshake**. There are three stages of this handshake – **synchronize**, or **SYN**; **synchronize-acknowledgment**, or **SYN-ACK**; and finally, **acknowledgment**, or **ACK**.

This is shown in *Figure 4.1*.

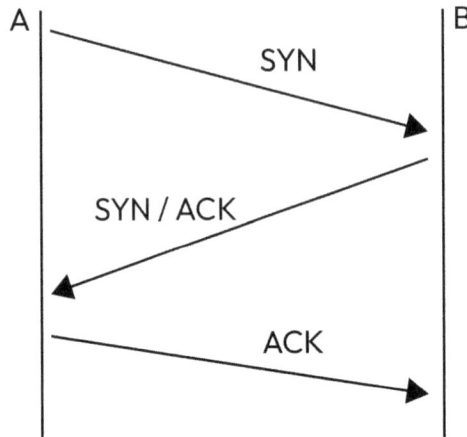

Figure 4.1: The TCP/IP three-way handshake

Figure 4.1 shows the sequence of packet exchanges that can create a session between **A** (the sender) and **B** (the receiver), through which they will later exchange data. This process is part of the TCP three-way handshake and consists of the following steps:

1. First, the sender (client) sends a **SYN** message to the receiver (server), indicating they wish to establish a connection and conveying the sequence number of its next packet.

2. The receiver (server) responds with a **SYN/ACK** message, indicating they are happy to establish the connection and signifying its next expected message.

3. The sender (client) replies with an **ACK** message, confirming receipt of the **SYN-ACK** message. At this point, the TCP session is established, and both parties can start exchanging data.

Once the session has been established, the TCP port sends data to the receiver, initiating data transmission. To ensure that all of the data has arrived, each part of the data exchange is regulated as follows:

Data transmission: When data is sent from one device (the sender) to another (the receiver) over a network, it is typically divided into smaller units called packets. These packets are sent individually to their destination.

Acknowledgment: The receiver verifies the received data and sends an ACK message to confirm successful delivery. This ensures reliability and helps manage retransmissions if any packet is lost or corrupted.

Error handling: If the sender doesn't receive an ACK message within a certain time frame, or if it receives a **Negative Acknowledgment (NACK)**, indicating an error, it can take the appropriate action(s). For example, it may retransmit the data packet to ensure reliable delivery.

The TCP process ensures reliability in communication, making TCP suitable for applications where data integrity is critical, such as web browsing, file transfers, and email. In an Ethernet network, the maximum size of a packet is known as the **maximum transmission unit** (MTU), which is 1,500 bytes.

User Datagram Protocol

UDP is connectionless, meaning it does not create a connection, unlike TCP. Because of this, it cannot guarantee delivery as it has no way to check that all of the packet has arrived. While this results in faster data transmission, it comes at the cost of reliability. This makes UDP the ideal choice for streaming video and online gaming, where speed takes precedence. In a UDP session, the application bears the responsibility of ensuring data reception. This is in contrast to TCP, which meticulously manages data integrity through its three-way handshake.

Generic Routing Encapsulation

Generic Routing Encapsulation (GRE) is a tunneling protocol created by Cisco that enables the encapsulation of various network layer protocols within virtual point-to-point connections. Essentially, GRE creates a private, secure pathway, or "tunnel," between two endpoints over a public network such as the internet. This enables the transport of packets of different protocols (such as **IPv4**, **IPv6**, or even **non-IP protocols**) across an IP network, effectively allowing for flexible and secure communication between distant networks. GRE is often used in VPNs to connect networks across different geographic locations, providing a seamless and secure connection as if the networks were directly connected.

Internet Protocol Security

IPsec, along with a three-way handshake, is covered in greater detail in *Chapter 2, Compare and Contrast Networking Appliances, Applications, and Functions.*

IPsec is a vital protocol for securing data across IP networks, especially over the public internet. It ensures that sensitive information can be transmitted securely and efficiently. IPsec is widely used in VPNs, secure communications, and protecting data at the network layer.

Protocols essentially govern the way in which interactions are carried out, and in the preceding example, we saw a straight connection between two parties. However, not every interaction in a network is one to one, and the final section of this chapter is about different types of interactions, or "traffic."

Traffic types

In networking, **traffic types** refer to the different ways data can be sent from one point to another over a network. These types determine how data is delivered to the destination(s). The main traffic types are unicast, multicast, anycast, and broadcast, each serving a different purpose depending on how many devices the data needs to reach.

Unicast, shown in *Figure 4.2,* is the most common type of network communication, where data is sent from one single sender to one single receiver. Think of it like a one-to-one conversation, where only two people are involved. For example, when you send an email to a friend, that email is transmitted from your device (sender) directly to your friend's device (receiver).

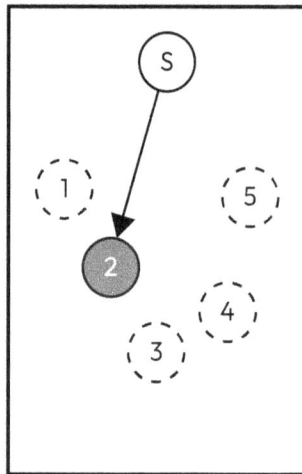

Figure 4.2: Unicast

Multicast, shown in *Figure 4.3,* involves sending data from one sender to a selected group of receivers. It's like a conference call where only those who are invited can listen in. This is commonly used in applications such as live video streaming or online gaming, where the same data needs to reach multiple users simultaneously, but not everyone in the network.

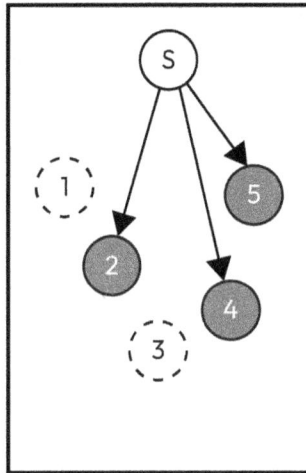

Figure 4.3: Multicast

Anycast , shown in *Figure 4.4,* is a method where data is sent from one sender to the nearest or most optimal receiver out of a group. Imagine a package being delivered to the closest store that can fulfill an order. In networking, this is used to route data to the closest server, improving speed and efficiency, often used in services such as DNS, where a user's request is directed to the nearest available server.

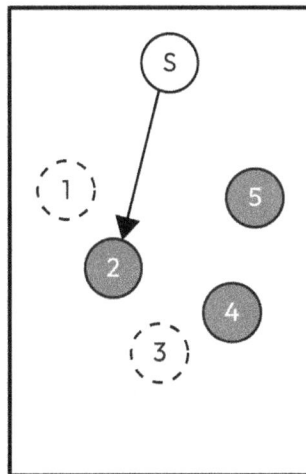

Figure 4.4: Anycast

Broadcast, shown in *Figure 4.5*, involves sending data from one sender to all possible receivers within a network. It's like a public announcement over a loudspeaker where everyone in the area can hear it. This method is used in scenarios such as **Address Resolution Protocol** (**ARP**), where information needs to be shared with every device on a local network.

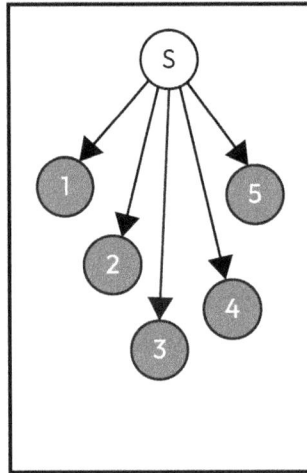

Figure 4.5: Broadcast

Summary

Networking ports, protocols, and services are essential components for communication over a network. Common protocols such as FTP, SSH, and HTTP use specific ports (e.g., FTP uses ports 20/21; HTTP uses port 80) to facilitate data transfer, secure connections, and web traffic. Protocols operate over different IP types, such as TCP, UDP, and ICMP, which define how data packets are transmitted and managed across the network. Traffic types such as unicast, multicast, anycast, and broadcast describe the ways data is distributed to devices. Understanding these protocols, ports, and traffic types is crucial for managing and securing network communications.

The knowledge gained in this chapter will prepare you to answer questions relating to exam objective 1.4 in the *CompTIA Network+ (N10-009)* exam.

Exam objective 1.4

Explain common networking ports, protocols, services, and traffic types

Protocols:

- **FTP (ports 20/21):** File transfer between computers
- **SFTP (port 22):** Secure file transfer using SSH
- **SSH (port 22):** Secure remote command-line access
- **Telnet (port 23):** Insecure remote command-line access
- **SMTP (port 25):** Email-sending protocol
- **DNS (port 53):** Domain name resolution
- **DHCP (ports 67/68):** Automatic IP address assignment
- **TFTP (port 69):** Simple, insecure file transfer
- **HTTP (port 80):** Web page delivery protocol
- **NTP (port 123):** Synchronizes time across network devices
- **SNMP (ports 161/162):** Network device management
- **LDAP (port 389):** Directory services access
- **HTTPS (port 443):** Secure web page delivery
- **SMB (port 445):** File and printer sharing on Windows
- **Syslog (port 514):** Logging system messages
- **SMTPS (port 587):** Secure email-sending protocol
- **LDAPS (port 636):** Secure directory services access
- **SQL Server (port 1433):** Database management system communication
- **RDP (port 3389):** Remote desktop access
- **SIP (ports 5060/5061):** Voice over IP communication

IP types:

- **ICMP:** Network error reporting
- **TCP:** Reliable, connection-based data transmission
- **UDP:** Unreliable, connectionless data transmission
- **GRE:** Encapsulates packets for tunneling
- **IPsec:** Secure IP communication (AH, ESP, IKE)

Traffic types:

- **Unicast**: Single-recipient communication
- **Multicast**: Communication to multiple specific recipients
- **Anycast**: Communication to the nearest of multiple nodes
- **Broadcast**: Communication to all nodes

Chapter review questions

Now that you've completed the chapter, you can check your knowledge using the practice questions provided in the online platform at https://packt.link/N10-009ch4. You can also use the QR code below. Accessing these questions requires you to unlock the accompanying online content first. Head over to Chapter 26 for detailed instructions.

5

Compare and Contrast Transmission Media and Transceivers

So far, you have seen the different appliances and applications in a wired network, as well as virtual counterparts in cloud-based systems. You have also seen how ports and protocols are used to help manage the data that goes through the network. Now, it's time to consider how that data is transferred between the appliances and applications. Understanding the various types of physical media that carry network signals (such as copper cables, fiber optics, and wireless signals) and the devices (transceivers) that send and receive these signals will allow you to design, implement, and maintain reliable and efficient network infrastructures. You should understand the strengths, weaknesses, capabilities, and limitations of each type of medium and transceiver, such as their speed, distance, cost, and susceptibility to interference. If you can't select the right combination of media and transceivers, your network will become slower and more expensive, harder to troubleshoot, and will experience more downtime.

This chapter explores the key differences and applications of wireless and wired transmission media, including emerging technologies such as 802.11 standards for Wi-Fi, cellular, and satellite connectivity, as well as traditional wired technologies such as Ethernet, fiber optics, and coaxial cables. Additionally, the chapter examines the diverse types of transceivers and connectors that enable seamless integration of devices in various networking environments.

This chapter covers the fourth objective in *Domain 1: 1.5 Compare and contrast transmission media and transceivers.*

Note

A full breakdown of objective 1.5 will be given at the end of the chapter

Wireless

In today's world, it's rare to encounter someone without at least one wireless device, especially in a busy office environment. Almost everyone carries a smartphone, and many also use tablets or laptops. Offices often include wireless printers and **internet of things (IoT)** devices such as smart lighting systems. All these devices contribute to crowded wireless networks, with many competing for the same frequencies. Without proper management, this could lead to chaos. However, modern wireless networks (such as Wi-Fi) use sophisticated rules and protocols to maintain order, allowing devices to communicate efficiently and securely.

Communication in a wireless network works like a conversation where only one person speaks at a time. It uses specific frequencies to send and receive data, but because wireless devices can't detect signal collisions directly, it uses a system to prevent them from talking over each other. This system is called **carrier-sense multiple access with collision avoidance (CSMA/CA)** and involves a device *listening* to see whether a channel, as defined by a frequency, is clear, sending the message, and then receiving an acknowledgment. The steps are as follows:

1. First, the device checks whether the communication channel frequency is currently being used. This is called the **carrier sense** part.
2. If the channel is already in use, the device will wait and then check again.
3. If the channel is free, the device sends the data packet.
4. When the receiver gets the data packet, it performs error checking.
5. If everything is fine, the receiver sends back an **acknowledgment (ACK)**
6. If the sender doesn't get an ACK, it tries sending the data again.

To further prevent interruptions, a device can send a **request to send (RTS)** signal, specifying its destination and how long it needs to send data. The receiving device replies with a **clear to send (CTS)** signal, and other devices in range wait their turn. This process ensures smoother communication by reducing the chance of collisions.

Wi-Fi networks usually work like a **hub-and-spoke system**, where a central device, such as a wireless router or **access point (AP)**, connects to multiple devices, such as phones or laptops, called **stations**, to create a wireless network.

Note

Types of networks will be covered in more detail in the next chapter, which is *Chapter 6, Compare and Contrast Network Topologies, Architectures, and Types.*

802.11 standards

There is a wide range of Wi-Fi-enabled devices from numerous manufacturers, each designed for different applications. Without standardization, it would be nearly impossible for these devices to communicate effectively. Fortunately, the **Institute of Electrical and Electronics Engineers (IEEE)** developed the **802.11** family of wireless **local area network (LAN)** standards, which define key parameters such as radio frequencies, data transmission rates, and signal behavior.

The 802.11 standards include amendments such as *802.11a*, *b*, *g*, *n*, and *ac*, each introducing improvements in speed, range, and reliability. These advancements ensure better performance and compatibility, enabling seamless communication across diverse devices. They are described in *Table 5.1*.

Standard	Max speed	Frequency	Range (indoors)	Description
802.11a	54 Mbps	5 GHz	35 meters	Early standard, faster but shorter range due to higher frequency
802.11b	11 Mbps	2.4 GHz	40 meters	Slower but longer range, and more interference due to the crowded 2.4 GHz band
802.11g	54 Mbps	2.4 GHz	40 meters	Backward compatible with 802.11b but faster, and still limited to the 2.4 GHz band
802.11h	54 Mbps	5 GHz	35 meters	Enhanced 802.11a with features to reduce interference with radar and meet EU regulations
802.11n Wi-Fi 4	600 Mbps	2.4 GHz and 5 GHz	70 meters	Introduced dual-band support, **multiple in/multiple out (MIMO)** antennas, and much higher speeds
802.11ac Wi-Fi 5	6.9 Gbps	5 GHz	35 meters	Focused on high speeds, and supports multiple devices and large data transfers

Standard	Max speed	Frequency	Range (indoors)	Description
802.11ax Wi-Fi 6	9.6 Gbps	2.4 GHz and 5 GHz	70 meters	Faster, more efficient, supports many devices, and works better in crowded areas and high-density environments

Table 5.1: 802.11 standards

The 2.4 gigahertz (GHz) frequency band is better for long distances and penetrating walls, but slower and prone to interference from microwaves, Bluetooth, and cell phones. The 5 GHz band is faster and suffers from less interference, but the range is shorter.

Starting with *802.11n*, Wi-Fi began using multiple antennas (MIMO), which significantly improved speed and reliability by sending multiple data streams at once. Newer standards, such as *802.11n* and *ac*, are compatible with older devices, ensuring that you can still connect to older equipment on your network.

Note

In October 2018, the names *Wi-Fi 4*, *5*, and *6* were introduced by the Wi-Fi Alliance to make it easier for non-technical users to understand the generation of Wi-Fi they're using or buying. For more details on frequencies and channels, see *Chapter 11, Given a Scenario, Select and Configure Wireless Devices and Technologies*.

Cellular

So far, you have looked at Wi-Fi, but of course, smartphones and many tablet computers can also connect to networks using cellular signals. **Cellular networks** are managed by telecommunications providers and work differently from private Wi-Fi. A cellular device connects to the nearest cell tower (base station), which links it to the larger network. The most common networks are **4G**, which means fourth generation, and **5G**, which means fifth generation. **Second generation (2G)** and **third generation** (**3G**) were deprecated due to low data rates in different countries. **Sixth generation** (**6G**) is currently being tested.

Long Term Evolution (LTE)

LTE was a big step forward because it let mobile networks work more like the internet, using the same technology to send and receive data. That's what made it faster and more reliable for things such as streaming, browsing, and apps. Current cellular networks mostly use 4G and 5G technology. The newest cellular standard, 5G, offers much faster speeds and lower delay, or latency, but requires more cell towers. Some types of 5G use **millimeter wave** (**mmWave**), which is very fast but only works at close range and struggles to pass through walls or windows.

Narrowband-IoT (NB-IoT)

NB-IoT is a low-power version of 4G that uses a smaller part of the network. It sends data slowly, about 20–100 **kilobits per second** (**kbps**), but that's fine because most sensors only need to send small bits of information quickly. NB-IoT is also better at getting signals through walls or underground, so it works well in hard-to-reach places such as tunnels or deep inside buildings.

For example, a water meter in the basement of a standard house can utilize NB-IoT to send daily usage data to the utility company. Even though it's deep underground, the signal still gets through thanks to NB-IoT's strong coverage.

Global System for Mobile Communications (GSM)

GSM is a worldwide standard for mobile networks. It uses SIM cards to identify and connect your phone to the network. This means you can easily switch phones by moving your SIM card, and you can use your phone in many countries if the network supports GSM.

Code division multiple access (**CDMA**) was another type of network, mostly used in the U.S. by carriers such as Verizon and Sprint in the past. Older CDMA phones didn't need SIM cards and were harder to switch between. But now, most networks, even former CDMA ones, use newer systems such as 4G LTE and 5G, which do use SIM cards.

If you're traveling from the U.S. to Europe and you have a GSM phone, you can just buy a local SIM card in the country you're visiting and use it in your phone to make calls or use data there. With older CDMA phones, this wouldn't be possible as you'd need a new phone or special arrangements.

To improve 5G coverage and reliability, networks use advanced technologies such as MIMO over multiple antennas to focus signals and connect to more devices at the same time.

Satellite

Cellular services have allowed devices to connect to networks outside of standard home and office environments. However, there are still plenty of places where even cellular networks are unavailable. Rural areas and inhospitable regions of the world, such as the Poles or deserts, do not have underground cables or cell towers, so often, the only way to connect is by using satellites.

Satellite communication uses dishes to send and receive signals from orbiting human-made satellites, but it has drawbacks. Because signals travel thousands of miles to space and back, there's a noticeable delay known as **latency**. This can affect activities such as online gaming or video calls. It is also more susceptible to adverse weather effects. Rain, snow, or storms can weaken the signal, causing slower speeds or temporary outages. Satellite communication can also be carried out with satellite phones. The signal from a satellite-enabled device transmits directly to the nearest satellite, which then sends the signal to the nearest gateway, or land-based center. It then transmits the signal to the receiving phone; the receiving phone can be a landline, cell phone, or another satellite phone.

There are two main types of satellite that can be used to access networks: **geostationary** (**GEO**) satellites and **low-earth orbit** (**LEO**) satellites.

GEO satellites are placed in high orbits, about 35,000 kilometers (22,000 miles) above the Earth, where they remain fixed over one location. This makes them easy to align with ground-based dishes, providing reliable coverage over large areas. However, one major drawback is increased latency. Signals must travel thousands of miles to the satellite and back, causing noticeable delays compared to land-based connections. This delay can affect real-time activities such as online gaming, video conferencing, or voice calls, making them feel laggy. Despite this, GEO satellites are widely used, especially in rural or remote areas where other internet options are unavailable.

LEO satellites orbit closer to Earth, reducing latency and improving performance. However, the dish must track moving satellites, requiring a motorized system. GEO requires fewer GEO satellites for inter-satellite communication because their distance from the Earth makes line of sight easier.

Satellites can also help devices such as smartphones determine their location by triangulating signals. Systems **GPS** (which stands for **Global Positioning System**) in the U.S. and **BeiDou** in China are commonly used worldwide.

Satellite communication is expanding, offering faster and more reliable services, but latency and weather remain challenges. For example, climbers typically use LEO satellites for communication through satellite phones. LEO satellites orbit much closer to the Earth (about 300 to 1,200 miles above the surface), which reduces latency and provides faster, more reliable connections compared to GEO satellites.

These phones connect directly to satellites, allowing climbers to make calls, send messages, and share GPS coordinates from almost anywhere on Earth. This capability is crucial for safety, enabling climbers to contact rescue teams or communicate with base camps during emergencies. However, satellite phones can be affected by weather conditions, such as heavy clouds or storms, which may disrupt the signal. Despite this, they remain a reliable lifeline for climbers in isolated and extreme environments.

Whether you use a smartphone to access the internet, connect your laptop to a wireless receiver, or use an Ethernet cable, most of the time, your data will eventually traverse a wired network, which we will cover next.

Wired

Despite continuing advances in wireless technology, most networks are still at least partially wired. **Wired networks** use physical cables to transmit data and are, on the whole, faster, more stable, more secure, and offer higher speeds than wireless counterparts.

This section introduces key wired technologies, including Ethernet standards, different types of fiber optic cables, specialized copper cables, cable performance speeds, and the importance of cable materials in specific environments.

Just as you saw in the section on wireless networks, for wired networks to perform efficiently, or even at all, there needs to be rules that allow devices to communicate on busy networks. Ethernet technology uses 802.3 standards set by the IEEE, which define how data is transmitted over physical cables in a LAN.

Ethernet standards define data transmission speeds, cable types, cable distances, and transmission modes. Transmission modes determine whether a cable carries data in only one direction at a time, which is known as **half-duplex**, or in both directions simultaneously, which is known as **full-duplex**.

Note

Transmission modes are covered in greater detail in *Chapter 10, Given a Scenario, Configure Switching Technologies and Features.*

Without these standards, different pieces of equipment from different manufacturers might not be compatible. For example, connecting a 10 Gbps high-speed cable to a switch that only supports lower data rates could lead to incompatibility or reduced performance. A device using **fiber optic cables** would be incompatible with a switch designed only for twisted-pair **Ethernet** unless both follow the same standard and include appropriate interfaces. Using devices that operate at different speeds will cause degradation in performance.

The *Table 5.2* summarizes various Ethernet standards, their specifications, and usage scenarios.

Ethernet standard	Max speed	Medium	Max distance	Description
10-BASE-2	10 Mbps	Coaxial thinnet	100 m	Thin coaxial cable, bulky and outdated
10-BASE-T	10 Mbps	Cat 3 twisted pair	185 m	Ethernet over twisted pair, early version
10-BASE-F	10 Mbps	Single-mode/ multimode fiber	2000 m	Ethernet over fiber for long-distance applications
100-BASE-TX	100 Mbps	Cat 5 twisted pair	100 m	Fast Ethernet, widely used in small networks
1000-BASE-T	1 Gbps	Cat 5e/6 twisted pair	100 m	Gigabit Ethernet, now standard for most modern networks
1000-BASE-SX	1 Gbps	Multimode fiber	220-500m	Short-range gigabit Ethernet over fiber
1000-BASE-LX	1 Gbps	Single-mode/ multimode fiber	5 km	Long-range gigabit Ethernet over fiber
10G-BASE-T	10 Gbps	Cat 6a/7 twisted pair	100 m	High-speed Ethernet over twisted pair cables
10-BASE-SR	10 Gbps	Multimode fiber	500 m	Short-range Ethernet for data centers

Ethernet standard	Max speed	Medium	Max distance	Description
10-BASE-LR	10 Gbps	Single-mode fiber	10 km	Long-range Ethernet for campus or backbone networks
40G-BASE-LR4	40 Gbps	Single-mode fiber	10 km	High-speed Ethernet for large networks and data centers
100G-BASE-LR4	100 Gbps	Single-mode fiber	10 km	Ultra-high-speed for cloud and large infrastructure

Table 5.2: Ethernet standards

Similar to Wi-Fi, wired networks are often crowded, and there needs to be methods to allow data flow from multiple devices in an efficient manner. The 802.3 standards use a method called **carrier-sense multiple access with collision detection (CSMA/CD)** to manage how devices share a network and avoid transmitting data at the same time. There are both similarities and differences between CSMA/CD and the CSMA/CA protocol that you saw for wireless networking, but first, let's take a brief look at the steps involved in CSMA/CD:

1. The network device listens to the network to check whether the cable is free or whether another device is already sending data. If the wire is busy, the device waits. If the wire is clear, the device sends its data. This is known as **carrier sense**.
2. All devices on the network share the same connection, so they take turns sending data when the cable is free. This is known as **multiple access**.
3. If two devices send data at the same time, their signals collide, causing the data to become garbled. Both devices detect the collision and stop sending data. This is **collision detection**.
4. After a random delay, the devices try sending the data again, going back to *step 1*. The delay ensures they don't collide again immediately. This is known as a **retry**.

Both CSMA/CA and CSMA/CD are designed to maximize fairness and efficiency in access networks, but because they are for different types of networks, there are some key differences. In wireless networks, where CSMA/CA is used, devices cannot directly detect collisions due to challenges such as signal attenuation and the hidden node problem. Instead, collision avoidance is done proactively. The device listens to the channel to ensure it is idle, waits for a random backoff time to reduce the chance of simultaneous transmissions, and then sends the packet. To confirm successful transmission, the receiver sends an ACK signal. If no ACK signal is received, the sender assumes a collision or error occurred and retransmits the packet.

In wired networks, where CSMA/CD is used, devices also check whether the channel (cable) is free before transmitting. However, they can detect collisions during transmission by monitoring the signal on the cable. If a collision is detected, the device immediately stops transmitting, sends a jamming signal to notify other devices, and retries after a random backoff period.

The part of a network where different devices can collide is called the **collision domain**, so if two laptops are connected to the same hub in a wired LAN, they are in the same collision domain, while a tablet device connected to the LAN by Wi-Fi will be in a different collision domain.

Wired networks, as the name suggests, use physical cables to connect devices. The most common types of cables are coaxial, twisted pair, and fiber optic, each with variations suited to specific needs. When designing a network, it is crucial to understand the capabilities and limitations of each type of cable. The following sections will explore these in detail, starting with fiber optic.

Fiber Ethernet and OM standards

Fiber Ethernet is a type of networking that uses **fiber optic cables** to transmit data as light signals. Fiber optic cables are faster because light pulses can travel longer distances in a shorter amount of time than electrical pulses through copper cables. They are also more reliable because they are not susceptible to **electromagnetic interference** (**EMI**).

For example, you might be setting up a network connection between two buildings that are 300 meters apart on a university campus. You have two choices, Ethernet cables or fiber optic cables:

- **Using copper Ethernet cable (for example, Cat 6)**:

    Standard Ethernet cables can only reliably transmit data up to 100 meters. Beyond that, the signal gets weak, causing data loss or no connection at all. To go 300 meters, you'd need repeaters or switches in between, which adds cost and complexity.

- **Replacing with fiber optic cables**:

    Fiber optic cables can transmit data much farther (even several kilometers) without signal loss. You can run a single fiber optic cable directly from one building to the other. It also provides faster speeds and is immune to electrical interference, which is great in outdoor or industrial areas.

Fiber optic cables are categorized by **optical multimode** (**OM**) standards, which define the cable's performance based on its speed, distance, and intended use. The higher the OM number, the higher the speed, measured in **gigabits per second** (**Gbps**), as shown in Table 5.2.

OM1	Older multimode fiber that supports up to 1 Gbps over up to 300 meters. Typically used with LED light sources.
OM2	Improved over OM1. Supports 1 Gbps up to 600 meters, and 10 Gbps up to 82 meters
OM3	Laser-optimized fiber. Supports 10 Gbps up to 300 meters, and 40/100 Gbps up to 100 meters.
OM4	Enhanced OM3. Supports 10 Gbps up to 550 meters, and 40/100 Gbps up to 150 meters.
OM5	Newest standard, designed for **shortwave wavelength division multiplexing (SWDM)**. Supports up to 100 Gbps over 150 meters, and aims to enable higher speeds with fewer fibers. Optimized for data centers and scalable upgrades.

Table 5.3: OM standards

Note

Fiber connectors will be covered later in this chapter.

Single-mode versus multimode fiber

Fiber optic cables come in two main types: single-mode and multimode. **Single-mode fiber** has a single, very thin core. It transmits light in one straight path (i.e., it is single-mode, which reduces signal loss and increases the distance the signal can travel) so it is ideal for long-distance communication. It is often used by telecom companies and **internet service providers (ISPs)** because, although it costs more than multimode, it offers higher bandwidths.

Multimode fiber has a wider core than single-mode, and this allows multiple light paths to travel simultaneously. There are potential signal distortions over long ranges due to modal dispersion, which is the increased chance of interference, but it is cheaper than single-mode, so it is best for short distances. Because it is cost-effective, it is commonly used in offices, campuses, and data centers.

Direct attach copper cables

Though fiber optic cables are efficient for short-range connections of around 10 meters or less, the setup can be cumbersome, which is why **copper cables** are still preferred in smaller environments to connect devices such as switches, routers, and servers. They require less power than fiber optics, and are more durable and cheaper. They are also easier to set up because there's no need to match or configure separate transceivers.

Direct attach copper (DAC) cables are made of twin axial copper and typically have transceivers attached to both ends, as shown in *Figure 5.1*.

Figure 5.1: DAC cable

Twinaxial, also referred to as **twinax**, means it has two insulated wires inside, twisted together rather than a single wire, as in a **coaxial cable**. Twinax is the foundation for DAC cables and supports high-speed data transfer while being more affordable than fiber optic cables. It also allows **InfiniBand** technology.

Note

InfiniBand is distinct from Ethernet and is used in high-performance computing environments, supercomputing, and data centers for tasks that require high bandwidth and very low latency, such as scientific simulations and large-scale data processing. It is unlikely to be covered in the exam.

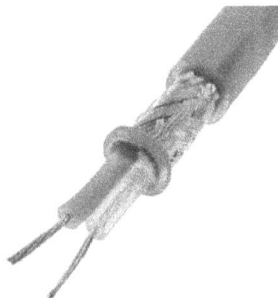

Figure 5.2: Twinaxial cable

Coaxial cable

Prior to the introduction of DAC and fiber into telecommunications networks, the dominant physical transmission method for most applications was the coaxial cable. These cables originally carried analog signals, such as radio and especially television signals. They were then used to carry digital signals in the early days of the Internet and were part of the first Ethernet standards. They are still in use, although they have mostly been replaced by the aforementioned twinaxial and fiber optic cables.

A coaxial cable, or coax, consists of a central copper core surrounded by an insulating layer, a metal shield, and an outer cover, as shown in *Figure 5.3*.

It supports longer distances than twinaxial cables but is not as fast, meaning it doesn't compete with fiber optics in terms of performance. However, coaxial cables are cheaper than fiber optics and easier to maintain, especially when the cable is frequently moved or disturbed. Coaxial is less prone to interference than twinaxial, making it a good option for long-distance signal transmission where fiber optics might be too fragile or not cost-effective.

Figure 5.3: Coaxial cable

Cable speeds

A major consideration while planning a network will be network speed. The speed of a cable depends on its type, quality, and specific use cases. Fiber internet speeds of 400 Gbps or even higher are crucial for specific, high-demand applications, but businesses with lower bandwidth requirements, such as around 10 **megabits per second (Mbps)**, may not need such high speeds. However, the importance of 400 Gbps fiber speeds lies in the capacity and future-proofing they offer.

Fiber optic cables offer the highest speeds, reaching 400 Gbps or more, making them ideal for long-distance, high-speed networks. DAC cables can reach speeds of up to 100 Gbps, making them well suited for short distances within data centers. Twinaxial cables offer speeds between 25–100 Gbps, making them suitable for high-speed, short-range connections. In contrast, coaxial cables generally support speeds ranging from 10 Mbps to 1 Gbps, and are primarily used for internet and cable TV applications. Each cable type is optimized for different scenarios, with fiber optic cables being the fastest and most capable for long distances, while coaxial and DAC cables are more suited to shorter-range applications.

Plenum versus non-plenum cable

Plenum cables are a specialized type of cable designed for use in plenum spaces, which are the areas in buildings used for air circulation in **heating, ventilation, and air conditioning** (**HVAC**) systems. These spaces often include the space above a dropped ceiling or below a raised floor. Because these areas facilitate airflow, they can also help spread flames and smoke in the event of a fire. Plenum cables are constructed with materials that are flame-retardant and emit low smoke and non-toxic gases when exposed to heat or fire. These features make them compliant with strict building safety codes for use in plenum spaces. They are more expensive than **non-plenum cables**, so to reduce costs, they tend not to be used in areas with low fire safety concerns.

Transceivers

A **transceiver** is a device that combines a **transmitter** and a **receiver** into a single module. It serves as the interface between a device (such as a switch, router, or server) and the network. The transceiver enables seamless communication by converting electrical signals from the device into optical signals for transmission over fiber optic cables, or vice versa. It is used in data centers, offices, and enterprise networks, enabling high-speed communication over long distances using fiber optics.

Transceivers are typically hot-swappable, meaning you can replace or upgrade them without shutting down the device, ensuring minimal downtime. For example, let's say you have a small office network. The network switch is in one room and needs to be connected to another switch 100 meters away, in another room. Ethernet cables won't work reliably at that distance, so you use fiber optic cable. The setup will be as follows:

1. You insert a **small form-factor pluggable** (**SFP**) transceiver (1 Gbps) into the SFP port on each switch.

2. Then you connect them with fiber optic cable (such as OM3 multimode).

3. The transceiver converts electrical signals from the switch into light signals, sends them over the fiber, and then the transceiver at the other end converts the light back into electrical signals.

Protocols

Protocols define the rules and standards for data communication between devices. They ensure that data is transmitted and received correctly, no matter the type of network or device.

Ethernet

Ethernet is the most widely used protocol in networking. It supports data transmission over both copper and fiber cables and comes in various speed standards, such as Fast Ethernet (100 Mbps), Gigabit Ethernet (1 Gbps), and 10/40/100 Gigabit Ethernet. Ethernet is typically used in LANs to connect computers, servers, and other network devices.

Fibre Channel Protocol (FCP)

FCP is a protocol specifically designed for high-speed data transfer, often used in **storage area networks (SANs)**. It supports the connection of servers to storage devices, offering high performance and low latency. While it uses fiber optic cables, it can also run over copper cables for short distances.

Form factors

Form factors describe the physical size, shape, and specifications of a transceiver module. Different form factors are used based on the type of network and the speed requirements.

Small form-factor pluggable (SFP)

SFP is a compact, hot-swappable transceiver widely used in networking equipment for Ethernet and fiber channel connections. It supports speeds of up to 1 Gbps (SFP) and 10 Gbps (SFP+). SFP is ideal for connecting switches, routers, and other devices to fiber optic or copper cables.

For example, let's take a university network that connects different buildings on campus using fiber optics. Each building has a network switch with SFP ports. They insert 1 Gbps SFP modules with **local connector** (LC) connectors into these switches, then run OM3 multimode fiber between them. This allows reliable, high-speed connections across campus without replacing the whole switch.

Quad small form-factor pluggable (QSFP)

QSFP is similar to SFP but designed for higher data rates. It supports speeds up to 40 Gbps (QSFP) or even 100 Gbps (QSFP28). It is often used in high-performance data centers and cloud environments where large volumes of data are transmitted.

For example, imagine a data center that interconnects high-performance servers and spine-leaf switches using QSFP+ modules that support 40 Gbps. The QSFP+ ports are connected with **multi-fiber push-on (MPO)** and/or **multi-fiber termination push-on (MTP)** connectors and OM3 or OM4 fiber, allowing fast backbone links.

Understanding transceivers, protocols, and form factors helps you make informed decisions about network design, troubleshooting, and upgrades. These elements are foundational to building scalable and efficient networks, whether in small businesses or large data centers.

Connector types

Once you have sorted out which cabling you require for which function or scenario, you also need to consider which devices the cable will attach to. The connectors at each end of the cable need to be suitable not just for the device, but also for the cables. To close this chapter, you will see a collection of common connectors and specific applications.

Figure 5.4: Subscriber connector

A **subscriber connector (SC)** is used in fiber optic connections, often in patch panels. It is square-shaped and has a snap-in design, and is commonly found in older fiber networks.

Figure 5.5: LC

An LC is commonly used in fiber optic connections, especially in modern networks. It is smaller than an SC and also features a snap-in design, making it ideal for high-density environments. LCs are most commonly used in data centers and high-density networks. They are also the most likely connector type found on an NIC when used with SFP or SFP+ transceivers, due to their compact size and compatibility with modern networking equipment.

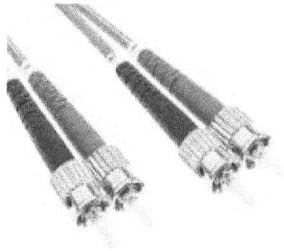

Figure 5.6: Straight tip

A **straight tip (ST)** connector is a fiber optic connection used in legacy systems. It is a round, bayonet-style connector with a twist-lock and is commonly found in older fiber optic systems.

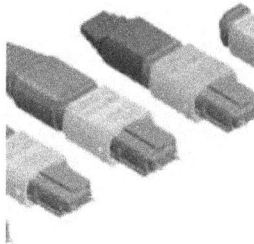

Figure 5.7: Multi-fiber push-on

An MPO connector is used for high-density fiber optic connections. It is a flat connector that houses multiple fibers and is commonly used in data centers and 40/100 Gbps networks. The MPO connector is designed to handle multiple fiber strands in a single connector, and it is commonly used with high-density transceivers such as QSFP.

Figure 5.8: Registered jack (RJ11)

A **registered jack 11 (RJ11)** connector is used in telephone and **digital subscriber line (DSL)** connections. It is small, with four pins, and is commonly used with landline phones and some DSL modems. It can be used by fax machines that use a telephone connection.

Figure 5.9: Registered jack (RJ45)

A **registered jack 45 (RJ45)** connector is commonly used with Ethernet cables, such as Cat 5, Cat 6, and Cat 7 cables. It is small with eight pins, and it connects computers, routers, switches, and other network devices to create LANs.

Figure 5.10: F-type

An **F-type** connector is a coaxial cable connection. It is screw-on and is used for cable TV and the internet.

Figure 5.11: Bayonet Neill–Concelman

A **Bayonet Neill–Concelman (BNC)** connector is a quick-lock connector used with coaxial cables for video, radio, and legacy networking. It's common in CCTV, RF equipment, and older Ethernet systems, offering easy, reliable connections.

Figure 5.12: BNC barrel connector

A **BNC barrel** connector is a small coupler used to join two BNC cables, extending their length. It's simple, cost-effective, and often used in CCTV systems or to bridge coaxial cable runs.

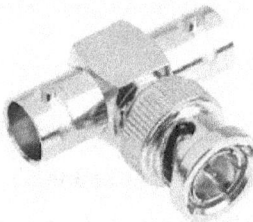

Figure 5.13: BNC T connector

A **BNC T** connector is a type of coaxial connector shaped like the letter *T* that has three ports. It is commonly used in networking, broadcasting, and instrumentation applications. It is most commonly seen in legacy setups.

Summary

This chapter covered the different ways in which devices are connected, both wired and wireless. Transmission media and transceivers are essential components of networking infrastructure, each serving distinct purposes. Transmission media include wireless technologies (e.g., 802.11 Wi-Fi standards, cellular, and satellite) and wired solutions such as Ethernet (802.3 standards), fiber optics (single-mode and multimode), DAC, twinaxial, and coaxial cables. These media differ in speed, range, and applications, from long-distance fiber connections to short-range copper setups. Transceivers, on the other hand, enable seamless data transmission by converting signals between devices and the network, using protocols such as Ethernet or FCP. Common transceiver types include SFP for standard speeds and QSFP for high-performance needs. Together, transmission media provide the physical path for data transfer, while transceivers act as the bridge, ensuring compatibility and efficiency across devices.

The knowledge gained in this chapter will prepare you to answer questions relating to exam objective 1.5 in your *CompTIA Network+ (N10-009)* exam.

Exam objective 1.5

Compare and contrast transmission media and transceivers

- Networking concepts:

    - **Wireless:**

        - **802.11 standards:** Wireless networking standards such as Wi-Fi

        - **Cellular:** Mobile network connectivity such as 4G and 5G

        - Satellite: Internet access via satellite signals

    - **Wired:**

        - **802.3 standards:** Ethernet networking standards

        - **Single-mode vs. multimode fiber:** Fiber types for long- or short-distance

        - **Direct attach copper (DAC) cable:** Short-distance, high-speed connections

        - **Twinaxial cable:** High-speed cable for data centers

        - **Coaxial cable:** Cable for TV, internet, and radio signals

        - **Cable speeds:** Data transmission rates of various cables

        - **Plenum vs. non-plenum cable:** Fire-resistant vs. standard cabling

- Transceivers:

    - **Ethernet protocol:** Networking protocol for wired connections

    - **Fibre Channel Protocol (FCP):** Protocol for high-speed storage networking

    - **SFP:** Small pluggable transceiver for fiber or copper

    - **QSFP:** Quad small pluggable for higher data rates

- Connector types:

    - **Subscriber connector (SC):** Fiber-optic connector

    - **Local connector (LC):** Compact fiber-optic connector

    - **Straight tip (ST):** Fiber-optic connector with twist-lock design

    - **Multi-fiber push-on (MPO):** High-density fiber-optic connector

    - **RJ11:** Connector for telephones

    - **RJ45:** Connector for Ethernet networking

    - **F-type:** Connector for coaxial cables

Chapter review questions

Now that you've completed the chapter, you can check your knowledge using the practice questions provided in the online platform at `https://packt.link/N10-009ch5`. You can also use the QR code below. Accessing these questions requires you to unlock the accompanying online content first. Head over to Chapter 26 for detailed instructions.

6

Compare and Contrast Network Topologies, Architectures, and Types

Just as IT networks serve a variety of purposes, there are also numerous ways to configure them. To create an efficient, secure, and reliable network, you need to make the right choices about how to set it up, which means understanding the various network topologies, architectures, and types used in designing and implementing a robust network.

Network topology refers to arranging elements such as links and nodes in a computer network, how the network is physically laid out, and whether intermediary devices are required. A topology can significantly impact performance, scalability, and fault tolerance. Meanwhile, **network architecture** describes the broader framework that defines the principles, design, and procedures that govern how the network is constructed and operates. Different architectures have different strengths and weaknesses, and understanding them is key to efficient network design. Finally, **network types** define the specific configurations or models used within a network to facilitate data communication.

In simple terms, networks consist of nodes and links. A node can either be an endpoint for information, such as a network interface that connects a PC or mobile device to the network, or a device such as a firewall, router, switch, or hub that controls the flow of data. Links refer to the connections between these nodes, which can be wired (such as Ethernet cables) or wireless (such as **Wi-Fi**, satellite, or even **Li-Fi**).

In this chapter, you will learn about the different types of network topologies, their advantages, and their disadvantages. You will also gain an overview of traffic flow.

This chapter covers the sixth objective in *Domain 1: 1.6, Compare and contrast network topologies, architectures, and types.*

> **Note**
>
> A full breakdown of objective 1.6 will be given at the end of the chapter.

Mesh

A **mesh network** is a type of network topology where each device, or node, is connected directly to multiple other nodes. This creates a web-like structure where data can travel along many different paths from one node to another. There are two types of mesh networks, **full mesh** and **partial mesh**.

In a full mesh network, every node is connected to every other node, enabling all devices in the network to communicate directly with each other without relying on a central router or a switch. If one connection or node fails, the data can use one of the other routes to send the data through other nodes, ensuring that communication continues. This redundancy makes mesh networks highly reliable and fault tolerant. Full mesh networks used to be common in small **local area networks**, but as can be seen in *Figure 6.1*, the larger they get, the more complex they are. A partial mesh, as the name implies, is where only some nodes are fully interconnected, while others connect to just a few nodes.

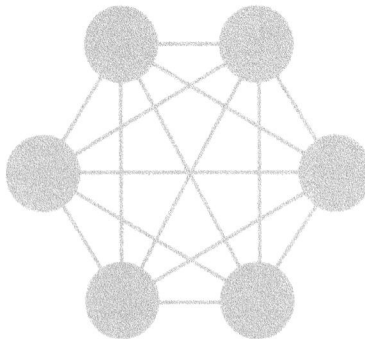

Figure 6.1: Full mesh network

Figure 6.1 shows a **full mesh** network. Even with just a small number of nodes, in this case 6, the number of connections is large, in this case 15.

This number can be calculated by using the formula $\frac{n(n-1)}{2}$. So, in our case, we have the following:

$$\frac{6(6-1)}{2}$$

$$\frac{6 \times 5}{2} = 15$$

As the number of nodes grows, the number of connections grows exponentially. Although the system is highly fault tolerant, it becomes difficult to manage and expensive to maintain because of all the cabling.

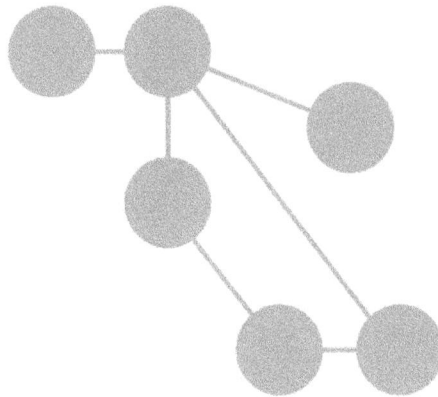

Figure 6.2: Partial mesh network

Figure 6.2 shows a **partial mesh** network. As you can see, only some nodes are fully interconnected, while others connect to just a few nodes. This makes connection management more efficient, but there is less redundancy, so partial mesh networks are less reliable. Full and partial mesh networks are commonly used in wireless networks, such as those in large buildings, outdoor areas, or communities where consistent and reliable coverage is needed.

Star/hub and spoke

In a **star**, also known as **hub-and-spoke**, topology, multiple nodes are connected to one central device. Data is passed through the central device, which then communicates it back to the other device or devices connected.

The simplest example is multiple computers connected to a single hub with either a cable or Wi-Fi.

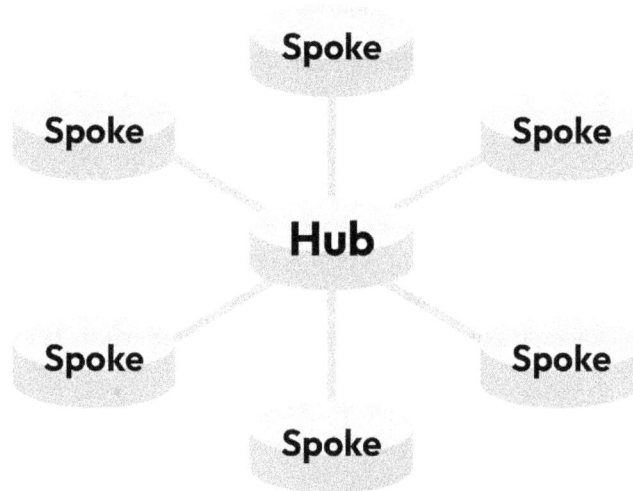

Figure 6.3: Star/hub and spoke

Figure 6.3 shows a typical star/hub-and-spoke topology with a central hub and six connections. The one-connection-per-machine model reduces costs and management overhead. Star topologies are convenient because it is easy to add a node with a single connection to the central point. In a star/hub-and-spoke network, if you need to update software or settings across the network, you can often push that update from the central hub to all connected devices. For example, there may be a new security patch for interface firmware, and by pushing it via the hub, all devices can be updated simultaneously, rather than having to patch individual devices at once. This can be important in environments in which keeping all devices up to date is crucial, such as in healthcare settings where medical devices must comply with strict regulatory standards, or in financial institutions where security vulnerabilities could expose sensitive data.

A centralized hub means that these topologies are more at risk of single points of failure – if the hub breaks, all the spokes will lose connection. However, these risks are mitigated with highly reliable equipment and by introducing redundancies with back-up hubs. The centralized hub could be replaced by a switch for faster communication.

Token ring topology

In a **token ring** topology, a token is passed around a number of nodes that are connected logically. A node is only able to transmit and receive information while it holds the token. A token ring topology is used in networks where precise timing and collision-free communication are critical, such as in industrial or manufacturing environments where delays could disrupt production processes. It ensures that only one device can transmit data at a time by passing the token around the network, reducing the chance of data collisions. While less common in modern office networks, token ring networks may still be found in legacy systems and may be important when maintaining or upgrading older infrastructure.

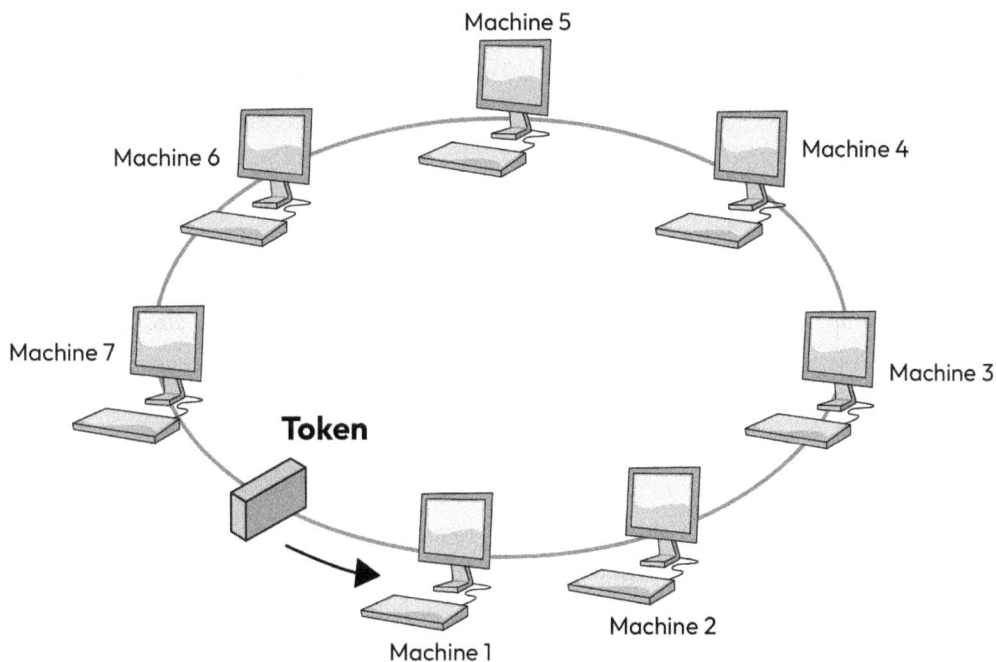

Figure 6.4: A token ring topology

In *Figure 6.4*, the token is traveling counterclockwise (although it can also travel clockwise) around seven desktop computers. At any time, a machine can seize the token, as long as it's not in use by another device, to transmit a message. Its ability to provide orderly and predictable network traffic is its main advantage in environments where timing and reliability are paramount.

Hybrid

A **hybrid network** combines two or more different types of topologies. In *Figure 6.5*, we combine a star/hub and spoke topology, on the left, with a token ring topology, on the right, connected by a switch or a bridge. This creates a network that benefits from the strengths of both.

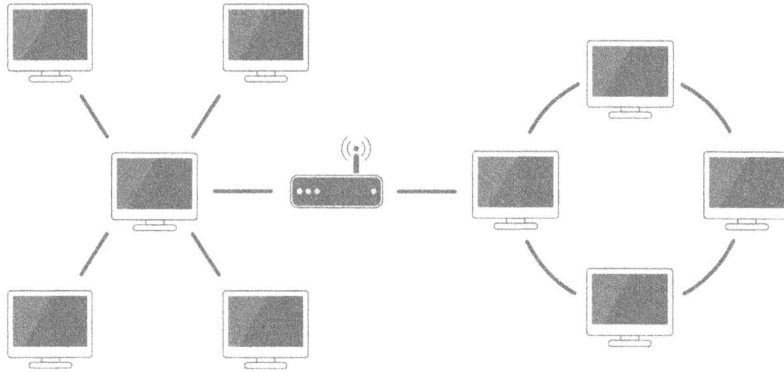

Figure 6.5: A hybrid topology

This hybrid network could be used in manufacturing setups. The left-hand side is used for general day-to-day company operations, such as project planning and informational storage, while the right-hand side is used to create precise and reliable data flow for machines or sensors that require strict timing and coordination.

Spine and leaf

A **spine-and-leaf** topology is made up of three sections, as shown in *Figure 6.6*. Each **leaf switch** connects to every **spine** switch, but not to each other. Each leaf switch connects to an end device.

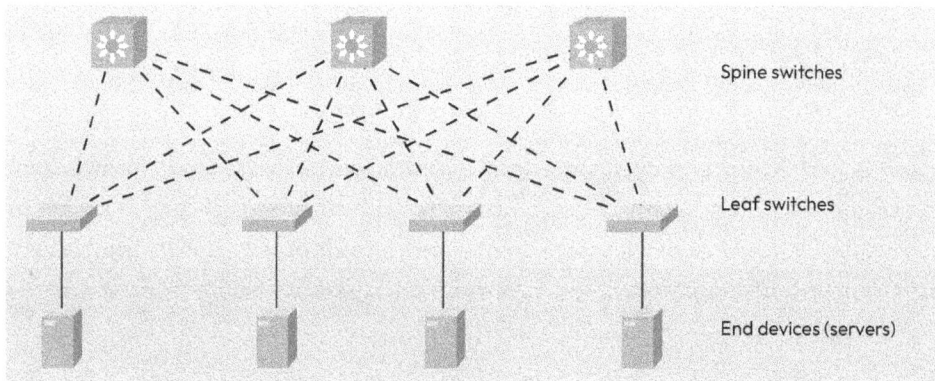

Figure 6.6: Spine and leaf

Figure 6.6 shows three **spine** switches, each connected to four **leaves**, which are in turn connected to one server each. This topology is highly reliable due to its redundancy – if one switch fails, multiple alternate paths are still available. Its performance is high because the numerous paths help reduce bottlenecks, and it offers low latency, as each leaf is connected through only one switch. Additionally, it is scalable, as adding a new device only requires connecting a new leaf to all existing spine switches.

The key benefit is that it allows for equal access to resources across the network. By distributing traffic efficiently across multiple paths, the network can balance loads dynamically, reducing the likelihood of congestion, meaning no single path gets overloaded with traffic. Spine and leaf is normally used in topologies where the devices are within one hop of each other.

Point to point

A **point-to-point** network is simply a single connection between two nodes. This kind of network can be implemented as a leased line, where a dedicated communication link is rented from a service provider to connect two locations or devices, as seen in *Figure 6.7*.

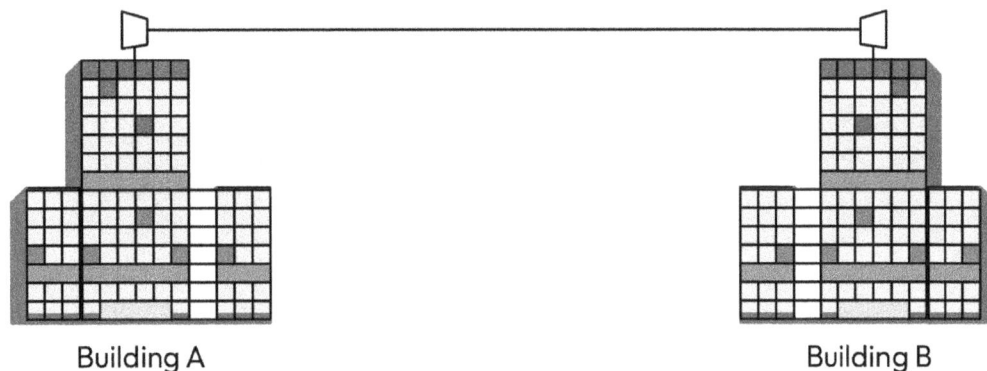

Building A   Building B

Figure 6.7: Point-to-point network

Figure 6.7 shows two buildings connected with a single link. This type of network is often used for secure, reliable, and constant communication between two points, such as between two offices or a branch and headquarters. The leased line ensures that the connection is always available, with consistent performance and without sharing bandwidth with other users. It is ideal for businesses that need a dependable and private link for sensitive data or high-priority communication. Point-to-point networks are often used by the military to ensure secure and dedicated communication between control centers, satellites, or other mission-critical devices. It is also how some IoT devices connect or could even refer to a single cable connecting your laptop and printer.

Three-tier hierarchical model

The **three-tier hierarchical model** is a network design that divides the network into three layers, the **core layer**, the **distribution layer**, and the **access layer**:

1. The **core layer** is the backbone of the network, responsible for fast and reliable data transfer across the network. It handles high-speed traffic and connects different parts of the network, ensuring that data can travel quickly and efficiently. This layer only handles connections, rather than any distribution, routing, or security policies.

2. The **distribution layer** is the middle layer and acts as a bridge between the core and access layers. It aggregates data from the access layer and routes it to the core layer. It also enforces network policies, such as security and routing decisions, to manage traffic flow and ensure efficient use of the network.

3. The **access layer** is where end devices such as computers, printers, and phones connect to the network. It's the closest layer to the users and handles local traffic, providing access to network resources and ensuring that devices can communicate with each other and with higher layers.

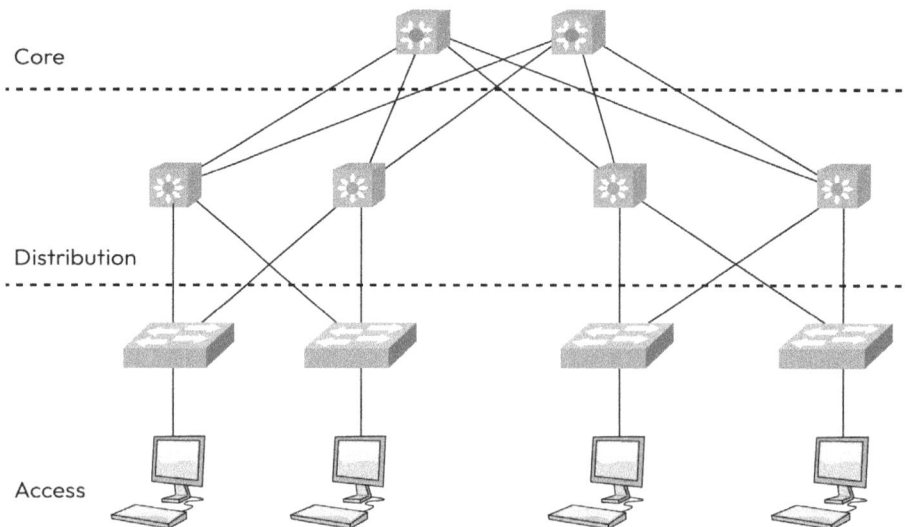

Figure 6.8: Three-tier hierarchical model

Figure 6.8 shows four workstations connected to **access layer** interfaces. Each interface is connected to multilayer switches on the **distribution layer**, which in turn connect to multiservice switches on the **core layer**. In this diagram, the workstations are essentially split into two groups, which could be geographically separated.

The **three-tier model** is common in large enterprises and offers several benefits. It is highly scalable, as each of the three layers can be expanded independently. This flexibility makes it easy to add new devices, user groups, or even entire sites without overhauling the entire network. The **distribution layer** plays a critical role by acting as the central point for implementing network-wide policies, such as traffic management and security enforcement. Centralizing control in this layer allows for efficient security patching, access management, and firewall policy enforcement, making it easier to standardize security and traffic control across a large network.

The three-tier hierarchy scales better than spine and leaf because it employs protocols such as the **Spanning Tree Protocol** (**STP**) to stop loops between switches. As such, this model is widely used in enterprise networks where a large-scale, reliable, and well-organized network architecture is essential.

> Note
>
> STP is covered in greater detail in *Chapter 10, Given a Scenario, Configure Switching Technologies and Features*.

Collapsed core

A **collapsed core** network design combines the core and distribution layers of the three-tier hierarchical model into a single layer. This simplifies the network by reducing the number of layers, which can be more cost-effective and easier to manage for smaller networks or organizations.

This is illustrated in *Figure 6.9*.

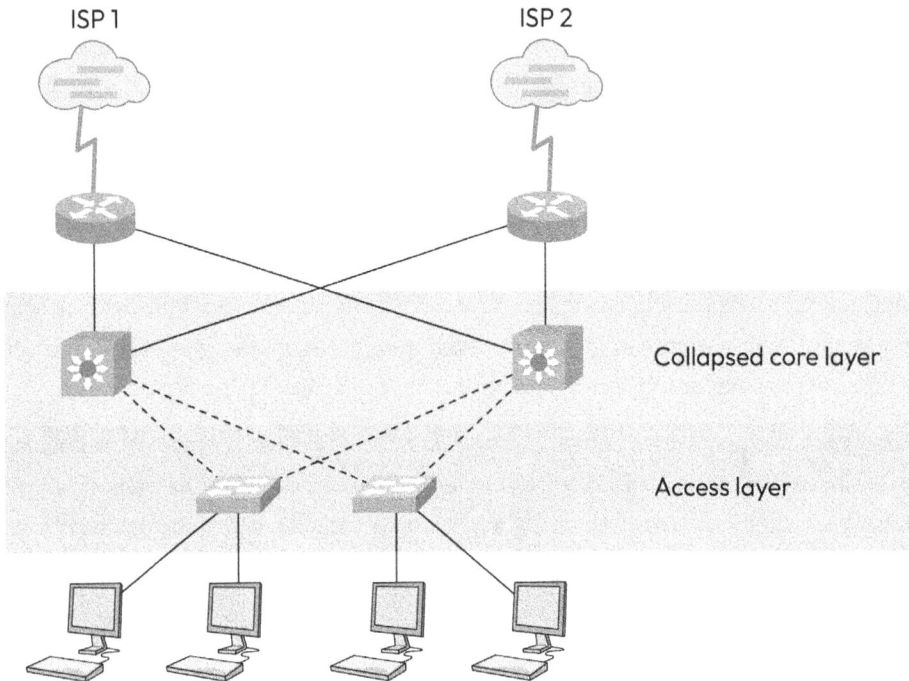

Figure 6.9: Collapsed core

Figure 6.9 shows the core and distribution layers merged together into the **collapsed core** layer in the middle. This layer handles both high-speed traffic routing (which would be the core's job in a standard three-layer hierarchy) and policy enforcement and aggregation (which would be the distribution layer's job). In the figure, it connects two ISPs. This design is commonly used in smaller networks where the full three-tier model might be overkill.

Traffic flows

Traffic flow refers to the paths through which data travels between different points in a network. Understanding traffic flow is crucial when analyzing or making decisions about a network because communication between points isn't always the same. For example, communication between internal points, such as two servers in the same data center, requires different considerations compared to communication between external points, such as your computer and the internet.

How efficiently data moves through a network impacts overall performance and user experience, but it's also essential to ensure that data remains secure. Network traffic is typically categorized into two types, which are **north-south traffic** and **east-west traffic**:

- **North-south traffic**: This refers to data flow that moves in and out of a data center or network, typically between users or external networks (such as the internet) and internal servers. Imagine a user accessing a website or a cloud service – this traffic flows vertically, from the top (the user) to the bottom (the server), hence the term *north-south*. With north-south traffic, security should be carefully considered, and controls such as firewalls are often used even though they can slow down data.

- **East-west traffic**: This type of traffic refers to data flow that occurs within a data center or network, specifically between servers or devices inside the same environment. For example, when one server communicates with another server within the same data center, the traffic moves horizontally, from side to side, so it's called *east-west*. Managing east-west traffic efficiently is crucial for optimizing performance within a data center. Security is still important, as there can always be internal threats, but efficiency is more important with east-west traffic.

Summary

This chapter covered the design and implementation of a network. These concepts are essential for analyzing and comparing network topologies, architectures, and types to create a system that meets the specific needs of an organization. Network architecture provides the overall framework for how a network is structured and operates, defining the principles and guidelines for building and maintaining the network. By understanding these aspects, organizations can select the appropriate design to ensure efficient data communication, optimal performance, and robust scalability in their networks.

The knowledge gained in this chapter will prepare you to answer questions relating to exam objective 1.6 in the *CompTIA Network+ (N10-009)* exam.

Exam objective 1.6

Compare and contrast network topologies, architectures, and types.

Mesh: Nodes interconnected for high reliability and redundancy

Hybrid: Combines multiple topologies for greater flexibility

Star/hub and spoke: Central hub connects all devices

Spine and leaf: Scalable, efficient data center design

Point to point: Direct connection between two devices

Three-tier hierarchical model:

- **Core**: Backbone of the network for high-speed data transfer
- **Distribution**: Middle layer, routing, and policy enforcement
- **Access**: Connects end devices to the network

Collapsed core: Combines core and distribution layers

Traffic flow: Direction of data movement in a network:

- **North-south**: Data flow between users and servers
- **East-west**: Data flow within the same network environment

Chapter review questions

Now that you've completed the chapter, you can check your knowledge using the practice questions provided in the online platform at https://packt.link/N10-009ch6. You can also use the QR code below. Accessing these questions requires you to unlock the accompanying online content first. Head over to Chapter 26 for detailed instructions.

7

Given a Scenario, Use Appropriate IPv4 Network Addressing

In *Chapter 6, Compare and Contrast Network Topologies, Architectures, and Types*, you saw how different network topologies and architectures offer advantages and disadvantages. However, in order for these networks to be implemented, there needs to be a system to direct data packets to the right place. The most widely used method of addressing on the World Wide Web and local networks is **IP version 4**, more commonly known as **IPv4**. It should be noted that both **IPv6** and various forms of **IaaS** have been rising in prominence in recent years – these will be looked at in more detail in later chapters.

As a network engineer, you will be required to use IPv4 to assign correct **IPv4 addresses, subnet masks,** and network configurations based on a specific use case or network design requirement. This means ensuring the proper use of **IP addresses** to ensure efficient, secure, and scalable infrastructure. To do this in both public and private networks, several types of IPv4 addresses are used, each with specific roles and characteristics.

This chapter will introduce core concepts in **IPv4 addressing**, including public and private addresses, subnetting, and the five main **classes of IP addresses.** You will explore how public addresses enable devices to communicate globally, while private addresses facilitate secure, local network communication. Additionally, you will see how subnetting and techniques such as **variable length subnet masking (VLSM)** and **Classless Inter-Domain Routing (CIDR)** allow for flexibility in managing address spaces and enhance network efficiency.

Finally, you will examine the IPv4 address classes A through E, each designed to serve different scales and types of network needs, from small networks to large global communications.

By understanding these elements, you will gain foundational knowledge of IPv4 addressing and be better equipped to make informed network configuration choices in any scenario. The chapter will start with an overview of what IP addresses actually are.

This chapter covers the seventh objective in *Domain 1: 1.7, Given a scenario, use appropriate IPv4 network addressing*.

> **Note**
>
> A full breakdown of objective 1.7 will be given at the end of the chapter.

Binary

Binary is the language that computers use to process and transmit data, so understanding it is essential for working with networking concepts such as **IP addressing** and **subnetting**. Binary is a number system that uses only two digits: 0 and 1. Everything in a computer is built on tiny electrical switches that are either off or on, and these two states are perfectly represented in binary:

0 = off

1 = on

A group of 8 binary digits is called an **octet**, and this is an important concept in IP addressing, which is made up of octets. Using an octet, we can represent numbers from 0-255. For example, if we want to represent the number 134 in binary, we use the bits that represent numbers that add up to 134. These are 128 + 4 + 2 = 134 as shown in *Table 7.1*.

	Octet values							
	128	64	32	16	8	4	2	1
134	1	0	0	0	0	1	1	0

Table 7.1: An octet representing the number 134

For a computer using binary, the number 134 is represented as 10000110.

If you wanted to convert 15 in decimal to binary, it would be as follows:

00001111 (1 + 2 + 4 + 8) or 1111 (leading zeros can be omitted)

54 = 00110110   (32 + 16 + 4 + 2)

95 = 01011111   (64 + 16 + 8 + 4 + 2 + 1)

The same can be done the other way around. The number 10001100 can be converted to decimal as follows.

10001100 = 128 + 8 + 4 = 140

and

01111000 = 64 + 32 + 16 + 8 = 120

Understanding how to convert between decimal and binary is a vital skill when looking at IP addressing and subnetting.

IP addresses

An IP address is a unique number assigned to every device that connects to a network, including the internet. IP addresses enable devices to locate and communicate with each other. Each IPv4 address is broken down into 4 octets, each comprising 8 bits – for example, 131.108.15.1; this is known as **dotted decimal notation** and **32-bit addressing**.

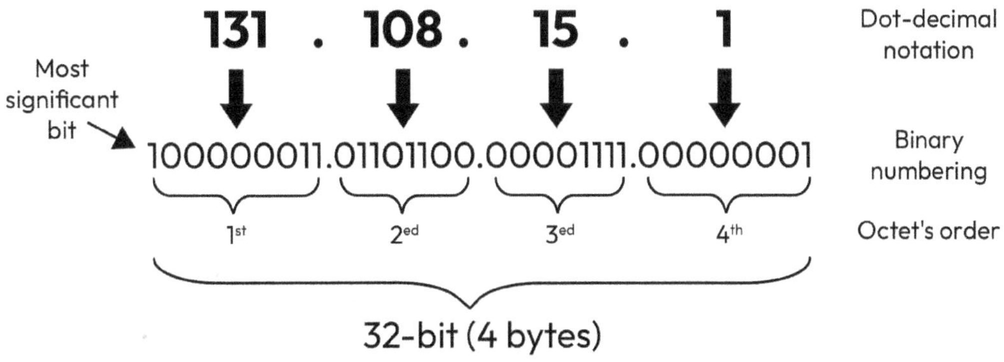

Figure 7.1: Four-octet breakdown

Figure 7.1 shows the breakdown of the IP address 131.108.15.1. Each octet has its binary numbering – for instance, 131 is transmitted as 10000011.

With 32 bits, the total number of addresses possible is 2^{32}, or 4,294,967,296 – around 4.3 billion. Although, as stated, IPv4 addresses are for identification, there are some large blocks that are reserved for special purposes to ensure proper functioning, management, and efficiency of the internet. These are as follows:

- `100.64.0.0/10`: Carrier-grade NAT, used by **ISPs** to manage large-scale address translation
- `192.0.0.0/24`: Reserved for IETF protocol assignments
- `192.88.99.0/24`: Used for 6to4 relay anycast, helping IPv6 and IPv4 coexist
- `198.18.0.0/15`: Reserved for network interconnection testing
- `192.0.2.0/24`, `198.51.100.0/24`, `203.0.113.0/24`: Set aside for **documentation** and **example purposes** in educational materials

These reserved IP ranges help avoid conflicts in real-world network operations and ensure that certain tasks, such as testing, example creation, and protocol development, are handled properly without affecting live Internet traffic. IP addresses are grouped into public and private, which we will look at now.

Public versus private

There are two types of IP addresses: **public** and **private**. A public IP address is visible to anyone on the internet, while a private IP address is used within a private network, such as a home or office network, and is hidden from the outside world. Private addresses are free, whereas public addresses are leased.

Public IP addresses

Public IP addresses are globally accessible and can be seen by other devices on the internet. When you go online, your network, which could be your router or ISP, typically uses a public IP address to communicate with websites and other networks around the world. It's like a public phone number because anyone on the internet can reach your network if they know the address.

Private IP addresses

Private IP addresses are only for use within a local network, such as a home or office. This is defined in **Request for Comments (RFC 1918)**. Devices with private IP addresses can communicate with each other within that network, but are "invisible" to the outside internet. Routers on the internet are designed to ignore private IP addresses and do not route them through the global internet. This behavior is intentional, as private IP addresses are specifically reserved for communication within local networks and help prevent conflicts with globally unique public IP addresses.

> **Note**
>
> RFC 1918, also known as `Address Allocation for Private Internets`, is an **Internet Engineering Task Force (IETF)** document that defines address ranges for private IP addresses used within local networks.

The private IP address ranges are as follows:

`10.0.0.0` to `10.255.255.255`

`172.16.0.0` to `172.31.255.255`

`192.168.0.0` to `192.168.255.255`

RFC 1918 is a set of rules that define specific IP address ranges reserved for private networks. These IP ranges are only used within local networks such as a home, office, or organization and are not routable on the public internet, as mentioned earlier in the chapter.

Private IP addresses are useful for security and address management. By using these ranges, organizations can create large internal networks without worrying about conflicting with public IP addresses. Only a router with public IP addresses can communicate with the internet on behalf of devices using private IP addresses.

Automatic private IP addressing (APIPA)

When a computer, server, or device is put on a network, it needs to have a mandatory requirement of an IP address and subnet mask. A default gateway is optional, but without this, you cannot access any remote networks, such as the internet. Just think what happens when your broadband router fails – you lose internet access. This is your default gateway.

There are some special IP address types that help networks stay functional and organized. One of them is **automatic private IP addressing (APIPA)**. APIPA assigns temporary IP addresses to devices when they cannot obtain one automatically from a **DHCP server**. Normally, when a device connects to a network, it broadcasts for an IP address from a DHCP server. However, if the DHCP server is unavailable due to technical issues – such as network connectivity problems, misconfiguration, or the DHCP server running out of assignable IP addresses – the device still needs an IP address to enable basic networking. After a set number of retries – typically, up to four DHCP discover attempts over about 60 seconds – the device gives up on the DHCP server and switches to APIPA mode. In this mode, the device self-assigns a randomly selected IP address from the APIPA range `169.254.0.1` to `169.254.255.254`, then checks to ensure that it is not already in use on the local network.

This **APIPA address** allows the device to communicate with other devices on the same local network that also have APIPA addresses, but it cannot communicate with any other IP address on the network. APIPA does not provide a default gateway, which means **APIPA messages** are never directly sent to a router and cannot be used to access the internet or external networks.

APIPA acts as a fallback mechanism, ensuring limited local network communication when the main network setup isn't functioning as expected. While using the APIPA address, the device continues to check for the DHCP server periodically, sending DHCP discover messages. If the DHCP server becomes available, the device discards the APIPA address and switches to the IP address provided by the DHCP server.

> **Note**
>
> RFC stands for **Request for Comment**. RFCs are produced by the **Internet Engineering Task Force (IETF)**, an open standards organization that develops and promotes Internet protocols and best practices. The IETF collaborates with experts and stakeholders worldwide to create RFCs, which cover standards, protocols, and guidelines for internet functionality, security, and interoperability. These documents are essential references for building and maintaining reliable, compatible networks and internet technologies.

Loopback/Localhost

The **loopback/localhost address** is 127.0.0.1 and is mainly used for diagnostic testing purposes and verifying that **TCP/IP** is working on your device. When you run a loopback test, usually by "pinging" 127.0.0.1, your device sends a message to itself through the TCP/IP stack. If you get a response, it confirms that TCP/IP is properly configured and functioning on your device. However, it only tests internal TCP/IP functionality on the device – not the connection to other networked devices or the internet. This is shown in *Figure 7.2*.

```
C:\Users\Administrator.WIN-HB5RLG5VD60>ping 127.0.0.1

Pinging 127.0.0.1 with 32 bytes of data:
Reply from 127.0.0.1: bytes=32 time<1ms TTL=128
Reply from 127.0.0.1: bytes=32 time<1ms TTL=128
Reply from 127.0.0.1: bytes=32 time<1ms TTL=128
Reply from 127.0.0.1: bytes=32 time<1ms TTL=128
```

Figure 7.2: Pinging the loopback address

Using the loopback address is helpful for troubleshooting and developing network-based applications, as it allows you to test network functions on your own device before connecting to external networks. You can achieve the same result using localhost. However, since I am using a Windows computer with a dual-stack configuration (supporting both IPv4 and IPv6), the system returns the IPv6 address by default. This is shown in *Figure 7.3*.

```
C:\Users\Administrator.WIN-HB5RLG5VD60>ping localhost

Pinging WIN-HB5RLG5VD60.Domain.local [::1] with 32 bytes of data:
Reply from ::1: time<1ms
Reply from ::1: time<1ms
Reply from ::1: time<1ms
Reply from ::1: time<1ms
```

Figure 7.3: Localhost returning IPv6 address

In such cases, you can force the use of an IPv4 address by adding the -4 flag to the end of the ping command. This indicates that you want an IPv4 output. This converts the output from IPv6 to IPv4, as shown in *Figure 7.4*.

```
C:\Users\Administrator.WIN-HB5RLG5VD60>ping localhost -4

Pinging WIN-HB5RLG5VD60.Domain.local [127.0.0.1] with 32 bytes of data:
Reply from 127.0.0.1: bytes=32 time<1ms TTL=128
Reply from 127.0.0.1: bytes=32 time<1ms TTL=128
Reply from 127.0.0.1: bytes=32 time<1ms TTL=128
Reply from 127.0.0.1: bytes=32 time<1ms TTL=128
```

Figure 7.4: Forcing localhost to return an IPv4 address

Note

More details on pinging and other useful network commands are given in *Chapter 25, Given a Scenario, Use the Appropriate Tool or Protocol to Solve Networking Issues.*

Beyond the special categories of addresses, IPv4 is split into five classes of addresses, as will be covered in the next section.

IPv4 address classes

Similar to how IP addresses can be separated into public and private, IP addresses can also be grouped into different classes, A-E, based on their size and the number of devices they can support. The classes are defined by the IP address range, as indicated in the first octet. This system, called **classful IP addressing**, helps organize networks of different scales, from large corporate networks to individual home connections.

Only classes A-C are allocated to devices and contain both private and public addresses. Class D is used for multicast groups, and Class E is reserved for experimental purposes, so it doesn't have the distinction between private and public addresses. The classes are as follows:

- **Class A** supports large networks with 16,777,214 host addresses
- **Class B** supports medium networks with 65,534 host addresses
- **Class C** supports small networks with 252 host addresses
- **Class D** is reserved for multicast groups, not for regular networks
- **Class E** is reserved for experimental purposes and is not publicly used

Table 7.2 shows the range of IP addresses, the default subnet mask, the number of networks in the range, and the number of hosts per network.

	Public IP range	Private IP range	Default subnet mask	Number of networks	Number of hosts per network
Class A	1.0.0.0 to 126.255.255.255	10.0.0.0 to 10.255.255.255	255.0.0.0	126	16,777,214
Class B	128.0.0.0 to 191.255.255.255	172.16.0.0 to 172.31.255.255	255.255.0.0	16,384	65,534
Class C	192.0.0.0 to 223.255.255.255	192.168.0.0 to 192.168.255.255	255.255.255.0	2,097,152	254
Class D	224.0.0.0 to 239.255.255.255	Multicast			
Class E	240.0.0.0 to 255.255.255.255	Experimental			

Table 7.2: IPv4 class A-E IP addresses

Although the 127.0.0.0–127.255.255.255 range is technically a block of Class A addresses it is not used by hosts as it is reserved for loopback addresses. The loopback address 127.0.0.1 is used for diagnostic testing and to verify that TCP/IP has been initialized.

Hosts

The formula for calculating the number of usable hosts in a subnet is as follows:

$2^n - 2 = x$

Where n is the number of bits used for the host portion of the IP address.

The -2 accounts for two addresses that cannot be used. They are as follows:

- The network address, which ends in 0 (e.g., 10.2.2.0) and identifies the subnet
- The broadcast address, which ends in 255 (e.g., 10.2.2.255) and is used to send data to all hosts on the subnet

These two addresses cannot be assigned to devices, so they are excluded from the total count of usable host addresses.

If I am using 4 bits for my subnets, the formula is as follows:

$$2^4 - 2$$

$$2 \times 2 \times 2 \times 2 - 2 = 14$$

By using 4 bits, I have up to 14 hosts.

If I want to use 6 bits for hosts, the calculation is $2^6 - 2 = 62$, so I have up to 62 hosts on my network.

Networks

The formula for calculating the number of networks in IP addressing is as follows:

$$2^n$$

Where n is the number of bits used for the host portion of the IP address.

- **Class A:** Uses 7 bits because the first bit is always set to 0 to indicate a **Class A** address.

  $2^7 = 128$ networks. You cannot use 127.x.x.x as it is the loopback address, and 0.x.x.x is reserved for special usage.

- **Class B**: Uses 14 bits because the first 2 bits are set to 10 to indicate a **Class B** address.

  $2^{14} = 16,384$ networks.

- **Class C**: Uses 21 bits because the first 3 bits are set to 110 to indicate a **Class C** address.

  $2^{21} = 2,097,152$ networks

Subnet masks

As mentioned, networks can be divided into smaller groups of hosts called subnets. Creating subnets is useful for managing large networks, as they help with things such as efficiency and broadcasting. Subnets are indicated by **subnet masks**, which show how the IP address is split between the network parts and host parts. A subnet mask can be identified as it starts with 255 in the first octet – for example, 255.255.0.0.

The **default subnet mask**, as shown in *Table 7.2*, is the mask for each class that indicates only 1 network. The default masks for each class are as follows:

- **Class A**: 1 octet for networks and 3 octets for hosts

  Dot-decimal: 255.0.0.0

  Binary: 11111111.00000000.00000000.00000000

  Networks: 126

  Hosts per network: 16,777,214

- **Class B**: 2 octets for networks and 2 octets for hosts

  Dot-decimal: 255.255.0.0

  Binary: 11111111.11111111.00000000.00000000

  Networks: 16,384

  Hosts per network: 65,534

- **Class C**: 3 octets for networks and 1 octet for hosts

  Dot-decimal: 255.255.255.0

  Binary: 11111111.11111111.11111111.00000000

  Networks: 2,097,152

  Hosts per network: 254

A subnet mask helps a device, such as a computer, determine whether a packet is "local" (on the same network) or "remote" (on a different network) by comparing the destination IP address to its own IP address. If it is remote, it is forwarded to the default gateway (router) for delivery; otherwise, it is delivered locally. The following describes how it works:

1. The device applies the subnet mask to both of the following:

   - Its own IP address
   - The destination IP address

2. **ANDing** (see next) is used to determine the network address to reveal the network ID of both addresses.

3. The device compares the two network IDs:

   - If the network IDs match, the destination is local, and the device sends the packet directly to the target device.
   - If they don't match, the destination is remote, and the packet is sent to the default gateway (a router) to reach the destination network.

ANDing is a bit-by-bit logical comparison between two binary numbers:

- 1 AND 1 = 1
- Anything else – for example, 1 AND 0, 0 AND 1,0 AND 0 = O

Example of ANDing

A user has computer A, which has the IP address 192.168.1.10 and is going to send a packet to computer B, whose IP address is 192.168.2.25. Both are using a subnet mask of 255.255.255.0. Using ANDing, we can determine whether it's local or remote delivery.

First, we will convert the IP address into binary, then we will perform ANDing.

Step 1

First, AND the first octet of computer A's IP address, 192.168.1.10, with a subnet mask of 255.255.255.0. This is done by converting the IP address and subnet mask into binary, then adding each bit.

The result is converted back into dot-decimal notation.

Computer A: 192.168.1.10				
	Octet 1	**Octet 2**	**Octet 3**	**Octet 4**
IP Address	11000000	10101000	00000001	00001010
Subnet Mask	11111111	11111111	11111111	00000000
AND	11000000	10101000	00000001	00000000
Network ID	192	168	1	0

Table 7.3: ANDing 192.168.1.10 with a subnet mask of 255.255.255.0

Step 2

Now we will do the same with computer B.

Computer B: 192.168.2.25				
	Octet 1	**Octet 2**	**Octet 3**	**Octet 4**
IP Address	11000000	10101000	00000010	00011001
Subnet Mask	11111111	11111111	11111111	00000000
AND	11000000	10101000	00000010	00000000
Network ID	192	168	2	0

Table 7.4: ANDing 192.168.1.10 with a subnet mask of 255.255.255.0

The network ID of computer A is 192.168.1.0, and the network ID of computer B is 192.168.2.0. This means these two computers are remote from each other, and the packet will be sent to a router for delivery. You will notice that if an octet in the subnet mask is 255, you will always end up with the same value as the corresponding octet in the IP address after ANDing. Likewise, a value of 0 in the subnet mask has a value of 0 in the corresponding octet after ANDing. Subnet masks can be customized when we break a network into smaller portions. This is described later in the chapter.

As shown in *Table 7.2*, each network can support a specific number of devices or hosts based on its size. Class C networks are small and can have up to 254 hosts. A medium network, Class B, can support 65,534 hosts, and a large network, Class A, can have 16,777,214 hosts. However, networks are similar to roads in that large amounts of traffic can cause issues. Just like too many cars can cause congestion, too many devices on one network can cause it to slow down. Networks must be carefully designed to avoid this issue, and the main way of doing this is by dividing large networks into smaller ones using a technique called subnetting.

Security also becomes an issue, as the higher the number of IP addresses, the greater the attack surface for potential intruders. Even unused IPs can be targeted with malicious traffic, leading to unnecessary network traffic or attempts to exploit vulnerabilities. Monitoring and securing such a vast range is challenging and requires more resources, with the administrative overhead growing even if there are unused addresses.

Broadcast messages, which are messages sent to all devices on a network, can also cause issues. If a message is sent to the entire network, it will slow down. Frequent broadcasting can also lead to network congestion, making it hard for devices to communicate efficiently. A **broadcast domain** refers to the number of hosts on the network. For example, a network with 150 hosts has a broadcast domain of 150.

Although Class C networks offer a solution by having a maximum of 254 IP addresses per network, large networks might have 16.7 million hosts. Think of a motorway with 16.7 million cars – there would be lots of traffic jams! As mentioned, subnetting has a solution, and this will be covered next.

Subnetting

As mentioned in the previous section, the classful system of IPv4 offers little flexibility in the size of networks, with only three options: a small number of networks with a large number of hosts (Class A), a large number of networks with a small number of hosts (Class C), or one option in between (Class B). However, the reality of modern networking requires far more flexibility to overcome the administrative, technical, and security issues mentioned earlier. The most obvious solution is to have a way of further dividing networks, so you can tailor the size, structure, and architecture to your needs, and this is exactly what subnetting is.

With subnetting, you can divide a large network into multiple smaller networks, called subnets. This is done logically by making further divisions of IP addresses and configuring devices such as routers and switches to recognize these divisions. For example, you might divide a network with 254 hosts into 4 subnets, each with 62 usable hosts. This division is done by customizing the subnet masks and creating subnets, which we will cover now.

Advantages of subnetting

Subnetting allows you to split large ranges into smaller, more manageable blocks, so you can match the IP range closely to your actual needs, and it can address many of the issues caused by the classful system of IPv4.

Without subnetting, every device in a Class A, B, or C network is essentially grouped into one large network. This means all devices will receive broadcasts meant for the entire network, which can slow down performance. In large networks, frequent broadcasting can lead to network congestion, making it hard for devices to communicate efficiently. Subnetting creates smaller networks, which can isolate broadcast traffic and help keep network performance smooth.

It can also help with security issues, as in a single large network without subnetting, all devices are accessible to each other, increasing the risk of unauthorized access and security breaches. With subnetting, different departments or groups can be separated by subnets. This way, sensitive data on one subnet can be isolated from other subnets, adding an extra layer of security and making it easier to control who can access what.

A large network with thousands of devices is challenging to manage, track, and troubleshoot. Without subnetting, any issue that arises – such as network congestion or device misconfiguration – can be hard to pinpoint in a massive pool of IPs. Subnetting lets administrators divide the network into smaller sections, which makes it easier to locate and resolve issues, as well as to manage IP addresses effectively.

Subnetting can be applied to both classful and classless networks. In classful networks, such as with Class A, B, and C IP ranges, subnetting divides the predefined IP address blocks into smaller sections. Classless networks, however, use CIDR to allow flexible subnetting without sticking to the strict Class A, B, or C boundaries, offering even more control over IP address allocation. This flexibility makes classless subnetting especially useful for efficiently managing modern networks.

Note

A subnet mask of /24 has a range of 256 IP addresses, but only 254 usable IP addresses for devices because x.x.x.0 is the network ID and x.x.x.255 is the broadcast address. Anything sent to a broadcast address will go to all devices in the network. This rule applies to every subnet, regardless of the size (subnet mask). The first address in the range is always the network ID, and the last is always the broadcast address.

For more information on how subnets are used in routing, refer to *Chapter 2*.

Devising subnets

As mentioned, in IPv4 addressing, the values are stored in binary. A value switched on is represented by a 1, and values switched off are represented by a 0. Each IP address has 4 octets, each comprised of 8 bits, which makes it 32-bit addressing. The 8 bits in an octet are arranged from right to left, with each bit representing a power of 2. The rightmost bit represents 2^0, doubling each time as you move left. So, the positions of the bits look like this:

128 | 64 | 32 | 16 | 8 | 4 | 2 | 1

When all values are switched on, the maximum number you can have in an octet is 255.

Table 7.5 shows the values of 72 and 250 in binary and how they are worked out.

Bit No	1	2	3	4	5	6	7	8
Value	128	64	32	16	8	4	2	1
72	0	1	0	0	1	0	0	0
250	1	1	1	1	1	0	1	0

Table 7.5: Working out the values of 72 and 250 in binary

There are a couple of tricks for working out binary values, which we will discuss here. Take the number 72. The first bit value is 128, which is greater than 64, so it is turned off, meaning the binary is 0. Bit number 2, which is 64, is more than half of 72, so it is turned on, meaning the binary is 1. This means we have 8 to find because 72 - 64 is 8. Bit number 3, 32, and bit number 4, 16, are both greater than 8, so they are both set to 0. Bit number 5 is 8, which is the number we are after, so that is set to 1. Because we have the target decimal number, the remaining bits are set to 0. Therefore, decimal 72 is represented as binary 01001000.

Another method is the "subtractive method." Take the decimal number 250. The maximum decimal value of the 8-bit octet is 255, because 1 + 2 + 4 + 8 + 16 + 32 + 64 + 128 = 255

You can easily work out that 255 - 250 = 5. Rather than going bit by bit and adding the numbers, look at all the bits and find the numbers you need for 5 and turn them off. Bit number 6 is 4, and bit number 8 is 1. These two bits should be 0 and the bits switched on leave 128 + 64 + 32 + 16 + 8 + 2 = 250.

Converting a full IP address into binary is simply a matter of working out the binary for each octet – for example, take the IP address 220.1.1.3:

220 in decimal = 11011100 in binary

1 in decimal = 00000001 in binary

1 in decimal = 00000001 in binary

3 in decimal = 00000011 in binary

11011100.00000001.00000001.00000011

It's simple to do the other way. Take the binary 01111100.00001100.00000100.00000001 and turn it into decimal:

01111100 = 124

00001100 = 12

00000100 = 4

00000001 = 1

This gives us an IP address of 124.12.4.1

The process of devising subnets for your network will start with the simple question of how many subnets you want and how many devices you need for each one.

Once you have decided on the numbers you need, you then need to calculate what the subnet mask will be. As stated earlier, the subnet mask determines what portion of the IP address is for the network/subnets and what portion is for the host or device. This portion is described by the number of bits. For example, in a standard Class A IP address, the first 8 bits (the first octet) are for the network ID, and the remaining 26 bits are for the host ID. Remember, each IP address is 32 bits.

When you create subnets, you increase the portion of the IP address used for the network ID and reduce the portion for the host by "borrowing" bits from the host ID. Think of going into a bar with $20 for beer, but after ordering a beer, you then purchase a packet of chips. This will reduce the amount of money left to buy more beer. In networking terms, the more bits you borrow from the host portion the more networks you will be able to create. However, each network will have fewer hosts.

Working out subnets with the Lone Ranger table

If you do not have any experience in subnetting, you can use a simple method to work out the masks and networks, as shown in *Table 7.6*. I call this method a *Lone Ranger* table.

Bits	1	2	3	4	5	6	7	8
Range	128	64	32	16	8	4	2	1
Subnet Mask	128	192	224	240	248	252	254	255
Networks	2	4	8	16	32	64	128	256

Table 7.6: A Lone Ranger table

This how to put the table together:

- Top row – **Bits**: Enter **1** to **8**, from left to right, as there are 8 bits in an octet.

Bits	1	2	3	4	5	6	7	8
Range								
Subnet mask								
Networks								

Figure 7.5: The Lone Ranger table – first row

- Second row – **Range**: Write the binary for each octet, 1 to 128, starting *on the right and going left*.

Bits	1	2	3	4	5	6	7	8
Range	128	64	32	16	8	4	2	1
Subnet mask								
Networks								

Figure 7.6: The Lone Ranger table – second row

- Third row – **Subnet mask**: Bringing the **128** down for bit **1**, add the value for bit **2**, and keep a running total. We therefore have the 128 and then add the **64**, which equals **192**. For bit **3**, we take the **192** and add **32**, which equals **224**, and repeat all the way through.

Bits	1	2	3	4	5	6	7	8
Range	128	64	32	16	8	4	2	1
Subnet mask	128	192	224	240	248	252	254	255
Networks								

Figure 7.7: The Lone Ranger table – third row

- Fourth row – **Networks**: Instead of using the formula 2^n, we simply start at **2** and then double it all the way through, from left to right.

Bits	1	2	3	4	5	6	7	8
Range	128	64	32	16	8	4	2	1
Subnet mask	128	192	224	240	248	252	254	255
Networks	2	4	8	16	32	64	128	256

Figure 7.8: The Lone Ranger table – third row

Note

If using this method, *do not take this exam online, as you will not have a paper and pen*, but will take it in an exam center, where they will provide you with a plastic board and pen. Ensure you can write this table out from memory. When you start the test, immediately write out your *Lone Ranger table* to make it easier to complete subnetting questions.

Subnetting involves borrowing bits from the host portion of the IP address to create more networks. This is done starting with the next available octet beyond the default network portion for that class.

Class A addresses have the default subnet mask 255.0.0.0, meaning the first octet is the network portion and the remaining three octets are for hosts.

- When subnetting a Class A address, you start by breaking into the second octet, borrowing bits from the host portion.

Class B addresses have the default subnet mask 255.255.0.0, so the first two octets represent the network.

- When subnetting a Class B address, you begin breaking into the third octet, again stealing bits from the host portion.

Class C addresses have the default subnet mask 255.255.255.0, with the first three octets as the network portion.

- When subnetting a Class C address, you break into the fourth octet, borrowing bits from the host portion.

Subnetting example

Your IT department has purchased the Class B IP address 131.107.0.0. Because it is Class B, it has the default subnet mask 255.255.0.0. This means the first two octets are the network ID and the second two octets are for hosts. The business requires 8 subnets. We use the *Lone Ranger table* and look for 8 subnets. From this, we can see that we need to borrow 3 bits from the host to create more networks. For the network/subnet ID, that means we will be customizing the third octet of the IP address. We can see from the lookup table that for 3 bits, the subnet mask is 224.

Bits	1	2	3	4	5	6	7	8
Range	128	64	32	16	8	4	2	1
Subnet mask	128	192	224	240	248	252	254	255
Networks	2	4	8	16	32	64	128	256

Figure 7.9: Using a look-up table for subnetting

This means that octet 3 for the subnet mask should be 224. So, the subnet mask is now 255.255.224.0. Because we have borrowed 3 bits from octet 3, there are 5 bits remaining, in addition to the last octet. The range is 32.

> **Note**
>
> The number of subnet divisions can only be a power of 2 (i.e., 2, 4, 8, 16). If you required 7 subnets, you would still create the subnet mask for 8 subnets, and would have one spare address.

The next thing to do is to work out the address ranges for each of the subnets. This can be done by using a table like *Table 7.6*. The object of this exercise is to find the *start IP address*, which is the numerically first IP address for a device in the network, and the *end IP address*, which is the numerically last IP address for a device in the network. The following table has all the subnets written down the left-hand side. The **Start IP address** and the **End IP address** columns have been left blank for the moment.

	Start IP address					End IP address			
Subnet 1									
Subnet 2									
Subnet 3									
Subnet 4									
Subnet 5									
Subnet 6									
Subnet 7									
Subnet 8									

Table 7.6: Blank subnet IP address table

Next, we are going to insert values into the table that will not change. The IP address that we purchased was 131.107.0.0, so the values in the first 2 octets will not change.

	Start IP address				End IP address			
Subnet 1	131	107			131	107		
Subnet 2	131	107			131	107		
Subnet 3	131	107			131	107		
Subnet 4	131	107			131	107		
Subnet 5	131	107			131	107		
Subnet 6	131	107			131	107		
Subnet 7	131	107			131	107		
Subnet 8	131	107			131	107		

Table 7.7: Subnet IP address table with static values

Next, we will insert the *start IP address* subnet portion, so we look at the *Lone Ranger* table and see that the range is 32. That means the start value for octet 3 is 0, with the subsequent values increasing by 32 with each subnet – so 32, then 64, then 96, and so on. The final value should match the same octet in the subnet mask (octet 3 in this case), or you have made an error. You can see they are both 224; therefore, no error has been made.

	Start IP Address				End IP Address			
Subnet 1	131	107	0		131	107		
Subnet 2	131	107	32		131	107		
Subnet 3	131	107	64		131	107		
Subnet 4	131	107	96		131	107		
Subnet 5	131	107	128		131	107		
Subnet 6	131	107	160		131	107		
Subnet 7	131	107	192		131	107		
Subnet 8	131	107	224		131	107		

Table 7.8: Subnet IP address table with start addresses entered

Next, we insert the network portion of the *end IP address*, which is one less than the start address of the next subnet. If *Subnet 2* starts at 32, then the end address of *Subnet 1* is one less, or 31. For *Subnet 2*, the end address is one less than for *Subnet 3*, so it is 63. Complete this, as shown in *Table 7.9*. On the last network, the end address is one less than 255; this means it is 254.

	Start IP Address				End IP Address			
Subnet 1	131	107	0		131	107	31	
Subnet 2	131	107	32		131	107	63	
Subnet 3	131	107	64		131	107	95	
Subnet 4	131	107	96		131	107	127	
Subnet 5	131	107	128		131	107	159	
Subnet 6	131	107	160		131	107	191	
Subnet 7	131	107	192		131	107	223	
Subnet 8	131	107	224		131	107	255	

Table 7.9: Subnet IP address table with end addresses entered

Finally, we enter the host portion. We know that an IP address for a host cannot start at 0; therefore, for each *start IP address*, the host portion is 1. We also know the IP address cannot end in 255; therefore, for each *end IP address*, the host portion is 254.

	Start IP Address				End IP Address			
Subnet 1	131	107	0	1	131	107	31	254
Subnet 2	131	107	32	1	131	107	63	254
Subnet 3	131	107	64	1	131	107	95	254
Subnet 4	131	107	96	1	131	107	127	254
Subnet 5	131	107	128	1	131	107	159	254
Subnet 6	131	107	160	1	131	107	191	254
Subnet 7	131	107	192	1	131	107	223	254
Subnet 8	131	107	224	1	131	107	255	254

Table 7.10: Subnet IP address table completed

The completed table will show the ranges of device IP addresses for all the newly created subnets. For example, the **Subnet 1** range is 131.107.0.1 to 131.107.31.254. Any address in that range will be in subnet 1. For **Subnet 4**, the range is 131.107.96.1 to 131.107.127.254.

In the *CompTIA Network+* exam, you might need to work out whether two devices are on the same subnet or whether the default gateway is correct. *Figure 7.10* shows three servers, with their IP addresses and subnet masks.

Server 1	Server 2	Server 3
158.17.31.254	158.17.32.1	158.17.60.1
255.255.224.0	255.255.224.0	255.255.224.0

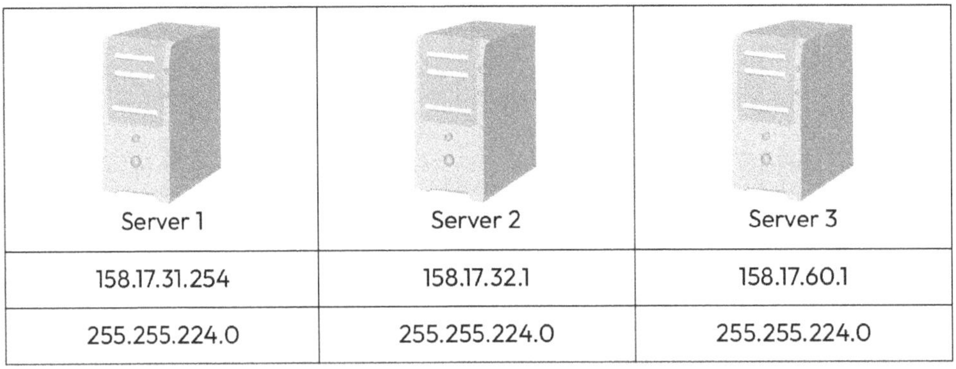

Figure 7.10: Three servers with their IP addresses and subnet masks

The first stage is to check that they all have the same subnet mask, which they do. Although the IP addresses 158.17.31.254 and 158.17.32.1 seem very close, you should not take it for granted. The third octet for the subnet mask is 224. Using the Lone Ranger table, you can see that this means there are 8 subnets, with a range of 32. In the same way we created the table earlier, we know that the range of subnet 1 is 158.17.0.1 to 158.17.31.254, the range of subnet 2 is 158.17.32.1 to 158.17.32.254, and the range of subnet 3 is 158.17.64.1 to 158.17.64.254.

We can see the following:

- **Server 1**: 158.17.31.254 is in **Subnet 1**
- **Server 2**: 158.17.32.1 is in **Subnet 2**
- **Server 3**: 158.17.60.1 is in **Subnet 2**

Therefore, server 2 and server 3 are in the same subnet. In this case, server 1 would not be able to communicate directly with server 2 and server 3. If this process seems long-winded, then there is a quicker way to work out whether devices are in the same subnet, as we will cover next.

Magic number

The **magic number** is a tool that will help you understand whether computers are on the same subnet without the need for any special tools – just a piece of paper. Practicing this technique will help you in the exam.

In the following question, we need to find out which of these machines can work on the same subnet. This uses the same example as before for comparison.

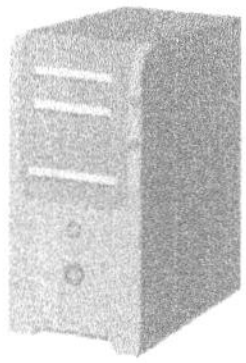 Server 1	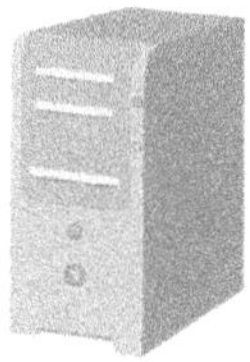 Server 2	 Server 3
158.17.31.254	158.17.32.1	158.17.60.1
255.255.224.0	255.255.224.0	255.255.224.0

Figure 7.11: Three servers with their IP addresses and subnet masks

- **Step 1**: Ensure that all the servers have the same subnet mask, which they do here.

- **Step 2**: Going from left to right, look at the first value that is not a zero. You can see this is 224.

- **Step 3**: Subtract the 224 from the magic number, which is always 256.

  $256 - 224 = 32$

  This gives us the range – in this case, 32.

- **Step 4**: Write out the first 4 subnets or until you cover all the numbers. Remember, the first subnet starts at 0, then we add 32.

Subnet 1	0	
Subnet 2	32	
Subnet 3	64	
Subnet 4	96	

Table 7.11: Subnet start points

The first subnet is 0 to 31, the second subnet is 32 to 63, the third subnet is 64 to 95, and the fourth subnet is 96 to 127.

Subnet 1	0	0 to 31
Subnet 2	32	32 to 63
Subnet 3	64	64 to 95
Subnet 4	96	96 to 127

Table 7.12: Subnet ranges

Because the mask is in the third octet, we only need the third octet from the IP addresses. Server 1 is 56, server 2 is 32, and server 3 is 30. Place those values against the relevant subnet.

Subnet 1	0	0 to 31	Server 3
Subnet 2	32	32 to 63	Server 1, Server 2
Subnet 3	64	64 to 95	
Subnet 4	96	96 to 127	

Table 7.13: Placing the ranges

With some practice, the magic number will help you identify which network different devices are in. This is a useful skill for real-world networking, as well as in the *CompTIA* exam.

So far, we've seen how subnet masking can be used to handle classful IP addresses in a more efficient manner by using bits from the host IP addresses to create new subnets. However, class-based IP addresses are still inherently inefficient because even when you divide up the network, you might still have wasted IP addresses. For instance, if you have been assigned a **Class B** address, which has 65,534 host addresses, you might need only a small portion of those addresses. Subnetting will help with architecture and routing, but there will still be wasted addresses. For this reason, class-based IP addresses are being replaced with CIDR, which you will read about in the next section.

Classless Inter-Domain Routing (CIDR)

CIDR allows for more flexible subnetting without sticking to class-based boundaries. For instance, instead of always using default subnet masks for class A, B, and C networks, with CIDR, we start with 32 bits in 4 octets:

11111111.11111111.11111111.11111111

Instead of having classes A, B, and C, there are no classes. If I want to borrow the first 15 bits for networks, I leave 17 bits for hosts. This means I could create 15 networks, each with a maximum of 131,070 ($2^{17} - 2$) hosts.

CIDR allows specifying the subnet mask directly using slash notation. For example, 192.168.1.0/24 means the CIDR mask is /24. CIDR is still IPv4, so it is still 32 bits. If an address has a CIDR mask of /23, then the first 23 bits from the left are the network address, leaving 9 bits for the host: - $2^9 - 2 = 510$ hosts per subnet.

Being able to fix the network size avoids wasting IP addresses, which is a problem with the class system. For example, a class C network provided 254 usable IP addresses, even though the organization only needed 50. With CIDR, an organization could buy an IP of /26, which leaves 6 bits for the hosts, giving a potential 62 assignable IP addresses, essentially stopping the wastage of 204 addresses. This flexibility is essential given the limited supply of IPv4 addresses.

CIDR's flexibility also makes it easier to add or adjust subnets as a network grows or changes. For example, an ISP might start with a /20 network and divide it into smaller subnets for customers as they sign up, adjusting subnet sizes as needed.

CIDR also enables **route aggregation**, also known as **supernetting**, where multiple IP addresses can be represented by a single routing entry. This might seem strange when you have just spent time breaking up networks into subnets, but in fact, it can also improve network management.

For example, a company might have two regional subnets, `10.1.0.0/16` for one region and `10.2.0.0/16` for another, and this could be combined into `10.0.0.0/15`. This reduces the number of entries in a router as well as the number of IP addresses that need to be advertised. It also reduces complexity if further subnets are created in the different regions. You will see how to actually work this out in the next section.

Supernetting

Your organization has three different networks – `192.168.4.0/24`, `192.168.5.0/24`, and `192.168.6.0/24` – and wishes to combine them. To achieve this, you will carry out **supernetting**, which is the process of creating a CIDR mask that incorporates all the bits that are the same.

The first two octets, `192.168`, are the same for all three networks, so we need to then look at the third octet and work out which bits are common.

We can see they all start with `192.168`; therefore, we look at the third octet in each and lay it out in binary. We take the lowest, `192.168.4.0/24`, and the highest, `192.168.6.0/24`.

	128	64	32	16	8	4	2	1
4	0	0	0	0	0	1	0	1
6	0	0	0	0	0	1	1	0
Commonality	✓	✓	✓	✓	✓	✓	x	x

Table 7.14: Supernetting

In *Table 7.14*, you can see that the first 6 bits are common; therefore, there are 16 bits for the first 2 octets and 6 for the third octet, making the CIDR mask /22. If we use a mask of /22, all three addresses can be used on the same subnet. They can now be aggregated as one entry into the routing tables instead of three.

Supernetting combines multiple smaller, contiguous subnets into one larger network using a shorter subnet mask – for example, combining a number with /24 into /22). This works because IP addresses are binary, and supernetting looks for a shared prefix in binary between the lowest and highest addresses in the group.

Converting CIDR notation to dotted decimal notation

As a network engineer, you need to be able to convert a CIDR mask (e.g., /24) to the standard dotted decimal format that we saw before. Both formats are used in different contexts, with some more modern CLI interfaces using / and other older devices using the dotted decimal. When troubleshooting, you may come across both, so it's handy to know how to translate between the two.

The conversion process is as follows.

- **Step 1**: Write out the bits based on the CIDR mask number, with 1s for network bits and 0s for the host bits. For /24, we have 24 bits that are 1s, followed by 8 bits that are 0s.

11111111111111111111111100000000

- **Step 2**: Divide the sequence into octets (groups of 8 bits):

11111111 | 11111111 | 11111111 | 00000000

- **Step 3**: Convert each octet to decimal:

255 | 255 | 255 | 0

Therefore, /24 in CIDR notation is equivalent to 255.255.255.0 in dotted decimal notation.

There are some common masks, as shown in the *Table 7.15*:

CIDR Notation	Dotted Decimal Notation	Number of Host Addresses
/8	255.0.0.0	16,777,216
/16	255.255.0.0	65,534
/24	255.255.255.0	254
/30	255.255.255.252	4

Table 7.15: Common masks

Variable length subnet mask (VLSM)

So far, we have seen how IP addresses and masks are used to divide networks into even-sized subnets. In reality, you may have an organization that requires a more nuanced system; for instance, you might have one office with data entry clerks and 50 computers on one network, while the head office has finance, research, and management, which all require smaller separate networks of 5 computers each. To achieve this, you can use a technique in which we create a **variable length subnet mask (VLSM)**.

Using a VLSM means you can use different network sizes for different parts of the network based on how many IP addresses each part needs. Each subnet will have only as many addresses as it needs, instead of forcing every subnet to be the same size.

For example, one department has 50 computers, another department has 20 computers, and a third department has just 10 devices. Without VLSM, you'd have to give each department the same size subnet, and you'd probably end up with wasted IP addresses.

When we use VLSM, we start with a large network and break it down into smaller pieces, each with its own custom subnet mask. So, for example, you have the IP address range 192.168.1.0/24, which means you have 256 IP addresses to work with (from 192.168.1.0 to 192.168.1.255). If you were to divide them into equal parts, you would need to do a mask of /26, giving four subnets of 62 usable addresses each. This creates an unneeded subnet (there are only three departments), along with the wastage of a lot of IP addresses. Instead, you can use VLSM to divide the network based on each department's needs:

- Department A needs 50 IP addresses.

- Department B needs 20 IP addresses.

- Department C needs 10 IP addresses.

Each department needs its own subnet, as follows:

- **Subnet for department A** (50 IP addresses): The smallest subnet that can hold 50 IP addresses is /26, which provides 64 IP addresses (62 usable). We will assign 192.168.1.0/26 to department A. This range goes from 192.168.1.1 to 192.168.1.61 (64 addresses).

- **Subnet for department B** (20 IP addresses). The smallest subnet that can hold 20 IP addresses is /27, which provides 32 addresses (30 usable). We will assign 192.168.1.64/27 to department B. This range goes from 192.168.1.64 to 192.168.1.95 (32 addresses).

- **Subnet for department C** (10 IP addresses). The smallest subnet that can hold 10 addresses is /28, which provides 16 addresses (14 usable). We will assign 192.168.1.96/28 to department C. This range goes from 192.168.1.96 to 192.168.1.111 (16 addresses).

There are still unused addresses in each subnet, but not as many as by dividing the network into equal parts. There are 144 addresses left over, 192.168.1.112 to 192.168.1.255. This range can also be divided up into subnets as needed.

Summary

The chapter covered essential topics relating to IP addresses. Understanding IP addressing concepts is essential for efficient network management. Public and private IP addresses distinguish between globally routable addresses and those reserved for internal networks, with APIPA providing automatic private IPs when no DHCP server is available. RFC1918 defines the specific IP ranges for private networks, while loopback addresses allow devices to communicate with themselves for testing. Subnetting techniques, such as VLSM and CIDR, allow flexible division and efficient use of the IP address space. Additionally, IPv4 addresses are grouped into classes (A, B, C for standard networks, and D, E for special uses) to help with addressing structures. Together, these concepts form the foundation of modern IP networking, supporting both large-scale internet routing and small private networks.

The knowledge gained in this chapter will prepare you to answer questions relating to exam objective 1.7 in the *CompTIA Network+ (N10-009)* exam.

Exam objective 1.7

Given a scenario, use appropriate IPv4 network addressing

Public versus private:

- **Public addresses** are globally routable.
- **Private addresses** are restricted to the local network.
- **Automatic Private IP Addressing (APIPA).** Assigns IP addresses 169.254.X.X when the DHCP server is unreachable.
- **RFC1918** defines IP address ranges reserved for private networks.
- **Loopback/localhost:** Used to test network connections on the same device.
- **Subnetting:** Divides networks into smaller, manageable sub-networks.
- **Variable length subnet mask (VLSM):** Allows flexible subnet mask sizes within a network.
- **Classless Inter-Domain Routing (CIDR):** Improves IP address allocation efficiency by using custom subnet masks.

IPv4 address classes:

- **Class A:** Supports large networks with 16 million addresses.
- **Class B:** Supports medium networks with 65,000 addresses.
- **Class C:** Supports small networks with 256 addresses.
- **Class D:** Reserved for multicast groups, not for regular networks.
- **Class E:** Reserved for experimental purposes; not publicly used.

Chapter review questions

Now that you've completed the chapter, you can check your knowledge using the practice questions provided in the online platform at https://packt.link/N10-009ch7. You can also use the QR code below. Accessing these questions requires you to unlock the accompanying online content first. Head over to Chapter 26 for detailed instructions.

8

Summarize Evolving Use Cases for Modern Network Environments

As network environments continue to evolve, businesses and IT professionals are turning to modern solutions to achieve greater scalability, security, and operational efficiency. Technologies such as **software-defined networks (SDNs)**, **software-defined wide area networks (SD-WANs)**, and **infrastructure as code (IaC)** are transforming how networks are designed, deployed, and managed.

This chapter introduces critical advancements, including centralized policy management, **zero trust architecture (ZTA)**, **secure access service edge (SASE)**, IPv6 adoption, and **Virtual Extensible LAN (VXLAN)**. These innovations enable the creation of agile, resilient, and cloud-ready infrastructures.

By understanding and applying these technologies, organizations can meet the demands of modern business, reduce risk, and improve network performance and flexibility. Let's explore the key technologies shaping the future of networking.

This chapter covers the eighth objective in *Domain 1: 1.8, Summarize evolving use cases for modern network environments.*

> **Note**
>
> A full breakdown of objective 1.8 will be given at the end of the chapter.

Software-defined network (SDN)

So far, you have seen how network devices such as **routers** and **switches** are configured to create network topologies. In a simple setup, a router uses **routing tables** to decide where a data packet should be forwarded next, based on the destination **IP address**. This approach works well for small networks, such as a small office or home network.

However, as networks have grown in size and complexity, with tens or even hundreds of individual devices, managing them has become an administrative burden. Adding a new network or changing the topology might require reconfiguring multiple devices, a process that is time-consuming and prone to errors.

One way to address this challenge is to centralize network management rather than leaving it to individual devices. This can be achieved through an SDN, which allows for centralized control and greater flexibility in managing complex networks. Instead of manually configuring a network, you can use code to set up and reconfigure devices.

In SDN, the network is divided into two main parts: the **control plane**, which decides how data should move through the network, and the **data plane**, which moves packets along their paths. The data plane is also known as the **forwarding plane**.

In traditional networking, both the control and forwarding functions are handled by each individual device. A router consults its routing table to determine the next hop for a packet based on the destination IP address. A switch, on the other hand, forwards packets based on their **MAC** addresses, using its MAC address table.

By separating these two functions or layers, an SDN makes networks easier to manage. It's like the brain/body dynamic. A central brain, or the software, makes the decisions, and the body, or the interconnected physical network devices, carries out the actions. This separation also allows for quicker improvements and updates to both layers.

The SDN also allows easy and efficient implementation of business logic or desired configurations, such as automatically setting up new LANs. *Figure 8.1* shows the structure and components of an SDN.

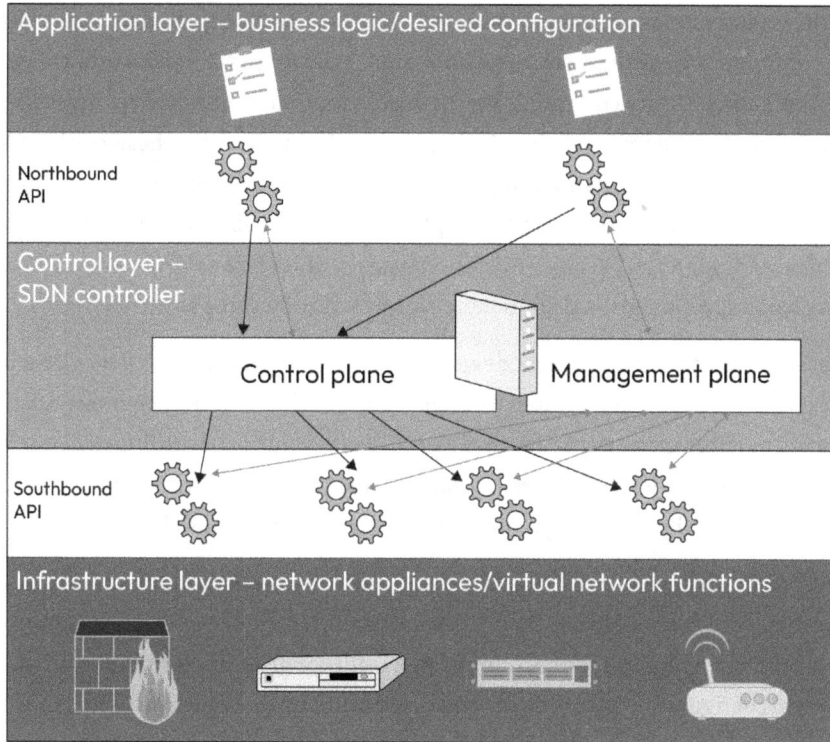

Figure 8.1: A diagram of an SDN

In *Figure 8.1*, you can see three layers of an SDN split by two APIs. The bottom is an **infrastructure layer,** which includes all the network appliances such as routers, firewalls, and switches. This is the data plane, the place where signals are physically directed. In the middle is a **control layer.** This includes the control plane, which makes the decisions about where data can go, and the **management plane,** which configures and monitors the network. The control layer sends instructions to the infrastructure layer through a **southbound API.**

At the top is an **application layer.** This is where business logic or network configurations can be defined by a user. It specifies what the network should do with regard to policies, traffic prioritization, and access controls. It interacts with the control layer through a **northbound API,** which translates high-level application requests into commands for the control layer.

Business logic can include things such as the following:

- Prioritizing video conferencing traffic during work hours to ensure smooth communication
- Automatically scaling bandwidth for e-commerce servers during peak shopping hours
- Blocking specific IP addresses to comply with security policies

For example, a network administrator will use a network application such as the **Cisco DNA Center** to configure a **quality of service (QoS)** rule. The application converts this into logic and uses northbound APIs to communicate these policies to the control layer, translating them into network-level configurations. Finally, the control layer executes these configurations by interacting with the data plane, ensuring that the devices in the network enforce the desired QoS rule. Simply put, business logic in the application layer enables policy-driven automation and dynamic reconfiguration based on operational goals. This allows the network to intelligently respond to changing demands and align more closely with the company's objectives.

In SDN-based environments, physical devices such as load balancers can be virtualized and delivered as software applications, often through NFV. Like their physical counterparts, software load balancers monitor incoming traffic and distribute it evenly or according to defined policies, ensuring no single server is overloaded. If a server fails, the load balancer detects the issue and redirects traffic to healthy servers, ensuring continuous service availability.

For example, during a flash sale on an e-commerce site, the company could quickly instruct the load balancer to redirect traffic to less busy servers, preventing the site from crashing and ensuring a smooth browsing experience for customers. In a traditional setup, this kind of change might require manual configuration of several devices or even adding more physical load balancers. This is cumbersome, time-consuming, and could be inefficient if the flash sale only lasts a short time.

Note

There is still some confusion in the tech world about SDN's exact structure and how the different layers (control, data, and applications) interact. To address these issues, the **Internet Research Task Force (IRTF)** has the **Software-Defined Networking Research Group (SDNRG)**, which sets guidelines to clarify these concepts based on research and standards.

For more information, visit https://www.rfc-editor.org/rfc/rfc7426.txt.

Software-defined wide area network

Because **wide-area networks (WANs)** are, by definition, dispersed across geographical areas, they create significant challenges for setup and maintenance. Having to add, reconfigure, and maintain devices across distances with complex and ever-changing security requirements is not easy and could require experts at many destinations working together over different time zones. Having a central network management point has an obvious advantage.

An SD-WAN enables businesses to connect their offices, remote workers, and data centers securely and efficiently. The goal of an SD-WAN is to optimize network traffic over long-distance connections using technologies such as **multi-protocol label switching (MPLS)**, broadband internet, and LTE. This provides a more efficient use of WAN resources, improving performance and reducing costs. SD-WAN focuses heavily on routing and managing traffic between multiple locations, often using internet-based links to replace or complement traditional MPLS circuits.

Instead of sending all traffic through a central hub, which can slow things down, SD-WAN allows direct, secure connections to the internet or cloud services and can automatically choose the fastest and most reliable path for data.

The SD-WAN is a use case application of an SDN, and as such, shares the same benefits, which will be discussed in the next section.

Key benefits of SDNs and SD-WANs

SDNs and SD-WANs can offer some key advantages over traditional networks, including being application-aware, having zero-touch provisioning, and central policy management.

Application-aware

The first advantage of using SDNs is the extent to which it is **application-aware**. Traditional networks are able to prioritize some types of applications, such as VoIP, using traffic classification based on IP headers. However, this is limited to how the individual router is configured to interpret the data packet, as well as handling forwarding instructions. In short, there is very little room for dynamic handling. By setting policies, an SDN can make real-time, dynamic decisions on prioritizing applications to ensure optimal performance.

For example, a policy can be set for video calls to take priority over large downloads. The SDN controller can see the entire network state, recognize that video call traffic is being delayed due to congestion on a certain link, and dynamically reroute that traffic to another path or adjust network policies to prioritize the call.

Zero-touch provisioning

SDNs and SD-WANs support **zero-touch provisioning (ZTP)**—a process where, upon first connecting to the internet, a device automatically retrieves its configuration from a central controller or specified URL and applies it without manual intervention. For example, a technician implementing a new SD-WAN router might simply plug it into the network, access a URL received via email, and watch as the device pulls down its network settings, routing policies, and security protocols from the cloud. This hands-off setup method not only ensures rapid, consistent deployment across remote or large-scale environments (such as branch offices of a financial institution) but also minimizes downtime, reduces the need for on-site expertise, and guarantees proper integration with the organization's existing security posture.

Transport-agnostic

Traditional WAN networks have been built using static routing on MPLS as the primary transport. Though other types of networks, such as cellular, can be used, they tend to be backup options to provide fault tolerance. SDNs, and thus SD-WANs, work with any type of transport. They can use real-time monitoring to determine the best transport for each application or data flow. Policies can be centrally defined, and the SD-WAN adapts to changing network conditions automatically. For example, a newly built remote office can use 5G temporarily until a fiber connection is available. SD-WANs use smart routing to decide the best path for data to travel based on speed and congestion. They also offer secure connections, which use encryption to protect data and ensure only authorized users access it.

Central policy management

With **central policy management**, all network policies—such as access controls, security rules, and traffic priorities—are managed from a single, centralized control panel. This simplifies administration and ensures consistent implementation of security protocols across the entire organization. It also allows a company to apply security updates or configuration changes to all branches at once, instead of managing each site manually. This centralized approach reduces the likelihood of misconfigurations and improves the speed and effectiveness of incident response.

When combined with the principle of least privilege, which ensures that users and devices are granted only the minimum permissions necessary to perform their tasks, overall network security is significantly enhanced. Limiting access in this way reduces the risk of unauthorized activity and minimizes the potential impact of a breach, since attackers would have fewer privileges to exploit.

For example, a pizza delivery chain has 30 branches across a city. In the past, each branch had to contact the central office for every order, inventory check, or update. This constant back-and-forth created delays and slowed down service. With an SD-WAN, each branch can connect directly to cloud-based systems. That means they can instantly receive orders, check supply levels, and update records without going through the main office. This results in faster deliveries, better coordination, fewer errors, and happier customers.

SDNs and SD-WANs are becoming increasingly important as IT networking becomes more complex, larger, and more geographically dispersed, and has to meet the demands of modern working habits, organizational structures, and data needs. It enables enterprises to create agile networks over large geographic areas.

For example, a global retail company has stores in North America, Europe, and Asia. Previously, each store routed all traffic back to a central data center over expensive MPLS links for security inspection and application access. This caused latency issues, especially for cloud apps such as Microsoft 365 and Salesforce.

Deploying SD-WAN offers the following benefits:

- Each store connects securely and directly to cloud services via local broadband or LTE

- The SD-WAN automatically chooses the best path (e.g., 5G, fiber, or MPLS) based on real-time performance

- Application-aware routing ensures that video conferencing is prioritized over software updates

- New stores can be brought online in hours using ZTP and cloud-based orchestration

- Central IT can push policy and security updates from headquarters to all branches instantly

- This reduces costs (by using less MPLS), improves performance, and simplifies operations. However, there are other modern networking technologies meeting the demands of modern industry, as you will see in the next section.

Virtual extensible local area network (VXLAN)

In *Chapter 7, Given a Scenario, Use Appropriate IPv4 Network Addressing,* you saw how IP addresses are used to create networks and subnets. In traditional Ethernet networks, VLANs are used to segment traffic into separate broadcast domains. VLAN IDs are 12 bits long, allowing for a maximum of 4096 VLANs. While this is sufficient for small and medium environments, it poses scalability challenges for large data centers and cloud providers, which may require thousands of isolated networks. Virtual Extensible LAN (VXLAN) addresses this limitation by encapsulating Layer 2 traffic over Layer 3 networks and expanding the identifier space to 24 bits, supporting up to 16 million logical networks. VLANs can also require physical changes because they are based on routers and switches directing data packets. For small offices and enterprises, this might not be an issue; however, larger, modern environments, such as data centers or cloud providers, need more agile and efficient solutions.

The answer is a VXLAN. Like VLAN, VXLAN is a technology that allows a single network to be split into many virtual networks. It is like having separate lanes on a highway, so different types of traffic don't interfere with each other. It is commonly used in large data centers to connect many devices and systems while keeping their traffic isolated. It has the ability to support 16 million **virtual network identifiers** (**VNIs**), each of which is one VXLAN. This dwarfs the traditional VLAN limitation of 4,096 IDs.

VXLANs enable cloud providers to extend their network infrastructure efficiently by creating scalable, isolated Layer 2 networks over existing Layer 3 infrastructure. This allows multitenant environments because the network segmentation enables millions of isolated virtual networks for different tenants or customers.

> **Note**
>
> VLANs are covered in more detail in *Chapter 10, Given a Scenario, Configure Switching Technologies and Features*.

Data center interconnect (DCI) with VXLAN

VXLAN allows organizations to connect physically separate data centers into one unified virtual network. This is especially useful for sharing resources, migrating workloads, and ensuring disaster recovery between sites—a practice known as **data center interconnect** (**DCI**).

VXLAN achieves this by using Layer 2 encapsulation over a Layer 3 network, making distant systems appear as if they're on the same local network. Each segment of the network is identified by a **VXLAN network identifier** (**VNI**), which helps direct traffic correctly.

The key component that makes VXLAN work is the **VXLAN tunnel endpoint** (**VTEP**). These devices or software functions encapsulate and decapsulate network traffic, acting as bridges between the physical and virtual networks. They also map VNIs to physical interfaces.

For example, an international e-commerce company has data centers in New York and Delhi:

- During a high-traffic event such as a holiday sale, VXLAN enables the company to balance traffic between both data centers, ensuring no one site is overwhelmed
- If the New York site experiences an outage, workloads can instantly shift to Delhi—without users noticing and without needing to change IP addresses
- On normal days, staff in New York can seamlessly access analytics or resources hosted in Delhi, as if they were in the same building

Zero-trust architecture

ZTA is a modern approach to cybersecurity designed to keep sensitive information safe, especially in today's world, where people work from many locations and use various devices. The basic idea behind ZTA is simple: *Never trust, always verify*. Even if someone or something is inside your network, it assumes they could still be a threat until proven otherwise. The way ZTA does this can be broken down into three main components: policy-based authentication; how identities are managed; authorization; the regulation of who can access resources; and least privilege access, which limits exposure to resources. These will be covered in the following sections.

Policy-based authentication

Policy-based authentication acknowledges that user identities can change over time and aren't fixed. Instead of granting access solely based on static credentials such as passwords, it evaluates the context and conditions under which a request is made. For example, rather than simply having access to a resource such as financial data being tied to a username and password, a policy can be put in place, such as "Allow access to financial data only during office hours" or "Require multi-factor authentication for all logins from unrecognized devices".

Policy-based authentication ensures that identity verification is not a one-time event but rather an ongoing process, dynamically adapting based on the user's current context, behavior, and the specific resources they want to access.

For example, someone logging in from their usual location might require standard verification, but a login attempt from a new device or unexpected location would trigger additional security measures such as two-factor authentication. This continuous monitoring enhances security while allowing legitimate users to work seamlessly. This dynamic security system is also known as **adaptive identity**.

This way of doing things ensures strong security rules because policies ensure that security decisions are consistent and predictable, meaning there is no guessing or human error. Access is tailored to each user or device, so there's no over-permission or unnecessary risk. Policies also make it easier for organizations to manage security, even as teams grow or systems become more complex, and since policies can be applied universally, you can keep the system safe and still allow people to access resources from multiple destinations.

In another example, imagine that a trusted employee starts acting in a suspicious way or tries to log in from an unusual location, their identity status adapts, and the system tightens the controls automatically. The system continuously monitors a user's behavior, location, device, and the resources being accessed. If the user is accessing from a different country or a VPN, then the system might adapt to require further authentication. If the user is accessing certain critical resources, such as financial details, at an unusual time, such as in the middle of the night, the system might block access entirely.

By continuously monitoring behavior, it's harder for hackers or malware to exploit accounts unnoticed. Security adapts to each user's specific context and habits, providing more precise safeguards.

Authorization

If you enter a bank, even if there are security checks at the door, you are still only allowed to access the public areas as a customer. Even employees will face restrictions, with only high-level managers being able to access the safe, for instance.

Network access and authorization in ZTA work much the same way. Even if you have been authenticated and can access the network, you may still be able to access only certain resources—those pertinent to your job, for instance. This could also be dynamic. For example, you may be able to edit documents at certain times of the day or access them from trusted locations, while you can only read the same documents at other times of the day or from less trusted locations.

Least privilege access

How to decide which adaptive identities can access what might sound like a complex process. Deciding which resources and networks should be restricted might become an arduous task in a dynamic company. One way to deal with this issue is with the concept of **least privilege access**. Rather than working out what should be restricted, least privilege access starts with the principle of restricting everything and only allowing what is necessary for the job. For example, if a new employee is a graphic designer, they are only given access to the design team's network, as well as being given selected read-only access to important documents such as company policies and human resources guidelines. If the employee needs access to other apps and devices to do their job, these can be granted on a case-by-case basis.

Under this system, the employee might not be able to access some fairly innocuous resources, and they may have to spend more time requesting permissions from other departments, for instance, marketing. However, it also means that if the employee's account is compromised by a hacker or some malware, the damage is minimized because the account's reach in the network is minimized.

By combining policy-based authentication, authorization, and least privilege access, ZTA reduces the potential damage any security threat can cause. For example, if a password is stolen, a malicious actor still needs to pass additional security checks, and even if the actor can access the account, they can only access limited systems.

The main components of ZTA are the control and data planes, which are shown in *Figure 8.2.*

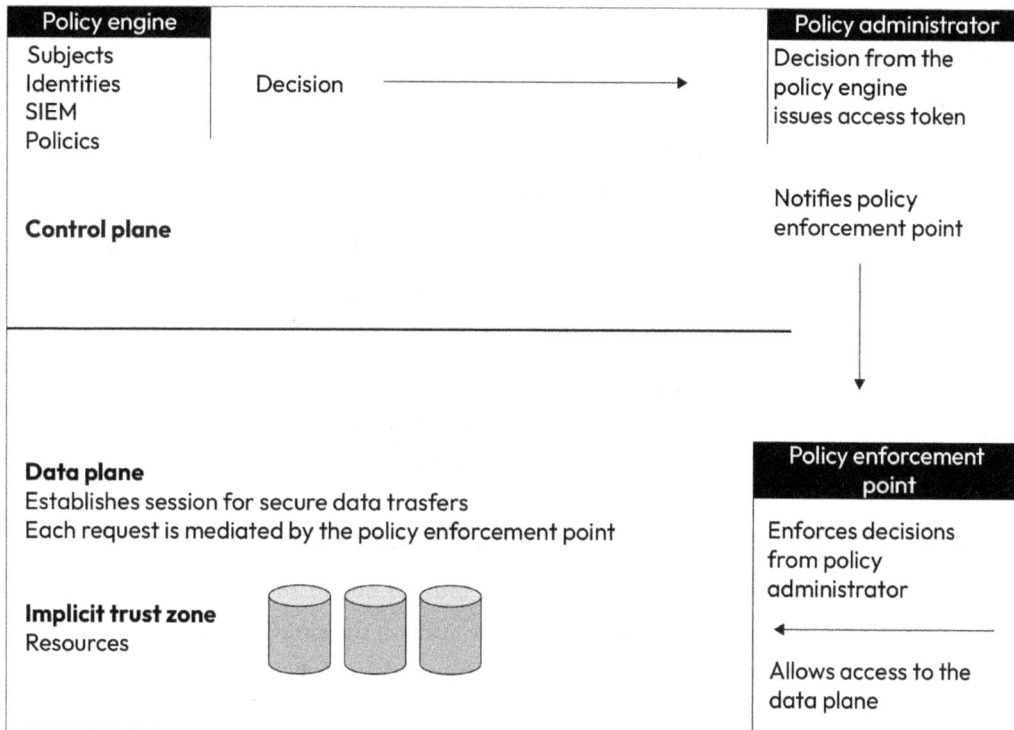

Policy engine		Policy administrator
Subjects Identities SIEM Policics	Decision ⟶	Decision from the policy engine issues access token
		Notifies policy enforcement point
Control plane		

Data plane
Establishes session for secure data trasfers
Each request is mediated by the policy enforcement point

Implicit trust zone
Resources

Policy enforcement point
Enforces decisions from policy administrator

Allows access to the data plane

Figure 8.2: ZTA

The **policy engine** is the "brain" of the system. It decides who can access what, using preset rules written by the security team. These decisions are based on multiple factors such as user details, device information, and threat intelligence. After analyzing all this data, it tells the **policy administrator** what actions to take.

The policy administrator serves as the bridge between the policy engine and the **policy enforcement point (PEP)**. It is responsible for executing the decisions made by the policy engine and ensuring they are properly enforced.

When access is approved, the policy administrator works with identity and access management systems, such as Entra ID (formerly Azure AD) or Okta, to generate and deliver the necessary credentials or access tokens.

It then communicates with the PEP, instructing it on how to apply the decision. For example, it may tell the PEP to grant a user read-only access to a specific resource for a limited time, based on the defined security policy.

The PEP serves as the final authority for access control and policy implementation. It evaluates the token or directive provided by the policy engine and ensures that only authorized users, devices, or actions are allowed.

The PEP may grant access to an **implicit trust zone**, which refers to areas of the network where limited access is given with minimal permissions. For example, an employee may only be allowed to view general resources such as company policies, but not sensitive data.

If required, the PEP can also grant access to a **secure zone**, which is a highly protected area of the network containing sensitive or critical information. This is only allowed after strict verification, such as multi-factor authentication and device compliance checks.

ZTA is a general term for any architecture that follows the principles we have covered in this section. However, it plays a crucial role in recent networking advancements as many enterprises move to entirely cloud-based solutions, as you will see in the next section.

Secure access service edge/security service edge

Many businesses now rely on cloud computing for most, if not all, of their network functions. This shift necessitates ensuring the same level of security in the cloud as is maintained for on-premises systems. Traditional perimeter-based security models—relying on firewalls, VPNs, and proxies—are becoming increasingly complex and less effective as network access originates from geographically dispersed locations, and more functions occur in remote data centers.

SASE and the related **security service edge** (SSE) address the issue by integrating security functions into cloud computing. They are both frameworks designed to provide secure, efficient access to resources regardless of a user's location or device.

Pronounced *sassy*, SASE integrates networking and security services into a unified, cloud-delivered framework. It combines SD-WAN and cloud-based delivery with ZTA and **firewall as a service** (**FWaaS**) functions. Essentially, it does away with data centers and puts security controls at the point of connection.

With SASE, resources are accessed directly from the cloud rather than having a user connect to an on-premises data center. This, coupled with SD-WAN, optimizes networking for wide geographic areas by finding the closest connection point, increasing efficiency, and bolstering scalability. Security is handled with ZTA, as described earlier, using **secure web gateways** (**SWGs**), which filter internet traffic, blocking harmful websites and malware. **Cloud access security brokers** (**CASBs**) monitor cloud service access and usage to prevent data leaks and ensure secure behavior. For example, it can block an employee from uploading sensitive files to untrusted sites. As mentioned, FWaaS replaces the traditional on-premises hardware firewall and normally has next-generation firewall capabilities.

SSE is essentially a type or component of SASE, focusing primarily on the security components of SASE. Though normally a part of SASE, as a framework, it can be used to bolster hybrid environments that include both on-premises networking and cloud access, offering the same SWG, CASB, and FWaaS capabilities already mentioned.

The final aspect of modern networking technologies you will look at in this chapter is the ultimate in applying logical, rather than physical, solutions to today's networking requirements. That is IaC.

Infrastructure as code

Businesses rely on **cloud service providers** (**CSPs**) to create and manage thousands of digital resources, such as **virtual machines** (**VMs**), storage spaces, and networks, on a daily basis. While this makes operations highly scalable and efficient, it also introduces a major challenge: human error.

Imagine a CSP setting up thousands of resources manually in a day. Even the most experienced team is prone to mistakes when handling such large volumes. A single typo or misconfiguration could lead to issues such as security vulnerabilities when sensitive data is left exposed and downtime if a resource fails due to being incorrectly configured. There might even be compliance violations if data protection rules have not been properly followed.

One solution is to automate the creation, configuration, and management of resources by using scripts or templates to define how everything should work using IaC principles. Instead of manually setting up each resource, IT teams can write code that specifies exactly how resources should be configured. This ensures a consistent setup every time, reduces human error, and allows tasks to be repeated or adjusted easily.

For instance, a company wants to deploy a web application in AWS. This environment includes a VPC for network isolation. A VPC in AWS provides a logically isolated virtual network where a company can deploy its resources securely. When deploying a web application, the VPC is typically divided into public and private subnets to enhance security and control.

The **public subnet** hosts resources that must be accessible from the internet, such as web servers or load balancers, which have public IP addresses and route traffic through an internet gateway.

The **private subnet** contains sensitive components such as databases or application servers that do not have direct internet access. These private resources communicate with the internet indirectly via a **network address translation (NAT) gateway** located in the public subnet, allowing them to download updates or access external services securely. This separation ensures that only necessary parts of the application are exposed to the internet, while critical data and backend services remain protected, following best practices for network segmentation and security.

The environment also includes two EC2 instances, which are VMs in the cloud that the company is renting. One is for the app and one for the database. It also has an S3 bucket, which is a virtual container, for storing static assets such as images and CSS files used to define HTML styles. Identity access is also needed to manage permissions. If done manually through the AWS Management Console, this process is prone to human errors, such as forgetting to assign correct **identity access management** (IAM) roles, which are used to define permissions, or misconfiguring security group rules and creating inconsistencies between environments, such as staging and production.

However, using IaC, the IT team can write a configuration file in YAML (a human-readable format often used for configuration) or HCL (HashiCorp Configuration Language, designed for tools like Terraform) to define the infrastructure. Every time this template runs, it creates an identical environment, ensuring staging and production are configured exactly the same. It reduces human error and increases efficiency.

Automation in IT is all about using tools and processes to make repetitive tasks faster, easier, and less prone to human error. Instead of setting up systems manually each time, automation lets us use pre-made instructions to handle tasks efficiently and consistently. It includes **playbooks**, which are sets of instructions designed to automate tasks such as setting up new servers, configuring applications, or running updates. They define what needs to be done and how, ensuring that the task is performed the same way every time.

Automation also includes **templates**, which define the configuration of systems or applications. For instance, if you need to create multiple VMs with the same settings, a template ensures each machine is identical without having to configure each manually. **Reusable tasks** are smaller components within playbooks or templates that can be used repeatedly. For example, a reusable task might include installing software, configuring security, or setting up network access.

Orchestration takes automation further by coordinating multiple automated tasks into a unified workflow. It ensures that all the automated tasks work together seamlessly to achieve a larger goal. For example, let's say you are deploying a new application, which might involve the following tasks:

1. Setting up servers
2. Configuring the network

3. Deploying the application

4. Setting up monitoring tools

Orchestration ensures that these tasks are executed in the proper order automatically by connecting various automated processes. It manages the order of execution and dependencies between tasks and ensures that tasks are completed successfully before moving to the next step.

The key differences between automation and orchestration are as follows:

- Automation refers to single tasks or actions. The scope is narrow and focused on specific processes, for example, automating backups or applying patches.

- Orchestration refers to coordinating multiple automated tasks into workflows. The scope is broad, managing end-to-end processes, for example, deploying a complete application or IT service.

Source control

Source control is a system used to manage and track changes to files, especially in software development. It ensures that multiple people can work on the same project without overwriting each other's work. It is essential for software teams to collaborate efficiently and maintain a history of all updates. The key features of source control are version control, central repositories, conflict identification, and branching and merging. They are covered in more detail here:

- **Version control**: This keeps a history of all changes made to files, allowing you to go back to earlier versions if mistakes occur or something breaks. It works like a "save history" in a video game, so you can reload an earlier point if needed.

- **Central repository**: This is a shared place where all project files and their change history are stored. Everyone on the team uploads their work here, ensuring it is always up to date. Think of it as a shared Google Drive folder that tracks all changes.

- **Conflict identification**: When two people edit the same part of a file, a conflict occurs. Source control systems identify these conflicts and allow the team to resolve them manually. It is like two people editing the same line of a document—source control flags it and asks whose changes to keep.

- **Branching and merging**: This allows developers to create separate copies (branches) of the project to work on features or fixes without affecting the main version. Once the work is complete, it can be merged back into the main project. It is like making a copy of a group project to try new ideas without changing the main project until it is finalized.

Source control is widely used in software development because it helps teams collaborate without overwriting each other's work. It keeps track of every code change, making it easy to undo mistakes. It manages conflicts when multiple people edit the same files. It enables branching for experimentation without affecting the main project.

For example, when building a mobile app, one developer can work on the login feature while another works on the profile page. Source control ensures their changes can be integrated smoothly without disrupting the project. Popular tools for source control in software development include Git, GitHub, GitLab, and Bitbucket.

IPv6 addressing

In *Chapter 7, Given a Scenario, Use Appropriate IPv4 Network Addressing*, you saw how **IPv4** uses a 32-bit address to identify networks, subnets, and devices. While, at the time of writing, this version is still the most common, it has one major drawback: **address exhaustion**. IPv4 has been around since 1982, and has fewer than 4.3 billion available addresses, with large numbers of those addresses reserved for special purposes. However, an updated version of the protocol is solving this issue.

> **Note**
>
> For more details on IPv4 addressing, see *Chapter 7*. For more details on address exhaustion, you can check the Wikipedia entry here: https://en.wikipedia.org/wiki/IPv4_address_exhaustion.

Mitigating address exhaustion

Internet Protocol version 6 (IPv6), released in 1999, is the most recent version of the protocol. It solves the issue of address exhaustion, offering 340 undecillion (i.e., 340 trillion trillion trillion) possible addresses, along with better performance and compatibility with new technologies.

The format of an IPv6 address is broken into eight hextets, or blocks, rather than the four octets of IPv4. Each hextet represents 16 bits (or 2 bytes) of the 128-bit address. The IPv6 convention is that these hextets are written in hexadecimal and separated by colons (:), rather than the decimal numbers and periods used by IPv4. This makes the address both compact and human-readable.

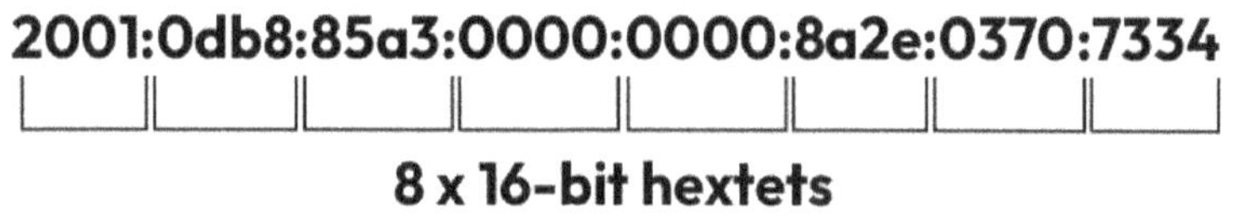

2001:0db8:85a3:0000:0000:8a2e:0370:7334

8 x 16-bit hextets

Figure 8.3: An IPv6 address separated into eight 16-bit hextets

To simplify the writing of IPv6 addresses, the IETF has created a way of shortening them in a standardized way, making them easier to read, write, and compare. This shortened form is called the **canonical address**.

The rules of canonical address are as follows:

- Leading zeros are removed, so 00b6 is written as b6, and 0004 becomes 4.

- Consecutive hextets containing all zeros are collapsed and replaced with ::, so 0000:0000:0000 becomes ::. This can only be done once in a single address to prevent confusion.

- Only the leftmost groups of consecutive zeros are collapsed, with further groups being shortened to :0:

Let's look at some examples:

Example 1

- The full IPv6 address is 2001:0db8:0000:0000:0000:ff00:0042:8329

- 0db8 becomes db8

- 0000:0000:0000 becomes ::

- 0042 becomes 42

- The canonical form is 2001:db8::ff00:42:8329

Multiple consecutive hextets of zeros in *Example 1* are collapsed to ::, representing 0000:0000:0000 will appear the same in the canonical form. You can easily work out what is being represented by counting the number of hextets, as there are always eight.

Example 2

- The full IPv6 address is 2001:0db8:0000:0000:0bcd:0000:0042:8329

- 0db8 becomes db8

- 0000:0000 becomes ::

- 0bcd becomes bcd

- 0000 becomes 0

- 0042 becomes 42

- The canonical form is 2001:db8::bcd:0:42:8329

In *Example 2*, we can see that the first two blocks of zero have been replaced by :: and then the second block of zeros has been replaced by :0:. After we count the six hextets, we then realise the :: is two hextets of zeros.

Example 3

- The full IPv6 address is 2001:0db8:0000:0000:0bcd:0000:0000:8329

- 0db8 becomes db8

- 0000:0000 becomes ::

- 0bcd becomes bcd

- 0000 becomes 0

- The next set of 0000 also becomes 0

- The canonical form is 2001:db8::bcd:0:0:8329

In *Example 3*, you can see that only the leftmost group of 0000 hextets is collapsed to ::, and subsequent groups become :0:0:

Similar to IPv4, IPv6 divides its 128-bit address into parts: the **network ID** and the **host ID**. The network ID is 64 bits and contains the routing information. The host, or **device ID**, is also 64 bits and is the unique address of the device.

The network ID is further split into two components. The first part is the **global routing prefix**, which includes a 3-bit prefix for the address type and a 45-bit network ID for the specific network. The second part is the subnet ID, which is 16 bits. This is shown in *Figure 8.4*.

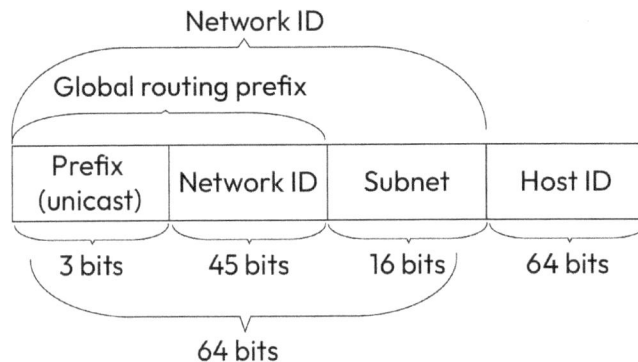

Figure 8.4: Breakdown of an IPv6 address

As shown in *Figure 8.4*, the first part of an IPv6 address contains a prefix indicating the address type—such as a 3-bit prefix for global unicast addresses, which are public IPv6 addresses. The host portion (interface identifier) was historically often derived automatically using the **EUI-64** (this stands for **extended unique identifier 64-bit**) method, which incorporates the device's MAC address, but today it is more commonly generated randomly or with privacy extensions to protect user anonymity.

Global unicast addresses in IPv6 fall within the prefix 2000::/3. This means that any address beginning with the first 3 bits 001 is part of the global unicast space, leaving the other 61 bits of network ID for different network addresses. The double colons are equivalent to 0000:0000:0000:0000:0000:0000:0000, so the range of addresses spans:

From: 2000:0000:0000:0000:0000:0000:0000:0000

To: 3fff:ffff:ffff:ffff:ffff:ffff:ffff:ffff

These addresses are routable on the public network and allocated in blocks (such as /48, /56, or /64) for different networks.

The different types of IPv6 addresses are shown in the following table.

Type	Prefix	Example
Global unicast	2000::/3	2001:0db8::1
Link-local unicast	fe80::/10	fe80::1ff:fe23:4567:890a
Multicast	ff00::/16	ff02::1
Link-local multicast	ff02::/16	ff02::1
Solicited-node multicast	ff02::1:ff00:0/104	ff02::1:ffab:1234
Unspecified	::/128	::
Loopback	::/128	::1

Here are the use cases for each of these types of address:

- **Global unicast** (2000::/3): These are publicly routable IPv6 addresses, similar to public IPv4 addresses. They are used to identify a device on the internet and are unique worldwide.

  Example format: 2001:0db8:85a3:0000:0000:8a2e:0370:7334

- **Link-local unicast** (fe80::/10): These addresses are automatically assigned to every IPv6-enabled device. They are only valid within a local network link similar to IPv4 private addresses, so they might be used in a home Wi-Fi or office network. The prefix (/10) defines how many bits must fit a defined binary format.

  Example format: fe80::1ff:fe23:4567:890a.

- **Multicast** (ff00::/8): In an IPv6 network, there is no broadcast address, so they use the multicast address. Multicast addresses are used to send data to multiple devices at once. Instead of sending separate messages to each device, one message can reach many.

  Example format: ff00::1

- **Link-local multicast** (ff02::/16): This targets devices on the same link, as in this example:

ff02::1	All nodes	All devices on the link
ff02::2	All routers	Devices routing traffic on the link
ff02::1:2	DHCP servers	Used for managing IP addresses

- **Solicited-node multicast** (ff02::1:ff00:0/104): This is a specialized multicast address used in neighbor discovery, allowing devices to find each other on a local network.

  Example format: ff02::1:ffab:1234, which is performed by appending part of a device's address to the prefix

IPv6 uses **neighbor solicitation (NS)** messages, part of the **Neighbor Discovery Protocol (NDP)**, to manage communication between devices on the same link. One key use is address resolution, where a device knows a neighbor's IPv6 address but needs its MAC address to send data. The device sends an NS message to the neighbor's solicited-node multicast address, and the neighbor replies with its MAC address in a **neighbor advertisement (NA)**. Another use is **duplicate address detection (DAD)**, which is where a device ensures its IPv6 address is unique on the network before using it. The device sends an NS message to the solicited-node multicast address of the intended address, and if no response is received, the address is considered unique:

- **Unspecified address** (::/128): This represents "no specific address" and is used by devices that don't yet have an address.

  Example format: :: (all zeros)

- **Loopback address** (::1/128): The loopback address performs the same function as the IPv4 127.0.0.1 address. It is used by a device to communicate with itself, often for diagnostic testing.

  Example format: ::1 (all zeros except the 128 bit that is set to 1)

As you can see, there are many similar functionalities with IPv4. However, the two protocols are not the same, and this can cause problems when they are both used concurrently. The solutions for these issues are covered in the next section.

Compatibility requirements

IPv6 and IPv4 are fundamentally different in their addressing formats and design, which makes them incompatible by design. IPv6 uses 128-bit addresses, while IPv4 uses 32-bit addresses. However, there are some compatibility techniques that allow the two protocols to coexist. These are tunneling, dual stack, and NAT64.

Tunneling

Tunneling is like placing a package inside another box for delivery. IPv6 packets are wrapped, or encapsulated, inside IPv4 packets so they can travel across IPv4-only networks. Once the packet reaches an IPv6-capable system, it's unpacked and processed normally. This process is called **6to4 tunneling**.

The 6to4 tunneling process begins with an IPv6 address that embeds an IPv4 address, formatted as `2002:IPv4-address::/48`. This IPv6 packet is sent to a network device, such as a router, that supports both IPv6 and IPv4. The router encapsulates the IPv6 packet by adding an IPv4 header, effectively placing the IPv6 packet as the payload of an IPv4 packet. This encapsulated packet is then transmitted over the IPv4 network to the destination. At the destination, a 6to4-capable device or router decapsulates the packet by removing the IPv4 header, extracting the original IPv6 packet, and forwarding it to the intended IPv6-capable device.

Dual stack

Dual-stack devices and networks run both IPv4 and IPv6 simultaneously, with each stack running independently of the other. This allows them to communicate with either IPv4 or IPv6 systems, depending on what's available. A dual-stack device can handle both IPv4 and IPv6 traffic, choosing the appropriate protocol based on the destination address.

NAT64

NAT for IPv6 to IPv4 allows IPv6-only devices to communicate with IPv4-only systems. **NAT64** acts as a translator, converting IPv6 addresses into IPv4, and vice versa. This is useful when transitioning from IPv4 to IPv6, as not all systems are IPv6-ready.

Neighbor solicitation

IPv6 introduces new mechanisms to manage addresses on local networks and ensure efficient communication between devices. NS is part of the NDP, which replaces the older ARP in IPv4. It allows devices to discover the link-layer address (such as a MAC address) of other devices on the same network and check whether an IPv6 address is already in use. The process is simple:

1. A device sends an NS message to the desired IPv6 address.
2. The target device responds with an NA message, providing its link-layer address. This ensures that communication is established efficiently and without conflicts.

Summary

This chapter covered modern networking concepts, which focus on agility, security, and efficiency to meet evolving IT demands. SDN and SD-WAN enhance application-aware traffic management, enable ZTP, work across diverse transports, and support centralized policy control for simplified operations. VXLAN provides scalable Layer 2 encapsulation and facilitates DCI for flexible data center networking.

ZTA enforces strict, policy-driven authentication, authorization, and least privilege access to secure critical resources. SASE and SSE integrate networking and security to ensure secure, distributed connectivity.

IaC introduces automation through reusable playbooks, templates, and dynamic inventories, ensuring compliance, reducing configuration drift, and simplifying upgrades. IaC also leverages source control with centralized repositories, version control, conflict resolution, and branching to streamline collaborative network management. These approaches are reshaping modern network environments with a focus on scalability, security, and operational efficiency.

The knowledge gained in this chapter will prepare you to answer questions relating to exam objective 1.8 in the *CompTIA Network+ (N10-009)* exam.

Exam objective 1.8

Summarize evolving use cases for modern network environments

SDN and **SD-WAN**: Simplify network with application awareness and zero-touch provisioning

- **Application-aware**: Tailors network behavior based on application needs
- **Zero-touch provisioning (ZTP)**: Automates network setup without manual intervention
- **Transport-agnostic**: Operates over any transport medium seamlessly
- **Central policy management**: Unified control for consistent network policies

VXLAN: Enhances scalability with Layer 2 encapsulation for data centers

- **Data center interconnect (DCI)**: Connects multiple data centers efficiently
- **Layer 2 encapsulation**: Supports extended networks over Layer 3 infrastructure

Zero trust architecture (ZTA): Strengthens security via strict authentication

- **Policy-based authentication:** Enforces access based on predefined policies
- **Authorization:** Ensures only permitted users can access resources
- **Least privilege access:** Limits user access to the bare minimum required

SASE/SSE: Converged network security and connectivity at the edge

Infrastructure as Code (IaC): Automates and manages network configurations

- **Automation:** Streamlines operations with reusable templates and dynamic inventories

    - **Playbooks/templates:** Standardize and reuse tasks for consistent automation
    - **Configuration drift/compliance:** Monitor and correct configuration discrepancies
    - **Upgrades:** Simplifies network updates through automation
    - **Dynamic inventories:** Automatically track and manage network assets

- **Source control:** Maintains versioning and collaboration for network configurations

    - **Version control:** Tracks changes to configurations over time
    - **Central repository:** Stores all configurations in a unified location
    - **Conflict identification:** Detects and resolves configuration conflicts early
    - **Branching:** Tests and develops changes without affecting live environments

IPv6 addressing: Future-proofs networks to handle address exhaustion

- **Mitigating address exhaustion:** Expands available IP addresses with IPv6 adoption
- **Compatibility requirements:**

    - **Tunneling:** Enables IPv6 communication over IPv4 infrastructure
    - **Dual stack:** Operates with both IPv4 and IPv6 simultaneously
    - **NAT64:** Facilitates communication between IPv6 and IPv4 systems

Chapter review questions

Now that you've completed the chapter, you can check your knowledge using the practice questions provided in the online platform at `https://packt.link/N10-009ch8`. You can also use the QR code below. Accessing these questions requires you to unlock the accompanying online content first. Head over to *Chapter 26* for detailed instructions.

Domain 2

Network Implementation

The second part of the book focuses on deploying and configuring network infrastructure. It examines routing technologies, switching features such as VLANs and trunking, wireless deployment and security, and the physical factors involved in installations. Candidates will learn how to apply practical skills in building wired and wireless networks, ensuring secure connectivity and reliable performance across enterprise environments.

This part of the book includes the following chapters:

- *Chapter 9, Explain Characteristics of Routing Technologies*
- *Chapter 10, Given a Scenario, Configure Switching Technologies and Features*
- *Chapter 11, Given a Scenario, Select and Configure Wireless Devices and Technologies*
- *Chapter 12, Explain Important Factors of Physical Installations*

9

Explain Characteristics of Routing Technologies

In *Chapter 7* and *Chapter 8*, you saw how IP addresses and software-defined networks, including infrastructure as code, are used to map out a network. The next stage to understand a network is to look at how devices use these addresses or mappings to direct data to the correct place in a process known as routing.

Efficient routing ensures data is transmitted accurately and swiftly between devices. Even with a well-designed network topology, efficient routing is crucial to ensuring fast, secure, and manageable communication between devices. Routing technologies encompass a wide range of protocols and mechanisms designed to direct traffic through a network, select optimal paths, and maintain communication reliability. This chapter will examine the key characteristics of various routing technologies, including static and dynamic routing protocols, route selection processes, and address translation methods. Additionally, you will explore concepts such as **First Hop Redundancy Protocol (FHRP)**, **Virtual IP (VIP)**, and the use of subinterfaces to gain a comprehensive overview of how these technologies contribute to robust and scalable network designs.

This chapter covers the first objective in *Domain 2: 2.1, Explain characteristics of routing technologies.*

> **Note**
>
> A full breakdown of objective 2.1 will be given at the end of the chapter.

Introduction

If you have only two devices in a network, for example, with toy walkie-talkies, then communication is relatively simple. You press the button, speak, and the signal goes to the right place. But as soon as you add more devices to a network, things become a lot more complex. *Chapter 2, Compare and Contrast Networking Appliances, Applications, and Functions*, covered all the devices you might have on a network, such as routers and switches. Routers are responsible for directing data packets, or network traffic, using **IP addresses** that indicate the destination of the traffic.

Each router a data packet passes through on its journey is called a **hop**. A **router** determines how to direct a message by referencing a **routing table**, which provides the **next hop**, that is, the next router, for the data packet based on its destination IP address. These routes, the directions given in the routing table, can be defined in two ways: **static routing** and **dynamic routing**, which will be covered in the first two sections of this chapter.

Static routing

Static routing is one of the simplest forms of routing used in networks. It involves **manually configuring** the routing table on a router or network device to determine the path data packets should take to reach a specific destination. Unlike dynamic routing, which automatically adjusts to changes in the network, static routing requires manual updates whenever there is a change in the network topology, such as adding a new route or changing the network structure.

Key characteristics of static routing

Because network administrators manually enter routes into the routing table, they have complete control over how data moves through the network; for smaller networks, this makes setup more straightforward than automatic routing. Static routing also does not consume network resources or bandwidth for route discovery and maintenance, unlike dynamic routing protocols, so there is no overhead. Because static routes are not influenced by network changes, they can lack flexibility and can't adapt quickly if a link goes down or the network changes.

To configure a static route, you'll need to use specific syntax depending on the device's operating system. The following bash command is an example of a static route set up using **Cisco Internetwork Operating System (Cisco IOS)**.

```
Router(config)# ip route <destination-network> <subnet-mask> <next-hop-ip-
address>
```

We can break down the code as follows.

- `<destination-network>`: This is the network address for the destination. It tells the router where the data should ultimately be delivered.

- `<subnet-mask>`: This is the subnet mask for the destination network. The subnet mask specifies the host and network portion of an IP address.

- `<next-hop-ip-address>`: This is the IP address of the next hop, which is typically the nearside gateway of a router closest to the destination network.

For example, we want to create a static route to connect two networks: `192.168.2.0`, and `132.12.0.1`.

In *Figure 9.1*, the source network is `192.168.2.0`, the nearside gateway to Router A is `192.168.1.1`, and the farside gateway is `15.12.0.1`, in the in-between network. The in-between network is `15.12.0.0` and has two gateways: `15.12.0.1`, connecting to the farside of Router A, and `15.12.0.254`, connecting to the nearside of Router B. The farside gateway on Router B is `132.12.0.1`, which is our destination gateway. The destination network is `132.12.0.0`.

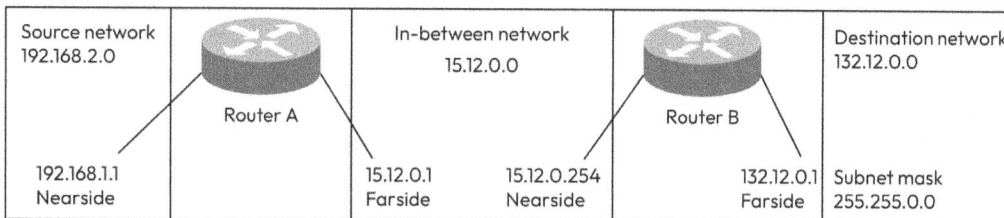

Figure 9.1: Network layout

The command is as follows:

```
Static route = Router(config)#  ip route 132.12.0.0 255.255.0.0
15.12.0.254
```

We can break down the code as follows:

- `132.12.0.0` is `<destination-network>`

- `255.255.0.0` is `<subnet-mask>`

- `15.12.0.254` is `<next-hop-ip-address>` (the nearside gateway of Router B, which is the router closest to the destination network)

> Note
>
> Subnets and network classes are covered in more detail in *Chapter 7, Given a Scenario, Use Appropriate IPv4 Network Addressing*.

When to use static routing

Static routing is best suited for small, straightforward networks with few routes and a stable topology that doesn't change frequently. It works well in stub networks, where there's only one entry and exit point, and in tightly controlled environments where you need to enforce specific traffic paths for security or policy purposes.

In most modern networks, static routing is uncommon. However, it is useful to understand not simply because you may be asked to deal with a network setup with static routing, but also because it will help you to analyze more advanced dynamic routing techniques, which will be covered next.

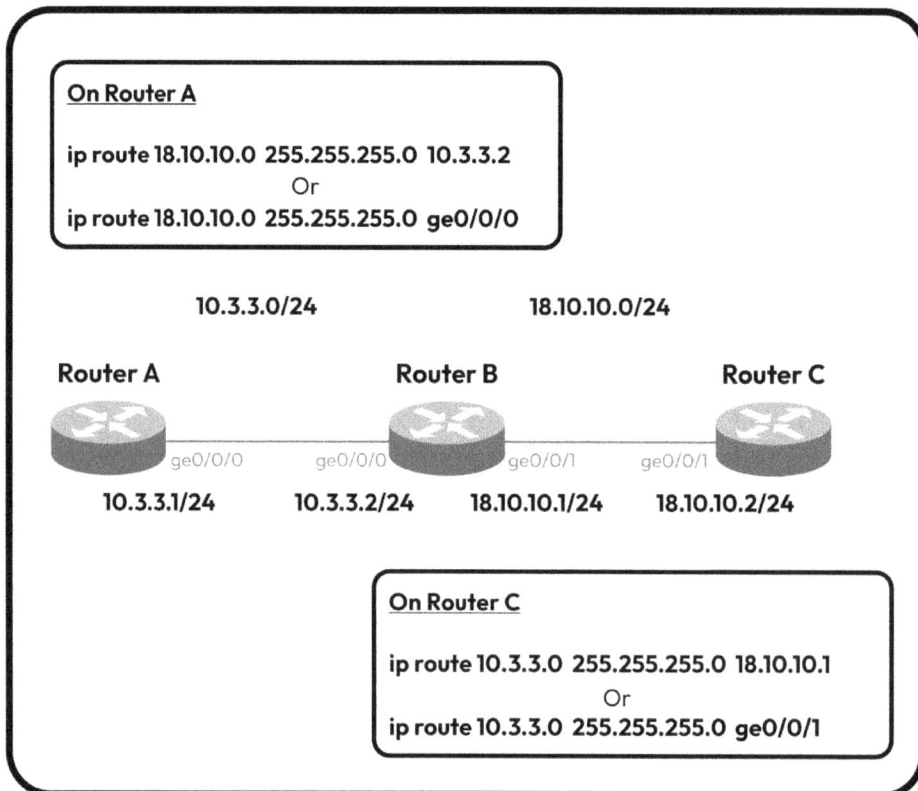

Figure 9.2: Static routes

Dynamic routing

With dynamic routing, routers automatically discover and maintain the best paths for data to travel across a network. Unlike static routing, where routes are manually entered, dynamic routing protocols help routers adapt to changes in the network, such as when a device goes offline or a new device is added. This adaptability makes dynamic routing ideal for larger and more complex networks.

In simple terms, dynamic routing is like the GPS system in your car. Just like a GPS will help you find the best route from your start point to your destination, dynamic routing helps network devices find the best path to send data between two points. This is done using protocols such as **Border Gateway Protocol (BGP)**, **Enhanced Interior Gateway Routing Protocol (EIGRP)**, and **Open Shortest Path First (OSPF)**.

Autonomous systems

Dynamic routing is essential in an **autonomous system (AS)**, which is a large network, or group of networks, managed by a single organization, such as an ISP or a big company, such as BT, Amazon, or Google. Each autonomous system has its own routing policy, meaning it controls how data is moved within its network. Autonomous systems are the building blocks of the internet, each identified by a unique number called an **autonomous system number (ASN)**, which is assigned by the **Internet Assigned Numbers Authority (IANA)**. Autonomous systems need to communicate with each other to make sure data can travel across the internet. This is done using automatic routing protocols, which are covered next.

Border Gateway Protocol (BGP)

Border Gateway Protocol (BGP) is the main protocol that allows different autonomous systems to communicate and exchange routing information on the internet. It uses ASNs to manage routing between different networks or organizations on the internet. As an EGP, BGP manages routing between these autonomous systems, making it essential for ISPs and large-scale network operators. You can think of BGP as the internet's master GPS system, helping data navigate across the global network by choosing efficient and policy-compliant paths. Without BGP, different parts of the internet wouldn't be able to communicate smoothly, making it difficult for users to access websites or use online services.

Unlike some protocols that prioritize speed, BGP selects the *best* route for data – not necessarily the quickest. It considers factors such as network reliability, stability, and routing policies to ensure data reaches its destination efficiently. Routing policy in BGP refers to the rules network administrators configure to influence how routes are imported, exported, or preferred.

When a user accesses a website hosted in another country, their internet traffic travels across many different networks – ISPs, **data centers**, and backbone providers. Each of these networks is part of a unique autonomous system. BGP is the protocol responsible for routing traffic between these autonomous systems.

For example, when a packet leaves a user's local ISP in the United States and needs to reach a web server hosted in Europe, BGP determines the best path by evaluating policies, reachability, and AS paths. It ensures that traffic can efficiently traverse multiple independently managed networks on the global internet.

Unlike protocols such as OSPF, EIGRP, or **Routing Information Protocol (RIP)**, which are **interior gateway protocols (IGPs)** used within organizations, BGP is specifically designed to route traffic across the public internet and between large-scale networks.

Enhanced Interior Gateway Routing Protocol (EIGRP)

EIGRP is an IGP commonly used in enterprise networks. It helps routers determine the best path for data by calculating a composite metric based on bandwidth, delay, and optionally, load and reliability.

EIGRP adapts automatically to network changes – such as when a link goes down – by quickly recalculating optimal routes using a **diffusing update algorithm** called **DUAL**. This ensures efficient and reliable data delivery even in large or rapidly changing networks. DUAL makes EIGRP fast, reliable, and responsive to network changes without causing routing loops or downtime.

Open Shortest Path First

OSPF is another dynamic routing protocol used within a single autonomous system. It uses link-state routing, which means each router advertises the state of its links (connections) to all other routers in the area.

Instead of simply counting the number of hops like some other protocols, such as **RIP**, OSPF uses a cost **metric** to determine the "shortest" or least-cost path to a destination. This cost is based on factors such as **bandwidth**, not actual time or latency. So, higher-bandwidth links are typically preferred, because they're more efficient for data transfer – even if they involve more hops.

OSPF continually updates its network map and recalculates routes using **Dijkstra's algorithm**, ensuring quick convergence and efficient routing in large and complex networks. An example of this is shown in *Figure 9.3*.

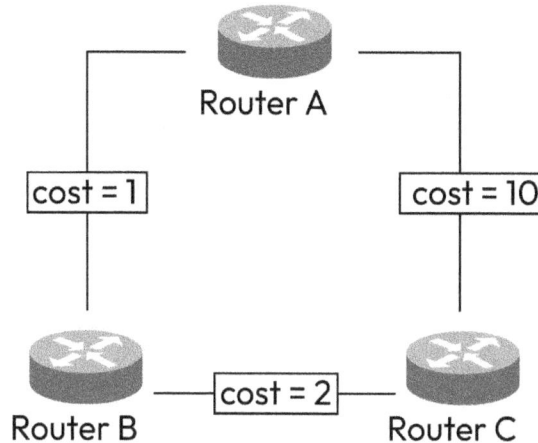

Figure 9.3: OSPF

In *Figure 9.3*, traffic is going from Router A to Router C. There is a direct path from Router A to Router C or an indirect path from Router A to Router C via Router B. Let us select the OSPF path, based on least cost routing, taking the route with the lowest cost. This means the quickest route, and ignores the distance involved.

- Path 1: A → B → C is Therefore the cost = 3
- Path 2: A → C directly. The cost = 10

OSPF will send the traffic using path 1 as it is faster with less latency. This is an example of route selection, which we will look at in more detail next.

Route selection

Route selection is the process by which routers decide the best path to send data across a network. When multiple routes are available, routers must choose the most efficient one to ensure that data reaches its destination quickly and accurately. This is done by using **prefix length**, **administrative distance (AD)**, and other metrics.

Administrative distance AD is a measure of the trustworthiness, or reliability, of a route. Because a **static route** has been manually set up by an administrator, it is given the value 1, which means it is the most trustworthy. Routes created by dynamic protocols are considered less trustworthy because they rely on protocol algorithms and updates from other routers, which can introduce potential inaccuracies or delays. For this reason, they get higher AD values.

Table 9.1 shows a list of administrative distances for some common routing protocols:

Type of route	AD score
Static	1 (most trusted)
BGP (external)	20
EIGRP (internal)	90
OSPF	110
BGP (internal)	200 (least trusted)

Table 9.1: Types of routes and their AD scores

These values help routers decide which route to choose when multiple paths to the same destination are available from different routing protocols. A static route would be preferred to anything else, and an EIGRP route would be preferred to an OSPF route.

For example, a network engineer is configuring a Cisco router that receives routes from multiple protocols: RIP, OSPF, and EIGRP. When each protocol advertises a route to the same destination, the router chooses one.

To do this, the router uses AD. It assigns the following values:

- EIGRP internal routes AD = 90
- OSPF routes AD = 110
- RIP routes AD = 120

Since EIGRP has the lowest AD, the router will select the EIGRP route.

Route selection in practice

You have seen some of the different factors considered when deciding the best route between two points. The processing of this is done by a router as it updates its **routing table**. It is carried out as follows:

1. First, the router receives multiple route options from different sources or protocols.
2. Next, the router checks the prefix length of the different routes. The one with the longest (most specific) **prefix** is preferred.
3. If the routes come from different protocols, the router uses AD to choose the most reliable route.
4. If multiple routes have the same prefix length with the same AD, the router compares their metrics, choosing the route with the lowest metric. The metric used is based on the protocol.
5. The routing table is updated.

Assigning AD to different routes can be useful even when a router isn't using dynamic routing protocols such as OSPF or EIGRP. For example, in a router not using dynamic protocols, the administrator still wants to ensure that if the primary route to a destination network becomes unavailable, a backup route will automatically be used.

To achieve this, the administrator configures two static routes to the same destination – one pointing to the preferred next-hop IP address (the primary route), and another pointing to a secondary next-hop (the backup route). By assigning a higher administrative distance to the backup static route, the router will prioritize the primary route as long as it is available. If the primary route fails, the router will automatically switch to the backup route due to the administrative distance mechanism.

Prefix length

The **prefix length** is determined by network administrators when they design and configure the network. In *Chapter 7, Given a Scenario, Use Appropriate IPv4 Network Addressing*, you saw how to divide the IP address space into networks and subnets. This process directly impacts the prefix length, which is the number of bits in an IP address, which defines the network portion. This is usually indicated with CIDR notation (i.e., /24). The prefix length indicates how specific a route is, and routers prefer routes with longer prefix lengths because they are more specific.

An IP address is similar to a standard address in that you use it to direct a piece of communication. You can split a standard address into different factors that describe the destination at different levels. The country is the least specific, then city, then district, street name, house or building number, and then maybe even apartment number, being the most specific. If you don't know the apartment number, you could still send it to the house and hope the right person picks it up, but you know that the more specific a postal address, the easier it is to deliver a package.

IP addresses work in a similar way. When a network administrator designs and configures a network, they decide how to divide the IP address space into networks and subnets. The first portion of the IP address, called the prefix, is the network or subnet, and the rest of the address is the host identifier or the specific interface on that network.

Here's an example:

- `192.168.1.0/24`

    - /24 means this IP address uses the first 24 bits for the network

    - The subnet mask is `255.255.255.0`

    - 256 total host IP addresses (254 usable)

- `192.168.1.0/26`

    - `/26` means this IP address uses the first 26 bits for the network
    - The subnet mask is `255.255.255.192`
    - 64 total host IP addresses (62 usable)

A `/26` prefix means fewer host IP addresses than `/24` – 62 usable addresses versus 256. So, `/26` is more specific.

Metric

While prefix length and AD are standards across protocols, though used in slightly different ways, the metric varies and measures different factors depending on the specific routing protocol. It measures various factors such as the number of hops, which is the number of routers a data packet will pass through before arriving at the destination, the bandwidth, or speed, which is measured as a delay. The lower the value of a metric, the more favorable it is. This is obvious with delay and the number of hops, but in the case of bandwidth, it is measured as the deviation from a standard optimal bandwidth. Therefore, the higher the number, the more it has deviated from the ideal, and the lower, the closer it is to the ideal.

Different routing protocols, such as the ones mentioned earlier, use their own methods to calculate metrics and distribute routing information. OSPF considers the bandwidth of the links. EIGRP considers bandwidth *and* delay as the default, but also takes into consideration other factors such as load, which is how much traffic the path is handling, and reliability. BGP routing decisions are based on path attributes rather than metrics. The main attributes are **AS-path**, which is the number of autonomous systems the data packet is travelling through, and policy-based decisions, such as business relationships between autonomous systems or security protocols.

For example, with EIGRP, the metric determines the best path to a destination based on bandwidth, delay, and optionally reliability and load.

You have two routes to reach the destination `192.168.1.0/24`:

Route via	Bandwidth	Delay	Calculated EIGRP metric
Router A	100 Mbps	10 ms	1000
Router B	10 Mbps	5 ms	2000

Table 9.2: EIGRP metric calculation

Even though Router B has a lower delay, Router A has a much higher bandwidth, resulting in a lower EIGRP metric. EIGRP will choose Router A because it has the lower metric—`1000`.

Route selection is one of the primary functions of a router. It ensures that traffic flows correctly and efficiently through networks. However, routing is not the only task a router performs. The IP addresses used within a network (internally) often differ from those used when communicating with other networks (externally). The process of converting or translating between these internal and external IP addresses is covered in the next section.

Address translation

When setting up a network, you give each of your devices a unique IP, so that they can be easily reached. However, if you connect your new network to a second one, either internally or on the internet, how can you be sure that there are no duplicate IP addresses? The answer is to use a system called **address translation**, which means a machine will have one private IP, used internally within the network, and a public IP, used externally. The mapping of these two IPs is done by a router either as one-to-one mapping in NAT, or one-to-many with **port address translation (PAT)**.

NAT

NAT is a process used by routers to let devices in a private network (such as your home or office) connect to the internet using a single public IP address. Devices inside your network use private IP addresses, which are not visible to the outside world. When one of these devices wants to access a website or online service, the router translates the private IP address into a public IP address. This public IP is used to send and receive information over the internet.

When the response comes back from the internet, the router knows which private device made the request and translates the public IP back to the correct private IP. The data is then forwarded to the right device.

This process also hides your internal network from external users – because the outside world only sees the router's public IP address, not the internal private addresses of individual devices. This adds a layer of security and privacy.

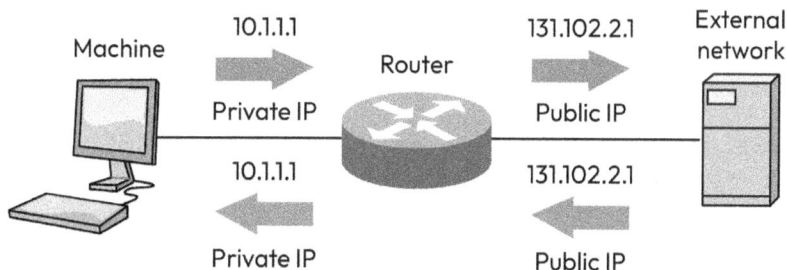

Figure 9.4: NAT

In *Figure 9.4*, you can see the machine's private IP, 10.1.1.1, going through the router, which gives it a new public IP, 131.102.2.1, with the reverse happening as data packets return. NAT avoids IP clashes with other endpoints across networks, which means that you can easily connect one network to another or even change your internet provider without having to reassign IP addresses to all your machines.

This not only allows internal devices to communicate externally but also provides a basic layer of security. Since internal IP addresses are never exposed directly, it becomes more difficult for outside attackers to target individual internal systems. Unsolicited inbound connections from the internet are typically blocked unless explicitly allowed through **port forwarding** or **firewall** rules.

In this way, NAT helps obscure internal network structure, offering both connectivity and a security benefit. However, because it's still one-to-one, there are still inefficiencies in large networks, which is where PAT comes in.

Port address translation (PAT)

While NAT provides a one-to-one mapping between internal and external IP addresses, PAT allows multiple internal devices to share a single external IP address. This is done by assigning each connection a unique port number. This is a more efficient use of IP addresses, especially in large networks. It is essentially a variation of NAT that enables multiple devices on an internal network to be mapped to a single external IP address. PAT distinguishes between devices by assigning unique port numbers to each device's connection.

When a device initiates a connection to the internet, the router assigns a unique **port number** to that session, effectively mapping the private IP address and port number to the shared public IP address. All devices within the internal network share a single public IP address when communicating with the internet.

When data returns from the internet, the router uses the port number to determine which internal device should receive the data. This allows multiple devices to communicate through one external IP address without confusion.

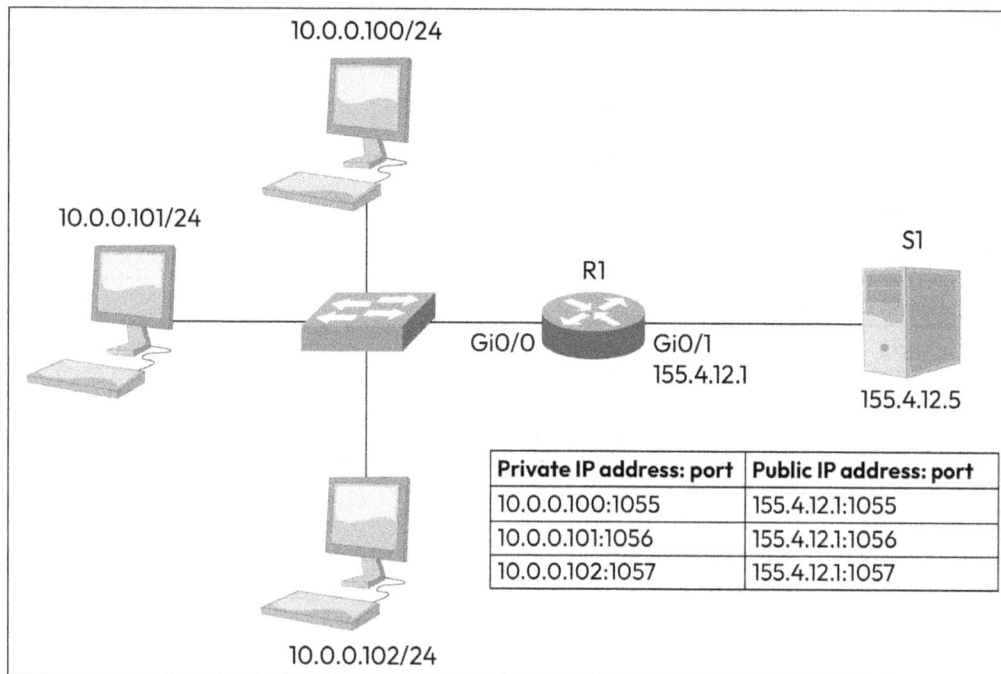

10.0.0.100/24

10.0.0.101/24

S1

R1

GiO/0   GiO/1
         155.4.12.1

155.4.12.5

Private IP address: port	Public IP address: port
10.0.0.100:1055	155.4.12.1:1055
10.0.0.101:1056	155.4.12.1:1056
10.0.0.102:1057	155.4.12.1:1057

10.0.0.102/24

Figure 9.5: PAT on three machines in one network

In *Figure 9.5*, you can see three machines with individual IP addresses translated into one public IP with different port numbers.

For example, in many small- to medium-sized networks, there is often only a single public IP address available for accessing the internet. However, multiple internal devices, such as laptops, phones, and servers, need to use that one public IP to browse the web, send emails, or access cloud services.

Having different IP addresses translated into one public PAT allows you to conserve public IP addresses by enabling multiple devices to share a single address. PAT is ideal for large networks where assigning a unique public IP address to each device would be impractical or impossible. Using PAT can lower the cost of maintaining an internet connection for a large number of devices.

First Hop Redundancy Protocol (FHRP)

First Hop Redundancy Protocol (FHRP) is a method used in computer networks to ensure that if your main router or gateway (the "first hop" your data takes when leaving your local network) fails, another router can automatically take over. This helps keep your network running smoothly without interruption. It provides redundancy because if the primary router goes down,

FHRP makes sure another router steps in immediately, so there's no downtime. This makes it reliable because it provides a backup path for data, ensuring your network stays connected even if something goes wrong with the main router.

FHRP is like having a spare tire for your network – ready to take over if the main one fails, keeping everything running without a hitch. *Table 9.3* gives a list of common FHRPs used by different vendors.

Protocol	Full name	Vendor
HSRP	Hot Standby Router Protocol	Cisco
VRRP	Virtual Router Redundancy Protocol	Open/Standard
GLBP	Gateway Load Balancing Protocol	Cisco

Table 9.3: Common FHRPs

If you are in an office where all computers send internet traffic through a router with the IP address 192.168.1.1, that router is the default gateway – the first hop to the outside world.

With an FHRP such as HSRP, VRRP, or GLBP, there's a second router on standby. Both routers share a **virtual IP address** (VIP) – for example, 192.168.1.1. The primary router handles the traffic under normal conditions. If the primary router fails, the backup router immediately takes over the VIP and starts forwarding traffic, so users don't notice any disruption. There is no need to change settings on computers – the switch is automatic. This system relies on the use of VIPs, which we will look into next.

Virtual IP (VIP)

A **virtual IP** (**VIP**) is an IP address that doesn't correspond to a specific physical device but rather to a group of devices or a service. It's typically used to increase the availability and reliability of network services. Multiple devices (such as **servers** or routers) can share the same VIP address, which acts as a single point of contact for network traffic. VIPs are often used in load-balancing scenarios. For example, if multiple servers handle the same service, the VIP distributes incoming traffic evenly among them. This prevents any single server from becoming overwhelmed.

The advantages of this are as follows:

- **Failover**: If the device currently handling the VIP goes down, another device in the group can take over the VIP seamlessly. This ensures that the service remains available without interruption.
- **High availability**: VIPs enhance network resilience by allowing multiple devices to provide a service. If one fails, another takes over, ensuring continuity.

- **Simplified access:** Users and applications don't need to worry about which specific device they're connecting to; they simply use the VIP, and the network handles the rest.
- **Efficient load distribution:** In scenarios where multiple servers provide the same service, a VIP can balance the load across them, improving performance and reliability.

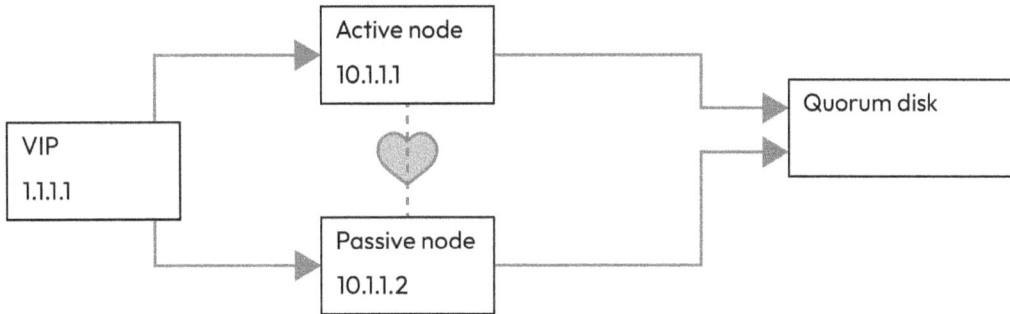

Figure 9.6: Cluster showing VIP

In *Figure 9.6*, the traffic will come through the VIP, 1.1.1.1. Though the VIP is connected to both nodes, the active node claims the VIP, and thus, all traffic will be passed through the active node to the quorum disk. The line between the active and passive node is known as a **heartbeat**; if the active node fails, it will cease sending the heartbeat, which is a signal to the passive node to claim the VIP and take over the communication to the quorum disk, maintaining connections. In this way, the system remains responsive without having to change the IP address, enhancing both reliability and efficiency in your network.

Subinterfaces

In the preceding example of VIPs, physical devices have been joined together logically with one virtual address. However, as you add endpoints to a network, you may be in a situation where you want to organize IPs connected to the same router into logical groups, such as **VLANs**. You will learn more about VLANs in the next chapter, but they are essentially a way of dividing physical networks into smaller segments for performance, management, and/or security reasons.

These groups are made possible by using a virtual interface created on a physical network. This is called a **subinterface**. A single physical interface on a router or switch can be split into multiple subinterfaces, and each subinterface can be assigned its own IP address, VLAN, or network.

Each subinterface is identified by appending a number to the physical interface name. For example, `GigabitEthernet0/1` could have the `GigabitEthernet0/1.1` and `GigabitEthernet0/1.2` subinterfaces, and each one has its own IP address on a different network or subnet. They are commonly used for inter-VLAN routing, routing between multiple subnets, and separating traffic types – for example, voice and data.

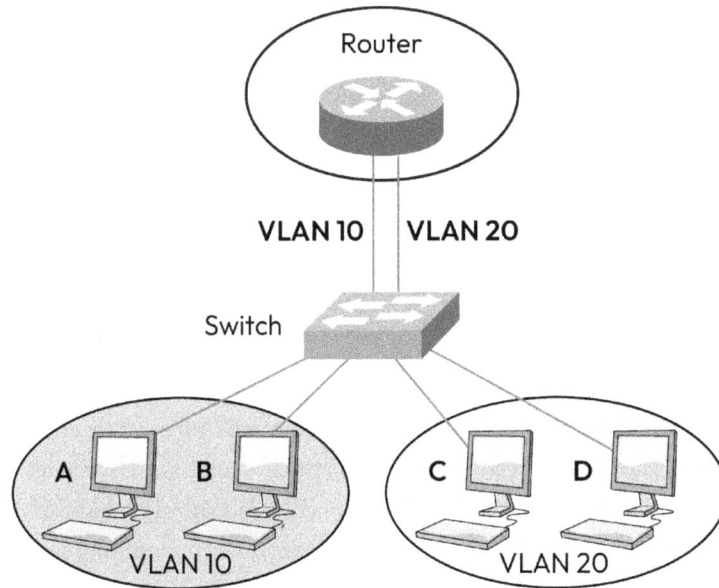

Figure 9.7: Logical separation on the same router

In *Figure 9.7,* you can see a router connected to a **switch**; the switch is connected to four machines. Although the machines are physically connected to the same switch, the router has logically separated them into two subinterfaces that have created two VLANs, VLAN 10 and VLAN 20. Communication between machines A and B would be done directly through the switch, while communication between VLAN 10 and VLAN 20 would be done through a router. The advantage of this could be that the different VLANs have different data access permissions, which are administered through the router. Unauthorized access between VLANs can be prevented with firewall rules. Administration is also easier; for instance, you can push patching and updates to devices in VLAN 10 without impacting VLAN 20.

Note

VLANs will be covered in more detail in *Chapter 10.*

Summary

This chapter covered routing technologies, which are critical for ensuring efficient and reliable data transmission across networks. They include a variety of protocols and mechanisms that guide traffic, select optimal paths, and maintain communication stability. Key characteristics of routing technologies encompass both static and dynamic routing methods. Static routing, which involves manual configuration of routing tables, is simple and reliable but lacks flexibility. Dynamic routing, on the other hand, uses protocols such as OSPF, EIGRP, and BGP to automatically adapt to network changes, making it suitable for larger networks. Route selection, a vital process, involves evaluating prefix lengths, metrics, and administrative distances to choose the most efficient path. Different protocols use different metrics.

Additional concepts, such as NAT and PAT enable efficient IP address management. With NAT, single private addresses within networks are translated into public IP addresses used to connect to other networks, including the internet. PAT also generates public IP addresses, but it can combine multiple devices under a single IP address by assigning unique port numbers to each device.

FHRP ensures network continuity by providing backup routing paths for when one path is unavailable. VIP enhances availability and load distribution by providing a single IP that can connect multiple devices or functions. Subinterfaces allow for the segmentation of a single physical interface into multiple logical interfaces, further optimizing network performance and scalability.

The knowledge gained in this chapter will prepare you to answer questions relating to Exam Objective 2.1 in the *CompTIA Network+ (N10-009)* exam.

Exam objective 2.1

Explain characteristics of routing technologies

Static routing: Manually configured routes, simple but inflexible

Dynamic routing: Automatically adapts to network changes, ideal for large networks

- **Border Gateway Protocol (BGP)**: Connects **autonomous systems**, critical for internet routing
- **Enhanced Interior Gateway Routing Protocol (EIGRP)**: Internal routing protocol, fast and adaptive
- **Open Shortest Path First (OSPF)**: Finds the shortest path, efficient for large networks

Route selection: Determines the best path based on prefix, metric, and distance

- **Administrative distance (AD)**: Ranks trustworthiness of routing sources
- **Prefix length**: Determines route specificity; longer is preferred
- **Metric**: Measures route efficiency; lower values are preferred

Address translation: Maps internal IPs to external IPs for communication

- **NAT**: Translates private IPs to public IPs
- **Port address translation (PAT)**: Multiple devices share one external IP

First Hop Redundancy Protocol (FHRP): Ensures backup routing if the primary fails

Virtual IP (VIP): Shared IP address for high availability and load distribution

Subinterfaces: Divides physical interfaces into multiple logical interfaces

Chapter review questions

Now that you've completed the chapter, you can check your knowledge using the practice questions provided in the online platform at `https://packt.link/N10-009ch9`. You can also use the QR code below. Accessing these questions requires you to unlock the accompanying online content first. Head over to Chapter 26 for detailed instructions.

10

Given a Scenario, Configure Switching Technologies and Features

Chapter 9, *Explain Characteristics of Routing Technologies*, looked at how routing technologies help to manage the movement of data throughout your network. Routers decide the direction of a data packet based on its destination address; however, for a physical route to be created, a switch is needed. Switches manage data traffic and network segmentation, and to do so effectively, network engineers need to ensure they are configured properly. This ensures that data travels through networks smoothly by optimizing traffic flow and reducing congestion. It also helps prevent data loops and improves efficiency and scalability.

The chapter explores essential concepts such as VLANs, which allow for the segmentation of a network into smaller, more manageable parts, and the various settings and features that enhance network performance, such as link aggregation, speed, and duplex configuration. Additionally, you'll see how technologies such as **Spanning Tree Protocol (STP)** help maintain network stability by preventing loops, making the overall network more reliable and efficient.

This chapter covers the second objective in *Domain 2: 2.2, Given a Scenario, Configure Switching Technologies and Features.*

> **Note**
>
> A full breakdown of objective 2.2 will be given at the end of the chapter.

Virtual local area network (VLAN)

As discussed in *Chapter 9,* a **VLAN** is a logical (rather than physical) segmentation of a network. Within a network that uses **VLANs**, a single **router**—or more commonly, a **Layer 3** switch—can facilitate communication between multiple **VLANs**.

VLANs operate at the **data link layer** (**Layer 2**) of the **OSI model** and allow network administrators to segment a single physical switch into multiple logical groupings of endpoints, such as by department or function. This segmentation reduces unnecessary broadcast traffic, simplifies network management, and enhances security by isolating traffic between departments.

For example, devices used by the HR and finance departments can be connected to the same physical switch, but assigned to different **VLANs**, ensuring that broadcast traffic and sensitive data do not cross departmental boundaries. Access control policies can be implemented at the **VLAN** or routing level to ensure that only authorized users can access specific resources—such as HR being restricted to personal employee files, and finance being limited to financial data. A **router** or **Layer 3 switch** is required for communication between **VLANs**, a process known as **inter-VLAN routing**. In this way, **VLANs** provide a method of departmental isolation at **Layer 2**, while still enabling secure, controlled communication when needed. I think of a **VLAN** as being departmental isolation on a switch.

VLANs also make it easier to troubleshoot network issues, reduce broadcast traffic, and offer flexibility and scalability, enabling quick adjustments without the need for physical changes. Overall, **VLANs** streamline the management process, making networks more efficient and easier to control.

VLAN database

A **VLAN** is established through the software on a network switch. Each individual **VLAN** has an identification tag, which is readable by switches. Data packets that move throughout the system include the **VLAN** identification tag so that when traffic arrives at the switch, the switch knows where to direct it. For the switch to know which physical port belongs to which **VLAN**, it needs some kind of reference. This is called a **VLAN database**.

The following figure shows a possible **VLAN** setup:

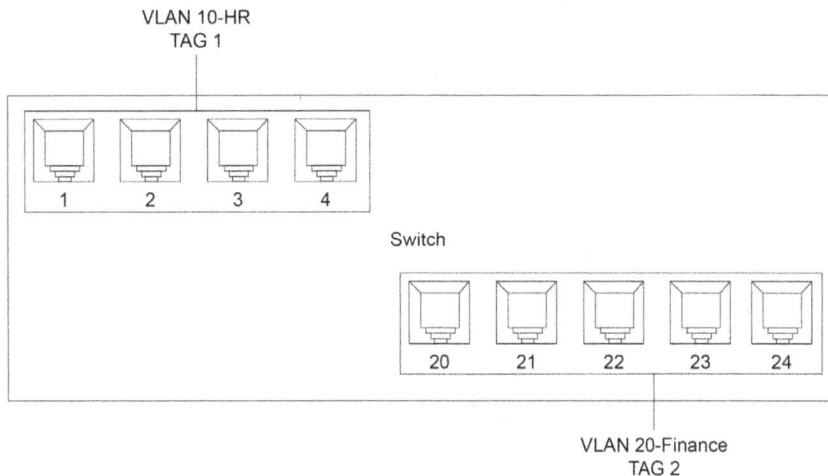

Figure 10.1: Two VLAN switches

In *Figure 10.1*, a switch with 24 ports has two VLANs set up. The HR VLAN is on ports 1–4, and the finance VLAN is on ports 20–24. These groups are created by the systems administrator using command-line interfaces (CLIs), graphical user interfaces (GUIs), or other network-defining tools. For example, the following code would create VLAN 10 for finance using a CLI:

1. Create the VLAN:

```
Switch(config)# vlan 10
Switch(config-vlan)# name Finance
```

This command creates VLAN 10 and names it "Finance".

2. Assign ports 20–24 to the VLAN:

```
interface range fastEthernet 0/20 - 24
switchport mode access
switchport access vlan 10
```

These commands select ports 20–24, set them to access mode (meaning they belong to one VLAN), and then assign them to VLAN 10.

3. View all VLANs:

```
show vlan brief
```

This command will display a list of all VLANs and the ports assigned to them.

This simple code will be repeated for all **VLANs**, but it's important to remember that once a device is placed in a **VLAN**, it cannot directly communicate with members of other LANs, even if they are on the same switch. However, there may be times when this is required, for example, if finance needs to access HR records for staff payroll. This can be achieved with a **switch virtual interface (SVI)**.

Trunk ports/links

A **trunk port** is a switch port configured to carry traffic for multiple VLANs across a single physical connection, unlike an **access port**, which handles traffic for only one VLAN. The trunk port uses VLAN tagging (typically **802.1Q**) to label each frame with its VLAN ID so that devices on the receiving end know which VLAN the traffic belongs to. The physical connection between two trunk ports is called a **trunk link**, and it is commonly used between switches or between a switch and a router, allowing VLAN traffic to pass through one cable while keeping each VLAN logically separated. This setup is efficient for networks with multiple VLANs, as it avoids the need for multiple physical links.

Switch virtual interface (SVI)

An **SVI** is a logical Layer 3 interface configured on a switch. While **VLANs** operate at **Layer 2** to logically separate devices within the same physical network, **SVIs** operate at **Layer 3** and allow traffic to be routed between **VLANs**—a process known as **inter-VLAN routing**.

An **SVI** is assigned an IP address and acts as the default gateway for all devices within its **VLAN**. When traffic needs to move from one **VLAN** to another—such as from a computer in the HR **VLAN** to a server in the finance **VLAN**—it is routed through the switch using **SVIs**.

SVIs are especially useful in networks that use both data and voice **VLANs**, as follows:

* The **data VLAN** handles regular user traffic (e.g., web browsing and email)
* The **voice VLAN** handles voice traffic from IP phones, which is often prioritized to ensure call quality
* By assigning an **SVI** to each **VLAN** (e.g., one for voice, one for data), the switch can keep data and voice traffic logically separate, while still allowing controlled communication between them if needed. This setup improves network organization, supports **QoS** policies, and enhances security by isolating traffic types.

In the following example, **SVIs** allow finance to directly access devices in HR to connect to personnel records:

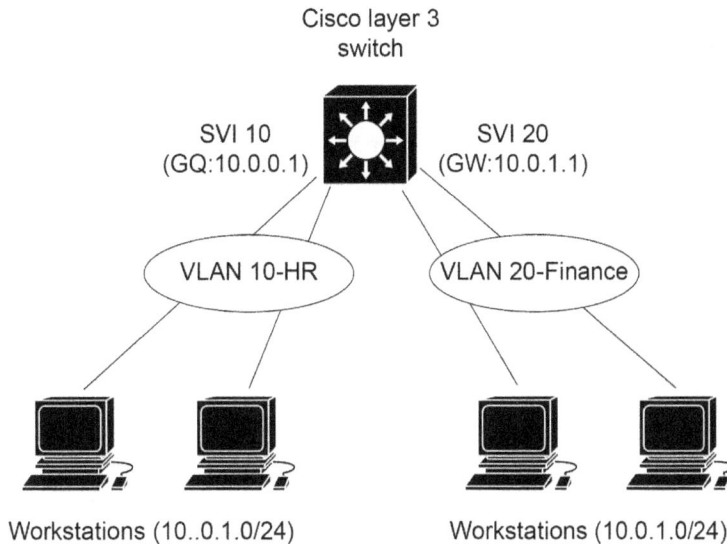

Figure 10.2: SVI

In *Figure 10.2*, as before, VLAN 10 is HR and VLAN 20 is finance. SVI 20 connects to VLAN 20 using the gateway protocol 10.0.1.1, while SVI 10 connects to VLAN 10 and has the gateway protocol 10.0.0.1. In simple terms, VLANs keep things separate at Layer 2, and the SVI acts as a bridge at Layer 3, helping them communicate when needed.

So far, we have seen a fairly simple example of how VLANs and SVIs can be used to create logic-based networks in a physical network. Though separating two groups of devices and communicating between them is important, in modern networks, things are much more complicated with large numbers of LANs and VLANs, and special usage of VLANs; these will be covered in the next section on configuring interfaces.

Interface configuration

Interfaces, in the context of networking, are the physical or virtual ports on a network device (such as a **switch**, **router**, or **firewall**) that connect to other devices or networks.

Depending on the device and use case, a single physical interface can host multiple logical interfaces, such as **subinterfaces** on a router. A **subinterface** on a router is a logical interface that is created from a single physical interface. **Subinterfaces** allow a single physical port to carry traffic for multiple **VLANs** or **IP subnets** by treating each **subinterface** as a separate virtual interface.

Though your architecture might be optimized for your specific setup, if interfaces haven't been properly configured, data flow will be inefficient. For example, incorrect speed settings can create bottlenecks, and if **VLANs** aren't set up correctly, data may be sent to the wrong places. Incorrect configurations of firewalls might cause security issues. Therefore, interface configuration is essential for efficient data flow, security, and network stability.

When configuring an interface, several key settings must be taken into account, including **VLAN** assignments, link aggregation, speed, and duplex modes. These configurations determine how data is transmitted across the network, how different types of traffic are separated or prioritized, and how links between devices are combined to increase bandwidth and provide redundancy. The following sections will look at these in more detail.

Native VLAN

You have already seen how VLANs can be used to group devices into a network. Data coming into a network is tagged so that it's directed to the correct VLAN, but what happens to untagged traffic? That's where the native VLAN comes in. The **native VLAN** is a special VLAN on a trunk port that handles untagged traffic. If a switch receives untagged frames on a trunk link, it assigns them to the native VLAN by default. When sending frames from the native VLAN over the trunk, the switch does not add a VLAN tag by default.

Think of a **VLAN** like creating separate lanes on a highway for different types of vehicles. Just as you might have one lane for cars, another for trucks, and a third for buses, **VLANs** separate different types of network traffic into their own lanes while still using the same infrastructure. Before vehicles are sorted into their designated lanes, they all enter the highway through a shared entry point without specific markings. Similarly, the **native VLAN** acts as a special lane that doesn't require additional tags or markings. It serves as the default path for untagged traffic unless explicitly assigned to a different **VLAN**.

Without a **native VLAN** configured, untagged traffic arriving on a **trunk port** would be dropped because the **switch** wouldn't know where to assign it. Configuring a **native VLAN** allows the **switch** to accept untagged frames and assign them to a specific **VLAN**, which can be isolated from other **VLANs** to create a controlled segment of the network. This setup helps protect critical infrastructure by limiting access.

However, a misconfigured **native VLAN** can create security risks by unintentionally allowing unauthorized devices to access sensitive network segments, potentially exposing the network to attacks.

For example, after relocating several users to previously used workspaces, a network administrator receives reports that these users are experiencing network connectivity problems. Investigation reveals that the switchports at the new locations still have the **native VLAN** configured for the previous users, which does not match the **VLAN** assigned to the relocated users' devices.

Because the **native VLAN** on the switchport doesn't match the **VLAN** of the connected devices, the untagged traffic from those devices is misclassified or dropped, causing communication failures. This **VLAN** mismatch prevents users from accessing network resources until the **native VLAN** settings on the ports are corrected to align with the devices' **VLANs**.

Voice VLAN

It's common for an access port to be configured with both a data **VLAN** and a voice **VLAN**, especially in networks that support IP phones using **VoIP** technology. A voice **VLAN** is a special **VLAN** specifically designed to carry voice traffic. It helps separate voice communication from regular data traffic such as emails, web browsing, or file transfers.

This separation is important because voice traffic is sensitive to delays, jitter, and packet loss. Even small interruptions can cause noticeable issues in call quality, such as echoes, distortion, or dropped calls. By assigning voice traffic to its own **VLAN**, the network can prioritize it and ensure it receives the bandwidth and low-latency delivery it needs.

In a typical setup, an access port connects to an **IP phone**, which often has a built-in switch to allow a computer to connect through it. The port is configured so that voice traffic from the phone is tagged and sent to the voice **VLAN**, while untagged data traffic from the computer is sent to the data **VLAN**. This way, both devices share the same physical port but operate on separate logical networks.

Using a voice **VLAN** not only improves call clarity and reliability but also enhances security by isolating voice traffic from the general data network. This structure ensures that voice services continue to function smoothly even during times of high network usage.

Private VLAN

In some network environments—especially in shared spaces such as data centers, **demilitarized zones (DMZs)**, or shared hosting platforms—there's a need to keep devices on the same subnet from communicating directly with each other. For example, in a hotel or a multitenant environment, you may want all clients to access the internet but not interact with each other's devices for security reasons. You can achieve this by implementing a **private VLAN (PVLAN)**.

A **PVLAN** is a **Layer 2** security feature that allows a network administrator to logically isolate ports on the same **VLAN** and subnet. While all devices can still access shared resources such as the default gateway, routers, or firewalls, they are prevented from communicating directly with one another. This enhances security without needing to create multiple subnets or complex routing rules.

PVLANs split a regular **VLAN** into multiple **sub-VLANs**, typically in the following roles:

- **Primary VLAN**: This is the main VLAN that all secondary VLANs belong to
- **Isolated VLAN**: Devices in this VLAN cannot communicate with any other device, not even other devices in the same isolated VLAN
- **Community VLAN**: Devices can communicate with each other, but not with other communities or isolated devices

All secondary **VLANs** communicate upstream (e.g., with a **router** or **firewall**) via the promiscuous port, which is typically the port that connects to the shared resource, such as a default gateway.

For example, a network administrator wants to prevent customer **VMs** that are in a cloud environment from accessing each other directly, while still allowing them to reach the internet. A **PVLAN** setup allows this. Each **VM** is placed in an isolated or community **VLAN**, while the **router/firewall** remains reachable via a promiscuous port.

802.1Q tagging

This chapter has already mentioned that data packets are tagged to ensure that data from each **VLAN** stays organized. This is done using the **802.1Q** standard, which creates what is essentially a label that identifies which **VLAN** the packet belongs to.

When a data packet is sent from a device that's part of a **VLAN**, typically a router or a switch, it adds an **802.1Q tag** to the packet in accordance with the **IEEE 802.1Q protocol**. The tag is inserted into the packet's header, which is a part of the packet that carries control information. The tag doesn't change the actual data being sent; it just adds a piece of information that the network needs to handle the packet correctly. This tag contains important information, including the **VLAN ID**, which is a unique identifier for the **VLAN** the packet belongs to.

When the tagged packet reaches a switch, it reads the **802.1Q tag**. The switch uses the **VLAN ID** in the tag to determine which **VLAN** the packet belongs to and then forwards the packet to the appropriate devices within that **VLAN**.

The **802.1Q** tag is inserted after the **Ethertype**, as shown in *Figure 10.3*.

Destination MAC address	Source MAC address	Ethertype (0x8100)	802.1Q tag	Payload	FCS

Figure 10.3: Ethernet packet showing the 802.1Q field

Figure 10.3 shows an **802.3 Ethernet packet**, which you covered in *Chapter 5, Compare and Contrast Transmission Media and Transceivers*. The fields are broken down into *Table 10.1*, *Table 10.2*, and *Table 10.3*.

Frame	Description	Size
Destination MAC address	The MAC address of the destination device	6 bytes
Source MAC address	The MAC address of the source device	6 bytes
Ethertype	Indicates the protocol type (0x8100 for 802.1Q VLAN tag)	2 bytes
802.1Q tag	See *Table 10.2*	**4 bytes**
Payload	Actual transmitted data	Varies
Frame check sequence (FCS)	Used for error checking the frame	4 bytes

Table 10.1: Data packet broken down into frames with 802.1Q tag highlighted

Table 10.1 shows a standard data packet with a VLAN tag inserted. As you can see, the Ethertype frame is 0x8100 to indicate that the next frame is an 802.1Q tag. Details on the other frames can be found in *Chapter 5*.

The 802.1Q tag is broken down further in the following table. The **tag protocol identifier (TPID)** is always 0x8100 to indicate that it's a **VLAN** tag. The actual details of the **VLAN** are in the **tag control information (TCI)**.

TPID	Identifies the tag as an 802.1Q tag, always 0x8100	2 bytes
TCI	Includes specific details about transmission; see Table 10.3	2 bytes

Table 10.2: The 802.1Q tag in more detail

The following table breaks down the specific parts of the TCI. The first indicates the priority of the data, known as the **priority code point (PCP)**. The lowest priority level is 0 for basic background traffic, up to 7, which is network control. Voice traffic, for instance, has a higher priority level than "best effort" traffic.

Note

The default priority is best effort, which is for standard communications, which is level 1, above 0 for background. Because it is the default, the 3 bits are, in binary, 000, which means that the lowest level is 001. This means that the lowest priority shows a PCP value of 1, with the next priority PCP value being 0. PCP values in order of priority are thus 1, 0, 2, 3, 4, 5, 6, and 7.

Next is the **drop eligible indicator** (**DEI**), which indicates that the frame can be dropped if there is congestion. 1 indicates eligibility to be dropped, and 0 indicates ineligibility. Finally, the VLAN ID indicates which VLAN the data packet is for. Value 0 or 0x000 is reserved and means there is no VLAN ID, and the value 4095 or 0xFFF is reserved for implementation, leaving 4,094 possible VLANs. *Table 10.3* shows this breakdown of the TCI data.

PCP	Indicates the traffic class	3 bits
DEI	For congestion management	1 bit
VLAN ID	Identifies the VLAN that the data packet is destined for	12 bits

Table 10.3: Breakdown of the TCI

The data in the 802.1Q tag is continuously read and rewritten by network devices. As you can see, it not only gives information about which VLAN the data is intended for but also its priority in communication. The PCP and DEI give values that devices use to keep data flowing smoothly and efficiently, though different devices, networks, and protocols will deal with it in different ways (*Chapter 9, Explain Characteristics of Routing Technologies*). The use of **802.1Q tagging** ensures that the packet doesn't get mixed up with data from other VLANs. This keeps the network organized and secure, as each **VLAN** can operate independently without interference from other VLANs. This is very important for **voice VLANs**.

Having too much data flow through one link creates obvious problems, and although data prioritization can help, the next section will look at another solution, link aggregation.

Link aggregation

Networks, like highways, can get congested when there's too much traffic. If you have too many vehicles using one route, then congestion will be a common occurrence, and the city may solve it by building an extra road. You can do the same thing for data traffic by combining multiple physical connections. By providing multiple paths for data to travel, it reduces congestion and increases overall network speed. This is called **link aggregation**. This is especially useful in environments with high data traffic, such as data centers or large office buildings, where fast and reliable data transfer is critical.

With link aggregation, you turn multiple physical network connections into a single logical link. This configuration is often referred to as an **EtherChannel**, **port bundling**, or a **port channel**. By aggregating links, you not only increase the available bandwidth between devices, providing better throughput, but you also enhance network resilience by adding redundancy. If one of the physical links fails, the remaining links continue to carry the traffic.

To manage and automate the process of link aggregation, many systems engineers often use **Link Aggregation Control Protocol (LACP)**. **LACP** is a part of the **IEEE 802.3ad** standard and allows network devices to negotiate and establish a dynamic link aggregation. With **LACP**, network devices can automatically detect which links can be bundled together and ensure that all links in the aggregation are properly functioning.

The following is a sample **Cisco IOS script** for configuring **link aggregation** using **LACP** on a Cisco switch. This script assumes you have multiple physical interfaces that you want to bundle together into a single logical interface (referred to as a port channel):

```bash
configure terminal

# Create a port-channel interface and assign ID
interface Port-channel1

# Specify the mode as active
channel-group 1 mode active

# Set the desired properties for the port-channel
switchport mode trunk
switchport trunk native vlan 10

# Exit the port-channel interface
exit
```

```
# Configure the physical interfaces for port-channel
interface GigabitEthernet0/1
channel-group 1 mode active
exit

interface GigabitEthernet0/2
channel-group 1 mode active
exit

# Verify the configuration
show etherchannel summary
show running-config interface Port-channel1

# Save the configuration to the startup-config
write memory
```

The script begins by entering global configuration mode, which allows you to make system-wide changes to the switch. You then create a port channel interface, which is basically the virtual link that will be used to aggregate multiple physical interfaces. It is then set as active so that it will try to form a link with another device. This script then configures the port channel as a **trunk port**, allowing it to carry traffic for multiple **VLANs,** and the **native VLAN** is set to 10. Any untagged frames will belong to VLAN 10.

Each physical interface that you want to include in the **LACP** group is configured individually. The channel-group command is again used to assign these interfaces to the port channel with the mode set to active. After the configuration, the script includes commands to verify the status of the port channel and ensure that the **LACP** setup is functioning correctly. Finally, the configuration is saved to ensure it persists across reboots.

All interfaces should be configured to allow **LACP.** If configured to be active, a device will look to other devices to set up an **LACP** connection. If set to passive, the device will allow a connection but will not create a connection, so if two devices are set to passive, no LACP connection will be created.

There are a number of benefits of using LACP to aggregate links. It can automatically configure and manage the link aggregation, simplifying the setup process. If a link in the aggregation fails or is disconnected, LACP can automatically adjust the bundle, continuing to send traffic over the remaining active links. LACP also helps in distributing traffic across the aggregated links, balancing the load to optimize network performance.

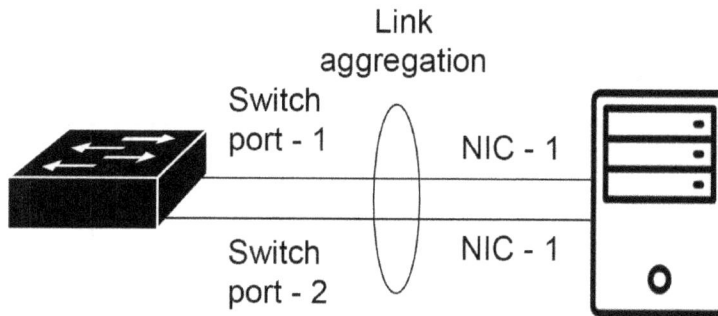

Figure 10.4: Link aggregation

In *Figure 10.4*, there are two separate connections between the switch and the server; they are using link aggregation, which provides them with twice the bandwidth and also redundancy if one connection fails.

Speed

Speed in the context of networking is all about how quickly data can be transmitted from one point to another. It's like the speed limit on a highway—the higher the speed limit, the faster you can get to your destination.

In networking, **speed** is usually measured in Mbps or Gbps. For example, a network speed of 100 Mbps means 100 million bits of data can be transferred every second. Faster speeds are crucial for activities such as streaming video, online gaming, or transferring large files, where delays or slowdowns can be frustrating.

The speed and reliability of a network are heavily influenced by the type of cable used. Different cables offer varying capabilities for data transmission, impacting factors such as maximum speed, bandwidth, and distance. While older cables such as **Cat 5** may suffice for basic needs, modern networks often require faster options such as **Cat 6a**, **Cat 7**, or **fiber optic** cables to handle higher data demands efficiently. Understanding the differences in cable types is crucial for optimizing network performance, whether for a home setup or a complex enterprise environment.

Cable type	Description	Max speed	Max length
Cat 7	High-performance cable with even better shielding than Cat 6a	Up to 10 Gbps	100 meters (328 feet)
Cat 8	The latest standard, designed for high-speed data centers and server rooms	Up to 40 Gbps	30 meters (98 feet)

Fiber: Single-mode	Uses light to transmit data, suitable for long distances and high speeds	100 Gbps or more	10 to 40 km or more, depending on the transceivers
Fiber: Multi-mode	Uses light to transmit data, typically used for shorter distances	Up to 100 Gbps	300 to 400 meters, depending on the transceivers
Coaxial cable	Used mainly for cable internet and television connections	Up to 1 Gbps (with DOCSIS 3.1)	500 meters (1,640 feet)

Table 10.4: Cable speeds

Duplex

Duplex refers to the ability of a network connection to send and receive data. A connection is either half duplex or full duplex:

- **Half duplex** is like a one-lane bridge that allows traffic to flow in only one direction at a time. If a car is crossing from one side, cars on the other side have to wait until the bridge is clear. In networking, this means that data can either be sent or received at any given time, but not both simultaneously. This can slow down communication, especially if a lot of data needs to be transferred.

- **Full duplex**, on the other hand, is like a two-lane bridge where traffic can flow freely in both directions at the same time. In a full-duplex network, data can be sent and received simultaneously, which makes communication much faster and more efficient. Most modern networks use full-duplex connections to ensure smooth and speedy data transfer.

Spanning Tree Protocol (STP)

The **STP** is a network protocol that prevents loops in **Ethernet** networks by creating a loop-free logical topology. In a network with multiple switches, loops can occur when there are redundant paths between switches, leading to broadcast storms, multiple frame copies, and **MAC** table instability. **STP** is designed to automatically detect and eliminate these loops by selectively blocking certain redundant paths while keeping one active path for data transmission. This ensures that only one active path exists between any two devices on the network, preventing the detrimental effects of loops.

STP works by electing a single switch in the network as the **root bridge**. The **root bridge** acts as a reference point for all path calculations. Each switch then determines the shortest path to the **root bridge** using a process called the **bridge protocol data units (BPDUs) exchange**. During this process, switches exchange BPDUs to identify which path to the **root bridge** is the shortest and therefore should remain active, while other redundant paths are blocked to prevent loops. The protocol dynamically adjusts to changes in the network, such as a switch or link failure, by recalculating the paths and unblocking previously blocked links if necessary to maintain connectivity.

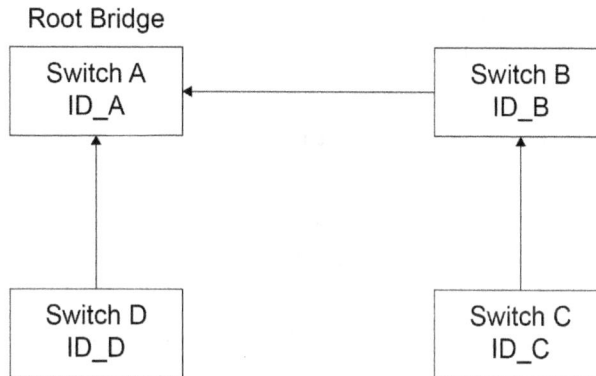

Figure 10.5: Spanning Tree Protocol

Figure 10.5 shows an STP topology, where *Switch A* is the **root bridge. STP** is used to prevent loops in a network with redundant links by disabling certain ports to create a loop-free topology.

The protocol is to prevent a switch from looping, which is very similar to broadcasting, where the traffic moves very slowly. **STP** has five different states for the ports; these are **blocking, listening, learning, forwarding,** and **disabled**:

- **Blocking** prevents the use of any redundant paths that could cause a network loop. In this state, the port does not forward any frames, does not learn MAC addresses, and only listens for BPDU messages. This state is essentially a "listening" mode where the port is aware of network topology changes but does not participate in data forwarding.

- **Listening** prepares the port to participate in the network by determining whether there are any loops. In this state, the port discards any data frames but still listens for BPDUs. The switch uses this time to ensure that no loops exist before moving to the next state. The port remains in this state for a set duration, known as the **forward delay timer** (typically 15 seconds).

- **Learning** allows the port to learn MAC addresses in preparation for forwarding. During this state, the port starts to populate the MAC address table by listening to incoming frames, but it still does not forward them. This state also lasts for the forward delay timer (typically 15 seconds). The goal here is to build a list of MAC addresses on the network so that when the port transitions to the forwarding state, it can make intelligent decisions about where to send traffic.

- **Forwarding** allows the port to forward data frames and actively participate in the network. In this state, the port fully participates in the network. It forwards data frames, processes and sends BPDUs, and continues to learn MAC addresses. This is the final operational state, where the port is considered fully functional.

- **Disabled** deems that a port is administratively down or not functioning. This state occurs when a port is manually shut down by the network administrator or if it is not operational due to a hardware issue. In this state, the port does not participate in STP, does not learn MAC addresses, and does not forward traffic

STP variants and modern usage

While the original **STP** (defined in **IEEE 802.1D**) is effective, it can be slow to react to changes, sometimes taking up to 50 seconds to re-establish a stable network after a topology change. To address this, several enhancements and variants have been developed, such as **Rapid Spanning Tree Protocol (RSTP, IEEE 802.1w)**, which significantly reduces convergence time to a few seconds, and **Multiple Spanning Tree Protocol (MSTP, IEEE 802.1s)**, which allows multiple spanning trees to be active simultaneously across different **VLANs**. These improvements ensure that modern networks are both resilient and efficient, allowing for faster recovery times and better management of large, complex networks.

For example, a company is expanding to a new floor in the same building. The network engineer sets up a new switch and configures it with the same **VLANs** as the existing switch stack on the main floor. After configuring the new switch, the engineer connects it to the existing switch stack.

Immediately after the connection is made, all users lose network connectivity. Devices cannot access resources, and network traffic spikes dramatically. The engineer investigates and discovers the network is flooded with broadcast traffic.

This issue is caused by an **STP** loop. When the new switch was connected, a redundant path was created without proper **STP** protection. Since **STP** was either not enabled or not configured correctly, the switch ports did not block the redundant link. This caused broadcast traffic to continuously loop through the switches, creating a broadcast storm that overwhelmed the network and caused the outage.

To prevent this, the engineer should ensure the following:

- Switches are connected using trunk ports when linking multiple VLANs

- STP is enabled and properly configured on all switches to detect and block redundant paths

- Network features such as **BPDU guard** are implemented to protect against accidental loops

By following these best practices, the network can avoid loops and maintain stable connectivity, even when expanding or adding new switches.

Maximum transmission unit

The **maximum transmission unit (MTU)** defines the largest size a data packet can be when sent over a network without needing to be broken into smaller pieces, which is a process called **fragmentation**. If the **MTU** is too small, data gets split into many smaller packets, which can slow down the transmission because each packet has overhead (extra information) that takes up space. This means more packets are needed to send the same amount of data, leading to increased network traffic and potential delays.

If the **MTU** is too large, a packet being received could be too big for the network to handle, and it has to be fragmented or dropped, causing **retransmissions**. This can also slow down data transfer and create inefficiencies.

When a packet is received, if it's been fragmented, the device needs to reassemble the pieces, which can add processing time and delay. If any fragment is missing or corrupted, the whole packet may need to be resent.

Sliding window

The **sliding window** technique controls how much data is sent before needing confirmation that it was received correctly. It's like a conversation where you say a few sentences, wait for the other person to nod in agreement, and then continue speaking.

If the window is small, you can only send a little bit of data before waiting for a response. This can make the transfer slower, especially if there's a delay in communication (such as on a long-distance network). A larger window allows you to send more data before stopping to wait for an acknowledgment. This can speed up the transfer, but if too much data is sent and not acknowledged (because of network issues), it could cause congestion or data loss.

The receiver uses the sliding window to tell the sender how much more data it can handle at any time. If the receiver's buffer (temporary storage) is full, it will reduce the window size, slowing down the data flow to avoid being overwhelmed.

Standard Ethernet frame

The standard size of an Ethernet **MTU** is 1,500 bytes. This means that the largest payload of data that can be sent in a single Ethernet frame without fragmentation is 1,500 bytes. This size does not include the Ethernet header and trailer, which add an additional 18 bytes to the frame, making the total frame size up to 1,518 bytes. This 1,500-byte **MTU** is the default size used in most Ethernet networks and is widely supported across different devices and network infrastructures.

Jumbo frames

Jumbo frames are oversized data packets that can be much larger than the standard **MTU** (typically 9,000 bytes compared to 1,500 bytes). By using larger packets, fewer packets are needed to send the same amount of data. This reduces the overhead (extra information in each packet) and makes data transfer more efficient. Handling fewer, larger packets can reduce the processing load on devices, as they don't need to handle as many individual packets. **Jumbo frames** are particularly useful in networks that handle large amounts of data, such as in data centers or video streaming services, where efficiency and speed are critical. The drawback with jumbo frames is that not all networks or devices support **them**, so they need to be used in environments where all equipment is compatible. Otherwise, the oversized packets might be fragmented or dropped, leading to inefficiency.

Summary

This chapter covered essential topics concerning switch technologies. When configuring switching technologies and features, it is essential to understand **VLANs**, which provide network segmentation within a physical network, and the **VLAN** database, which stores these configurations. **SVIs** enable routing between **VLANs**. Interface configuration involves setting parameters for network ports, including defining a **native VLAN** for untagged traffic and a voice **VLAN** for voice traffic. **802.1Q** tagging is used to add **VLAN** identifiers to Ethernet frames. Link aggregation combines multiple links to increase bandwidth, while adjusting speed and duplex settings ensures optimal data transmission. STP is crucial for preventing network loops, and configuring the MTU, including the use of jumbo frames, allows for the efficient handling of larger data packets.

The knowledge gained in this chapter will prepare you to answer questions relating to exam objective 2.2 in the *CompTIA Network+* (*N10-009*) exam.

Exam objective 2.2

Given a scenario, configure switching technologies and features

Virtual local area network (**VLAN**): Network segmentation within a physical network

- **VLAN database**: Stores VLAN configurations
- **Switch virtual interface** (**SVI**): Virtual interface for VLAN routing

Interface configuration: Settings for network ports

- **Native VLAN:** Default untagged VLAN on a trunk port
- **Voice VLAN:** Dedicated VLAN for voice traffic
- **802.1Q tagging:** VLAN tagging on Ethernet frames
- **Link aggregation:** Combining multiple links for increased bandwidth
- **Speed:** Data transmission rate on a network interface
- **Duplex:** Simultaneous data transmission in both directions

Spanning tree: Prevents network loops

Maximum transmission unit (MTU): Largest data packet size

- **Jumbo frames:** Larger-than-standard Ethernet frames

Chapter review questions

Now that you've completed the chapter, you can check your knowledge using the practice questions provided in the online platform at https://packt.link/N10-009ch10. You can also use the QR code below. Accessing these questions requires you to unlock the accompanying online content first. Head over to Chapter 26 for detailed instructions.

11

Given a Scenario, Select and Configure Wireless Devices and Technologies

A quarter of a century ago, wireless technologies were an exception within a standard network, but now it's not uncommon to have entire networks connected by wireless routers. Especially with the increase in remote working, smartphones, tablets, and laptops, wireless is now the default for many network devices.

Whether deploying a simple home network or a complex enterprise-grade wireless system, selecting and configuring the right wireless devices and technologies is essential for optimal performance and security. This chapter explores the critical elements of wireless network configuration, including channel management, frequency options, and network types. Key considerations, such as channel width, non-overlapping channels, and regulatory impacts such as the **802.11h** standard, are examined to ensure compliance and reduce interference. Additionally, the chapter delves into frequency bands, such as **2.4 GHz**, **5 GHz**, and the emerging **6 GHz** options, alongside the concept of band steering to optimize device performance.

This chapter covers the third objective in *Domain 2.3: Given a scenario, select and configure wireless devices and technologies.*

> **Note**
>
> A full breakdown of objective 2.3 will be given at the end of the chapter.

Channels

In *Chapter 5, Compare and Contrast Transmission Media and Transceivers*, you saw how different technologies carry wireless signals, such as satellite and cellular networks.

As mentioned in the introduction, a wireless network is normally implemented on three frequency bands, 2.4 GHz, 5 GHz, and 6 GHz, with each band divided into **channels**. In wireless networking, a channel is a specific frequency range used for transmitting data. For the three channels just mentioned, the frequency band is divided into channels spaced 5 MHz apart, with a few exceptions, which will be mentioned. 2.4 GHz, which remains the most common **Wi-Fi** frequency band, is split into 14 channels, with the 14th being 12 MHz above the thirteenth channel. Different jurisdictions have different restrictions on the use of channels. In most of the world, you use all 14 channels, though in some places, channel 14 is restricted for government use. In the US and Canada, channel 14 is reserved, and 12 and 13 are not recommended due to channel overlap, which you will read about in a moment. So, the US and Canada effectively only have 11 channels available. Channel 14 is only permitted in Japan, and only for 802.11b devices.

Channel width

Channel width refers to how wide the channel is, measured in MHz. The wider the channel, the more data it can carry, which means faster speeds. However, wider channels are more prone to interference because they overlap with other channels. A 20 MHz channel might be slower but experiences less interference, while a 40 MHz or 80 MHz channel can carry more data but might have more interference from nearby networks.

For the 2.4 GHz frequency band, channels have a width of 22 MHz; so, for example, channel 6 has a fundamental, or central, frequency of 2,437 MHz (2.437 GHz). This puts its range at 2,426-2,448 MHz, and it may share this frequency range with other devices, such as microwave ovens (around 2.45 GHz), baby monitors, and Bluetooth devices. This could lead to interference; however, cell phones use separate licensed bands and typically do not interfere with these Wi-Fi channels.

Non-overlapping channels

As you can see in *Figure 11.1*, channels are separated by 5 MHz, but have channel widths of 22 MHz, which means that channels actually overlap with each other. This means that if you, for instance, use channel 1 for one device and channel 2 for another device, the two signals will interfere with each other. For this reason, it is important to try to use a non-overlapping channel.

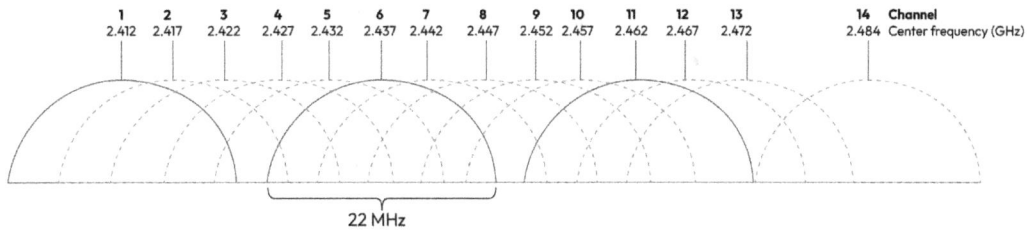

Figure 11.1: The channels of the 2.4 GHz frequency band

In the 2.4 GHz frequency band, there are only three **non-overlapping channels** (1, 6, and 11). Using these non-overlapping channels reduces the chances of interference between different wireless networks, leading to a more stable and reliable connection. So, for example, you might set up your first device on channel 1, then a second device on channel 11. If you need a third device, this would go on channel 6.

In the 5 GHz band, there are many more non-overlapping channels, which is one reason it often experiences less interference. Next, we will look at wider channel widths, 40 MHz, 80 MHz, and 160 MHz.

Wider channel widths

While 20 MHz channels are standard in the 2.4 GHz band due to limited space and high interference, wider channels are more commonly used in the 5 GHz and 6 GHz bands, where there is more available spectrum. The next section will look at how each wider channel option functions.

40 MHz channels can be used in both the 2.4 GHz and 5 GHz bands, though they are not recommended for 2.4 GHz. They offer double the bandwidth of 20 MHz, which can improve speed and throughput. However, in the 2.4 GHz band, using 40 MHz typically causes interference with adjacent channels because the band only supports three non-overlapping 20 MHz channels.

In the 5 GHz frequency band, there is a larger range of channels available compared to the 2.4 GHz band. Because of this wider spectrum, it is possible to use 40 MHz-wide channels without causing as much overlap or interference between neighboring channels. This means that using 40 MHz channels in the 5 GHz band is more practical and effective, allowing for higher data speeds while still maintaining good performance and minimizing interference. In contrast, the 2.4 GHz band has fewer channels overall, so using 40 MHz channels there often leads to overlapping signals and more interference.

80 MHz channels are available only in the 5 GHz and 6 GHz bands. They provide higher throughput, making them ideal for streaming, gaming, and other bandwidth-heavy applications. However,

using 80 MHz results in fewer non-overlapping channels, which can be problematic in high-density deployments. This channel width is best suited for environments with minimal nearby Wi-Fi networks or interference.

160 MHz channels are available in the 5 GHz and 6 GHz bands and are primarily used in Wi-Fi 6 and Wi-Fi 6E networks. They offer very high data rates, suitable for advanced applications such as 4K/8K video streaming, augmented reality, virtual reality, or high-performance enterprise networks. Because they use a large portion of the spectrum, there are very few non-overlapping channels available, so this option is best in low-interference or dedicated network environments. It may not be practical in areas with dense Wi-Fi usage, as overlapping channels will degrade performance.

Wireless reflection occurs when signals bounce off surfaces such as walls or metal, causing interference through multipath propagation, which can weaken or distort the connection.

Regulatory impacts

Just like the rest of the radio spectrum, the frequency bands used for wireless communication are regulated by governmental bodies. The standards set out by the **IEEE** are commonly adopted, but licensing and enforcement are handled by local agencies such as the **Federal Communications Commission (FCC)** in the US and **Ofcom** in the UK.

The rules and regulations ensure that wireless devices don't interfere with each other and operate safely, as well as ensuring that certain channels can be used by special organizations such as the military or satellite communications companies. There may also be regulations as to the power usage on certain channels, allowing them to be used but only for short-distance communication.

Regulations impact specifications for commercially available wireless devices. This is important to remember when configuring wireless devices, because some channels might not work by design in different places. For example, channel 14 is available in Japan, but a router purchased in the US is likely unable to use that channel due to regional restrictions.

802.11h

802.11h is a specific standard related to the 5 GHz frequency band. It was introduced to help reduce interference and improve the performance of wireless networks, especially in areas where there are many devices or networks operating. 802.11h includes features such as **dynamic frequency selection (DFS)**, which automatically switches the channel if interference is detected, and **transmit power control (TPC)**, which adjusts the power of the signal to avoid causing interference to other networks. This is particularly important in regions where the 5 GHz band is also used by other important services, such as weather radar and satellites.

Frequency options

Different **frequency options** offer different advantages and disadvantages. Lower frequency bands offer longer ranges, but have slower data transmission speeds because the bandwidths are narrower. So, 2.4 GHz has a standard range of 140 m and an ideal data speed of 450 Mbps. 5 GHz has a range of about 60 m and an ideal data speed of around 1,300 Mbps. In reality, there are a number of different factors that impact range and speed, such as environment, network equipment, and the specific implementation of the wireless standard. For the three main frequency bands, the key points are as follows:

- **2.4 GHz band**: Offers longer range but is more prone to interference and has fewer non-overlapping channels.

- **5 GHz band**: Provides faster speeds and more non-overlapping channels, but with a shorter range compared to 2.4 GHz. It is also more prone to obstruction by obstacles such as thick walls than 2.4 GHz.

- **6 GHz band**: Introduced with Wi-Fi 6E (802.11ax), it offers the highest speeds and the most channels, but with the shortest range due to higher frequency.

Wireless standard	Frequency band	Wireless speed
802.11a	5 GHz	54 Mbps
802.11b	2.4 GHz	11 Mbps
802.11g	2.4 GHz	54 Mbps
802.11n	2.4 GHz and 5 GHz	Up to 600 Mbps
802.11ac	5 GHz	Up to 6.93 Gbps
802.11ax	2.4 GHz and 5 GHz	Up to 9.6 Gbps

Table 11.1: Wireless standards frequency table

Band steering

Because some wireless standards include two frequency bands, routers and other network devices offer the choice of which band to use: 2.4 GHz, 5 GHz, or even 6 GHz. Because the best band will differ by device, placement, and even the current needs, the best band to use will also change dynamically and might not always be clear to the user. **Band steering** is an intelligent feature found in routers and other network devices that helps enhance the efficiency and performance of Wi-Fi networks by automatically managing device connections to the most suitable frequency band, normally for smartphones, tablets, and laptops.

When a device tries to connect to the Wi-Fi network, the router analyzes factors such as the device's capabilities, current network congestion, and signal strength. Based on this analysis, the router "steers" or directs the device to connect to the best available band. For instance, if a device is close to the router and supports the 5 GHz or 6 GHz band, the router may steer it to those bands for faster speeds. If the device is farther away, the router might steer it to the 2.4 GHz band, which has a better range.

Band steering is also important because some older devices might only work on 2.4 GHz, so the 5 GHz band should be utilized more to stop overcrowding. *Figure 11.2* depicts a router with band steering on and off.

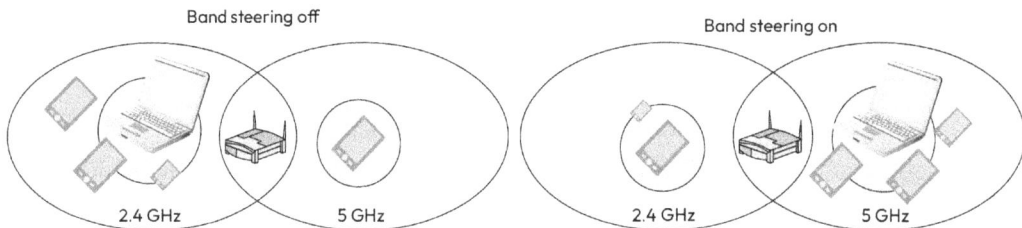

Figure 11.2: Band steering on and off

As you can see in *Figure 11.2*, while band steering is off, there are four devices on the 2.4 GHz band. This would cause data transfer speeds to slow down. In the image on the right, more devices have been automatically added to the 5 GHz band, giving them quicker data transfer. The two devices that need to be on 2.4 GHz, either because of the age of the device or the distance from the transmitter, also experience faster transfer because the band is less crowded. Some routers will have band steering turned off by default, so this should be checked during configuration.

Service set identifier (SSID)

The **service set identifier** (SSID) is essentially the name of a wireless network. When you connect to Wi-Fi, you see a list of available networks with names such as "HomeNetwork," "CoffeeShop WiFi," or "OfficeNet." These names are SSIDs. The SSID is what allows you to identify and connect to the right wireless network, especially when there are many networks nearby. It is a good idea to give an easily recognizable SSID, but always be aware that anyone can see it. Avoid using personal information or anything that could be used to guess the password.

Basic service set identifier (BSSID)

The BSSID is a unique identifier assigned to each AP within a wireless network. An AP is a device that allows wireless devices to connect to a wired network. The BSSID is usually the MAC address of the access point's wireless interface.

For example, one company in a large office building may have multiple access points spread across different floors, but all with the same SSID. Each access point would have its own BSSID. This could be something such as 00:14:22:01:23:45, which uniquely identifies that particular access point.

Extended service set identifier (ESSID)

The ESSID is the identifier for the entire wireless network, especially when there are multiple access points involved. If a network has several access points to provide better coverage across a large area, all these access points will share the same SSID, but each will have a different BSSID. The term ESSID is often used when referring to a network that spans multiple access points.

In that same office building, the network name you see on your device might be "Office WiFi." This is the ESSID, which all access points in the building use, allowing you to move around and stay connected without having to manually switch networks.

Think of the SSID as the name of a Wi-Fi network (such as the name of a restaurant), the BSSID as the specific table number you're sitting at in that restaurant, and the ESSID as the fact that all tables (APs) in the restaurant are part of the same dining area (network). When you move from one table to another (one access point to another), you're still in the same restaurant (network), just in a different spot, thanks to the ESSID.

Network types

As you saw in *Chapter 6, Compare and Contrast Network Topologies, Architectures, and Types*, once you get beyond more than two or three devices, there are various ways to configure a network. In wireless networking, different network types are used to meet various connectivity needs. Because range is such a factor with wireless devices, you need to consider the most efficient way to get the right coverage for your physical network area. Beyond a small four-room apartment, you may consider adding **wireless** APs, to avoid having areas in which devices cannot connect.

Different network types have their own structures and advantages, ranging from self-healing mesh networks to centralized infrastructure setups. In this section, we will look at the different types of networks.

Mesh network

As covered in *Chapter 6*, in a **wireless mesh network**, each device, also known as a node, is connected directly to multiple other nodes. To create a wireless mesh network, you connect multiple wireless access points together, allowing them to act as nodes that share the connection and extend coverage across a larger area without relying on a central router.

A **mesh network** is a type of network topology where each device, also known as a node, is connected directly to multiple other nodes.

In a mesh network, every node can communicate with any other node without relying on a central router or switch (remember, a node is any device in a network). If a connection or node fails, the data can be rerouted through alternative nodes, ensuring communication remains uninterrupted. This redundancy makes mesh networks highly reliable and fault tolerant.

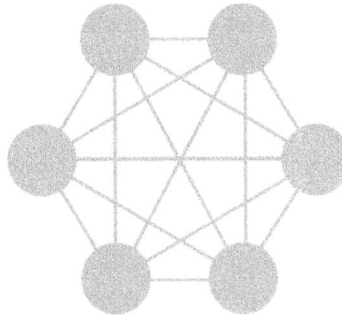

Figure 11.3: Full mesh network

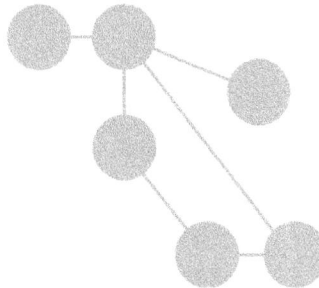

Figure 11.4: Partial mesh network

As you saw in *Chapter 6*, there are two types of **mesh networks: full mesh** and **partial mesh**. *Figure 11.3* shows a full mesh network where every node is connected to every other node directly, which provides maximum redundancy but can be expensive and complex to set up. *Figure 11.4* shows a partial mesh network, where only some nodes are fully interconnected, while others connect to just a few nodes. A partial mesh has less redundancy but still offers some backup and is cheaper and easier to administer.

Mesh networks are commonly used in wireless networks, such as in large buildings, outdoor areas, or communities where consistent and reliable coverage is needed.

Ad hoc network

An **ad hoc network** is a simple and temporary type of wireless network where devices connect directly to each other without using a central AP such as a router. It's a "peer-to-peer" setup, meaning each device communicates directly with others in the network. This type of network is useful in situations where a quick and easy connection is needed, such as when sharing files between two laptops or setting up a temporary network for a small group of devices in an area without existing infrastructure.

Imagine you and a friend want to share files between your laptops while sitting in a park. If there is no established network, then you could create an ad hoc network, allowing your laptops to connect directly to each other and exchange files without needing any other equipment.

Point to point

A **point-to-point** wireless network is a direct connection between two devices or locations using wireless technology, typically involving two antennas aimed at each other to create a focused, high-speed link over a distance. This setup is often used to connect buildings or sites where cables are impractical, enabling data transfer between them as if they were on the same network.

Infrastructure wireless network

An **infrastructure wireless network** is the most common type of wireless network you encounter in homes, offices, and public places. In this setup, devices connect to a central access point, usually a Wi-Fi router, which manages the network and allows devices to communicate with each other and access the internet. The access point acts as a hub, directing traffic between devices and ensuring everything stays connected efficiently.

When you connect your smartphone, laptop, and smart TV to your home Wi-Fi, you're using an infrastructure network. The Wi-Fi router is the central access point that all your devices connect to, enabling them to communicate with each other and connect to the internet.

There are numerous considerations when configuring wireless networks, such as the physical area, including any structures or items that can block radio signals or cause interference, the need for reliability, and cost and administrative load. Additionally, with any system that can be accessed without a physical connection, the security of your network should remain paramount. With every wireless AP, you increase the opportunity for a malicious actor to gain access to your information. How you deal with this is covered in the next section.

Encryption

Open system authentication lacks encryption and is inherently insecure, so we must implement a method to secure our wireless network. Wi-Fi networks are secured by advanced encryption standards such as WPA2, known for its robust protection, and WPA3, which offers even stronger encryption and improved security features. These encryption standards ensure that the data transmitted over your network is scrambled and secure, making it difficult for hackers to intercept or tamper with your information. This section will look at the importance of each.

Wi-Fi Protected Access 2 (WPA2)

WPA2 is a security standard designed by the Wi-Fi Alliance to protect a Wi-Fi network from intruders. It keeps your Wi-Fi connection safe using data encryption protocols. **Wi-Fi Protected Access-Counter Mode CBC-MAC Protocol**, better known as **WPA2-CCMP**, is the protocol inside WPA2 that does the actual encryption of data using 128-bit AES. Devices are connected to a WPA2-protected Wi-Fi network using two methods: using a **pre-shared key (PSK)** or a **Wi-Fi-protected setup (WPS)**.

The PSK is the password for your Wi-Fi network. You should only need to input it into a device once, the first time it is introduced to the network, so a complex password shouldn't be a burden as you do not have to remember it. The security of your network largely depends on the strength of this password and how it is managed. For example, a coffee shop might want to display the password clearly so customers can easily access the network; however, an office might want to only tell staff the password and change it regularly.

WPS is a shortcut that helps you connect devices to your Wi-Fi without typing in the password. WPS often includes a feature where you can press a button on your router to quickly connect a device to your Wi-Fi network without needing to enter a password. On the router, there will be a button labeled *WPS* (it might have the WPS symbol, which looks like two arrows forming a circle). Pushing the *WPS* button usually activates WPS for a short period (around two minutes). In most situations, it's a good idea to disable this because it can make the network more vulnerable to hackers.

WPA2-Personal is a wireless security mode that uses a PSK for authentication. In this setup, all users connect to the Wi-Fi network using the same password. It's simple to set up and commonly used in home networks and small businesses where ease of access is prioritized over strict security and user control. However, because the password is shared, it does not allow for identifying or tracking individual users. If one person shares the password or leaves the organization, the key must be changed for everyone to maintain security, which can be inconvenient and insecure in larger environments.

WPA2-Enterprise, on the other hand, provides a much higher level of security by using an authentication server such as a RADIUS server that works with a directory service such as **Active Directory** (**AD**). Instead of a shared password, each user logs in with their own unique credentials, which are verified by the RADIUS server against the AD database. This allows administrators to track and log each user's activity, enforce individual access policies, and easily revoke access by disabling a user account. WPA2-Enterprise is ideal for large organizations, schools, or any environment that requires secure, accountable, and scalable network access.

Wi-Fi Protected Access 3 (WPA3)

WPA3 was released in 2018 and it is more secure than WPA2. WPA3 primarily relies on **Simultaneous Authentication of Equals** (**SAE**) for key establishment and encryption compared to WPA2's 128-bit encryption.

The key features of WPA3 include **Protected Management Frames** (**PMF**), WPA3-Enterprise, SAE, Wi-Fi Easy Connect, and Wi-Fi Enhanced Open:

- PMF protects management frames (such as disassociation and deauthentication messages) from forgery. This prevents common Wi-Fi attacks such as session hijacking and deauthentication flooding, which is a way for hackers to spam fake "disconnect" messages causing your devices to keep dropping off Wi-Fi.

- WPA3-Enterprise is suitable for government and finance departments, in contrast to WPA2, which only supports 128 bits. WPA3-Enterprise uses **Elliptic-Curve Diffie-Hellman Ephemeral** (**ECDHE**) for the initial handshake.

- SAE replaces WPA2-PSK using a very secure DH handshake called **Dragonfly** and protects against brute-force attacks. It uses **perfect forward secrecy** (**PFS**), which ensures that your session keys cannot be compromised.

- Wi-Fi Easy Connect simplifies connecting to IoT devices, such as a smartphone, by simply using a QR code.

- Wi-Fi Enhanced Open is an enhancement of WPA2 open authentication that uses encryption. It can be used in public areas such as hotels, cafés, and airports where no password is required. It also prevents eavesdropping as it uses PMF.

Guest networks

Guest networks offer a secure way to allow visitors access to your Wi-Fi without compromising your main network. To further enhance security and manage guest access, **captive portals** can be used to control and secure access to a Wi-Fi network by guests. When someone tries to connect, they're directed to a special web page where they might need to enter a password, agree to terms, or provide some information to verify who they are, such as their email address or Facebook or Google account, before they can use the internet. This helps ensure that only authorized users can access the network, protects your main network from potential threats, and allows you to manage who is using your Wi-Fi.

Authentication

Authentication protocols are a set of rules through which relevant parties are required to prove their identities. They play a crucial role in corporate networks by ensuring secure access and enabling effective user tracking and policy enforcement, thereby bolstering corporate accountability and protecting digital assets. These protocols include the following:

- **Protected Extensible Authentication Protocol (PEAP)** is a version of **Extensible Authentication Protocol (EAP)** that encapsulates and encrypts EAP data using a certificate stored on the server. For this reason, PEAP is more secure for WLANs.

- **802.1x** is an overarching access control standard. It allows access only to authenticated users or devices and is therefore used by managed switches for port-based authentication. 802.1x needs a certificate installed on the endpoint (client or device), which is used for authentication. For wireless authentication, the switch needs to use a RADIUS server for enterprise networks.

- **EAP-TLS** is a specific, secure version of wireless authentication that requires a certificate stored on the endpoint (client or device) to verify identity and authorization.

- **EAP-TTLS** uses two phases. The first is to set up a secure session with the server by creating a tunnel using certificates that are stored on the server and seen by the client. The second is to authenticate the client's credentials.

- **EAP-FAST**, developed by Cisco, is used in wireless networks and point-to-point connections to perform session authentication. It is the only one of these authentication protocols that does not use a certificate.

Enterprise wireless authentication

When a company has a large network with many users and devices, it needs a secure and organized way to control who can connect to the Wi-Fi. This is where **enterprise wireless authentication** comes in. Rather than a simple password (like a home Wi-Fi), enterprise authentication uses a more secure and flexible method to ensure that only authorized people can access the network.

Enterprise-level wireless authentication uses RADIUS with an AD domain controller. RADIUS provides secure centralized authentication for wireless networks. The process is as follows:

1. A user logs in via a RADIUS client. This could be a VPN server, 802.1x managed switch, or wireless access point that the user connects to the RADIUS server by using a shared secret (such as a password).

2. RADIUS checks whether someone trying to connect to the Wi-Fi has the right login details by contacting the AD domain controller.

3. AD stores and manages these login details for all users in the organization. It also verifies that the person has the right to log in remotely.

Antennas

There are two main types of antennas used to manage wireless signals: omnidirectional and directional antennas. In the following section, we will describe both of these.

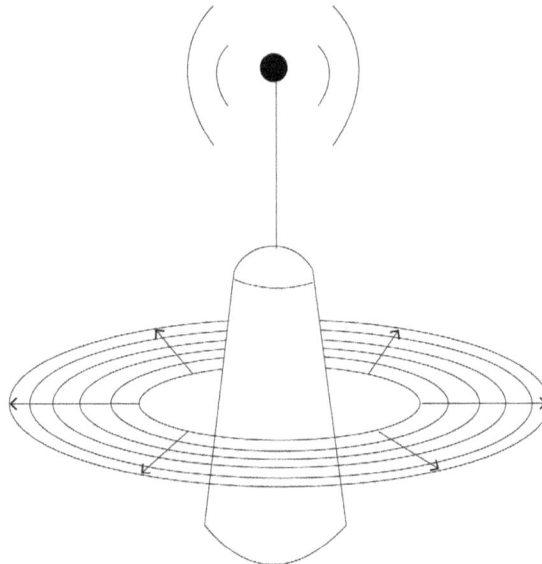

Figure 11.5: Omnidirectional antenna

The omnidirectional antenna in *Figure 11.5* broadcasts signals in all directions to provide broad coverage. A directional antenna, as shown in *Figure 11.6*, concentrates signals in a specific direction to achieve an extended range.

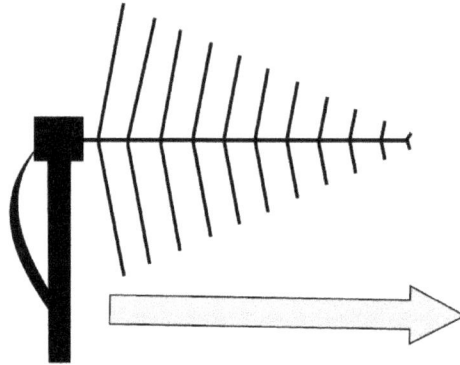

Figure 11.6: Directional antenna

Autonomous versus lightweight access points

When setting up a Wi-Fi network, it's important to understand the difference between autonomous APs and **lightweight APs (LWAPs)**, as they each serve different purposes depending on the size and needs of the network. Autonomous APs work on their own. They do everything needed to manage Wi-Fi connections by themselves, making them good for small networks where you don't need a lot of devices. LWAPs, on the other hand, don't work alone. They connect to a central controller that handles most of the important tasks, such as setting up the network and keeping it secure. This makes them great for larger networks where you have many access points spread out in different places. The central controller helps manage all of them easily.

Summary

This chapter covered wireless networks and their configurations. Wireless networks optimize performance through channel width, non-overlapping channels, and regulated frequencies such as 2.4 GHz, 5 GHz, and 6 GHz, with band steering directing device connections. SSIDs manage network identification, while different network types offer various coverage options. Security is ensured with WPA2/WPA3 encryption and guest network controls such as captive portals. Authentication ranges from simple PSKs to enterprise solutions, and antennas can be omnidirectional or directional. Autonomous APs are standalone, while LWAPs need central management.

The knowledge gained in this chapter will prepare you to answer questions relating to exam objective 2.3 in the *CompTIA Network+ (N10-009)* exam.

Exam objectives 2.3

Given a scenario, select and configure wireless devices and technologies.

Channels:

- **Channel width:** Determines data throughput by controlling the bandwidth of the wireless channel
- **Non-overlapping channels:** Minimizes interference by using separate, non-interfering frequency bands
- **Regulatory impacts:** Legal constraints affecting wireless channel usage in specific regions:
  - **802.11h:** Standard addressing interference and power control in the 5 GHz band

Frequency options:

- **2.4 GHz:** Offers wider coverage but is more prone to interference
- **5 GHz:** Higher speeds, less interference, but shorter range
- **6 GHz:** Newest option, more channels, reduced congestion
- **Band steering:** Directs devices to the optimal frequency band for better performance

Service Set Identifier (SSID):

- **BSSID:** Unique identifier for individual access points within a network
- **ESSID:** Identifier for a network, shared across multiple access points

Network types:

- **Mesh networks:** Devices act as nodes, providing robust, self-healing coverage
- **Ad hoc:** Direct, peer-to-peer device communication without an access point
- **Point to point:** A direct connection between two distinct network devices
- **Infrastructure:** Centralized network with devices connecting via access points

Encryption:

- **Wi-Fi Protected Access 2 (WPA2):** Strong encryption standard for wireless security
- **WPA3:** Enhanced security over WPA2, with better encryption and protection

Guest networks:

- **Captive portals:** Web page prompts for guest authentication before accessing the network

Authentication:

- **Pre-shared key (PSK)**: Simple password-based authentication for small networks.
- **Enterprise**: Centralized authentication, usually via RADIUS, for larger networks.

Antennas:

- **Omnidirectional**: Broadcasts signal in all directions for broad coverage.
- **Directional**: Focuses the signal in one direction for an extended range

Autonomous vs lightweight access point:

- **Autonomous**: Standalone, fully functional access point with local management
- **Lightweight**: Relies on a central controller for management and configuration

Chapter review questions

Now that you've completed the chapter, you can check your knowledge using the practice questions provided in the online platform at https://packt.link/N10-009ch11. You can also use the QR code below. Accessing these questions requires you to unlock the accompanying online content first. Head over to Chapter 26 for detailed instructions.

12

Explain Important Factors of Physical Installations

In the previous three chapters, you examined how messages are transmitted across networks using routing and switching technologies and explored the configuration of wireless communication systems. With a strong foundation in logical network operations established, we will now shift our focus to the physical infrastructure that supports and sustains network performance.

Proper installation of cabling, along with the strategic deployment of **main distribution frames (MDFs)** and **intermediate distribution frames (IDFs)**, is critical to ensuring the reliability, throughput, security, and operational safety of a network environment.

As a network engineer, it is essential to understand how environmental factors—such as humidity, temperature, and the physical placement of components—influence both hardware performance and the overall security posture of the network.

This chapter covers strategic equipment placement in IDF/MDF locations, appropriate rack sizing, organized cabling, and proper cooling management. Additionally, power management through **uninterruptible power supplies (UPSs)** and **power distribution unit (PDU)** systems, along with maintaining optimal environmental conditions such as temperature and humidity control, ensures long-term network performance.

This chapter covers the fourth objective in *Domain 2*: *Explain important factors of physical installations.*

> **Note**
>
> A full breakdown of objective 2.4 will be given at the end of the chapter.

Important installation implications

As you have seen in previous chapters, the installation of network infrastructure is not simply a case of placing the equipment in a room and being done with it. There are a number of factors that need to be taken into consideration, such as the types of networks, the size and location of the network, and how different parts of the network will be separated. How to best place essential network equipment and how to set it up so it runs efficiently and safely are core considerations.

One of the first decisions to be made is the placement of distribution frames, which are the central points that handle the connections of the network. The two distribution frames you will most often come across are the **main distribution frame**, or **MDF**, which, as the name suggests, is the central hub of network infrastructure, and the IDF, which is a secondary hub used in larger networks.

The MDF is the central hub of a network infrastructure, acting as the primary point where external network connections, such as the internet, enter the building; see *Figure 12.1*. From the MDF, the network is distributed to various IDFs throughout a building or campus.

Figure 12.1: Main distribution frame

The MDF houses critical network equipment such as **routers, switches,** and **servers,** making it the backbone of the network. It is often located in a dedicated server room or data center with controlled environmental conditions to ensure the safety and performance of the equipment. The MDF is responsible for managing and distributing network connections efficiently, ensuring that data flows smoothly throughout the network.

An IDF is a secondary hub within a network infrastructure, strategically placed closer to the end users or devices that require network access. It serves as an intermediary point, connecting devices to the MDF via structured cabling. Instead of running individual cables from each device directly to the MDF, which can be inefficient and complicated, the IDF allows for shorter, more manageable cable runs. This setup improves network performance by reducing the distance data must travel and helps maintain organized and efficient cabling. For large networks, each floor or section of a building will typically have its own IDF, allowing for better distribution and management of network connections across the premises. MDFs and IDFs have a massive impact on the speed, security, and reliability of your network, so it is worth carefully considering their placement, as you will see in the next section.

Locations

The location of both the IDF and MDF is crucial for the overall efficiency, security, and scalability of the network. The MDF should be centrally located in a secure area, ideally within a dedicated server room or data center, to protect sensitive equipment and provide easy access to external network connections. Proper placement ensures that the MDF can effectively manage and distribute network traffic across the building. For example, the MDF could be placed in a centralized server room on the ground floor, close to the building's incoming fiber optic line from the internet service provider.

On the other hand, IDFs should be strategically positioned near areas with high concentrations of users or devices to minimize the distance data must travel. This reduces latency, improves network speed, and makes it easier to manage and troubleshoot the network. Additionally, choosing appropriate locations for these distribution frames allows for better scalability and future-proofing of the network, while taking security into account, ensuring it can grow and adapt to changing needs.

However, location isn't the only thing that will influence IDF and MDF performance. You also need to consider how well equipped they are to deal with the number of devices and connections, as you will see in the next section.

Rack size

When considering your central and secondary hubs, it's important to think about the actual physical space needed for all those routers, switches, cables, and patch panels. Anyone who has ever visited a server room will know that they aren't just left on the floor; they are placed on racks. Two factors that we need to consider before placing a device in a rack are the device depth and device height. Racks need to have enough space to fit all the equipment on, but they also need to allow enough space between different pieces of equipment to allow for airflow and avoid overheating.

Racks are the physical structures that house network equipment such as servers, switches, routers, and patch panels. They enable high **compute density**, allowing you to install and organize more devices efficiently. Choosing the right rack is essential not only for fitting your current equipment but also for ensuring proper airflow and allowing room for future expansion.

Figure 12.2: A 42U rack

Figure 12.2 shows the most common rack size for network equipment, which is the **42U**. The *U* stands for *rack unit*. 1U is the smallest unit of space for a piece of network equipment, which is 44.45 mm (1.75 inches) in height, while the width and depth are standard. It is also nicknamed a pizza box because it is wide, long, and shallow. A 42U rack provides 42 rack units of vertical space. The number of devices a 42U rack can hold depends on the height of each device, measured in *U* units. Servers, switches, and routers will often be 1U, so you could, in theory, fit 42 on one 42U rack. Larger servers and other specialized equipment are 2U, allowing for 21 devices, and large storage arrays or appliances are 4U, so a 42U rack could fit 10 devices, with some space.

In practice, however, the rack's usable space is reduced by factors such as the space taken by **power distribution units (PDUs)** and cable management trays. A PDU is a device in a server rack that works like a big power strip, letting all the equipment share electricity safely and neatly. As mentioned earlier, you also need to consider airflow and ventilation, so you should leave space between devices. Proper ventilation is critical to the longevity and performance of your network equipment. When racks are too tightly packed, airflow is restricted, which can cause devices to overheat. Look for racks designed to promote good airflow, such as those with perforated doors and side panels. Additionally, consider using blanking panels to fill unused rack spaces, which helps guide airflow more efficiently through the equipment that needs it most. Airflow and cooling considerations are not just confined to racks, as you will read in the next section.

Port-side exhaust/intake

In data centers, servers and network devices generate significant amounts of heat. Too much heat can cause systems to slow down or malfunction. Most hardware will have optimal operation temperatures and will shut down if they overheat. To manage this heat efficiently, IT equipment that could overheat will have fans fitted that control **intake** and **exhaust**. The intake side is where cool air is drawn into the device to keep it from overheating. The exhaust side is where hot air is expelled from the device. Typically, rack-mounted devices take in cool air at the front and exhaust it out of the rear.

Switches differ because they are used in different environments and different conditions. When rack-mounted, network engineers prefer to have the ports facing the front to easily configure cables; thus, the cool air should be taken in through the side that has the ports. This is called **port-side intake**. In other scenarios, such as telecommunications rooms, switches are placed with the port side facing the wall. In this case, the cool air should be taken in from the side not facing the wall, with hot air pushed out through the port. This is called **port-side exhaust**. Many switches will have variable airflow, and it is important to ensure settings match the cooling setup, whether in a server room or a distribution closet.

Cabling

As you have seen so far in this chapter, the placement of devices is important for the efficiency, reliability, and safety of your network. But getting the right devices in the right places, with the right setup, is only part of the task. All these devices need to be connected, and getting the **cabling** right is just as crucial for your network. Poor installation practices include exceeding cabling lengths, improper space, poor cabling shielding, and piling cables on top of each other, which can crush the lower cables.

These practices can be detrimental to the network; they can negatively impact signal integrity and network reliability and increase the risk of electromagnetic interference and tampering or unauthorized access. Not having the right types or lengths of cables can degrade network speed and increase costs, while poorly organized systems will be difficult to troubleshoot and scale. Bad cabling can also be a safety hazard.

When building or managing a network, it's important to know about the different types of cables and what they do. Each type of cable has a specific purpose, such as connecting computers and devices to the network or linking different parts of the network together. This section will look at some of the most common cables that you will come across.

T568A and T568B wiring standards

Ethernet cables typically have eight individual wires, twisted into four pairs. Each pair consists of one solid-colored wire and one striped (white plus the color) wire:

- **Green pair**: Green, white/green
- **Orange pair**: Orange, white/orange
- **Blue pair**: Blue, white/blue
- **Brown pair**: Brown, white/brown

At the end of each cable, it is "terminated." This means a connector is attached to the raw end of the cable so it can be plugged into something else, or that is connected directly to a patch bay, which will be discussed further in this chapter.

The difference between T568A and T568B is the order of these color pairs when terminating an Ethernet cable. Most modern systems use T568A.

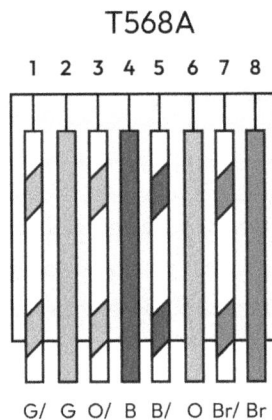

Figure 12.3: T568A

Table 12.1 shows the pin details of T568A.

Pin Number	Wire Color	Pair
1	White/green	Pair 3
2	Green	Pair 3
3	White/orange	Pair 2
4	Blue	Pair 1
5	White/blue	Pair 1
6	Orange	Pair 2
7	White/brown	Pair 4
8	Brown	Pair 4

Table 12.1: T568A

T568B

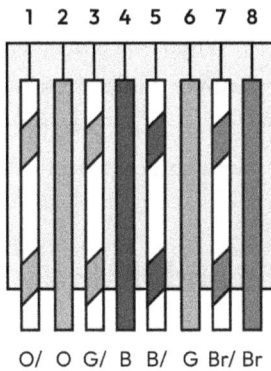

Figure 12.4: T568B

Table 12.2 shows the pin details of T568B.

Pin Number	Wire Color	Pair
1	White/orange	Pair 2
2	Orange	Pair 2
3	White/green	Pair 3
4	Blue	Pair 1
5	White/blue	Pair 1
6	Green	Pair 3

Pin Number	Wire Color	Pair
7	White/brown	Pair 4
8	Brown	Pair 4

Table 12.2: T568B

Note

For color versions of the preceding figures, please visit `https://packt.link/aLt82`.

T568A starts with the green pair on pins 1 and 2, while T568B starts with the orange pair on pins 1 and 2. T568B is more commonly used in the US, while T568A is more common in international settings and is the preferred wiring standard for federal government installations in the US.

When both ends of the cable are terminated using the same standard (either T568A or T568B), it is known as a **straight-through cable**. This is the standard for most Ethernet applications, such as connecting a computer to a switch. When one end is terminated with T568A and the other with T568B, the cable becomes a **crossover cable**. Crossover cables were historically used to directly connect two devices without the need for a network switch or router, such as connecting two computers directly. Straight-through and crossover cables will be looked at in more detail in the next section.

Different types of cables and their uses

When building or managing a network, it's important to know about the different types of cables and what they do. Each type of cable has a specific purpose, such as connecting computers and devices to the network or linking different parts of the network together. *Chapter 5, Compare and Contrast Transmission Media and Transceivers*, covered different categories of Ethernet cables. This section will look at some of the most common cables that you will come across:

- **Backbone cables**, also known as vertical cables, are responsible for connecting the MDF to IDFs. These cables typically carry the network's main signals across long distances, linking floors or buildings. In large networks, backbone cables are used to interconnect different sections of a building or multiple buildings. They're often fiber optic cables because fiber provides high bandwidth and long-distance signal transmission. To protect backbone cables, they should be run through raceways and conduits, taking into consideration environmental factors such as temperature, humidity, and even vermin that might chew through wires. Fiber optic cables especially have strict guidelines on how far you can bend the cable.

- **Drop cables** are shorter cables used to connect individual devices, such as computers, phones, or access points, to the network within a local area. You will find drop cables in the IDF, connecting patch panels to the end user devices. They are normally Ethernet cables. The path of a drop cable should be planned to avoid too many obstacles. Cable trays, J-hooks, and other support systems are designed to prevent sagging or tension on the cables and help the cables last longer.

- **Straight-through cables** are Ethernet cables where the wire configuration is identical on both ends, using either the T568A or T568B standard. These cables are primarily used to connect devices of different types, such as a computer to a switch, a switch to a router, or any other end device to a network.

- **Crossover cables** are Ethernet cables where the wiring is crossed, meaning the transmit and receive pairs of wires are swapped on one end. This allows direct device-to-device communication without a switch or hub. Crossover cables are traditionally used to connect two similar devices, such as switch to switch or computer to computer, directly without using a network device. If you're an admin configuring a new switch and there's no network connection yet, you might use a crossover cable to directly connect your laptop to the switch for configuration purposes.

The length of the cable can significantly impact the network's performance because the signal degrades as it travels over long distances, a phenomenon known as attenuation, the loss of signal strength. The maximum length for ethernet cables should be 100 meters, with extra allowed for patching at each end. Longer distances can be achieved with switches, repeaters, or Ethernet extensions.

Within any complex cabling setup, there needs to be a way to connect cables in an organized way; this is done with a patch panel, which we will look at in the next section.

Patch panels

A **patch panel** is a hardware component that provides a physical interface for connecting and organizing multiple cables. It functions as a hub, where various cables from different devices come together and are "patched" or connected. For example, in a network setup, Ethernet cables from different computers or switches can be routed to a patch panel, allowing the connection of devices to network switches or routers more cleanly.

A typical patch panel is shown in *Figure 12.5*.

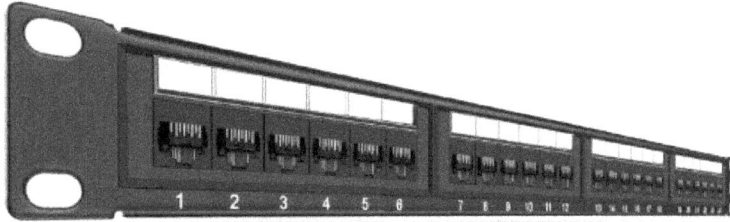

Figure 12.5: Cat7 1U patch panel – front

Patch panels also make it easier to maintain and troubleshoot network connections because you can identify and access specific connections quickly without having to deal with a tangled mess of cables. *Figure 12.6* shows the back of a patch panel.

Figure 12.6: Rear of a patch panel

In *Figure 12.6*, you can see the punch-down blocks at the rear of the patch panel. These blocks secure a wire by cutting through its insulation, making a connection with the patch panel and holding it in place. Technicians use a punch-down tool to complete this process, as shown in *Figure 12.7*.

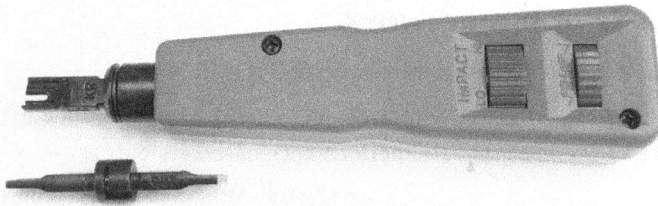

Figure 12.7: A punch-down tool

A **fiber distribution panel**, as shown in *Figure 12.8*, is similar to a patch panel but is specifically designed for fiber optic cables. Fiber cables are more fragile than copper cables (such as Ethernet cables), so a fiber distribution panel helps protect these cables and minimizes the risk of damage or signal interference. This panel allows you to route and manage fiber optic cables between switches, servers, and storage devices more efficiently.

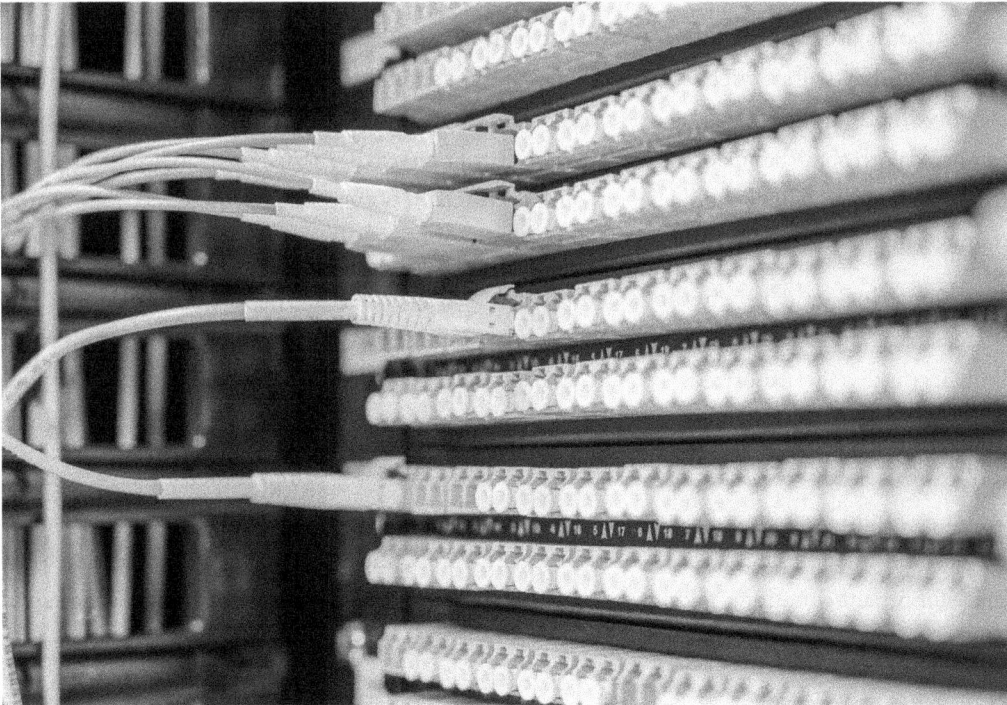

Figure 12.8: Fiber distribution panel

Lockable parts of the network

When setting up a physical network infrastructure, it is important to consider security and organization as part of the installation. Physically securing networking equipment is crucial to maintaining the safety, integrity, and performance of the system. The easiest way to secure important equipment and setups is with the use of physical locks to protect either small individual devices, nodes, or entire rooms.

Lockable cabinets are secure, enclosed storage units that hold networking equipment such as switches, servers, and routers. They are typically found in server rooms or network closets (IDFs or MDFs) and can be locked to prevent unauthorized access. It is important that only authorized personnel have access to the equipment inside, protecting it from tampering, accidental damage, or theft. Cabinets should also be labeled clearly, so if maintenance is required, the correct equipment can be accessed quickly without confusion.

Server rooms are the central location for critical network equipment such as servers, storage systems, and network switches. Access to these rooms should also be highly controlled to protect sensitive data and hardware. Server rooms contain valuable and sensitive equipment that, if tampered with or mishandled, can cause severe disruptions to the network or lead to data breaches. Unauthorized individuals should not have free access to these areas, as this could lead to accidental damage, malicious activity, or network downtime.

Traditional lock-and-key methods can be effective in protecting parts of the network, but increasingly, more high-tech locking systems are being used. **Key card systems**, for instance, limit access to only authorized personnel and also allow you to monitor who enters and exits the server room and when. **Biometric systems** are also common in more secure environments, and fingerprint or retina scanners can be used to add an extra layer of security.

Systems should keep logs of everyone who enters and exits, and surveillance cameras can also be used for an additional layer of monitoring. Emergency access procedures should also be in place for urgent situations, taking into consideration the security of the network and the safety of personnel.

Power

When setting up or maintaining a network, understanding how power is managed is just as important as knowing about network cables. Power systems ensure that your network devices, such as switches, routers, and servers, stay operational, even during power outages or fluctuations. Without stable and reliable power, network devices can experience outages, performance issues, or even damage, which impacts the entire network's functionality.

Sudden power outages can cause unsaved data to be lost, particularly in servers, workstations, or computers that are actively processing or storing information. Even small interruptions can cause data loss or corruption. This can be prevented by using an uninterruptible power supply (UPS), which is a backup battery system that provides temporary power to network devices when the main power source fails. It typically uses batteries to keep equipment running long enough to either restore power, start a backup generator, or shut down devices safely. A UPS ensures that critical devices such as servers and switches do not go down abruptly during a power outage, protecting the network from data loss, downtime, or hardware damage. UPS systems typically support both 110 V (standard in the US and parts of Asia) and 240 V (standard in Europe and other regions). It's important to use a UPS that matches the voltage of your power system to avoid incompatibility or failure.

Even when the power supply is running, it is important that all devices in a network receive the right amount of power. A PDU ensures that all devices receive the right amount of power and often includes monitoring features. PDUs help manage power distribution efficiently and safely across multiple devices, ensuring there are no overloads or power imbalances, which can cause downtime or hardware damage. A UPS allows the network administrator to turn off the power in a controlled manner, also called "shut down gracefully", preventing data corruption. Like UPS systems, PDUs are designed to handle 110 V or 240 V, depending on the region, and it's important to ensure the PDU matches the voltage standard of your power system.

Power load

Power load refers to the total amount of power being used by all the devices in your network setup. Each device adds to the overall power load, and it's essential to make sure the power system can handle the combined demand without overloading. Most networks and offices use single-phase (phase 1) power, which is typically used in low- to medium-power applications. It supplies power through a single **alternating current** (**AC**) waveform. Single-phase power is used in most small to medium-sized network environments because it's efficient and sufficient for powering standard networking equipment such as servers, switches, and routers. Monitoring the power load and understanding whether you're using single-phase or higher-phase power helps prevent overloading the system, which could cause outages or even damage equipment. It's essential to balance the power load across your UPS and PDU to ensure the network runs smoothly.

Voltage

Voltage (**V**) refers to the force of the electrical current supplied to the network equipment, while **amperage** (**amps**) is the measure of the electrical current flowing through the equipment. **Wattage** (**W**), the total power consumed by a device, is calculated using the following formula:

$W = V \times A$

So, for example, if a network switch operates at 120 V and uses 2 amps of current, its wattage consumption would be as follows:

$120 \times 2 = 240$

This means the switch consumes 240 W of power.

How many devices can a 30-amp circuit support?

To calculate how many devices can run on a 30-amp circuit, you first need to know the voltage of the circuit and the wattage consumption of each device. In most network environments, the voltage will be either 120 V or 240 V.

For example, the calculation for a 120 V circuit is as follows:

$120\,V \times 30\,A = 3{,}600\,W$

For a 240 V circuit, it is as follows:

$240\,V \times 30\,A = 7{,}200\,W$

To determine how many devices can be supported, divide the total wattage available by the wattage consumption of each device. For example, consider that each switch consumes 240 W.

For a 120 V, 30-amp circuit, the calculation is as follows:

$3{,}600 \div 240 = 15$

That means 15 devices.

For a 240 V, 30-amp circuit, the calculation is as follows:

$7{,}200 \div 240 = 30$

However, to prevent overloading the circuit, it's recommended to use only about 80% of the total capacity. For example, on a 120 V, 30-amp circuit, first you work out 80% of 3,600 watts, then do the same calculation as previously:

$3{,}600 \times 0.8 = 2{,}880$

This gives you 2,880 W:

2,880 ÷ 240 = 12

So, you can safely run 12 devices. Similarly, for a 240V, 30-amp circuit, the calculation is as follows:

7,200 × 0.8 = 5,760

This gives you 5,760 W:

5,760 ÷ 240 = 24

This makes 24 devices.

Always check the power requirements of your equipment and the circuit ratings to ensure that you stay within safe operating limits to avoid overloading your circuit, which could cause electrical failures or fire hazards.

Environmental factors

Server rooms are the heart of any data infrastructure, and managing the environment within them is critical to ensure smooth operation, longevity of equipment, and overall safety. Three key environmental factors—humidity, fire suppression, and temperature—must be monitored and controlled to avoid damage, downtime, and potential data loss. **Humidity** refers to the amount of moisture present in the air, and maintaining the correct humidity levels in a server room is crucial for the health of your equipment. Both excessively high and low humidity levels can cause problems.

If the humidity level is too high, condensation can form on internal components of the servers, leading to short circuits and potential equipment failure. High humidity levels can also promote the growth of mold and mildew, which can affect both the equipment and air quality in the server room. On the other hand, if humidity levels are too low, static electricity becomes a major risk. Static discharge can damage sensitive components within servers and other network devices, leading to system failures or data loss, so you should follow good anti-static procedures to protect equipment.

Typically, the **ideal relative humidity range** for a server room is between 40% and 60%. This range helps prevent condensation and static electricity, keeping equipment in optimal operating condition. To do this, you can use either a humidifier to keep humidity above 40%, a dehumidifier to keep it below 60%, or a combination of both.

Environmental monitoring systems can be used to continuously monitor humidity levels in the server room. Specialized sensors can be connected to a control system, which can then automatically adjust the operation of humidifiers and dehumidifiers based on real-time conditions. Many advanced systems include alerts that notify staff if the humidity goes beyond the set thresholds.

Fire suppression in a server room is critical, as traditional fire-fighting methods, such as water-based systems, are not suitable. To control and suppress fire hazards, you can use a **clean agent fire suppression system**. These systems release a gas such as FM-200 or Novec 1230 that extinguishes fires without damaging electronic equipment. They are the preferred choice for data centers and server rooms as they do not leave residue, unlike water-based systems. **Pre-action sprinkler systems** are water-based but do not release water unless both smoke and heat are detected. This minimizes the risk of accidental water damage. They are often used as a backup to gas-based systems.

Early detection is key to preventing major damage. Server rooms often use smoke detection systems with high sensitivity, which can detect the smallest traces of smoke before a fire escalates. The server room itself should be designed with **fire-resistant building materials**, such as fire-rated doors, walls, and ceilings, which will help contain a fire and prevent it from spreading.

It is best practice to implement a **dual-layer fire suppression system**. You can use a clean agent system as the primary method of fire control and a pre-action water system as a backup, along with early smoke detection systems for maximum protection.

Temperature control is perhaps the most well-known factor in server room management. Servers generate a significant amount of heat, and if the room gets too hot, it can cause the servers to overheat, leading to hardware failures, data loss, and, in extreme cases, fires. There are several cooling methods, including air conditioning units, hot/cold aisle containment, and liquid cooling.

Computer room air conditioning (CRAC) units are specialized air conditioners designed for server rooms that maintain both temperature and humidity, ensuring stable conditions. HVAC systems help control the temperature, airflow, and humidity in server rooms. They provide general cooling to the room and are often the first line of defense against overheating. As mentioned earlier in the chapter, racks are arranged in rows, where one aisle contains cold air (intake) and the other hot air (exhaust). By containing these aisles, the cooling system becomes more efficient by reducing the mixing of hot and cold air.

Some high-density server environments utilize **liquid cooling**, where a liquid coolant absorbs heat directly from the equipment and dissipates it through radiators or external cooling systems. This method is more efficient than air cooling but is more complex to implement.

The **recommended temperature range** for server rooms is generally between 20°C (68°F) and 25°C (77°F). Keeping the room at this temperature ensures optimal performance and minimizes the risk of overheating. Server rooms often use raised floors to create space for airflow. Cool air is pushed through the floor and directed toward the intake side of servers, while hot air is removed through ceiling vents. This helps create a more efficient cooling cycle.

Summary

This chapter covered effective physical installations, showing how they are key to network reliability and efficiency. Key considerations include equipment placement in IDF/MDF locations, proper rack sizing, efficient cooling, and organized cabling. Power management through UPSs, PDUs, and careful load planning is crucial, as is maintaining optimal environmental conditions such as temperature and humidity control.

The knowledge gained in this chapter will prepare you to answer questions relating to Exam Objective 2.4 in your *CompTIA Network+ (N10-009)* exam.

Exam objective 2.4

Explain important factors of physical installations

Important installation implications:

- **Locations**: Place equipment in an IDF/MDF for optimal connectivity and management:

    - **IDF**: Localized hub for network connections, close to user areas

    - **MDF**: Central hub for managing and distributing network connections

- **Rack size**: Choose appropriate racks for equipment fit, airflow, and expansion.

- **Port-side exhaust/intake**: Ensure proper airflow to prevent overheating of devices.

- **Cabling**: Use patch panels and fiber distribution panels for organized cabling:

    - **Patch panel**: Organizes and connects network cables for easy management

    - **Fiber distribution panel**: Manages and distributes fiber optic connections efficiently

- **Lockable components**: Secure network equipment with lockable racks and cabinets

Power:

- **UPS**: Provide backup power during outages
- **PDU**: Distribute power efficiently across network equipment
- **Power load**: Ensure the power load is balanced to avoid circuit overloads
- **Voltage**: Match correct voltage levels to protect equipment from damage

Environmental factors:

- **Humidity**: Control humidity levels to prevent corrosion and static damage
- **Fire suppression**: Install systems to protect equipment from fire hazards
- **Temperature**: Maintain optimal temperature to ensure network equipment longevity

Chapter review questions

Now that you've completed the chapter, you can check your knowledge using the practice questions provided in the online platform at `https://packt.link/N10-009ch12`. You can also use the QR code below. Accessing these questions requires you to unlock the accompanying online content first. Head over to Chapter 26 for detailed instructions.

Domain 3

Network Operations

This domain emphasizes the processes and tools used to maintain operational networks. It introduces documentation practices, life cycle and configuration management, monitoring technologies such as SNMP and SIEM, and disaster recovery planning. Candidates will also explore IPv4/IPv6 services, DNS, NTP, VPNs, and remote management methods, equipping them to ensure network availability, resilience, and recoverability.

This part of the book includes the following chapters:

- *Chapter 13, Explain the Purpose of Organizational Processes and Procedures*
- *Chapter 14, Given a Scenario, Use Network Monitoring Technologies*
- *Chapter 15, Explain Disaster Recovery (DR) Concepts*
- *Chapter 16, Given a Scenario, Implement IPv4 and IPv6 Network Services*
- *Chapter 17, Compare and Contrast Network Access and Management Methods*

13

Explain the Purpose of Organizational Processes and Procedures

In networking, as with any kind of engineering pursuit, the designing and building part is only part of the battle. Maintaining, troubleshooting, and scaling architecture is part of the core duties of a network engineer, but if you are working as part of a team or are working on a network someone else has built, then the lack of familiarity can cause challenges. This is why it is important to ensure the right documentation, processes, and procedures are in place. These structured approaches ensure consistency, reduce errors, and enable smooth operations.

Key elements of this include documentation, which provides clear records of physical and logical setups, network diagrams, asset inventories, **IP address** management, and service-level agreements. Life-cycle management ensures hardware and software are effectively maintained, updated, and decommissioned when outdated. Change management tracks and approves network modifications to avoid disruptions, while configuration management maintains current, backup, and baseline configurations for recovery and optimization. Together, these processes streamline network management, improve troubleshooting, and support long-term organizational success. In the following section, we will explain these components.

This chapter covers the first objective in *Domain 3: 3.1, Explain the purpose of organizational processes and procedures.*

Note

A full breakdown of objective 3.1 will be given at the end of the chapter.

Documentation

When it comes to networking, **documentation** is like having a map to navigate your IT environment. It helps you understand how everything is set up, so you can troubleshoot problems, make changes, or expand the network without getting lost. Think of it as a blueprint that ensures everyone working on the network knows what's happening, even if they're new to the team. Good documentation saves time, prevents errors, and makes maintaining a network much easier. In the following sections, we show different types of network documentation.

Physical diagrams versus logical diagrams

A **physical diagram** shows the actual hardware setup and what type of cables join it. It might, for example, be a map of your office showing where servers, routers, and switches are physically located, along with how they're connected by cables. If a device needs repair or replacement, you know exactly where to find it.

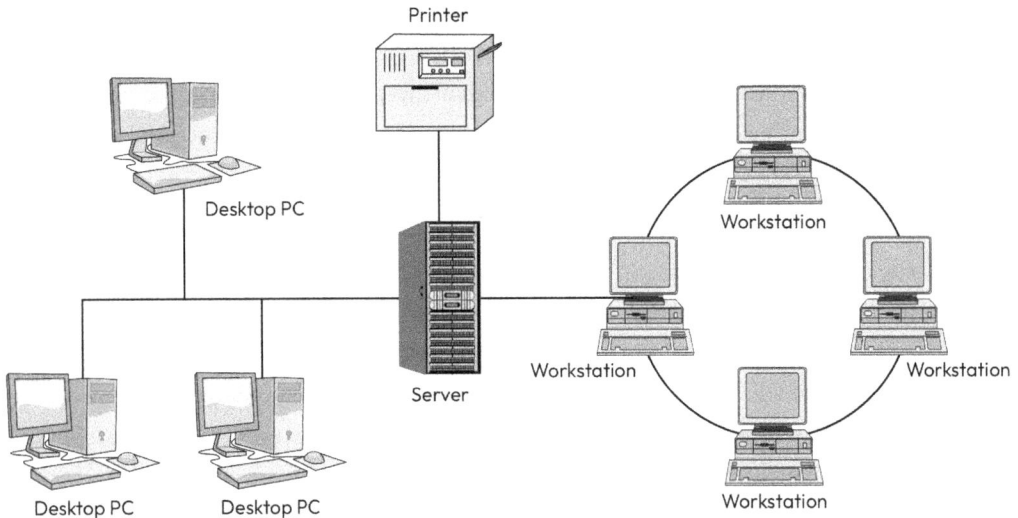

Figure 13.1: Physical network diagram

Figure 13.1 shows a server connected to a printer, a workstation ring, and three desktop PCs. The image can help an engineer work out which device should be physically connected to what.

A **logical diagram** shows how devices communicate rather than where they're located. For example, it might show that your laptop connects to a router, which then connects to the internet. It can aid in troubleshooting.

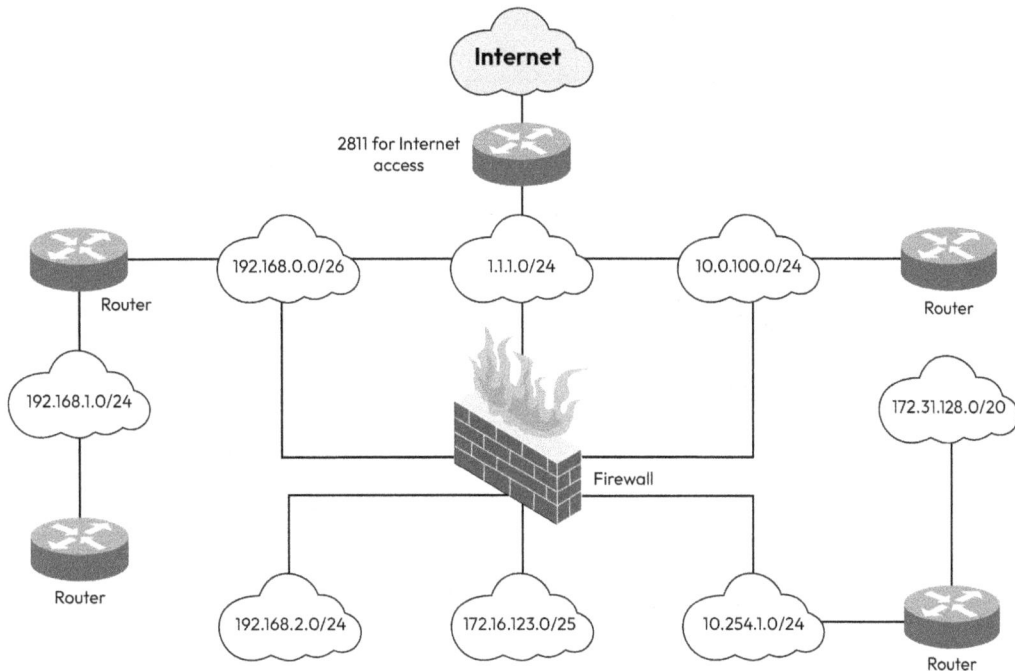

Figure 13.2: Logical network diagram

In *Figure 13.2*, you can see a network setup where multiple internal subnets are connected via routers, all protected by a central firewall, and accessing the internet through a designated router with an IP range for internet access. Subnets are represented by clouds and show the IP addresses for each one. This is useful when you need to check the security settings or scale up the network. It makes it easy to trace communication paths and isolate faults by understanding how different network segments are connected.

A **rack diagram** shows the devices installed in a rack with their location, including the names of devices, IP addresses, and VLAN addresses.

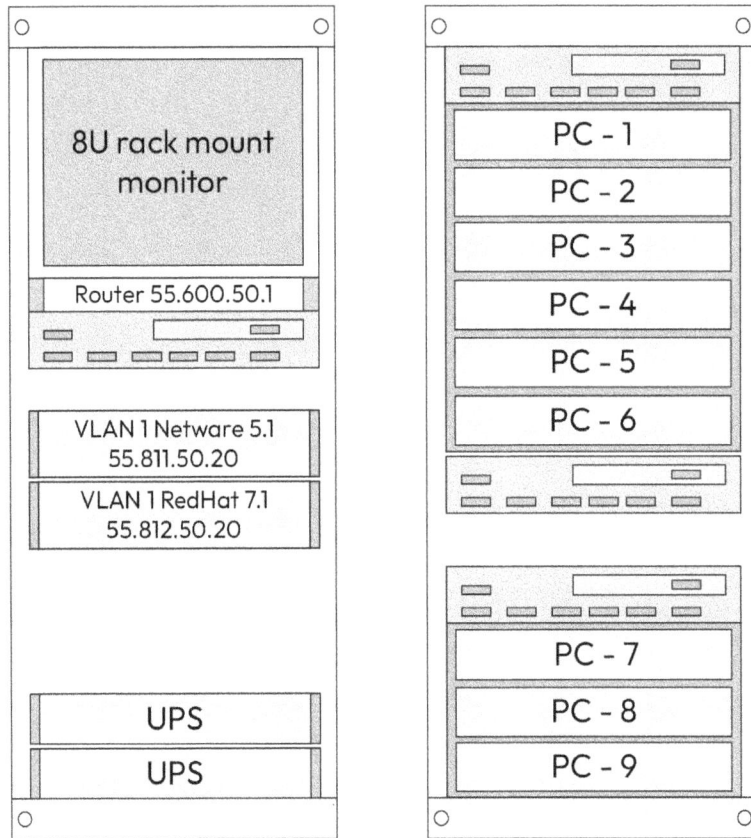

Figure 13.3: Rack diagram

Figure 13.3 shows a rack with a router, multiple VLANs, power supplies, and several connected PCs. Like the previous two diagrams, this visual representation of a rack is useful because it improves network visibility, simplifies management, and ensures efficient operations by clearly showing how devices are connected and organized.

Cable maps and diagrams also provide a visual representation of how devices are linked via cables. For instance, they might illustrate a cable connecting a computer to a wall port, passing through conduits to a patch panel, and then connecting to a switch in the server room. These diagrams are useful for identifying problems such as disconnected cables for organizing future installations efficiently. Cable types such as **twisted pairs** and **fiber optics** might be represented in different colors, helping to identify where each cable type is utilized.

Network diagrams

The **OSI** model, as covered in *Chapter 1*, helps break down the network into different layers of abstraction. This way of considering a network is incredibly useful in the troubleshooting process because it helps to narrow the type of issue (i.e., hardware) and configuration before you can start to pinpoint the exact issue. When looking into issues, it's often useful to refer to diagrams for the first three layers: **physical**, **data link**, and **network**. Creating and maintaining diagrams for each of these can help with ongoing maintenance and scaling of a network. *Figure 13.4* shows an example network diagram.

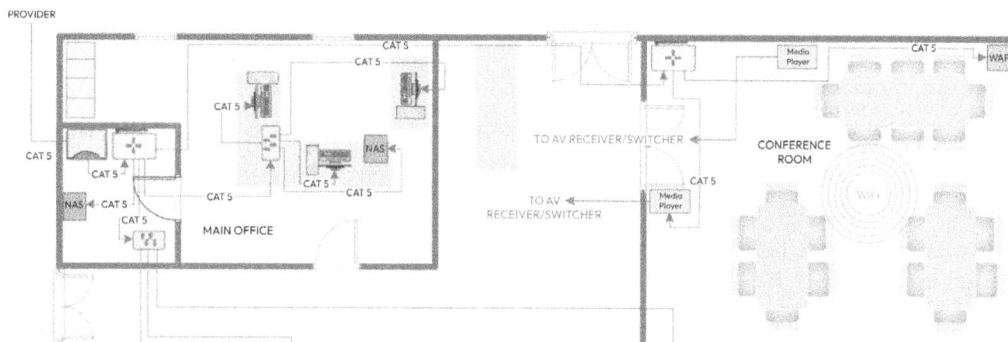

Figure 13.4: Sample section of a physical layer diagram

Layer 1 (physical layer) diagrams typically show cable connections and wall/patch panel/switch port labels. You should use color-coding or varying line styles to differentiate cable types, ensuring a legend accompanies the diagram to clarify the chosen scheme. For instance, you can use solid black lines for Ethernet cables, dashed blue lines for fiber optic cables, and solid green lines for coaxial cables. Additionally, label each cable connection to indicate the port number and termination points, so a line labeled "A1-P5" might indicate that wall jack A1 is connected to switch port 5.

Layer 2 (data link layer) illustrates the connections between switches and trunk links, highlighting asset identifiers (or the management IPs of the devices), interface IDs, link-layer protocols, and bandwidth details. Bandwidth can be represented using varying line thickness, but adding explicit labels is advised for clarity. Additionally, it is important to display VLANs and their corresponding VLAN IDs.

Layer 3 (network layer) shows the IP addressing and routing, detailing how devices interact across different networks. It includes the IP addresses of router interfaces, along with any static IP assignments, firewalls, and links that display the IP network ID, subnet mask, VLAN ID (if applicable), and DHCP scopes. This layer is essential for understanding how data flows between offices or across the internet.

Troubleshooting often starts from the lowest layer and moves upwards, using diagrams to check connections methodically. For example, a retail company faces network downtime at one of its stores, causing payment systems to fail. The IT team will check the layer 1 diagram to identify the connection between the store's switch and the data center and replace a faulty fiber cable. Once the cable is replaced, the issue persists, so they turn to the layer 2 diagram, which reveals a VLAN mismatch between the store's switch and the trunk port on the router. After correcting the VLAN tagging, some systems still cannot connect. Finally, the layer 3 diagram highlights a misconfigured static route on the router, preventing traffic from the store's subnet from reaching the payment gateway. By leveraging all three layers' diagrams, the team quickly resolves the issue, restoring network connectivity and minimizing revenue loss.

Using different diagrams is useful for general maintenance as it gives a quick, holistic reference to different parts of a network. It is important to maintain them, implementing any changes, so there is one source of truth for all network engineers, and any job handovers can be done smoothly. However, it is also important to understand the status of individual assets, such as cables and network devices, and this is done with an **asset inventory**, which we will cover in the next section.

Asset inventory

Knowing a network layout is important, but it's also important to consider the different individual components of a network. How old is each piece of equipment? When was it last maintained? How many of each device do you have in your network, and are there any missing?

An asset inventory involves meticulously tracking and managing all the hardware, software, licenses, and warranty details within an organization. Companies often invest hundreds of thousands or even millions of dollars in IT resources, making it essential to maintain an organized inventory to maximize value, reduce costs, and prevent misuse. Each asset is typically labeled with a unique asset tag – a barcode or identifier that allows for easy tracking, whether it is a laptop, server, or software license. The main assets are **hardware**, such as computers or physical routers; **software**, such as Microsoft 365; **licensing**, which controls the use of software; and **warranty support**.

Hardware

Hardware encompasses the tangible devices owned by a company, including computers, servers, networking equipment, and peripherals. Tracking these devices using asset tags ensures that every piece of equipment is accounted for, properly maintained, and deployed where needed. This is especially important because high-end hardware such as enterprise-grade servers or storage systems can cost tens of thousands of dollars each. Asset inventory helps prevent loss, streamline replacements, and avoid the unnecessary purchase of new equipment by reallocating existing resources effectively.

Software

Software includes all the applications and systems a company uses to perform tasks, ranging from productivity tools such as Microsoft 365 to specialized programs such as accounting or design software. Software inventory tracks details such as version numbers, installation locations, and associated asset tags. Companies often pay hundreds of dollars per user annually for software licenses, making it critical to ensure they are compliant and not overspending on unused licenses. Proper inventory helps identify which software is underutilized, enabling cost-saving decisions and preventing legal issues related to license overuse.

Licensing

Licensing is important to be recorded in an inventory. Software vendors often issue licenses that specify how many users or devices can access the software, and mismanaging these licenses can result in overpayments or fines for exceeding usage limits. By tracking licenses with asset tags and recording expiration dates, companies can ensure compliance, avoid unnecessary renewals, and optimize software use. For example, unused licenses for expensive enterprise software can quickly add up to hundreds of thousands of dollars annually in wasted costs if not managed effectively.

Warranty support

Warranty support ensures that hardware and software are covered for repairs or replacements within a specific period, saving companies significant repair costs. Asset tags are instrumental in tracking devices and warranties. For instance, a server under warranty could qualify for a free replacement part, avoiding a costly repair bill. Keeping this information up to date ensures companies fully utilize their warranties before they expire and helps plan for replacements after coverage ends.

IP address management

IP address management (IPAM) is a comprehensive toolset designed to help organizations effectively plan, deploy, manage, and monitor their IP address systems. It streamlines the process by automatically detecting IP address infrastructure and **DNS** servers on the network, providing centralized control through an intuitive interface, and ensuring optimal utilization of IP addresses.

> **Note**
>
> Microsoft has a web page that details the management of IPAM, which can be found at: https://learn.microsoft.com/en-us/windows-server/networking/technologies/ipam/manage-ipam

Service-level agreements (SLAs)

An **SLA** is a contractual arrangement between a service provider and a recipient that outlines the expected level of service. It defines specific metrics to measure service standards, response, or resolution times, and usually includes remedies or penalties for the provider if the agreed-upon service levels are unmet. An SLA might guarantee a 4-hour fix for critical server issues, holding the provider accountable for quick action. When a service desk receives a ticket, it must be prioritized according to its criticality and the amount of time to act in accordance with its SLA. Otherwise, the company must compensate the customer according to the penalties in the SLA.

Wireless survey

We've all been in situations where we've been trying to connect to a network from a device, and either the connection keeps dropping or is too weak to be useful. *Chapter 2, Compare and Contrast Networking Appliances, Applications, and Functions*, discusses how **APs** can be used to ensure full coverage across an office space. However, just placing wireless APs randomly is not enough; you need to find the "dead areas," or places without good coverage, to enable the best placement of APs. The best way to do this is by conducting a **wireless survey**.

A wireless survey, sometimes called a **site survey**, includes checking the building layout to spot obstacles and then designing and optimizing AP placement. If the wireless **SSID** is seen in some parts of the wireless network but not others, we must use a site survey and heat map to identify why there is not full coverage. The steps to complete a site survey are as follows:

1. **Review the layout**: Start by looking at the blueprints or floor plans of the building. These help you understand the layout and spot obstacles that might block or interfere with Wi-Fi signals, such as thick walls or metal objects.

2. **Conduct a visual check**: Walk around the space to spot anything not shown on the plans, such as metal shelves or other features that could cause signal problems. This helps ensure that even tricky spots get good coverage.

3. **Plan wireless AP placement**: Each AP needs to connect to the network through a network port and have power. This could be a separate power outlet or, more commonly, **PoE**, where the AP gets power through the same cable it uses for data. Knowing where these ports are located helps with planning.

4. **Design the network**: Create a plan that shows where each AP will go, along with the areas they cover, known as the **basic service areas** (**BSAs**). Place APs close enough to prevent dead zones but not so close that their signals interfere with each other.

5. **Optimize the setup**: Ensure APs are spaced so that no single AP is overloaded while others nearby are underused. This ensures an even distribution of devices and reliable performance across the network.

Once the APs are installed, or if you are checking an area that already has APs, it is useful to create a visual representation of the signal strengths. A **heat map** shows the signal strength by using colors to indicate the strength of the signal; areas shaded in red and orange typically represent strong signal coverage, while blue areas highlight weaker or non-existent coverage. These blues areas are in the top left corner. Weak spots like this might indicate issues such as misconfigured or malfunctioning wireless APs, which could be the root cause of the problem, as shown in *Figure 13.5*.

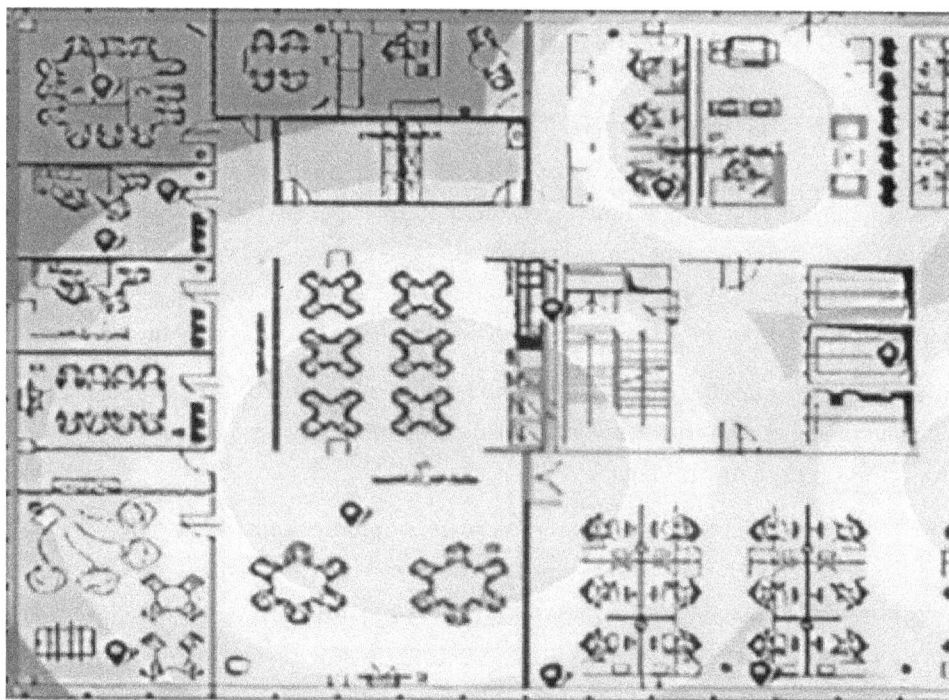

Wireless signal strength

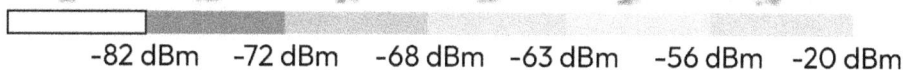

-82 dBm   -72 dBm   -68 dBm   -63 dBm   -56 dBm   -20 dBm

Figure 13.5: Heat map

In *Figure 13.5*, the center of the map and the top right show very strong signals, while the top left shows a very weak signal.

> **Note**
>
> You can find a color version of 13.5 at the following link: `https://packt.link/aLt82`

The process of documentation, including various mapping, SLAs, and IPAM, makes it easy to plan, maintain, and troubleshoot your network based on business requirements. In the rest of the chapter, you will look at other important processes, which are more focused on the handling of different devices and responding to the evolving needs of the network. **Life-cycle management** deals with the proper management of devices as they age through to the end of usage. **Change management** sets out the right way to deal with alterations to the network, and **configuration management** covers how devices should be set up.

Life-cycle management

As a network grows and becomes more complex, all assets, including network and IoT devices, risk becoming a breach point. Maintenance and monitoring of all devices should be proactive, ensuring that all equipment is optimized to work effectively and securely. Life-cycle management refers to the comprehensive process of overseeing a device, from installation to decommissioning. This includes regular patching to ensure all new security risks are mitigated and tracking.

Regular maintenance ensures that hardware and software remain functional, secure, and efficient throughout their use. Two critical stages are **end-of-life (EOL)** and **end-of-support (EOS)** – the device at this time is known as **legacy**.

When a product reaches EOL, the manufacturer ceases its production and sale. While the product may still function, it no longer receives updates or enhancements. The manufacturer will honor existing warranties and sell any spare parts that they have on their shelves. For instance, a software application at EOL will not get new features or improvements, and a hardware device will not get any upgrades.

EOS signifies that the manufacturer has stopped providing any type of support, and no warranties will be valid. If a device is EOS, you need to decommission the device and then purchase the latest version of the device, as it is insecure.

The key differences between EOL and EOS are that EOL focuses on the end of a product's production and sale, indicating no further development or new versions, while EOS pertains to the cessation of support services, meaning no more updates, patches, or technical assistance.

Continuing to use products past their EOS date can lead to security vulnerabilities, compatibility issues, and a lack of technical support. It is advisable to plan for replacements before reaching this stage to maintain security and efficiency.

Software management

Software also needs life-cycle management, and it is especially important to address weaknesses in software that can be exploited by malicious actors. Software management involves overseeing and maintaining various software components to ensure systems operate efficiently and securely by regularly applying **patches and bug fixes** provided by software vendors to resolve problems such as security vulnerabilities and software bugs or to improve features and functionality.

Operating systems such as Windows, macOS, and Linux require regular maintenance. Since they often interact directly with hardware and networks, they can present a significant attack surface. Vendors typically notify users about smaller updates, which should be applied regularly. However, larger system updates, such as upgrading to a completely new version, should be approached with caution – especially if you're running software or hardware that may not be compatible with the upgraded OS.

Firmware, the specialized software embedded in hardware devices, controlling their functions, should also be regularly updated, as it addresses vulnerabilities and introduces new features. It is essential for maintaining device security and performance.

Decommissioning

The **decommissioning** phase is the final stage in the life cycle of an asset. This phase involves the systematic removal, decommissioning, and disposal of assets that are no longer in use or have reached the end of their operational life. Proper disposal is crucial because it mitigates the risk of unauthorized access and data breaches and maintains regulatory compliance. It ensures that no residual data is left on any data drives, especially if the device was used to access classified data. Let's look at some aspects of disposal/decommissioning.

Destruction

Techniques such as incineration, pulverization, and degaussing (for magnetic media) render the media unusable. Destruction can be carried out by shredding or pulverizing, incineration, pulping, or crushing. The vendor carrying out the destruction will provide you with a destruction certificate.

Sanitization

Sanitization is a process that erases data while preserving the media for future use. For **hard disk drives** (**HDDs**), overwriting data multiple times with patterns of zeros, ones, and random data enhances security. Many drives support a **secure erase** (**SE**) command, which performs a thorough data wipe. For **solid state drives** (**SSDs**) and flash-based storage, traditional overwriting is less effective due to wear-leveling mechanisms. In such cases, invoking the SE command marks all blocks as empty, prompting the drive's firmware to erase data over time.

Change management

There will always be a need to make changes to a network, whether it involves upscaling as an organization grows, adjusting the architecture to meet evolving business requirements, or transitioning entirely, such as moving from on-premises to cloud infrastructure. Modern networking devices and techniques can make smaller network changes seamless, but for larger changes, it's essential to have a well-defined process to minimize downtime, prevent data loss, and avoid chaos.

For example, an organization may wish to set up a new VLAN to segment network traffic for the Finance department, aiming to enhance security and optimize performance. Without a formal process, there may be IP address conflicts if the VLAN's IP range overlaps with an existing VLAN. The VLAN might also be created without adequately updating firewall rules and **access control lists** (**ACLs**). If the change is not scheduled correctly, it could result in downtime during peak areas, and if stakeholders are not informed, it could result in an increase in helpdesk requests as users are not able to connect to the older network. Finally, without a rollback plan, any errors during setup might take hours or even days to fix.

To avoid these scenarios, it's important to have **change management** processes for major changes to an IT environment. Change management involves a series of steps to ensure that modifications to IT systems are introduced smoothly and effectively. This includes planning, testing, implementing, and reviewing changes to maintain system integrity and performance. A critical change management component is the request process tracking or service request system. This system allows IT teams to manage and document change requests systematically.

A typical change management process will be as follows:

1. **Submission**: A user or stakeholder submits a change request detailing the desired modification, outlining the costs and any savings to be made.

2. **Review**: A **change advisory board** (**CAB**), which is responsible for considering and approving changes, evaluates the request to assess its feasibility, potential impact, and alignment with organizational goals.

3. **Approval:** Authorized personnel approve or reject the request based on the review findings.

4. **Implementation:** If approved, the change is planned, tested, and implemented in a controlled manner.

5. **Documentation:** All steps and outcomes are documented for future reference and accountability.

Change management should consider the impact of change, stakeholders and other affected people, and risks. There should also be back-out plans in case the change throws up issues that were unforeseen, and there is a need to roll back to the original setup quickly.

It's also useful to have a process when dealing with changes or assistance requested by people in your organization. This is called service request management and is described next.

Service request management is a structured approach to handling user-initiated requests for services, information, or assistance. This process ensures that requests are addressed efficiently, consistently, and in accordance with SLAs, helping maintain the quality and reliability of IT services.

While **service request management** primarily deals with standard, low-risk tasks (such as password resets or software installations), tracking the request process improves visibility and accountability. It allows IT teams to monitor performance, identify trends, and optimize response times.

However, tasks involving system configuration changes or environment alterations typically fall under change management or configuration management, which include more rigorous evaluation and risk assessment steps.

Configuration management

The section on the life-cycle management of devices stressed the importance of regular monitoring of devices, especially patching, to ensure security. In fact, the configuration of a device is as important as the device itself. Poorly configured **firewalls**, for instance, are security risks if the traffic rules are not kept up to date. If the quality of service and VLAN configurations are inconsistent across routers, data bottlenecks can occur, severely slowing down your network. By employing good **configuration management** processes, you can not only help the security of the system but can also increase the efficiency of upscaling or adapting your network. There are some key aspects to configuration management, including **production configuration**, **backup configuration**, and **baseline** or **golden configuration**.

Production configuration refers to the active setup of a system or application that is in use and producing the desired output. It includes all settings, software versions, and hardware components that are operational. For example, an e-commerce site might operate a live website that handles thousands of customer transactions daily. The production configuration would include all the settings, software, and hardware that enable the website to function seamlessly. So, the frontend might use **React.js version 17.0.2**, and the website might be hosted on **AWS** with **EC2** instances in a load-balanced cluster.

Production configuration for on-premises setups would also include the settings of network devices; for instance, if a switch needs to be replaced, the new one would have to be set up with the current production configuration to work perfectly in that specific environment. Managing the production configuration involves monitoring and documenting any changes to ensure the system runs smoothly and meets user needs.

A backup configuration is a saved copy of the system's settings and data at a specific point in time. These backups are crucial for recovery, enabling IT professionals to restore the system to a prior state in cases of failure. This could be a device breaking down or needing to be replaced, or a cyber attack that reconfigures a firewall to allow malicious actors to access the network. As mentioned earlier, backup configurations are also important if changes to the network are being made, in case the change doesn't go to plan, or turns out to be worse than the original configuration.

The baseline or golden configuration is a reference point representing a system's optimal and approved state. It serves as a standard for comparison when assessing changes or updates. Establishing a baseline helps in identifying deviations, managing updates, and ensuring that the system remains aligned with organizational standards and requirements.

Summary

This chapter covered the processes and tools used to maintain, troubleshoot, and scale network infrastructures. Proper documentation, including physical, logical, rack, and cable diagrams, is important for planning and maintenance. Asset inventories, IP address management, and SLA agreements also help to maintain a healthy network. Wireless surveys and heat maps are used to optimize AP placement, mitigating weak signal areas.

Life-cycle management for hardware, software, and firmware includes EOS and EOL. Change management processes help to plan, approve, implement, and document network changes to reduce risks and disruptions. Service request management helps to handle standard user requests, while configuration management focuses on maintaining production, backup, and baseline configurations to ensure operational stability, security, and efficiency.

The knowledge gained in this chapter will prepare you to answer questions relating to Exam objective 3.1 in your *CompTIA Network+ (N10-009) exam*.

Exam objective 3.1

Explain the purpose of organizational processes and procedures

Documentation: Records network designs, setups, and inventory for clarity and troubleshooting.

- **Physical diagrams**: Show actual hardware layout and physical connections.
- **Logical diagrams**: Illustrate data flow and virtual connections between devices.
- **Rack diagrams**: Visualize equipment placement in server racks.
- **Cable maps and diagrams**: Show how devices are physically connected.
- **Network diagrams**: Show how the network is mapped out.

    - **Layer 1**: Illustrate physical device connections.
    - **Layer 2**: Highlight switches and VLAN communications.
    - **Layer 3**: Show IP routing between different networks.

- **Asset inventory**: Tracks all assets

    - **Hardware**: Tracks physical devices such as servers and switches.
    - **Software**: Monitors installed applications and tools.
    - **Licensing**: Ensures proper use of licensed software.
    - **Warranty support**: Tracks repair and replacement coverage.

- **IP address management (IPAM)**: Manages and organizes IP address allocations.
- **Service-level agreement (SLA)**: Defines performance expectations with service providers.
- **Wireless survey/heat map**: Visualizes signal strength and wireless coverage.

Life-cycle management: Manages hardware/software from purchase to decommissioning.

- **End-of-life (EOL)**: When equipment or software is no longer sold.
- **End-of-support (EOS)**: When vendor support is no longer available.
- **Software Management**

    - **Patches and bug fixes**: Regular updates to fix bugs and improve security.
    - **Operating system**: Updates to keep systems running efficiently and securely.
    - **Firmware**: Updates for device firmware improvements.

- **Decommissioning**: Safely retiring outdated hardware or software.

Change management: Tracks and approves network updates to avoid disruptions.

- **Request process tracking**: Logs and manages requests for network changes.

Configuration management: Maintains and backs up network device settings for reliability.

- **Production configuration**: Current settings actively used in the network.

- **Backup configuration**: Stored copies of settings for recovery purposes.

- **Baseline/golden configuration**: Ideal reference configuration for consistency and troubleshooting.

Chapter review questions

Now that you've completed the chapter, you can check your knowledge using the practice questions provided in the online platform at `https://packt.link/N10-009ch13`. You can also use the QR code below. Accessing these questions requires you to unlock the accompanying online content first. Head over to Chapter 26 for detailed instructions.

14

Given a Scenario, Use Network Monitoring Technologies

Even the best-designed networks will run into issues at some point. Equipment will break, there will be security attacks, or unexpected demand might create traffic bottlenecks. Knowing what to do when this happens is important, but it is also important to know when it is happening. Issues that go unnoticed can lead to a loss of productivity or customers, increased security weaknesses, and expensive emergency fixes.

Knowing how to use the right network monitoring technologies is essential for the performance, security, and reliability of your network. The methods and tools covered in this chapter include enabling real-time traffic analysis, device management, and anomaly detection through methods such as **SNMP**, log aggregation, and packet capture. We'll cover advanced solutions such as baseline metrics, port mirroring, and **API integration** that streamline monitoring, while network discovery, traffic analysis, and performance tracking ensure comprehensive oversight. Together, these technologies help identify issues, optimize operations, and ensure compliance across diverse network environments. In the following section, we will outline how SNMP works.

This chapter covers the second objective in *Domain 3: 3.2, Given a scenario, use network monitoring technologies.*

> **Note**
> A full breakdown of objective 3.2 will be given at the end of the chapter.

Methods

Depending on the scenario, different methods and technologies are used for monitoring a network. For example, you may wish to understand how different components, such as **routers** and **switches**, are functioning or determine whether the flow of data through the network is as expected. Alternatively, you might need to inspect individual packets to identify potential threats or diagnose why specific devices are experiencing high packet loss.

Common methods for network monitoring include SNMP, which monitors and manages network devices by gathering data such as device status, bandwidth utilization, and error rates, and **flow data**, which provides insights into traffic patterns and detects anomalies such as spikes in bandwidth or unauthorized transfers. **Packet capture** analyzes individual data packets to identify threats, troubleshoot connectivity issues, or resolve performance bottlenecks, while baseline metrics establish normal performance levels to detect deviations that signal potential problems. **Log aggregation** consolidates logs from various devices to identify patterns and correlate events, and API integration allows tools to share data and streamline monitoring processes through automation.

The following sections will look at these technologies.

SNMP

While various technologies provide raw data from different parts of a network, allowing engineers to monitor activity across devices, tracking all this information manually becomes challenging in large networks. Instead of constantly checking individual values on different devices, using a system that monitors components and sends alerts when issues arise is more efficient – and often more accurate. SNMP is a protocol specifically designed for this purpose. It provides statuses and reports on network devices by using a **management information base** (**MIB**), which is detailed next.

An MIB is like a dictionary that helps manage devices on a network. It works with the SNMP to turn network events into information that people can understand. This makes it easier for network engineers to monitor and manage devices.

The MIB lists all the things, known as **objects**, that can be watched or controlled on the network – for example, routers, switches, and printers. Each object has a unique ID, similar to a name tag, called an **object identifier** (**OID**). The SNMP uses the OIDs to recognize the device, and it helps network administrators check the health of devices and fix problems more easily.

The SNMP works using software components that run on network devices, such as routers, switches, servers, or printers, called **SNMP agents**. These agents exchange information about the devices' statuses and performance with a central monitoring system called an **SNMP manager**, which is made up of management software and **network management systems (NMSs)**. Metrics, such as bandwidth usage, errors, and uptime, are defined in the MIB. SNMP agents can be set up to send alerts, called **traps**, when something unusual happens, such as hardware failure or high network usage. Each data point within the MIB is associated with an OID, functioning as a unique address for that information.

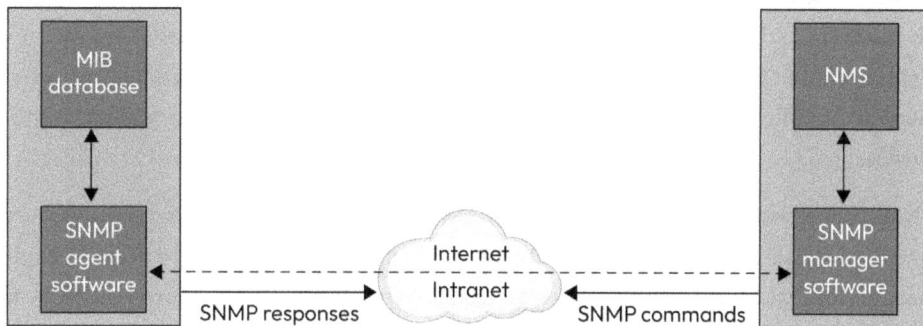

Agent devices (routers, switches, etc)   SNMP manager

Figure 14.1: SNMP components

In *Figure 14.1*, you can see an example of SNMP architecture. On the left is SNMP agent software, which connects to the MIB database, and on the right is the NMS and SNMP management software, which is the control center. The whole system works on the network, which could be an intranet or the internet.

SNMP can be a proactive guard against issues that cause outages. For instance, you may have a corporate network with multiple devices, including routers, switches, servers, printers, and workstations. If a switch port goes down or a router experiences high CPU usage, the SNMP agent on the device sends a trap to the SNMP manager, notifying the IT team. The SNMP manager can also be set up so that it can flag issues such as unusually high network traffic. If this is flagged up on a router interface, for example, a network engineer can investigate the issue by querying detailed SNMP data, such as the source and destination of the traffic.

While SNMP is a powerful protocol, it has limitations. It can be chatty, meaning it can send too much data, consuming bandwidth in large networks. **SNMPv1** and **SNMPv2c** lack strong security, making them unsuitable for sensitive environments.

SNMP versions

Over time, SNMP has evolved, with newer versions offering better security and functionality:

- SNMPv2c is currently the most widely used version. It includes basic security through community strings (shared passwords), but it's not very secure. It uses UDP port 161.

- **SNMPv3** adds strong authentication and encryption, making it more secure. It ensures that only authorized users can access or modify the data. It uses UDP port 162.

For authentication, SNMP uses **community strings**, which are passwords that control access to devices. The default for read-only is `public`, and the default for read-write is `private`. Leaving the defaults as they are can lead to a security risk, as an intruding agent that knows the common default will be able to see network configurations. With read-only access attackers can see device/network details, but with read-write access, attackers can reconfigure or disrupt the network device.

SNMPv3 authentication ensures that the data being exchanged comes from a trusted source. It uses user credentials and encryption to protect the information. For example, a network engineer may be monitoring a router using an SNMP manager. When the CPU usage surpasses 90%, the SNMP agent on the router sends a notification, known as a trap, to the SNMP manager. This prompts the IT administrator to take action, such as optimizing network traffic, to avert a possible outage.

Flow data

While SNMP excels at monitoring the performance and health of individual devices in a network, it is equally important to understand the movement of data across the network. For example, SNMP can alert you when a device is experiencing high traffic or nearing capacity. However, flow monitoring tools such as **NetFlow** go a step further by providing detailed insights into the traffic itself, revealing where the data is coming from, where it is going, and even the type of data being transmitted.

Flow data provides information about how data moves through a network. It is made up of key details, such as where the data is coming from, where it is going, and how much data is being sent. Importantly, flow data does not capture the actual traffic content, making it a lightweight and privacy-friendly way to monitor network activity.

NetFlow, created by **Cisco**, is an advanced technology designed to collect and analyze flow data, enabling effective monitoring and evaluation of network traffic. It has since evolved into an industry standard known as **IP Flow Information Export** (**IPFIX**), making it accessible for devices from various manufacturers. NetFlow defines a "traffic flow" based on common attributes, such as the source and destination **IP addresses** and the type of protocol (e.g., HTTP or FTP). These shared characteristics, referred to as keys, are used to group packets into flow labels. Traffic matching a specific flow label is recorded as a flow record, which can then be exported and analyzed.

For example, an office worker is accessing a website that is being monitored by NetFlow. As the user's device communicates with the website, the router processes multiple packets for this session as follows.

- **Source IP Address**: 192.168.1.10 (user's device)
- **Destination IP Address**: 203.0.113.5 (web server)
- **Source Port**: 56789 (ephemeral port on the user's device)
- **Destination Port**: 443 (HTTPS traffic)
- **Protocol**: TCP
- **Type of Service (ToS)**: 0x10 (for quality of service)
- **Input Interface**: Where the packet enters the Cisco device

Every packet with the preceding key will be given a single flow label by the router that has been configured using NetFlow. The router stores records based on the label, which includes the number of packets, the amount of information transferred in bytes, start and end times, and the duration of the flow. These records are then transferred to a central monitoring tool and can be analyzed by a network administrator.

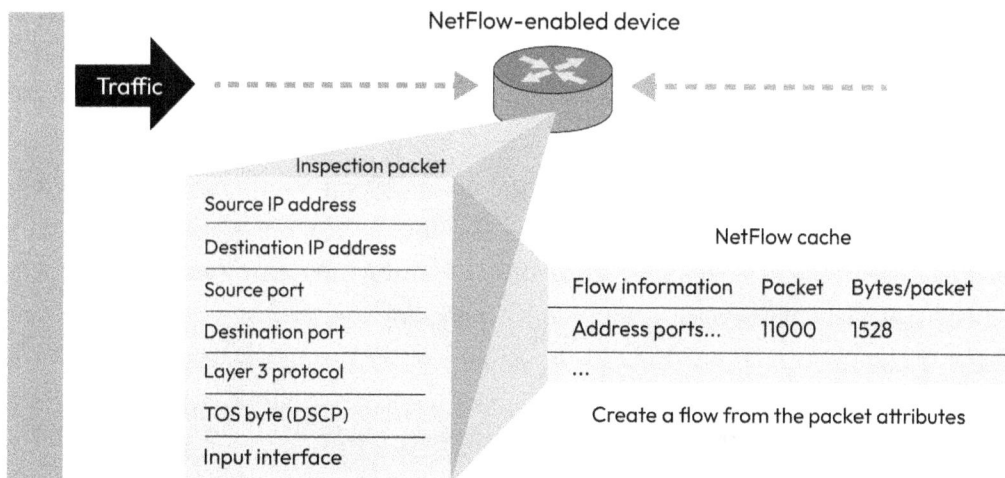

Figure 14.2: Creating a flow label

A **NetFlow analyzer** can transform this data into meaningful insights, such as identifying the top bandwidth users, tracking traffic trends, and spotting potential bottlenecks. This capability is particularly useful for troubleshooting network issues, planning for future capacity needs, and ensuring efficient network operations.

One of the significant benefits of NetFlow is its ability to detect anomalies in traffic patterns. For example, it can identify unusual spikes in data usage, which may indicate a security threat, such as a denial-of-service attack. By providing alerts to the network team, NetFlow ensures quick responses to potential problems. Additionally, it can help identify applications consuming more network bandwidth than usual, allowing administrators to address performance issues or optimize usage.

While NetFlow was initially designed for Cisco devices, the adoption of the **IPFIX** standard allows similar functionality across multi-vendor environments.

Packet capture

NetFlow can provide many insights into how data flows through a network, but it's kind of like examining a crowd from a high vantage point. You can see where people are going and where they came from, and even identify bottlenecks. However, sometimes you need to know who the individual people are – for example, if you believe there are thieves in the area. Similarly, you may need to know more details about a data packet, such as the protocol or the payload.

Packet capture is the process of looking at individual packets as they travel through the network. Packet capture tools are known as **packet sniffers** or **protocol analyzers**, common examples of which are **Wireshark**, the Linux-based **tcpdump** and the Windows-based **WinDump**, which is fully compatible with tcpdump. These tools perform **traces**, which are detailed records of packets captured on a network.

An example of packet capturing is troubleshooting why a user did not receive an IP address from a **DHCP server** that automates IP address allocation. Automatically allocating an IP address is done by the exchange of four packets: **DHCP Discover**, **DHCP Offer**, **DHCP Request**, and **DHCP Acknowledgement**. If the cybersecurity administrator only sees the first packet but no second packet, they know there is a problem with the DHCP server; for example, it may have run out of IP addresses to allocate, or there is a network connectivity problem. For troubleshooting purposes, you would install Wireshark on the client and the server.

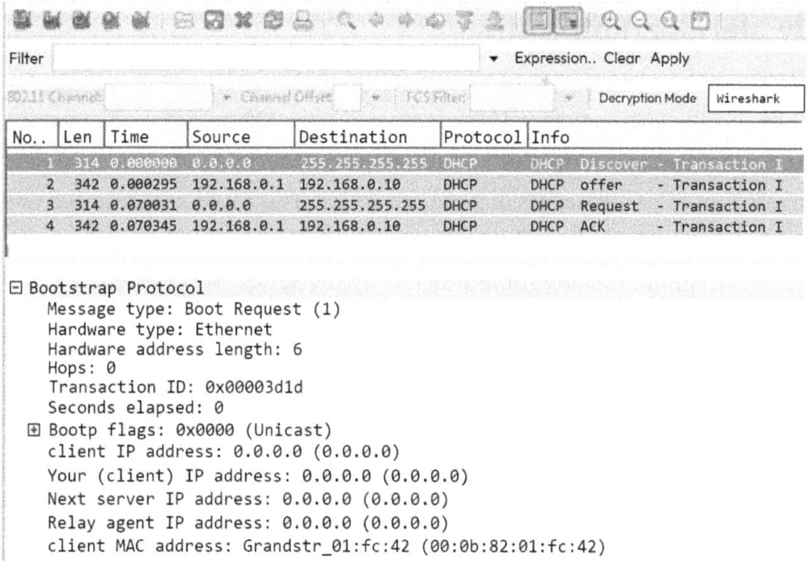

No..	Len	Time	Source	Destination	Protocol	Info
1	314	0.000000	0.0.0.0	255.255.255.255	DHCP	DHCP Discover - Transaction I
2	342	0.000295	192.168.0.1	192.168.0.10	DHCP	DHCP offer - Transaction I
3	314	0.070031	0.0.0.0	255.255.255.255	DHCP	DHCP Request - Transaction I
4	342	0.070345	192.168.0.1	192.168.0.10	DHCP	DHCP ACK - Transaction I

```
⊟ Bootstrap Protocol
      Message type: Boot Request (1)
      Hardware type: Ethernet
      Hardware address length: 6
      Hops: 0
      Transaction ID: 0x00003d1d
      Seconds elapsed: 0
  ⊞ Bootp flags: 0x0000 (Unicast)
      client IP address: 0.0.0.0 (0.0.0.0)
      Your (client) IP address: 0.0.0.0 (0.0.0.0)
      Next server IP address: 0.0.0.0 (0.0.0.0)
      Relay agent IP address: 0.0.0.0 (0.0.0.0)
      client MAC address: Grandstr_01:fc:42 (00:0b:82:01:fc:42)
```

Figure 14.3: DHCP handshake

> **Note**
>
> DHCP is introduced in *Chapter 4, Explain Common Networking Ports, Protocols, Services, and Traffic Types.*

Baseline metrics

The three network monitoring techniques mentioned so far – SNMP, packet capture, and flow data – all have different uses. SNMP provides information on the performance of individual devices. Flow data is used to monitor and analyze traffic patterns. Packet capture is used to identify specific issues, such as application-layer problems, security breaches, or protocol errors.

To be able to identify anomalies, or deviations from normal values, an administrator needs to understand what normal values are in the first place. These normal performance indicators are called **baseline metrics**. They quantify typical network activity under normal conditions, such as bandwidth usage, latency, and server response times.

Establishing baselines allows you to know what is normal and healthy for your network. It makes it easier to identify unusual activity that could signal issues such as a system failure or a security breach.

Anomaly alerting/notification

For example, if your baseline shows 30% CPU usage during regular business hours but suddenly spikes to 90%, it indicates that something is wrong. This 90% usage is an anomaly, and with monitoring tools, you can set up **alerts** to notify your security team immediately of unusual activity, ensuring prompt awareness of potential issues. This proactive approach allows you to address problems such as cyberattacks, hardware failures, or misconfigured systems before they escalate, helping to minimize downtime and improve overall network reliability.

Take a network that usually handles 500 connections per second and suddenly jumps to 5,000; an alert might notify you of a possible **DDoS** attack. A jump from 500 to 5,000 obviously needs attention, but what about a jump to 1,000? What about a jump to 600? If the monitor reacted every time connections jumped to 600, this might mean too many alerts for standard traffic fluctuations. However, if the alert is not set low enough, a doubling of traffic, which could indicate an issue, might be missed.

The process of deciding what levels alerts should be set at is called **alert tuning**. It is the process of adjusting and refining alerts to ensure they are meaningful and actionable, avoiding unnecessary distractions or missing critical alerts. In other words, alert tuning is essential to avoid **false positives** and **false negatives**. A false positive is when the monitoring system thinks that an event has occurred when manual inspection reveals that no event has occurred. With a false negative, the monitoring system does not know that an event is happening, but manual inspection detects the event. This means the monitoring system might need an update. Although not alerting when there is an issue means you might not catch critical issues, too many alerts can cause **alert fatigue**, which means you get too used to alerts, or you may have too many to analyze and might miss problems due to the large volume of alerts.

One useful technique is, instead of setting simple values, you can calibrate monitoring systems to measure a second metric, such as time. For instance, rather than sending alerts for every minor bandwidth fluctuation, you could configure alerts to only trigger when bandwidth usage exceeds 80% for more than 10 minutes.

Log aggregation

As your system monitors the network, records or logs will be kept at all levels, from individual agents to whole networks. Records can be kept when someone logs in, when a file is accessed, or when there's an error or a problem. When a device or a system crashes, logs can show unusual activity, such as someone trying to hack into the system. It can be especially helpful if it is no longer possible to pull details from the system or device.

> **Note**
>
> Some industries, such as healthcare or finance, require keeping logs to meet legal or regulatory standards.

Log aggregation is important because it collects logs from different systems, devices, and applications into one central location. This makes it much easier to manage and analyze the data. Instead of searching through logs on each individual device, IT teams can quickly find problems, identify unusual activity, and respond to security threats more efficiently. It saves time, improves security, and helps keep everything organized.

Two tools that are used for log aggregation are **Syslog** and **security information and event management (SIEM)**.

Syslog

Syslog is a standardized protocol used by systems and network devices to send log messages to a central server, known as a Syslog collector. This collector receives, stores, and organizes logs, enabling IT teams to monitor, analyze, and troubleshoot systems from a single location. Think of it like a central mailbox that gathers status updates and alerts in the form of logs from every device in the network.

Each syslog message includes important metadata, such as facility (the source of the message) and severity level (how critical the message is). These two elements combine to form a priority value, which helps systems categorize and filter logs efficiently. Syslog collectors can be configured to filter incoming messages based on their priority, ensuring that only relevant or critical events are stored or acted upon.

The structure of a typical Syslog message includes the following components:

- **PRI code**: This is a number that represents the type of event **(facility)** and how important it is **(severity level)**.
- **Header**: This includes details such as the timestamp (when the event happened) and the hostname (which device sent the message).
- **Message**: This contains a **tag** that identifies the source of the event (e.g., which application or process) and content describing what happened. This format depends on the application and might use spaces, commas, or key-value pairs.

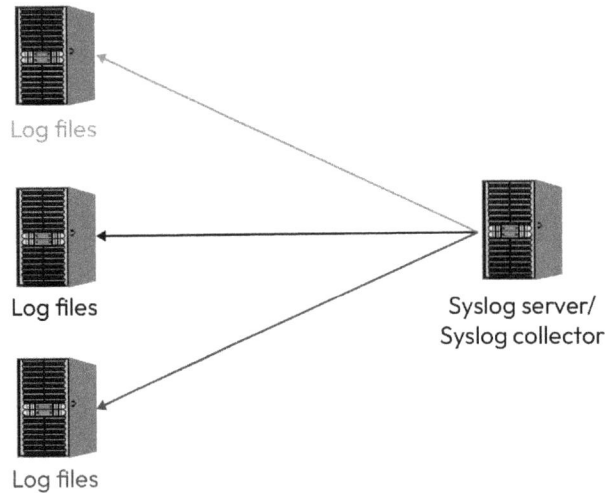

Figure 14.4: Syslog server

Syslog severity levels help prioritize logs since thousands of events can occur daily. Each level has a number (from 0 to 7) and describes the urgency:

0 – Emergency: The system is unusable (e.g., complete failure)

1 – Alert: Action must be taken immediately (e.g., database unavailable)

2 – Critical: Critical condition (e.g., hardware failure)

3 – Error: Non-urgent error (e.g., application crash)

4 – Warning: Something is wrong but not critical (e.g., disk nearing full capacity)

5 – Notice: Normal but significant events (e.g., configuration changes)

6 – Informational: General information about system operations (e.g., user login)

7 – Debug: Detailed diagnostic information used by developers for troubleshooting

To illustrate these levels, let's consider a company's web server and the different severity levels.

0 – Emergency:

    Event: The web server is completely down, and the website is inaccessible.

    Example log message: `EMERGENCY: Web server unavailable! Immediate action required.`

    Action: IT teams must act immediately to restore the server.

1 – Alert:

Event: The database supporting the website is unresponsive.

Example log message: `ALERT: Database connection failed. Unable to retrieve data.`

Action: Fix the database issue right away before it affects customers.

2 – Critical:

Event: The server's CPU is overheating and might cause hardware failure.

Example log message: `CRITICAL: CPU temperature exceeds safe limits.`

Action: Investigate and resolve before the hardware is damaged.

3 – Error:

Event: A software application crashed, but the system is still running.

Example log message: `ERROR: Application 'Payment Gateway' failed unexpectedly.`

Action: Restart the application and check logs for the cause.

4 – Warning:

Event: The disk space on the server is at 90% capacity.

Example log message: `WARNING: Disk space is running low (90% used).`

Action: Free up space or add more storage before it causes problems.

5 – Notice:

Event: A new admin user was added to the server.

Example log message: `NOTICE: Admin user 'JohnDoe' created successfully.`

Action: Log the event for security and compliance records.

6 – Informational:

Event: A user logged into the server successfully.

Example log message: `INFO: User 'JaneDoe' logged in at 2:00 PM.`

Action: No immediate action—this is just recorded for tracking.

7 – Debug:

> **Event**: The server is generating detailed logs about its internal processes for troubleshooting.
>
> **Example log message**: DEBUG: Process ID 1234 started successfully.
>
> **Action**: Use these logs for developers to debug issues.

SIEM

Like syslog, SIEM is a system designed to assist IT and security teams in monitoring and safeguarding networks in real time. SIEM tools are services or applications, hardware or software, or even cloud-based solutions, that combine security information management and **security event management** (**SEM**). They gather data, including logs and events, from various devices and systems across the network, such as firewalls, antivirus programs, routers, switches, servers, and applications. SIEM acts as a central hub, gathering this information using protocols such as SNMP, HTTP, or **Windows Management Instrumentation** (**WMI**), ensuring that every system and device is monitored. It works by collecting data, aggregating it, sending real-time alerts, and generating reports.

- **Data collection**: A SIEM system will gather data from various sources, such as end user devices, services, and wireless **APs**; applications on servers and the cloud; security systems; firewalls; routers and switches; and security software. This data collection is achieved either through agents installed on hosts to collect and forward data or by configuring hosts to send data directly to the centralized SIEM manager.

- **Correlation/aggregation**: Once the data is collected, the SIEM system organizes and combines it in a process called data aggregation. This step ensures that duplicate entries are removed, and the information is cleaned up to provide a clear picture of what's happening on the network. For example, if multiple systems report the same event, the SIEM combines those reports into one entry, making it easier to understand without being overwhelmed by repeated messages.

  The most powerful feature of SIEM is its ability to analyze and correlate data from multiple sources. By finding connections between seemingly unrelated events, the SIEM can detect patterns that indicate potential security issues. For example, it could detect a failed login attempt from an unexpected location, followed by unauthorized attempts to access sensitive files and, subsequently, a significant data transfer. These individual events might seem harmless on their own, but when analyzed together, they could indicate a cyberattack. This correlation ability allows SIEM to spot threats that would be difficult for humans to detect manually.

- **Alerts:** When a SIEM system detects unusual behavior or a potential threat, it generates alerts to notify the security team, enabling them to take prompt action. In some cases, it can even trigger automated responses, such as blocking an IP address or disabling a compromised account.

- **Reports:** In addition to real-time alerts, SIEM generates detailed reports and visual graphs that help security teams investigate incidents and understand the overall health of the network. These reports are also useful for meeting compliance requirements and preparing for audits, and can be archived.

- SIEM systems are complex to set up and require a lot of calibration and maintenance. They are primarily focused on security monitoring for large networks because it works by correlating different data points in real time and thus detecting security threats. For example, a SIEM system could detect a significant spike in outbound traffic from a server outside of normal business hours, along with multiple failed login attempts on the same server, originating from various global IP addresses. The SIEM would then flag a correlation between this activity and known malicious IP addresses listed in threat intelligence feeds.

Application programming interface (API) integration

An API is a bridge that allows different software programs to talk to each other. Instead of manually moving data between tools or systems, the API lets them share information and perform actions automatically. For example, if one system needs to get data from another or tell it to do something – such as running a scan or checking settings – the API makes that possible behind the scenes. This saves time, reduces errors, and helps systems work together smoothly.

It allows you to safely control access, manage systems from a distance, and keep activity logs, which makes it great for monitoring networks.

Example 1

A company uses the network monitoring tool **Cisco Meraki**. Through its API, the IT team can do the following:

- Securely control who can access different parts of the network
- Remotely manage devices such as routers and switches from anywhere
- Log activities to track network usage and detect issues

This helps the company keep its network running smoothly – even when the IT team isn't on-site. It is useful to have a way for these tools to work together to share data and reports. Through API integration, one system can access the functions or data of another system using automated scripts.

Example 2

A configuration monitoring tool can have an API that lets a security system (such as a SIEM) do things such as starting a scan, getting the results, and using that data right away. This makes it easier for different systems to work together and share information automatically.

Port mirroring

While summarized data from **SIEM systems**, or even multiple monitoring tools joined by APIs, can alert you to large systematic threats or failures, there are often instances when you need to look at what is happening at a certain point of your network at a granular level. As discussed earlier in the chapter, packet capture can give important insights into the actual data passing through a system. However, in a large network, how can a tool performing packet capture know where to look? **Port mirroring** is a technique that works by creating a copy of the data, or traffic, passing through one port of a switch and sending that copy to another port where a monitoring tool, such as a network analyzer or security system, is connected, as shown in *Figure 14.5*.

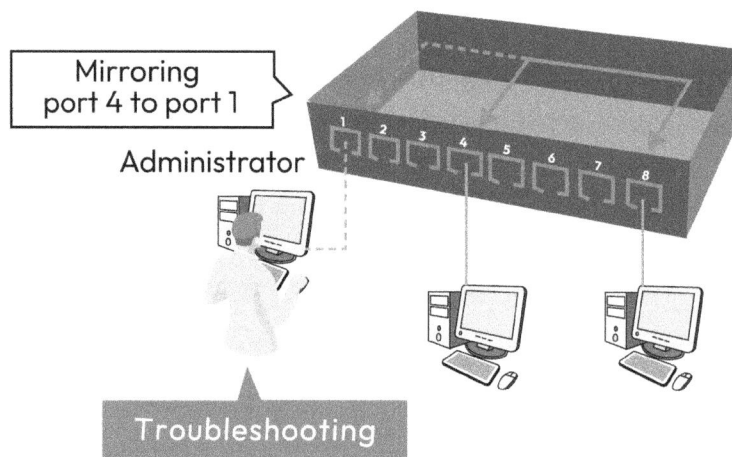

Figure 14.5: Port mirroring

Port mirroring relies on the switch's CPU to create a copy of all traffic flow, which can create performance issues, especially under high traffic loads. This might cause the switch to drop packets during high traffic loads or due to switch limitations. Although **application-specific integrated circuits (ASICs)** can help to reduce the load on the CPU, they cannot eliminate the risks of performance degradation.

The solution to this is a **test access point** (TAP), which is a hardware device that is plugged into a network at a specific point and creates a passive copy of all data passing through, which can then be transferred to a network monitoring tool. TAPs ensure uninterrupted monitoring without affecting the network's performance or introducing noticeable latency, so they're often used in high-security environments. For example, you could place the TAP between the router and the switch to monitor incoming traffic. *Figure 14.6* shows a TAP.

TAP placement

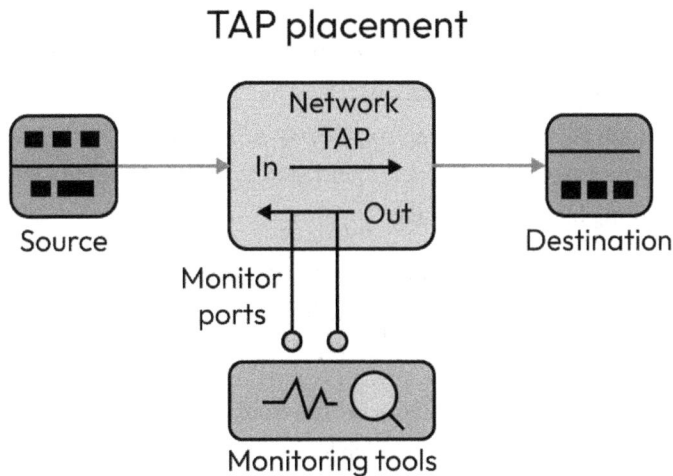

Figure 14.6: Network TAP

Without port mirroring or a **network TAP**, a packet capture tool would only see the traffic directly sent to or from the device running the tool. Port mirroring ensures that the capture tool can observe traffic not directly addressed to it, such as communications between other devices on the network.

Port mirroring and TAPs are useful when a performance issue has been narrowed down to a specific connection – for example, a company's internal file-sharing application is experiencing intermittent slowdowns. The network administrator suspects a problem with traffic between the application server and users' devices, but isn't sure whether it's due to network congestion, application behavior, or another issue.

By configuring port mirroring on the switch that connects the application server to the network, all traffic to and from the server can be mirrored to a designated port. A packet capture tool such as Wireshark can be connected to the mirrored port to analyze the traffic. In this case, the administrator can see that the application is causing excessive retransmissions due to improper **TCP** window sizing, which is leading to network congestion and slowdowns. The administrator can use this information to adjust the application's configuration or work with the development team to optimize its network behavior.

Solutions

This chapter so far has covered the main network monitoring methods, from using agents to monitoring devices in SNMP to port mirroring to track traffic. We've also covered how concepts such as flow data and log aggregation can create big-picture analysis, and API integration can help different tools to work with each other. All these are helped by establishing baseline metrics to help identify anomalies.

Network management is about ensuring smooth communications, reliable connections, and optimized performance. To do this, administrators need to know some common solutions to identify potential problems, optimize resource allocation, and monitor various aspects of network health. These solutions use some of the tools mentioned so far to ensure data flows where it needs to go while maintaining high performance.

If methods are the "how" of network monitoring, the solutions are the "why" or "what." Methods are the mechanisms that enable you to gather and interpret information about network behavior, and solutions are the overarching objectives or outcomes you aim to achieve using the methods.

The most important solutions to know about are **network discovery**, which looks at devices and connections in a network; **traffic analysis**, which looks at the data flow; **performance monitoring**, which tracks how well a network is working; **availability monitoring**, which tracks availability; and **configuration monitoring**, which checks that network devices are set up to specification.

The next sections will examine these solutions individually, offering examples, starting with network discovery.

Network discovery

Network discovery involves identifying devices and their connections within a network. It serves as a foundational step in gaining insight into and managing the network, ensuring that all devices and resources are properly identified and documented. There are two main methods for network discovery: **ad hoc discovery** and **scheduled discovery**.

- Ad hoc discovery is performed on demand. Administrators manually run a scan or use a tool to check the network when needed. This is useful for one-time checks, troubleshooting, or when adding new devices. So, for example, an administrator might run an ad hoc discovery to see what devices are connected after a new server is installed.

- Scheduled discovery conducts regular, automated scans for network inventory updates. Administrators automate the process by running scans at regular intervals. This ensures continuous visibility and helps maintain an updated inventory of devices in the network. So, a company might set up weekly scans to automatically detect any new devices added to its network.

Ad hoc and scheduled discovery are different ways of troubleshooting with network discovery, depending on the specific instance. It may be done in an ad hoc manner or might be part of scheduled maintenance. It might be on local networks, the cloud, or even hybrid, and could be security-focused or focused on a specific device. Knowing the right steps to take when troubleshooting is important for network engineers, so that you can be efficient when issues arise. The following examples will give you an idea of the variety of approaches you can take.

Example of ad hoc network discovery for troubleshooting

A company's IT team notices that an application is experiencing connectivity issues. To diagnose the problem, they use a network discovery tool such as Nmap to scan the network and identify all connected devices. During the scan, they discover an outdated switch causing the issue. By replacing or reconfiguring the switch, they resolve the problem and restore network performance.

Example of scheduled network discovery for asset management

An organization sets up scheduled scans using a tool such as **SolarWinds Network Performance Monitor**. These scans run weekly to automatically map all devices and update the network inventory. Over time, the IT team notices new devices appearing on the network. With this visibility, they can check whether these devices are authorized and ensure they comply with security policies.

Example of network discovery in cloud environments

A company migrating to the cloud uses a discovery tool such as **AWS Config** to map all cloud-based resources, such as virtual machines, databases, and storage buckets. The tool identifies configurations, tags, and relationships between these resources, helping the IT team monitor usage and costs effectively. *Figure 14.7* is an extract from the *AWS Config Developer Guide*.

> **Note**
>
> The guide can be found at https://docs.aws.amazon.com/config/latest/
> developerguide/how-does-config-work.html.

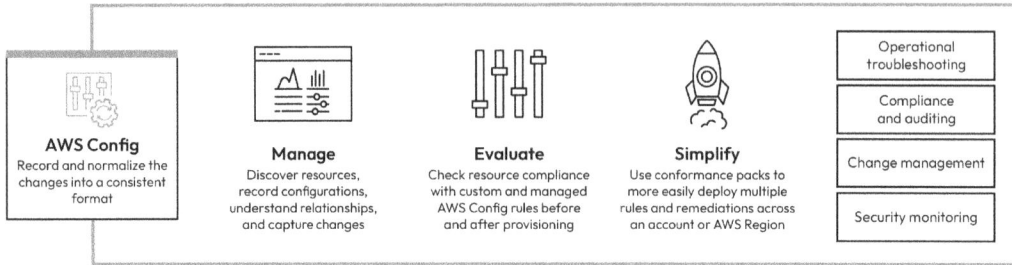

Figure 14.7: AWS Config

Example of discovery in hybrid networks

An enterprise with a mix of **on-premises** and **cloud** environments uses tools such as Microsoft **System Center Configuration Manager (SCCM)** or **ServiceNow Discovery**. These tools identify physical servers, virtual machines, routers, and software running across the hybrid network. This helps the team maintain a centralized inventory and monitor compliance.

Security-focused network discovery

A company concerned about potential unauthorized devices on its network uses a tool such as Wireshark to monitor network traffic and identify unknown IP or **MAC** addresses. They find a rogue device connected to their Wi-Fi, which they immediately isolate to prevent security risks.

IoT device discovery

A hospital deploying **IoT** devices such as smart monitors and sensors can use a tool such as Aruba ClearPass to identify and onboard new devices securely. This ensures all IoT devices are visible, properly configured, and compliant.

Traffic analysis

The primary goal of **traffic analysis** is to ensure that a network operates efficiently and securely. By monitoring data flow, IT teams can detect patterns, prioritize critical applications, and pinpoint areas where performance might be lagging. For example, during peak hours, understanding traffic can help prevent congestion by reallocating bandwidth or prioritizing essential services such as voice calls or real-time applications.

There are six key reasons to use traffic analysis:

1. Better network visibility
2. Compliance
3. Robust performance

4. Capacity planning

5. Network analysis

6. Cost reductions

Traffic analysis gives insights into bandwidth usage, enabling a business to scale its infrastructure efficiently while avoiding unnecessary expenses on excess resources. In addition to performance and security, traffic analysis helps optimize resource usage. It provides insights into bandwidth allocation, helping businesses scale their infrastructure effectively without overspending on unnecessary resources. By continuously analyzing traffic, organizations can adapt to changing demands and ensure a seamless experience for their users.

Traffic analysis uses packet and network monitoring tools mentioned in the *Methods* section of the chapter, such as TAPs, port mirroring, Wireshark, NetFlow, and other SNMP-based tools. Captured data is used to analyze issues such as available bandwidth, bottlenecks, overloaded hardware, and inefficient application behavior.

Another important use of traffic analysis is monitoring packet loss, error rates, discards, and drops. If data packets don't make it to their destination, network performance is affected, and this can lead to slower application performance and poor user experiences. For example, voice and video transmissions can experience latency.

Another important tool in traffic analysis is a **bandwidth speed tester**, which measures how fast your network can upload and download data. Popular tools include **Speedtest.net**, **Fast.com**, and *Figure 14.8* is a screenshot of Ookla. The download speed in this network should be 1,130 Mbps.

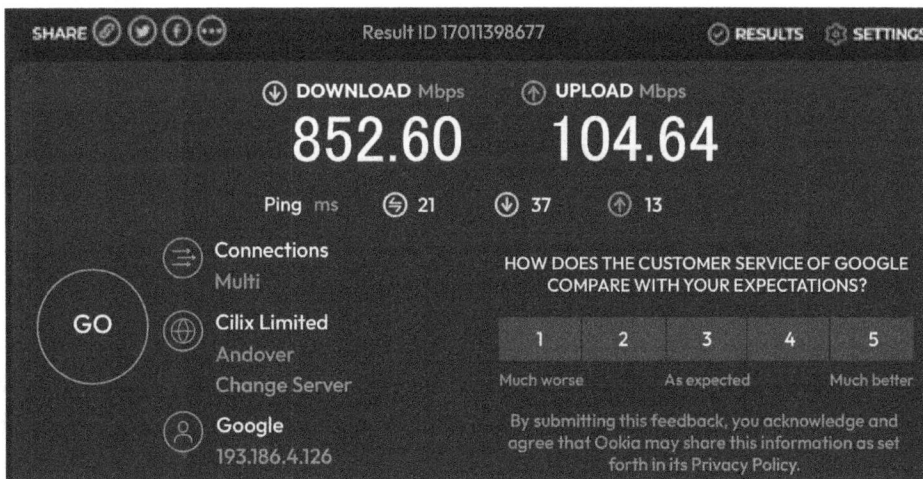

Figure 14.8: Bandwidth speed test

While checking that the overall traffic flow of a network is optimized, it is also important to be able to prioritize different types of traffic within a network – for example, **VoIP**. Network traffic prioritization and classification can be achieved using **Differentiated Services (DiffServ)**, which is a method for prioritizing network traffic. It assigns different levels of importance to various types of data, ensuring high-priority traffic, such as video calls, gets faster delivery compared to lower-priority tasks, such as file downloads.

> **Note**
>
> For more details on the prioritization of data packets, such as voice packets, see *Chapter 2, Compare and Contrast Networking Appliances, Applications, and Functions.*

Using DiffServ, the network categorizes and prioritizes traffic into classes based on its importance. These are **expedited forwarding (EF)**, **assured forwarding (AF)**, and **best effort (BE)**. They are covered in *Table 14.1*.

Category	Priority	Use case	Details
EF	High	Real-time, delay-sensitive applications such as video conferencing and VoIP calls	Packets tagged with **EF** are given the highest priority and are processed first to ensure minimal delay and jitter.
AF	Medium	Moderately important traffic, such as emails or document-sharing applications	**AF** traffic gets higher priority than **BE** but lower than **EF**. It is further divided into subcategories to ensure reliable delivery under different network conditions.
BE	Low	Web browsing and casual file downloads	These packets are given standard, low-priority treatment and are processed only when higher-priority traffic does not consume the bandwidth.

Table 14.1: DiffServ network categories

Take, for example, a busy corporate office with a network that sees a lot of traffic as employees are engaged in different activities. Some of them are on important video conference calls, while others are downloading large files or streaming videos during their breaks. Without any prioritization, all data packets would be treated equally, potentially causing delays in the video conference.

Using DiffServ, the network administrator ensures that video conferencing traffic is tagged with EF while downloads and streaming traffic are tagged as BE. When packets travel through the network, routers and switches process high-priority video conferencing traffic first, ensuring smooth and uninterrupted communication. Meanwhile, lower-priority tasks such as file downloads may experience slight delays during high-traffic periods. This way, DiffServ allows the network to deliver the most critical services efficiently, ensuring a seamless user experience for priority tasks.

DiffServ prioritizes traffic by tagging packets so that network devices process them in a specific order. However, there are other needs when it comes to traffic control in a network. Rather than prioritizing different types of data, sometimes there is a need to control the rates of data transfer in certain parts of a network, and this can be achieved with **traffic shaping**.

Traffic shaping is the process of controlling how data flows through a network to prevent congestion. It prioritizes important traffic while delaying less critical data. It works across three main "planes": the **control plane**, the **data plane**, and the **management plane**.

The control plane defines the rules for how traffic should be managed, such as which applications get priority. The data plane implements those rules by managing the flow of data packets, and the management plane provides tools for administrators to configure and monitor traffic policies.

For example, consider a household where multiple devices are using the internet simultaneously. One family member is streaming a 4K movie, another is engaged in an online gaming session, and a third is syncing files to a cloud storage service. The 4K movie could be using 15-25 Mbps. 25 Mbps produces good-quality video.

Without traffic shaping, all activities would compete equally for the available bandwidth, potentially causing the movie to buffer and the online game to lag. To avoid these issues, traffic shaping is applied. The router recognizes that the movie stream requires high bandwidth for smooth playback and assigns it a higher share of the available bandwidth.

The gaming session, which is sensitive to latency, is given low-latency handling to avoid delays. Meanwhile, the cloud sync, which is less time-sensitive, is allocated a smaller share of the bandwidth. As a result, the movie plays without interruptions, the game runs smoothly, and the cloud files continue syncing in the background without impacting the other activities. Traffic shaping ensures an optimized and balanced internet experience by dynamically managing the flow of data.

Performance monitoring

Performance monitoring is the practice of continuously tracking the behavior and efficiency of systems to ensure they operate as expected. It's essentially a health check of a computer or server, just like a doctor monitors a patient's vitals, and it helps IT professionals identify issues early, optimize system performance, and ensure a smooth user experience.

One of the main objectives of performance monitoring is tracking **system resource utilization**, which monitors **CPU usage**, **memory**, and **storage**. Monitoring CPU and memory usage ensures that the system isn't overloaded. High usage levels can slow down performance or cause crashes. For example, if an application uses too much memory, other processes might struggle to run smoothly.

Monitoring available storage helps prevent issues such as the inability to save files or performance drops due to insufficient space.

Performance monitoring also focuses on how well users interact with the system using user experience metrics such as **response time** and **error rate**. Response time measures how long it takes for a system to respond to a user's request, such as how long it takes for a web page to load, which is its response time. Faster response times make for a better user experience, while delays can lead to frustration.

The error rate tracks the number of errors during system operations. For example, if users encounter database connection issues or broken links, these are logged as errors. A high error rate indicates instability, which could harm user satisfaction and productivity.

Figure 14.9 shows **Microsoft Performance Monitor** (**PerfMon**), which is a tool built into Windows that helps monitor system performance. It provides both a graphic view and a report view of performance metrics.

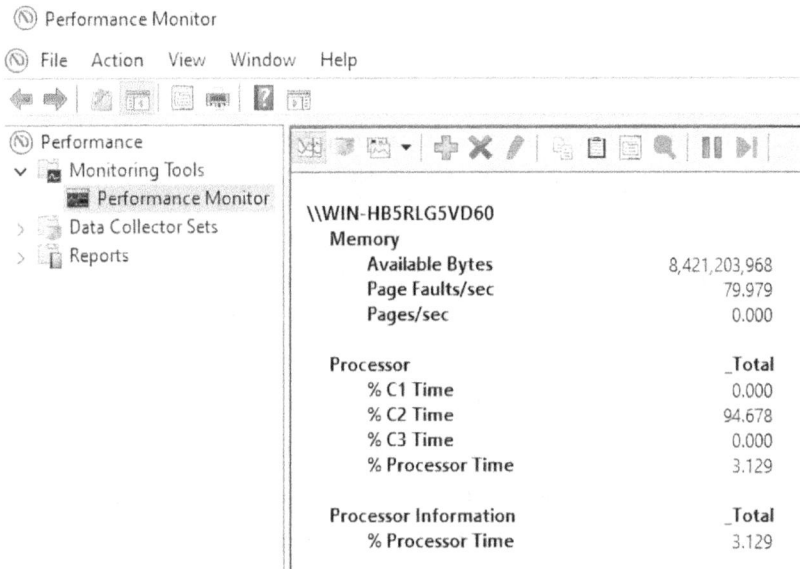

Figure 14.9: Report view for PerfMon

Figure 14.9 shows metrics related to memory and the processor. The most pertinent is memory pages per second, shown under **Memory** as **Pages/sec**.

- **Pages/sec** tracks how often the system accesses the disk to fetch data because there's not enough space in RAM. High values might indicate insufficient memory or heavy usage of swap files.

- **Processor Time** shows how much time the CPU spends processing tasks. A high percentage means the CPU is consistently busy, which could signal a need for optimization or hardware upgrades. This should be about 70% utilization. At 100% utilization, the processor is fully utilized and will struggle to execute tasks.

- **Reads/writes per second** measures the number of read and write operations performed on a disk. High values indicate heavy disk activity, which could lead to slower performance for other applications, especially if the disk is a bottleneck (e.g., on **HDDs** or busy **SSDs**).

Availability monitoring

Availability monitoring is the process of checking whether systems, devices, and applications are operational and accessible when needed. This ensures that services such as websites, databases, and network resources are always up and running for users. If something goes down (e.g., a server crashes), availability monitoring tools immediately alert IT teams so they can fix the issue quickly. The main things monitored are **outages**, **security threats**, and **network connectivity**.

Availability monitoring tools often include uptime monitors or heartbeat checks, which continuously verify whether services are operational. These tools detect outages as soon as they occur, enabling IT teams to respond quickly. For example, if a company's website goes offline, a monitoring tool such as **Pingdom** (see the tools section below) immediately alerts the IT team to investigate and resolve the issue before it impacts users significantly.

Detecting irregular access patterns or sudden spikes in traffic during availability monitoring can signal potential **security threats**, such as a **denial-of-service** (**DoS**) attack. Tools such as **Splunk** and **Datadog** integrate availability monitoring with security analysis, allowing IT teams to respond swiftly to secure affected services. For example, if a flood of unauthorized requests targets a web server, the monitoring system can trigger alerts and block malicious traffic.

Availability monitoring also extends to **network connectivity**, ensuring that data flows without interruptions. Tools such as **Zabbix** or **ManageEngine OpManager** can detect issues such as network congestion, broadcast storms, or switching loops. For example, if a network device starts to misbehave and causes a loop, the monitoring tool can alert administrators, who can quickly intervene to stabilize the network.

The following table has some common tools used for availability monitoring.

Tool name	Function
Pingdom	Monitors website and server uptime.
Nagios	Monitors the availability of servers, applications, and network devices.
Zabbix	Tracks availability and sends alerts when systems go offline.
SolarWinds Network Performance Monitor	Provides detailed availability insights for large networks.
Splunk	Integrates availability monitoring with security analysis.
Datadog	Analyzes the technology stack to keep applications and services running smoothly.
ManageEngine OpManager	Monitors the performance metrics of network devices.

Table 14.2: Availability monitoring tools

Consider a company that relies on a database server to process customer orders. Availability monitoring tools constantly check whether the server is online. One day, the server goes offline unexpectedly. The monitoring tool alerts the IT team, which quickly restarts the server, minimizing downtime and ensuring customer orders are not delayed.

Configuration monitoring

The configuration of systems and devices in your network, whether intentional or accidental, has the potential to cause disruptions or failures. Poor configuration is a security risk if default passwords are not changed, the firewall has the wrong rules, ports are left open, or encryption settings are not configured to use secure, modern protocols. Routing tables may be misconfigured, or static routes may be outdated, causing misdirected data packets and network degradation.

One of the main causes of misconfiguration is human error, so automated configuration monitoring can be an important tool in the overall health of a network. In fact, many industries have regulatory requirements that mandate specific configuration settings for security. For example, the **Payment Card Industry Data Security Standard (PCI DSS)** and the **Health Insurance Portability and Accountability Act (HIPAA)** require proactive measures to protect individual data.

Configuration monitoring ensures that the settings and configurations of systems, devices, and applications in a network remain correct, consistent, and secure. It involves tracking changes to configurations, detecting unauthorized alterations, and maintaining backups to quickly restore settings if something goes wrong. One critical concept in configuration monitoring is the use of baselines.

Configuration baselines are similar to the baseline metrics discussed earlier in the chapter in that they provide a reference point for automated checks. However, they have not measured values, such as bandwidth, but rather an ideal or approved configuration setting for a system or device. These settings have been tested, validated, and optimized, and a configuration monitoring tool will check the current configuration of network components against the baseline values and alert the administrator in the case of any anomalies.

In a network environment, the baseline for a firewall might include specific rules for allowed traffic, blocked IP addresses, and port configurations. Over time, administrators change the firewall configuration to accommodate new services, troubleshoot issues, or respond to security threats. Maybe a junior administrator accidentally modifies a firewall rule, opening an unnecessary port (e.g., port 23 for **Telnet**). This port is a common target for attackers because it transmits data in plaintext. A configuration monitor will detect the change and send the alert to the IT team, allowing them to review and revert the modification promptly.

The following table has some tools that can be used with configuration monitoring.

Tool	Usage
SolarWinds Network Configuration Manager	Tracks device configurations and reports changes
ManageEngine Network Configuration Manager	Monitors and automates configuration management for network devices
Puppet	Automates configuration management for servers and applications
Ansible	Ensures consistent configurations across systems

Table 14.3: Configuration monitoring tools

Availability and configuration monitoring often go hand in hand. For example, if a server becomes unavailable, configuration monitoring might reveal that an incorrect setting caused the issue. Together, these practices provide a comprehensive approach to managing and maintaining IT systems.

> **Note**
>
> Configurations are covered in more detail in *Chapter 13, Explain the Purpose of Organizational Processes and Procedures*.

Summary

This chapter covered the importance of network monitoring technologies, which ensure efficient network management. Tools include **SNMP** for device control, flow data, and packet capture for traffic analysis, and log aggregation tools such as **SIEM** for security insights. Features such as baseline metrics, **API** integration, and port mirroring help detect anomalies and optimize performance. Solutions such as network discovery, traffic analysis, performance monitoring, and configuration tracking ensure real-time oversight, compliance, and reliable operations.

The knowledge gained in this chapter will prepare you to answer questions relating to Exam objective 3.2 in the *CompTIA Network+ (N10-009)* exam.

Exam objective 3.2

Given a scenario, use network monitoring technologies

Methods:

- **SNMP**: Protocol for managing network devices, including traps and MIBs.
- **SNMP versions**: v2c for simplicity, v3 adds security and authentication.
- **Community strings**: Passwords for SNMP device access.

Authentication: Verifies identity to secure network access and operations.

Flow data: Monitors traffic patterns and bandwidth usage.

Packet capture: Analyzes individual packets for troubleshooting.

Baseline metrics: Establishes normal performance, triggers anomaly alerts.

- **Anomaly alerting/notification**: Detects and notifies of performance deviations

Log aggregation: Centralizes logs for analysis and troubleshooting.

- **Syslog collector**: Gathers logs from network devices for centralized monitoring.
- **Security information and event management (SIEM):** Correlates logs for security insights.

API integration: Enables automated network monitoring and management.

- **Port mirroring**: Copies traffic for analysis without disrupting operations.

Solutions:

Network discovery: Identifies devices via ad hoc or scheduled scans.

- **Ad hoc**: Performs immediate, one-time scans to identify devices.
- **Scheduled**: Conducts regular, automated scans for network inventory updates.

Traffic analysis: Examines network traffic for optimization or troubleshooting.

Performance monitoring: Tracks network performance metrics in real time.

Availability monitoring: Ensures devices and services remain online.

Configuration monitoring: Tracks changes to network configurations for compliance.

Chapter review questions

Now that you've completed the chapter, you can check your knowledge using the practice questions provided in the online platform at `https://packt.link/N10-009ch14`. You can also use the QR code below. Accessing these questions requires you to unlock the accompanying online content first. Head over to Chapter 26 for detailed instructions.

15

Explain Disaster Recovery Concepts

Disaster recovery is essential for ensuring that an organization can quickly resume operations after a disruption. It involves key metrics such as **recovery point objective (RPO)** and **recovery time objective (RTO)**, which define acceptable data loss and downtime until the time when we are back in an operational state. Disaster recovery also includes strategies such as cold, warm, and hot sites for backup, as well as high-availability approaches such as active-active and active-passive configurations. Regular testing, through tabletop exercises and validation tests, is crucial to ensure the effectiveness of disaster recovery plans.

This chapter covers the third objective in *Domain 3: 3.3, Explain disaster recovery concepts.*

> **Note**
>
> A full breakdown of objective 3.3 will be given at the end of the chapter.

Disaster recovery metrics

Making your network reliable and resilient is core to its operation. The reliability of your physical installations and logical configurations is important, but you should also know what to do when your network goes down due to circumstances outside of your control. This is where disaster recovery comes in. However, disaster recovery planning isn't simply about knowing what to do in case of an emergency. It's also about the efficient use of resources, such as backup, redundancy, and engineering time.

You might assume that disaster recovery should be done as quickly as possible, and that no data can be lost, which might sound ideal. However, backing up takes compute power, and setting a system back up takes an engineer's time. It would be inefficient to have all data backed up every second or have five engineers on call at all times. So how do you balance the requirements of disaster recovery with those of efficiency?

By setting objectives such as the acceptable amount of data loss or the maximum amount of downtime, you can better understand the disaster planning needs. There are a number of measurements that can be used to do this, which are covered here:

- **RPO**: The RPO, in simple terms, is the data backup frequency and is measured in time. It is determined by identifying the maximum age of files or data that an organization can afford to lose without experiencing unacceptable consequences. This can be influenced by many factors, including company policy and legislation requirements. For instance, if a company sets an RPO of *3 hours*, it means the organization must perform backups at least every three hours to prevent any data loss beyond this acceptable threshold.

- **RTO**: The RTO is the shortest amount of time a business targets to restore its operations to a functional level following a disruption. In a practical scenario, if a disruption occurs at 1:00 P.M. and the RPO is set at *3 hours*, the organization aims to have its operations restored by 4:00 P.M. If the restoration process extends beyond the defined RPO, it could potentially have detrimental effects on the business and lead to loss of revenue, reputation, and customer trust.

- **Mean time to repair (MTTR)**: MTTR signifies the average duration needed to restore a malfunctioning system to its optimal operating condition and is measured in time. For instance, if a router malfunctions at 2:00 P.M. and it is back online by 3:00 P.M., this means it took 1 hour to repair. If it malfunctions again but takes 30 mins to repair, the mean time is 45 mins because $(60 + 30) \div 2 = 45$.

- **Mean time between failures (MTBF)**: MTBF is the average time between the failure of a piece of equipment or system and determines the lifespan of a device. If a server fails on March 1, then 90 days later on May 30, then 110 days later, on September 17, and it fails again 40 days later, on October 27, then the MTBF is 80 days because $(90 + 110 + 40) \div 3 = 80$. This would imply an unreliable piece of equipment.

  There are no ideals for any of these metrics, and decisions are entirely based on business needs, conditions, and efficiency. Printers, for instance, might have an MTBF measured in days, because they have a lot of moving parts, and a lot of non-engineers using them.

However, they don't have a critical impact on other parts of the network; that is, they don't store information or connect other nodes, and they have a short MTTR, measured in minutes, so having a high MTBF isn't necessarily a priority.

Disaster recovery sites

In the previous section, we looked at the different metrics that can be used when making plans if the individual devices or sections of your network have failed. But there are also larger risks that could impact entire offices, buildings, or campuses. Large disasters such as floods, storms, fires, or terrorist attacks can have a devastating impact. Many organizations choose to have backup sites that can be used when the main site is out of operation. For this to be effective, planning is needed, and considerations such as budget, criticality of operations, and acceptable downtime all need to be taken into consideration.

There is a range of options, from simple empty buildings to fully set up offices, which are detailed here:

- **Cold site**: Where the budget is very limited, a cold site presents an economical choice. Unlike hot and warm sites, a cold site is essentially an empty shell. It provides essential infrastructure, such as a power and water supply, but lacks staff, equipment, and data. This absence of pre-loaded data and operational readiness makes a cold site the slowest option to get up and running in the event of a disaster. Organizations opting for a cold site must be prepared for a more extended period of downtime during recovery.

- **Warm site**: A warm site is fully functional but has no customer data on site. During a disaster, data may be sent to the warm site by courier or other means, resulting in a delay of 3–4 hours compared to the primary site. This setup allows for a reasonably swift recovery while being more cost-effective than a hot site.

- **Hot site**: A hot site is the best site for rapid recovery. It is a fully operational site that mirrors your primary data center or infrastructure. This site is up and running with staff loading data into the systems immediately as it is replicated. This could be an automated procedure. This immediate response capability makes hot sites the most expensive option to maintain, but also the fastest to recover from downtime.

  With more companies using the cloud, **cloud-based hot sites** have similarly increased in popularity. By building these recovery sites in the cloud, companies not only ensure the rapid disaster recovery characteristic of hot sites generally but also obtain the flexibility to scale resources dynamically, optimizing both resilience and cost-effectiveness. It allows for almost instant recovery, without the need to physically travel to a secondary location.

High-availability approaches

High-availability (HA) means keeping a system up and running, even if something breaks. **HA** approaches focus on minimizing downtime by using setups such as clustering, where we group multiple servers or nodes together to operate as a single system. Clustering involves an active node and a passive node that share a common quorum disk, reinforced by a witness server, heartbeat communication, and a **virtual IP address** (**VIP**) at the forefront.

Figure 15.1 represents a HA cluster architecture using an active-passive failover setup.

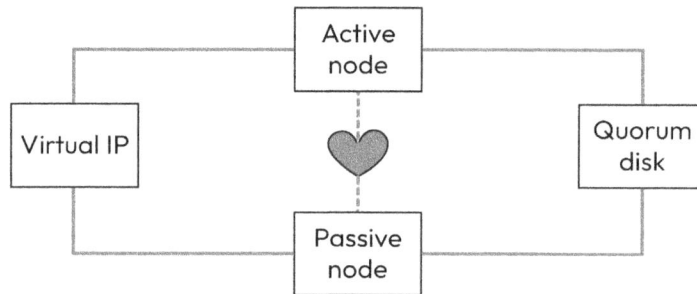

Figure 15.1: Active-passive cluster

At the forefront of the clustering setup is the VIP, which is to the left in *Figure 15.1*. It's the public-facing interface of the cluster, acting as the entry point for external requests. The VIP ensures that even if the active node experiences any failures, the cluster remains accessible to users without disruption. This monitors a seamless transition from active to passive, all while maintaining uninterrupted service, which is a hallmark of this configuration's robustness.

Heartbeat communication is communication between active and passive nodes and is facilitated through a heartbeat mechanism in the center of *Figure 15.1*. This heartbeat is analogous to the rhythmic pulse of a living organism, involving regular exchanges of status updates, or a "node heartbeat." The passive node continuously monitors the active node's heartbeat. If it detects an absence or irregularity in the node heartbeat, it knows that the active node has failed.

The **quorum disk**, which is on the right-hand side of *Figure 15.1*, is a shared storage resource that members of the cluster share. It acts as a neutral arbiter, storing critical configuration and state information that both the active and passive nodes access. This shared resource serves as the backbone of decision-making within the cluster.

Figure 15.1 shows an active-passive node configuration. Both nodes are accessed by a virtual IP on the frontend and share the same disk, the quorum disk, on the backend. The passive node remains in standby, synchronized with the active node, and ready to take over if the active node fails.

In an **active-active node configuration** setup, both nodes are active simultaneously, working in tandem to handle requests. Each node has its own designated tasks, but they share the workload, ensuring better resource utilization and higher availability. Both nodes are accessed via a shared virtual IP on the frontend, distributing the load between them. The nodes are synchronized to ensure data consistency, and they often share a common storage backend, allowing seamless failover or load balancing. If one node fails, the other continues to handle the load without interruption, providing continuous service availability.

For an additional layer of reliability, a **witness server** can be added. This is an impartial entity that assists in determining the state of the cluster. If network issues cause an active node to lose communication, the other server adopts the active role for both. A witness server helps determine which node should remain active. The witness server helps prevent split-brain scenarios and ensures that the cluster operates smoothly. Split brain happens when two nodes can't see each other (due to network issues) and both think they should be active, which can cause data corruption or conflicts. It is prevented by the witness acting as a tie-breaker.

Testing

So far in this chapter, you have seen how different metrics can help you make the right decisions when it comes to planning for downtime. You have also seen how different types of backup sites can be used in the event of large disasters. However, to be adequately prepared, organizations need a means to assess, refine, and validate their disaster recovery strategies. There are a couple of ways this can be done: tabletop exercises and validation tests.

- **Tabletop exercises** are a valuable tool for testing your disaster recovery plan in a controlled, hypothetical setting. During a tabletop exercise, key stakeholders gather around a table to discuss and strategize how they would respond to a disaster scenario. This exercise allows participants to identify gaps in their plans, such as missing procedures, lack of knowledge (training), or lack of required technology. It also helps refine communication channels and assess decision-making processes. This is the easiest testing exercise to set up, as it is paper-based.

- A **validation test** is a process used to perform the required actions to confirm that a product, system, or model meets the specified requirements and performs as intended in its intended environment. In the following section, we will look at different types of validation tests.

- **Failover testing** is another important test. Failover mechanisms are a testament to resilience in action as they enable the seamless transfer of operations to backup systems or data centers in the event of a system failure or disruption. By testing failover procedures, organizations can verify the reliability of these critical processes, ensuring that minimal downtime occurs and that essential services remain uninterrupted.

- **Simulations** introduce an element of competitiveness and urgency into disaster recovery exercises. The exercise typically involves a white team overseeing and assessing responses based on a predefined disaster scenario from the recovery plan. These drills simulate real-world cyberattacks, enabling organizations to test their incident response plans in a controlled environment. Simulations help identify gaps and improve coordination among teams to refine security measures. Like a flight simulator for pilots, the intent is to mimic the real danger so that, when disaster does strike, they already know exactly what to do. They take some time to set up, but they are the closest functional test to the real thing.

Summary

This chapter covered disaster recovery, which is a critical process that ensures an organization can swiftly resume operations after a disruption. It involves defining key metrics such as RPO and RTO to establish acceptable levels of data loss and downtime. Disaster recovery strategies include various site options, such as cold, warm, and hot sites, each offering different levels of readiness and cost. High-availability configurations such as active-active and active-passive nodes further enhance system resilience. Regular testing through exercises such as tabletop simulations and validation tests is essential to confirm the effectiveness of disaster recovery plans and ensure preparedness for real-world disruptions.

The knowledge gained in this chapter will prepare you to answer questions relating to exam objective 3.3 in your *CompTIA Network+ (N10-009) exam.*

Exam objective 3.3

Explain disaster recovery (DR) concepts

DR Metrics:

- **Recovery point objective (RPO)**: Maximum acceptable data loss duration.
- **Recovery time objective (RTO)**: Targeted system recovery time after disruption.
- **Mean time to repair (MTTR)**: Average time to fix a failure.
- **Mean time between failures (MTBF)**: Average operational time between system failures.

DR Sites:

- **Cold site**: Basic infrastructure, slowest recovery.
- **Warm site**: Partially equipped, moderate recovery speed.
- **Hot site**: Fully operational, fastest recovery.

High-availability approaches:

- **Active-active:** Both nodes active, shared load.
- **Active-passive:** One active, one standby, seamless failover.

Testing:

- **Tabletop exercises:** Hypothetical disaster scenario discussions.
- **Validation tests:** Confirm system performs as intended

Chapter review questions

Now that you've completed the chapter, you can check your knowledge using the practice questions provided in the online platform at `https://packt.link/N10-009ch15`. You can also use the QR code below. Accessing these questions requires you to unlock the accompanying online content first. Head over to Chapter 26 for detailed instructions.

16

Given a Scenario, Implement IPv4 and IPv6 Network Services

In *Chapter 7* and *Chapter 8*, you saw how **IPv4** and **IPv6** provide an addressing system so data across networks can be sent to the correct hosts. However, this is only part of the story. Over the internet, for example, people use human-readable web addresses, which need to be translated into IP addresses. Devices need to be synchronized to enable data transfer, and IP addresses need to be assigned.

Luckily for network engineers, these issues are solved with services that address dynamic addressing, name resolution, and time protocols. Being able to implement them is essential for building efficient, secure, and reliable network environments. Dynamic addressing ensures that devices can seamlessly connect to networks by assigning IP addresses automatically, while name resolution translates human-readable domain names into machine-friendly IP addresses for efficient communication. Time protocols maintain synchronization across devices, which is vital for accurate data transfer, logging, and security functions.

This chapter covers the fourth objective in *Domain 3:3.4, Given a scenario, implement IPv4 and IPv6 network services*.

Note

A full breakdown of objective 3.4 will be given at the end of the chapter.

Dynamic addressing

In *Chapter 7, Given a Scenario, Use Appropriate IPv4 Network Addressing*, you covered how IP addresses are used to identify networks, subnets, and devices. Assigning IP addresses to devices on a small network that doesn't change much can be done manually with minimal fuss. These IP addresses are configured on the host and don't change unless configured again. They are known as **static IP addresses**. However, in larger networks, things are not so straightforward. There are large numbers of devices, perhaps spread over numerous networks. Portable devices such as laptops and tablet PCs are continually joining and leaving. There may even be network changes, such as moving subnets or scaling up.

As a network administrator for a domain with constant users and devices in the thousands, managing IP addresses efficiently is crucial. Rather than having a single IP address configured on the host, IP addresses can also be assigned as devices join the network. These are called **dynamic IP addresses**, and they are pulled from a pool of IP addresses maintained by the ISP or network admin. Dynamic IP address allocation allows you to automatically assign and update IP addresses as needed, saving time and reducing manual errors. They can be set to last as long as a device is on a network, or there can be time limits. They are set dynamically by a **Dynamic Host Configuration Protocol** (**DHCP**) server, which will be discussed in the next section.

Dynamic Host Configuration Protocol

A DHCP server dynamically allocates IP addresses to host machines that log in each morning. The process involved the client broadcasting a `DHCPDISCOVER` packet to find a DHCP server, inserting its MAC address as its identifier. On receipt of this packet, the DHCP server replies with a broadcast packet called `DHCPOFFER`, looking for the host machine's MAC address. The host then replies with a `DHCPREQUEST` packet. The final stage is `DHCPACK` (acknowledgment), in which the IP address, 8-day lease time in a Windows environment, and DHCP options such as router and DNS server are provided.

To remember this process, you can use the mnemonic **DORA**.

DORA

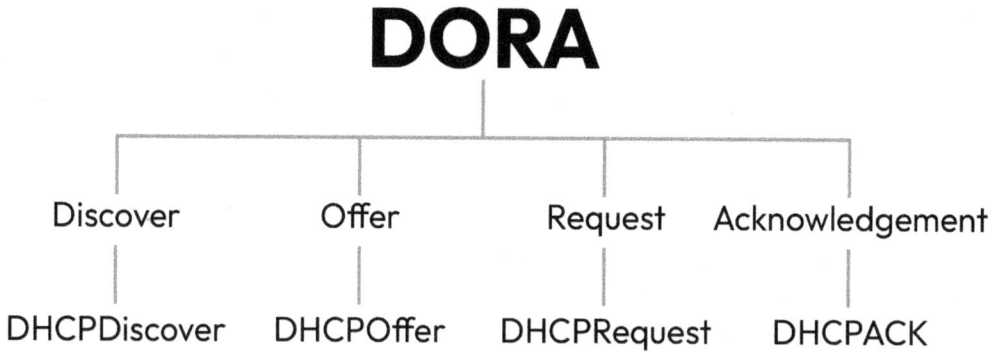

Figure 16.1: The DORA mnemonic

Figure 16.1 shows you the handy DORA mnemonic. You will need to know this handshake for the troubleshooting process.

The handshake process is shown in *Figure 16.2*.

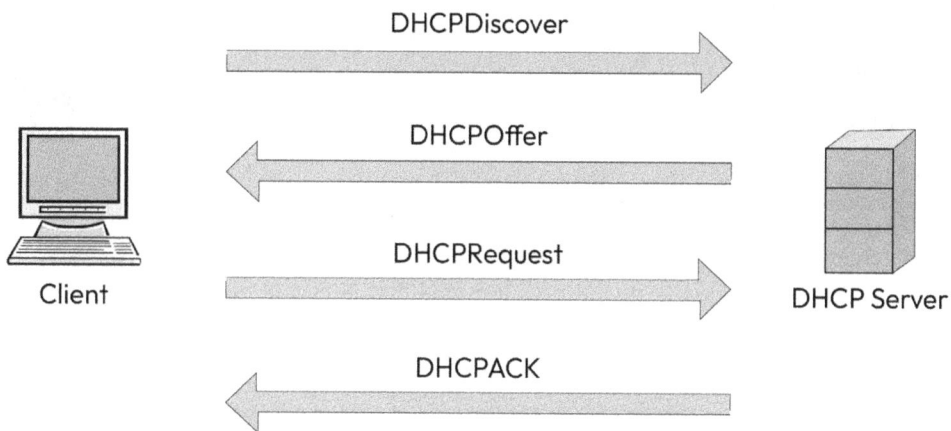

Figure 16.2: DHCP handshake

If a host cannot obtain an IP address because of network connectivity or the DHCP server has run out of IP addresses, then it will self-generate an **automatic private IP address (APIPA)** in the IP address range 169.254.0.0 to 169.254.255.255 with a subnet mask of 255.255.0.0, also written as 169.254.0.0/16. The APIPA does not allocate a default gateway address; therefore, the traffic cannot be routed. It is an aid to network troubleshooting as it lets the admin know that the client cannot obtain a DHCP IP address, normally due to connection problems, but occasionally when the DHCP server has run out of IP addresses.

When setting up a DHCP server, you will need to configure it so that it meets the needs of your network, taking into consideration what IP addresses are available, those that should be reserved, and how long IP addresses should be leased for. These settings are covered next, starting with scope.

Scope

The **scope** is the range of IP addresses that can be allocated to a single subnet. You can amend the IP address range, but you will need to delete and recreate the scope if the subnet mask changes. Insert all of your IP addresses that you can allocate into the scope so that you can keep track of them. After that, you can add exclusions so that they are reserved for servers and important network devices.

Figure 16.3 shows the New Scope Wizard in a DHCP server configuration tool:

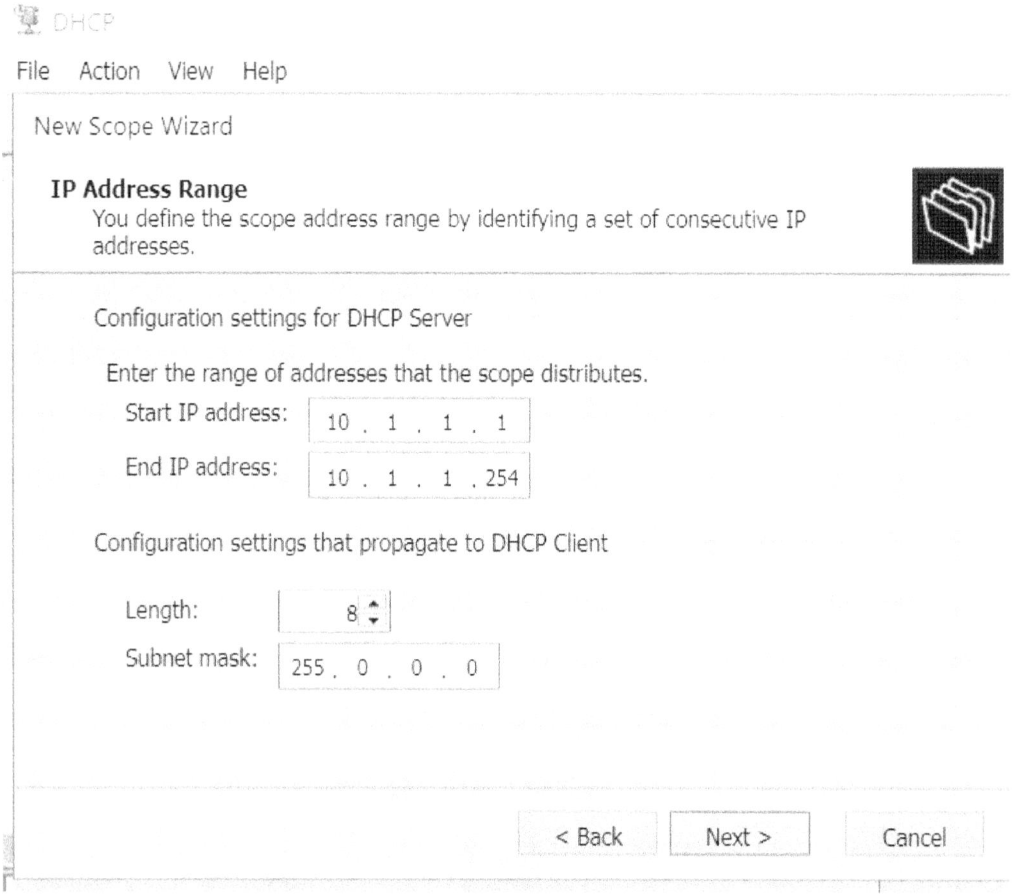

Figure 16.3: DHCP scope

The wizard in *Figure 16.3* shows the scope with the start IP address 10.1.1.1 and the end IP address 10.1.1.254. This indicates the full range of IP addresses that the DHCP server will assign to devices. You cannot insert an IP address that starts with 0 or 255, as they are the Net ID and broadcast addresses. The length is the prefix length (**CIDR notation**) that determines the subnet mask, in this case /8. The subnet mask is also shown, in this case 255.0.0.0. The subnet mask is set so that devices know whether the packets are for local or remote destinations. You can adjust the scope IP address range for expansion as long as the subnet mask remains the same. If you need to change the subnet mask, then you need to delete the current scope and create another.

Exclusions

Exclusions are IP addresses that need to be excluded from the scope, such as those that have been manually configured, normally for your servers, firewalls, routers, printers, and critical network appliances. The DHCP server will not allocate these IP addresses to any other host.

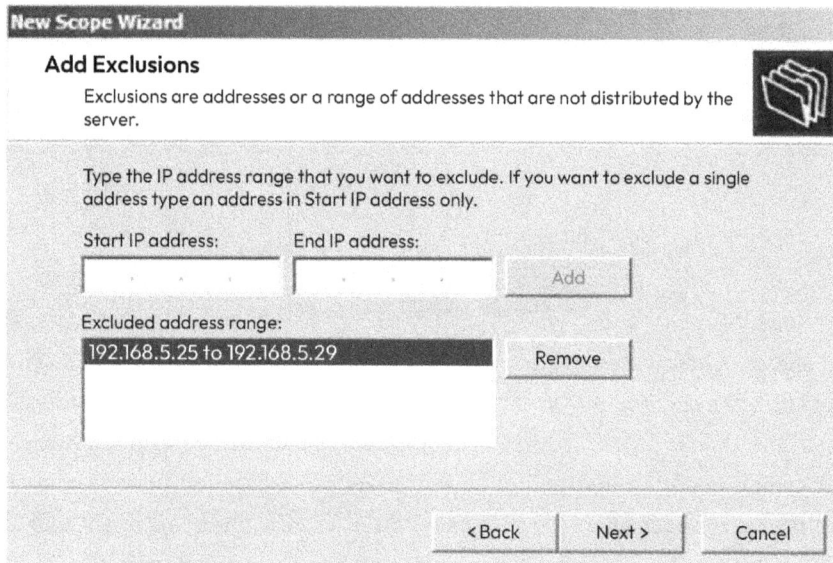

Figure 16.4: DHCP exclusions

Reservations

A **reservation**, also known as a **client reservation**, is where you need a host to be allocated the same IP address; this is instead of configuring them manually. This is useful for devices such as printers that need to be connected reliably.

You need to have the MAC address of the host; when you type it into the wizard, you omit the dashes, as shown in *Figure 16.5*.

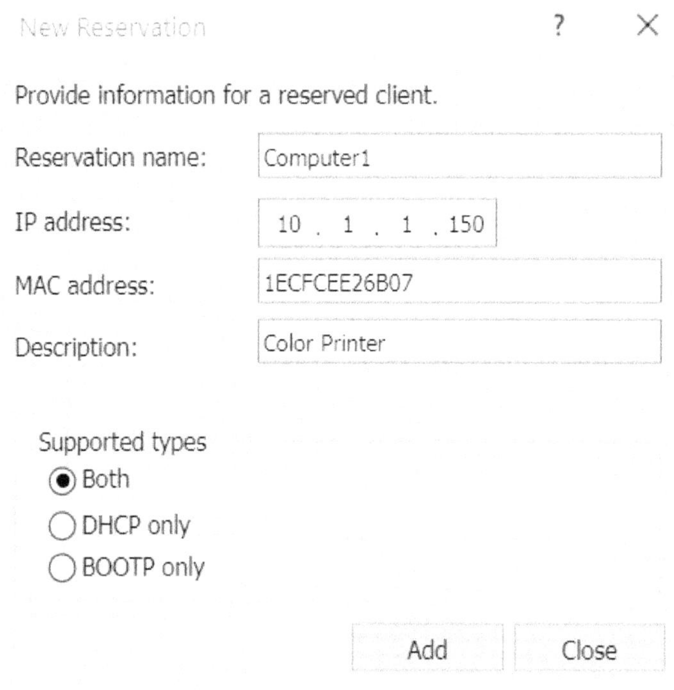

Figure 16.5: Client reservation

Figure 16.5 shows the **New Reservation** screen for the DHCP configuration tool. The reservation names show the client name, in this case, Computer1, then its reserved IP address, in this case, 10.1.1.150, then the MAC address, 1ECFCEE26B07, and then a description, which is Color Printer. A printer needs a consistent IP so that users can reliably connect to it via the same address. When the reserved client broadcasts for an IP address, then Computer1 will always be allocated 10.1.1.150. This address will not be allocated to any other host.

Lease time

With networks that have a limited number of IP addresses but a large number of devices connecting and disconnecting, it's important to make sure that IP addresses are not taken up by devices for extended periods of time. If there are too many IP addresses assigned to addresses that have left the network, then there may not be enough to assign to new devices.

The **lease time** is the length of time an IP address will be assigned to a device before being removed. *Figure 16.6* shows a lease time of 8 days, which is the normal default duration.

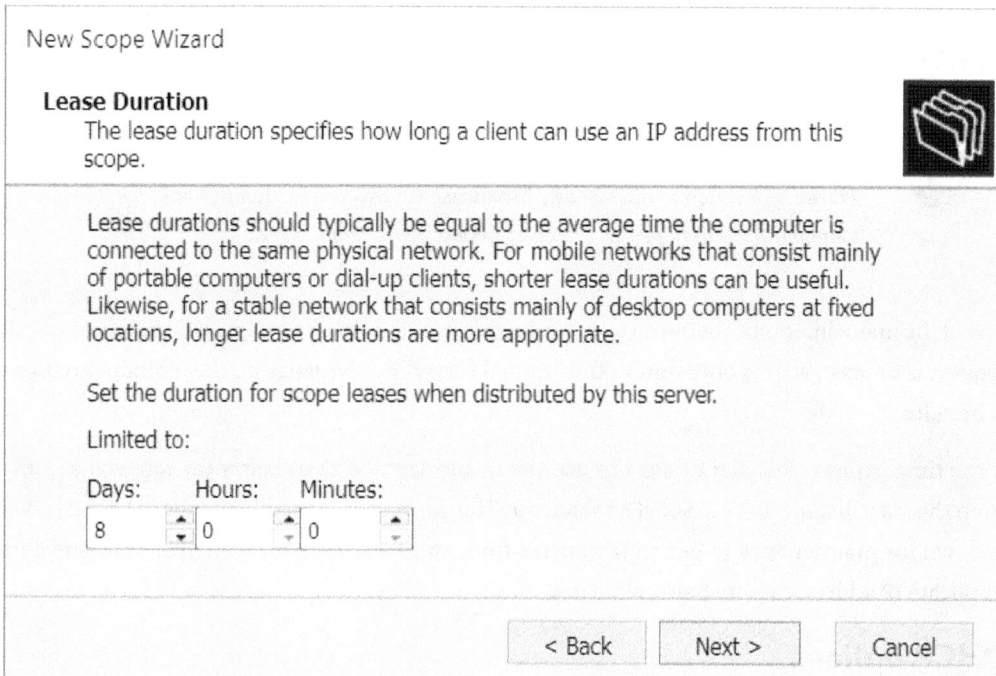

New Scope Wizard

Lease Duration
  The lease duration specifies how long a client can use an IP address from this scope.

Lease durations should typically be equal to the average time the computer is connected to the same physical network. For mobile networks that consist mainly of portable computers or dial-up clients, shorter lease durations can be useful. Likewise, for a stable network that consists mainly of desktop computers at fixed locations, longer lease durations are more appropriate.

Set the duration for scope leases when distributed by this server.

Limited to:

Days: Hours: Minutes:

  8   0   0

  < Back   Next >   Cancel

Figure 16.6: DHCP lease

Figure 16.6 shows the **Lease Duration** page of **New Scope Wizard** with the duration set to 8 days, but the number can be changed. For instance, a company with a limited number of IP addresses, but that has a day shift and a night shift, might reduce it to 12 hours. A coffee shop, which has customers coming and going, might have a lease time of 10 minutes.

Lease renewal

At the end of the lease duration, the IP address returns to the pool of available IP addresses. If a device whose lease has ended needs to continue on the network, then it will have to go through the discovery process again. This process is inefficient, especially when leases are set to short durations, so devices can instead follow a **lease renewal** process.

In the renewal process, the client attempts to renew its lease at 50% of the renewal time by sending a DHCPREQUEST packet to the DHCP server. If the server responds with DHCPACK the lease is renewed and the timer resets. If it does not receive a reply, then it will attempt to renew every

5 minutes by sending a DHCPREQUEST packet until it reaches 87.5% of the lease duration. At this stage, it reaches the rebinding phase, and it will then broadcast to any other DHCP server on the network. The rebinding phase in DHCP is the last attempt a client makes to keep its IP lease valid before it expires.

> **Note**
>
> Traffic types such as unicast and broadcast are covered further in *Chapter 4, Explain Common Networking Ports, Protocols, Services, and Traffic Types*.

One of the main differences between a renewal request and a rebinding request is that the renewal request is unicast, so it is only sent to the original server. By comparison, the rebinding request is broadcast.

If the time expires, the client does not use the IP address and then starts the renewal process from the start, using a DHCPDISCOVER broadcast. This process allows a client whose DHCP server is down for maintenance to get an IP address from another DHCP server. DHCP also prevents duplicate IP addresses from being allocated.

DHCP options

DHCP options are the dynamic settings that a host machine might need. The most common are listed here:

- 003 Router: Specifies the default gateway (router) IP address that clients should use to reach other networks
- 004 Time Server: Provides the IP address of a server to synchronize time (e.g., via NTP)
- 005 Name Servers: Specifies the IP address of a name resolution server (e.g., DNS server)

Figure 16.7 shows the DHCP options to allocate DNS servers.

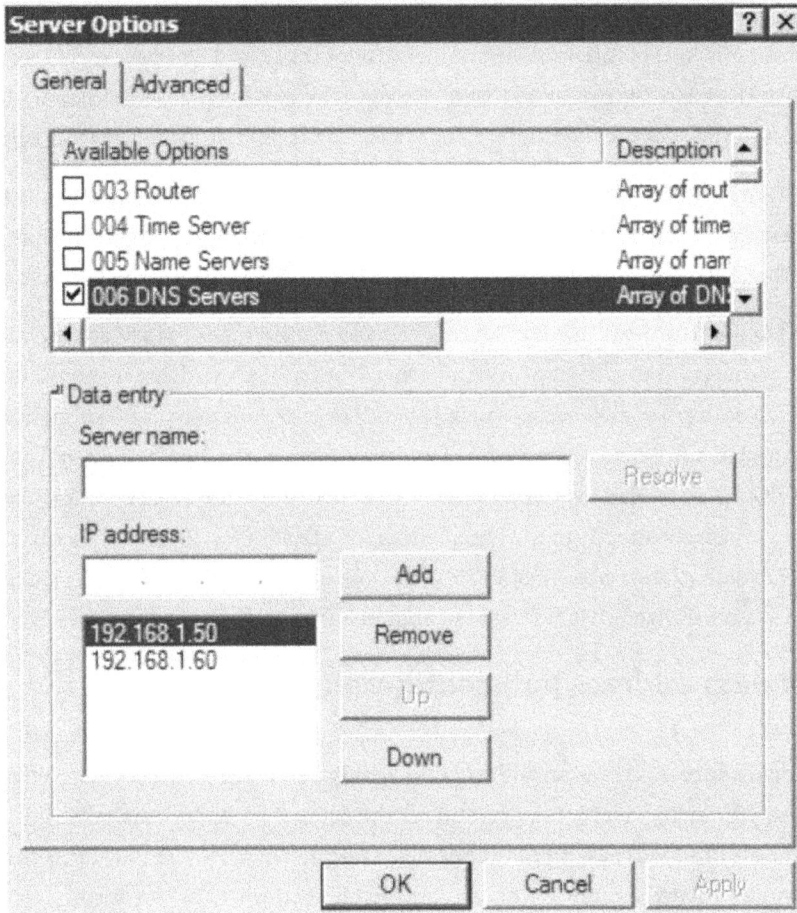

Figure 16.7: DHCP options

At certain times, these settings might need to change, for instance, if a piece of hardware, such as the router, needs to be changed or if the network is upgraded. If this happens, the DHCP server needs to ensure that all clients update their configurations immediately, and so the DHCP server will issue a DHCPNACK message to force the hosts/clients to drop the current configuration immediately and renew.

DHCP relay/IP helper

To ensure smooth connection and communication, each subnet should ideally have a dedicated DHCP server. This ensures that devices on the subnet can receive IP addresses and other configuration settings necessary for network communication. Occasionally, there will be small subnets where the number of hosts on that subnet is very low, and the cost of placing a DHCP server on that subnet cannot be justified. Most routers do not forward broadcast traffic by default; however, if the router is RFC 1542-compliant or has UDP ports 67 and 68 open, it can act as a DHCP relay agent. In this case, the router effectively bridges the gap between the client and the server, which enables the devices on the small subnet to receive IP addresses and network configurations.

The other alternative is to install a **DHCP relay agent** as an extra function on an existing server. This will intercept the DHCP clients broadcasting traffic and ask the DHCP server for an IP address. It will have the DHCP server IP address and forward the requests using unicast traffic.

The **Cisco IP helper** feature is used on routers and Layer 3 switches to forward broadcast traffic, such as DHCP requests, from one network to another. Normally, a broadcast sent by a computer (for example, when asking for an IP address using DHCP) does not leave its local subnet. If the DHCP server is located in a different subnet, the client would never reach it. The `ip-helper-address` command solves this problem by telling the router to take those broadcast requests and forward them as unicast packets directly to the specified server's IP address. By default, it forwards DHCP and a few other essential services (like TFTP and DNS), making it possible for devices in different subnets to use a centralized DHCP server without needing one in every network.

IPv6 stateless address autoconfiguration

IPv6's **stateless address autoconfiguration** (**SLAAC**) allows hosts to self-configure by generating a **link-local address**. This is an address that is only valid within the local network segment, also known as a **link**. To ensure it does not have the same IPv6 address as other devices on the link, it verifies its uniqueness with **neighbor discovery** (**ND**). After the link-local address is set up, it uses **router advertisements** (**RAs**) or **router solicitations** (**RSs**) for further configuration or DHCPv6 direction.

Name resolution

Name resolution takes a friendly name, such as a website or service, and converts it to an IP address. With the legacy system, NetBIOS, the name had to be less than 15 characters. However, with the name resolution we use today, **Domain Name System** (**DNS**), each label can be greater than 15 characters. For example, when you type www.packtpub.com into a web browser, the DNS resolution converts it to an IP address so that it can be found.

The full process is described in the following section.

DNS

When a user enters a URL into a web browser, **DNS resolution** occurs to identify the website's IP address. This process involves several steps, as shown in *Figure 16.8*.

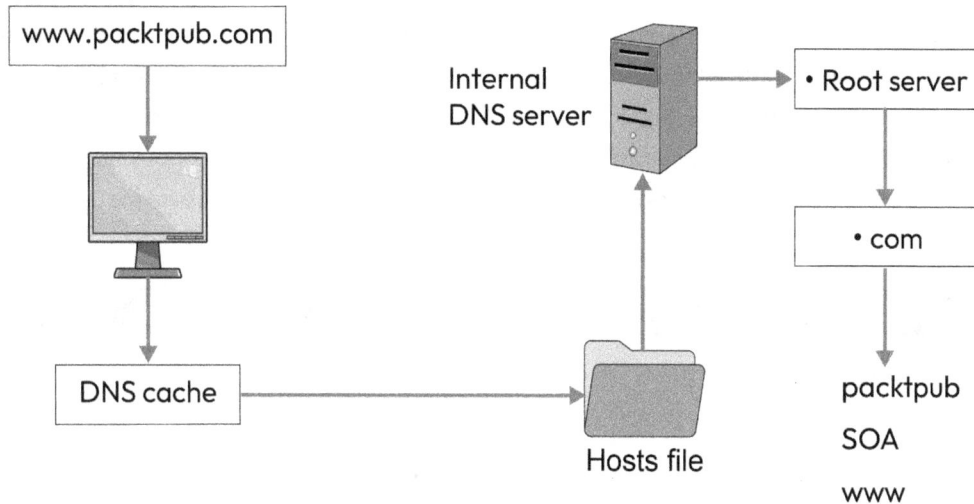

Figure 16.8: DNS resolution process

Figure 16.8 shows the process of converting the site name into the IP address. The DNS resolution starts when someone who wants to visit the Packt website types the URL www.packt.com into their web browser, and then the DNS resolution takes place.

The computer's operating system first checks the locally stored **DNS cache** for the IP address. It is worth noting that this cache is a frequent target for attackers due to its priority in the resolution process.

If the cache does not contain the required information, the system refers to the hosts file, which is a local text file that maps hostnames to IP addresses. In a Windows computer, the hosts file can be located in C:\Windows\System32\Drivers\etc\hosts. On macOS and Linux, it's located in /etc/hosts.

After checking its cache and hosts file, the DNS server (resolver) may query the root server, which refers it to the appropriate top-level domain (TLD) server, for example .org. The TLD server then provides the nameservers (NS records) for the next level down (e.g. example.org). When the resolver contacts one of these authoritative servers, it returns the A or AAAA record, for example www.example.org, which contains the actual IP address of the host. These records are cached locally.

The authoritative server may also provide a **Start of Authority** (**SOA**) record, which identifies the main DNS server responsible for the zone and contains administrative details (like refresh times and zone's serial number). While SOA is important for DNS management and replication, the clients main goal in this process is to obtain the A/AAAA record so it can connect to the host.

One issue within this system is the risk of malicious actors engaging in **DNS cache poisoning**, where they inject fraudulent IP addresses into DNS caches. For instance, if an online bank's domain name is stored in a DNS cache, an attacker could replace the legitimate IP address with one that redirects users to a fraudulent website. This is known as IP poisoning. This malicious site might be designed to steal usernames, passwords, or other sensitive information from banking customers.

You can check the DNS cache by using the following commands in the command prompt as follows:

```
ipconfig/displaydns
```

The output is shown in *Figure 16.9*.

```
Microsoft Windows [Version 10.0.19045.5796]
(c) Microsoft Corporation. All rights reserved.

C:\Users\Administrator.WIN-HB5RLG5VD60>ipconfig /displaydns

Windows IP Configuration

    105.210.168.2.in-addr.arpa
    ----------------------------------------
    Record Name . . . . . : 105.210.168.2.in-addr.arpa.
    Record Type . . . . . : 12
    Time To Live  . . . . : 173607
    Data Length . . . . . : 8
    Section . . . . . . . : Answer
    PTR Record  . . . . . : WIN-RJPN5B0RRLK.mshome.net


    login.microsoftonline.com
    ----------------------------------------
    Record Name . . . . . : login.microsoftonline.com
    Record Type . . . . . : 5
    Time To Live  . . . . : 2
    Data Length . . . . . : 8
    Section . . . . . . . : Answer
    CNAME Record  . . . . : login.mso.msidentity.com
```

Figure 16.9: DNS display

To erase all the DNS entries, you can use the following command:

```
ipconfig/flushdns
```

This results in the following output:

```
C:\Users\Administrator.WIN-HB5RLG5VD60>ipconfig /flushdns

Windows IP Configuration

Successfully flushed the DNS Resolver Cache.
```

Figure 16.10: Output of ipconfig/flushdns

Although this is one way to check DNS records, there are ways to prevent DNS records from being poisoned. This will be covered in the next section.

Domain Name System Security Extensions

Domain Name System Security Extensions (**DNSSEC**) is a suite of tools that secures DNS traffic by verifying the authenticity and integrity of DNS responses, protecting users from attacks such as spoofing and cache poisoning. It uses public-key cryptography, with private keys signing DNS records and public keys verifying them. These signatures are stored in **resource record signature** (**RRSIG**) records, and the public keys are stored in **DNSKEY** records, establishing a "chain of trust" from the DNS root zone to individual domains. DNSSEC works with standard DNS protocols (UDP/TCP on port 53) but doesn't encrypt queries. Instead, it ensures that DNS responses are authentic and untampered by validating the RRSIG signatures with the DNSKEY records. This process strengthens DNS security and helps users connect to legitimate websites and services. It can prevent DNS cache poisoning and DNS spoofing attacks. DNSSEC ensures that the records on a name server are authentic, but it does not protect DNS queries from being intercepted or tampered with during transit. To secure DNS queries, two main protocols are used, namely, **DNS over Transport Layer Security (DoT)** and **DNS over HTTPS (DoH)**:

- **DoT** encrypts DNS traffic using **Transport Layer Security** (**TLS**). It authenticates the digital certificate of the DNS server to confirm its legitimacy, minimizing the risk of connecting to a fraudulent DNS server. After verification, all DNS traffic is encrypted, with DoT utilizing TCP port 853 for communication.
- **DoH** encrypts DNS traffic and validates the certificate of the DNS server. It encapsulates DNS queries within HTTPS packets using the standard port TCP/443. This disguises DNS traffic as regular HTTPS activity, enhancing privacy. However, the additional HTTP headers can increase data overhead.

Both protocols improve privacy and security by ensuring DNS queries cannot be tampered with or intercepted by attackers.

DHCP snooping

DHCP snooping works by monitoring DHCP traffic on the network and allowing it only from trusted ports (usually where the real DHCP server is connected). All other ports are considered untrusted, and DHCP messages from them are blocked or logged.

nslookup

If a network administrator wants to double-check what IP address a DNS server holds for a particular computer or website, they can use a tool called nslookup:

```
Microsoft Windows [Version 10.0.19045.5796]
(c) Microsoft Corporation. All rights reserved.

C:\Users\Administrator.WIN-HB5RLG5VD60>nslookup www.packt.com 8.8.8.8
Server:  dns.google
Address:  8.8.8.8

Non-authoritative answer:
Name:    www.packt.com
Addresses:  2606:4700:10::ac43:a6e
          2606:4700:10::6816:42b4
          2606:4700:10::6816:43b4
          104.22.67.180
          104.22.66.180
          172.67.10.110
```

Figure 16.11: Output of nslookup

In *Figure 16.11*, we want to check the IP address of the packt.com website. We insert nslookup www.packt.com, but by adding 8.8.8.8 at the end of the command, we are using Google DNS, a very reliable source. Another source is Cloudflare's DNS server 1.1.1.1. In the output, you can see more than one IP address, which suggests that they are using a web array, which is multiple web servers used for performance and redundancy.

DNS record types

A DNS server uses different record types for different purposes. Some of these are listed in the following table:

Record type	Name
A	IPv4 host
AAAA	IPv6 host
CNAME	Canonical name – shortened alias
MX	Mail exchange – mail server
TXT	Text – stores domain information
NS	Name server – DNS server
PTR	Pointer – reverse lookup information

Table 16.1: DNS record types

In the following section, we will describe the use of each of these DNS records.

A or AAAA

The **A** record is used to indicate an IPv4 host on the network, while **AAAA** records indicate an IPv6 host. To create a new A or AAAA record in your DNS manager, right-click and then choose **New host** (A or AAAA, as they use the same wizard) as shown in *Figure 16.12*. The A or AAAA record will be created according to the IP address format that you use.

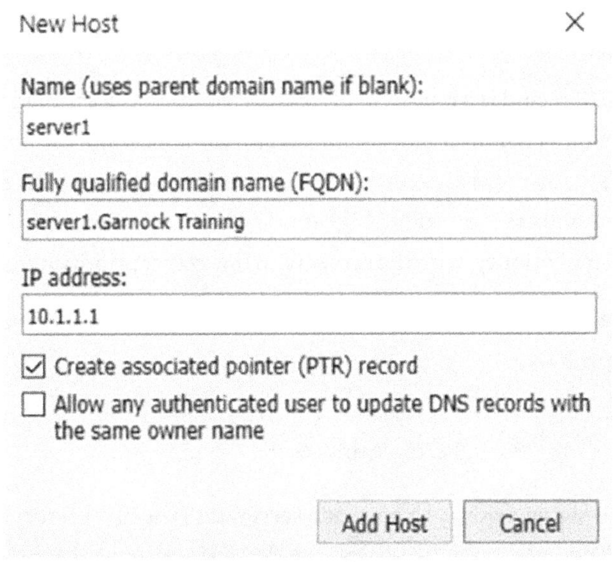

Figure 16.12: A new A record

Figure 16.12 shows a new A record being created. The **Name** section is the hostname you want to create, for example, server1. The **Fully qualified domain name (FQDN)** section automatically combines the hostname (server1) with the parent domain name (Garnock Training), resulting in server1.Garnock Training. Next is the IP address you want to map to the hostname. In this case, it is 10.1.1.1. The **Create associated pointer (PTR) record** checkbox option creates a reverse lookup record that maps the IP address (10.1.1.1) back to the hostname (server1. Garnock Training). It is stored in the reverse lookup zone as 1.1.1.10.

Canonical name

A **canonical name** (**CNAME**) is a type of DNS record that maps an alias or alternate domain name to a canonical (true) domain name. For example, it could be used internally to give a host with a long filename a shorter name, or to give your web server a more unique name. You might call your web server server1, but you might use an alias of www.packtpub.com.

You might be using a third-party blogging service with a URL such as myblog.thirdparty.com, but you want it to appear as if the blog is hosted on your own domain. To achieve this, you can create a CNAME (alias) record that maps blog.domain.com to myblog.thirdparty.com. However, most DNS providers do not allow you to use a CNAME record for the root of your domain (e.g., domain.com) due to technical limitations.

Mail exchange

A **mail exchange** (**MX**) record is a type of DNS record used to specify the mail servers responsible for receiving emails on behalf of a domain. It directs email messages sent to your domain, for example, user@domain.com, to the correct mail server for processing. Each MX record has a priority number, with lower numbers indicating a higher priority. When an email is sent, the mail servers are contacted in order of priority, with the server with the lowest priority number being tried first.

In the following example, mail1.example.com is the primary mail server, and the number after IN MX is the priority number:

```
example.com. IN MX 10 mail1.example.com.
example.com. IN MX 20 mail2.example.com.
```

You can use the mail server priority to have one server with the low priority outgoing, but with the MX from the internet. We could then change the low priority to mail2.example.com and have different mail servers as the primary outgoing and primary incoming. If we want to load balance the mail traffic, we keep the priority the same.

This is shown in the following example:

```
example.com. IN MX 10 mail1.example.com.
example.com. IN MX 10 mail2.example.com.
```

In this example, the number after IN MX is the mail priority; both mail1 and mail2 have the same priority, so the traffic will be load-balanced.

Text

A **text (TXT)** record stores any arbitrary text string, so it can be used to store various bits of information. One key use is to improve email deliverability and protect against spoofing and phishing attacks. A **sender policy framework (SPF)** is a record of which mail servers are authorized to send email on behalf of your domain. When a recipient receives an email from your domain, it can check back to the SPF record on your server to see whether it is genuine by checking the IP address.

Name server

A **name server (NS)** is a server that holds all the DNS entries for your domain. Without a name server, visitors would not be able to navigate your site, so it is important to ensure its reliability. One solution is to have numerous name servers, with redundancy ensuring availability. The main NS is called the authoritative name server and is indicated by an SOA record.

To ensure that all name servers have the same records, they are updated with **zone transfer** using TCP 53. With zone transfer, the main server sends a zone file, which is a text file that contains mappings between domain names and IP addresses, along with other related information, to all the secondary servers.

If you change the IP address of a DNS server, you need to update the NS record in DNS immediately.

Zone types

In DNS, a zone is a container that holds information about a specific portion of a domain's namespace. There are different types of zones, including primary, secondary, stub, forward lookup, and reverse lookup zones.

The **primary zone** is the main zone where all the DNS records are managed and stored. Since the records in this zone are writable, they can be edited as needed. These records are also replicated to other DNS servers. This is also known as the master server. The **secondary zone** is a backup copy of the primary zone used for redundancy. These are read-only and cannot be edited, but are used to reduce the load on a primary zone server.

The main difference between primary and secondary DNS servers is where the DNS records are created and managed. The primary DNS server is the main source of truth for a domain. The secondary DNS server holds a read-only copy of the primary server. It helps provide redundancy and handles queries if the primary server is unavailable.

The **stub zone** contains only the necessary information to find records in another zone. It optimizes name resolution by forwarding DNS queries to the authoritative servers for a specific domain and only includes the SOA, NS, and A/AAAA records.

The **forward lookup zone** resolves hostnames to IP addresses for your domain.

Reverse lookup zones resolve IP addresses to hostnames. They use a special domain called in-addr.arpa, designated for reverse DNS lookups in IPv4. While standard DNS translates domain names into IP addresses, reverse DNS performs the opposite function: it maps IP addresses back to domain names.

An IPv4 address, such as 192.168.1.1, is reversed to 1.1.168.192. The reversed IP is then appended with .in-addr.arpa, resulting in 1.1.168.192.in-addr.arpa. Reverse lookup zones rely on PTR records to provide the mapping.

Email servers often use reverse DNS to verify the identity of incoming connections, helping to reduce spam.

DNS authority

Within DNS, servers are categorized based on the information they provide: authoritative and non-authoritative. **Authoritative DNS servers** store and provide the definitive records for specific domain names. When queried, they respond with accurate and up-to-date information about a domain, such as its IP address. So, for example, if you own yourdomain.com, your hosting provider's DNS server is authoritative for that domain, holding all its DNS records.

Non-authoritative DNS servers don't hold official records themselves. Instead, they retrieve information from authoritative servers on behalf of users. After fetching data from authoritative servers, they temporarily store (cache) this information to answer future queries more quickly. This means that when you access a website, your ISP's DNS server may act as a non-authoritative server, fetching and caching the site's DNS information to speed up future visits.

The key differences are that authoritative servers own and maintain the DNS records; non-authoritative servers do not. Authoritative servers provide original data, while non-authoritative servers may offer cached data, which could be outdated if the original records have changed. Understanding these distinctions helps in grasping how internet domain names are resolved and how data flows across the network.

Caching-only DNS server

A **caching-only DNS server** is a simple type of DNS server that temporarily stores (or caches) DNS query results, acting like a memory bank for website addresses. When you type a website name, the server retrieves the matching IP address from another DNS server and caches the answer. This allows it to respond faster if the same query is made again.

Unlike other DNS servers, a caching-only server doesn't store permanent records about websites. It only keeps the cached answers for a limited time, determined by the **time to live** (**TTL**) value associated with the DNS record. Once the TTL expires, the cached information is discarded, and the server must fetch it again if requested. You can reduce the TTL so that the DNS records are updated more frequently and up to date.

Caching-only DNS servers are commonly used to improve internet speed and efficiency in environments such as offices, schools, or home networks. By caching recent DNS information, these servers reduce the load on primary DNS servers and provide smoother browsing experiences.

A **recursive DNS server** is a server that does the work of finding the answer to your query. When you type a domain name, it goes out to other servers starting at the root hints, the ultimate authority in DNS, which redirects it to find the IP address or records you need and brings the answer back to you. It's like a helper that does all the searching for you.

A hosts file comes after the DNS cache in the DNS name resolution process and can be used as a filter before the DNS server is queried. If we have a server called Sneaky Beaky that should only be accessed by three members of the Special Forces group, then we would go to the hosts file that is located in C:\Windows\System32\drivers\etc\hosts, and place an entry for Sneaky Beaky only on those three computers.

As shown in *Figure 16.13*, a DNS entry would allow everyone to access Sneaky Beaky; this is the main reason to use the hosts file.

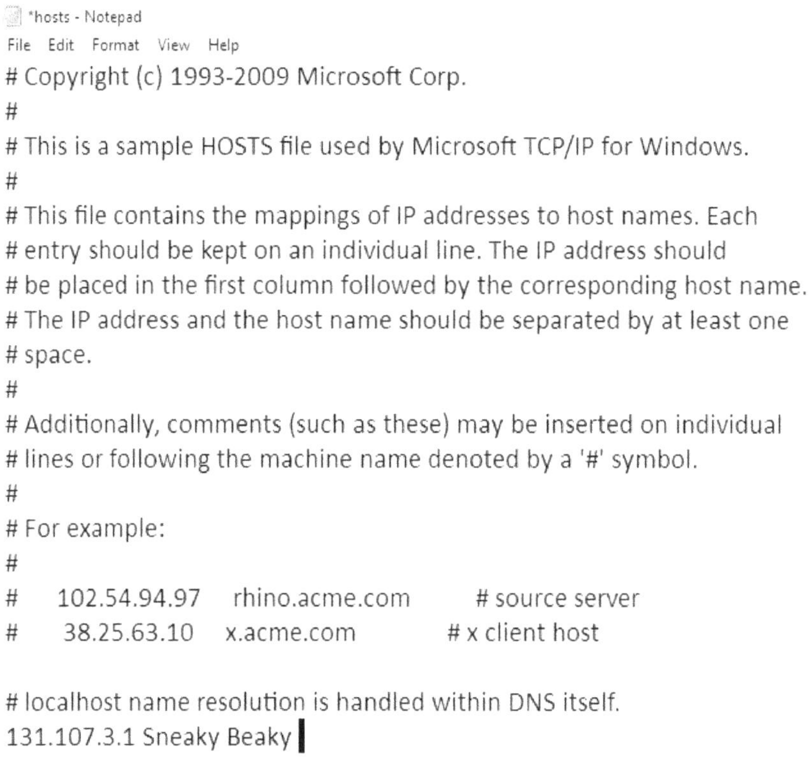

```
*hosts - Notepad
File   Edit   Format   View   Help
# Copyright (c) 1993-2009 Microsoft Corp.
#
# This is a sample HOSTS file used by Microsoft TCP/IP for Windows.
#
# This file contains the mappings of IP addresses to host names. Each
# entry should be kept on an individual line. The IP address should
# be placed in the first column followed by the corresponding host name.
# The IP address and the host name should be separated by at least one
# space.
#
# Additionally, comments (such as these) may be inserted on individual
# lines or following the machine name denoted by a '#' symbol.
#
# For example:
#
#      102.54.94.97     rhino.acme.com        # source server
#       38.25.63.10     x.acme.com           # x client host

# localhost name resolution is handled within DNS itself.
131.107.3.1 Sneaky Beaky |
```

Figure 16.13: Example HOSTS file

Time protocols

Many network applications rely on accurate time synchronization across hosts to function effectively. For example, in databases, transactions might need to occur in a precise sequence to avoid data corruption. Examples include authentication systems, auditing and logging mechanisms, scheduling tools, and backup software. The **Network Time Protocol** (**NTP**) plays a critical role in enabling this synchronization by operating over UDP on port 123.

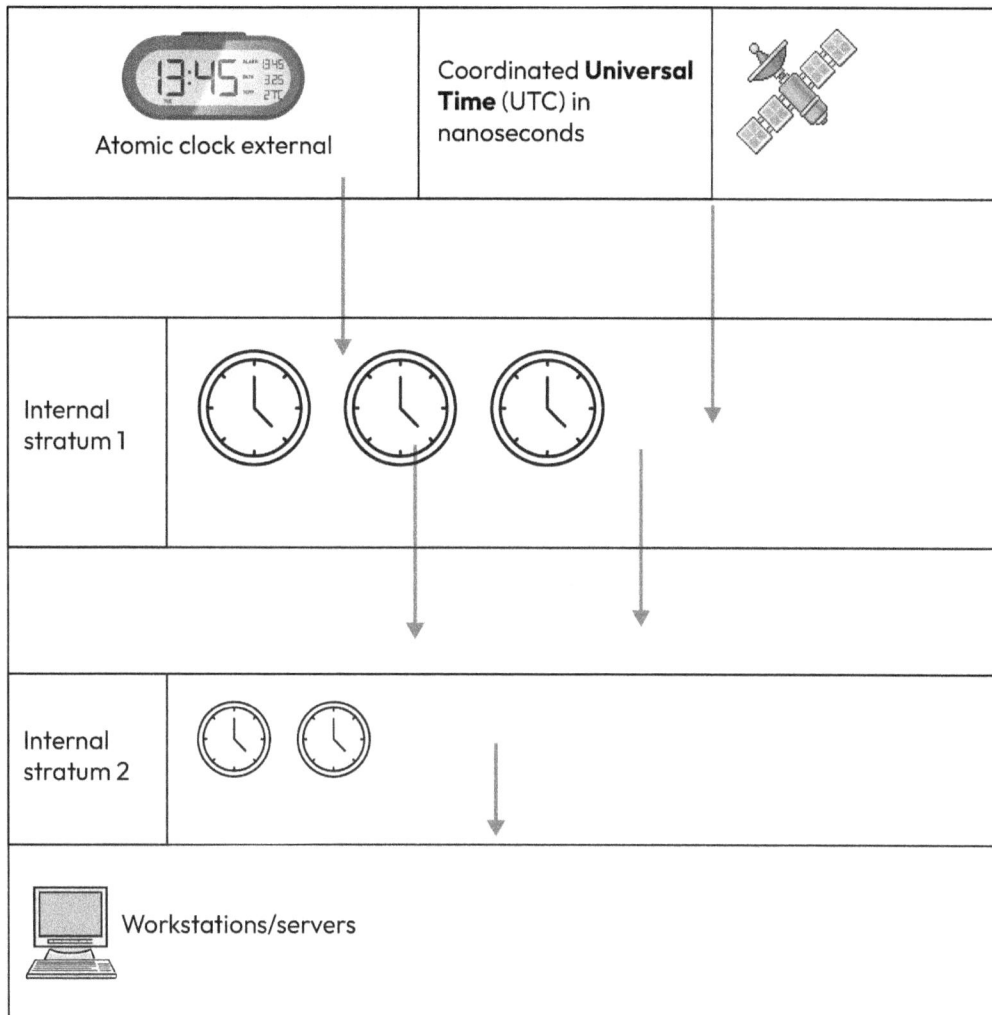

Figure 16.14: Time sources

NTP servers are classified based on their proximity to the original time source. *Stratum 1* servers obtain **Coordinated Universal Time (UTC)** directly from nanosecond-precise sources, such as an atomic clock or the **Global Positioning System (GPS)**. These servers serve as the primary time source for *Stratum 2* servers, which synchronize their clocks with *Stratum 1* servers over a network. If a local *Stratum 1* server is unavailable on the network, the time source can be set up using one or more public NTP server pools such as time.google.com, time.windows.com, or time.apple.com.

Stratum 2 servers act as time sources for lower-stratum servers or client devices, including network equipment such as switches and routers, which can be configured as local time servers for hosts.

Directory servers such as **Active Directory** often handle time synchronization for their networks. To maintain accuracy and reliability, devices should be configured with multiple reference time sources, preferably three or more, and set up as peers. This redundancy allows the NTP algorithm to correct for drifting clocks or inaccurate time values, ensuring synchronized and precise time-keeping across the network.

Time drift happens when a device's clock slowly becomes inaccurate over time. Just like a watch might run a little fast or slow, computers and other devices can have clocks that gradually lose or gain time. This can happen because the internal components used to keep time aren't perfect and can be affected by things such as temperature or small manufacturing differences.

If time drift isn't corrected, it can cause problems. For example, communication issues, errors in logs, and security problems. Devices that rely on the same time to communicate (such as servers, phones, or computers) might not sync properly. Events recorded in different systems might show incorrect times, making it harder to track what really happened. Some systems rely on accurate time for security checks, such as verifying passwords or securing financial transactions.

To fix time drift, devices often connect to a trusted time source, such as an internet time server. These servers provide the correct time, and the devices adjust their clocks regularly to stay accurate. This process is called **time synchronization**, and it helps ensure everything runs smoothly and consistently.

Precision Time Protocol

For most everyday uses, NTP provides sufficient precision, typically keeping devices synchronized within milliseconds. However, when timing needs to be extremely accurate, down to the microsecond or even nanosecond range, NTP might not be sufficient. This is where **Precision Time Protocol (PTP)** comes into play. It is designed for applications where precise timing is critical, such as 5G networks, where accurate timing ensures smooth and fast data transmission, or industrial processes that need to synchronize machinery.

Other important uses of PTP include medical applications that require precision for surgery or diagnostics, stock markets that need to accurately record and validate transactions, and broadcast media that need to sync audio and video.

Similar to NTP, PTP uses a hierarchy of clocks to synchronize devices with a leader or **grandmaster clock** at the highest level of the PTP network. **Boundary clocks** are found in switches and other devices that connect the networks. They receive time from the grandmaster and pass it on to other parts of the network. **Ordinary clocks** are found in servers or end devices and receive time from the grandmaster or boundary clocks. The **transparent clock** is found in advanced network switches, measures the delay as time passes through the network, and adjusts messages to maintain accuracy.

In a 5G network, a grandmaster clock could be located at a central base station, while boundary clocks ensure all regional towers are synchronized at the same time. In financial trading, a grandmaster clock might reside in a data center, ensuring all trading systems in different locations operate on an identical timestamp.

Network Time Security

To address potential risks such as unauthorized time sources or tampering with synchronization data, **Network Time Security (NTS)** provides enhanced protection for NTP, using TLS to establish secure connections and exchange keys. It then uses **authenticated encryption with associated data (AEAD)** to secure communications between clients and time servers. NTS ensures that time synchronization data remains secure during transmission. Earlier versions of NTS operated over TCP port 4460.

NTS strengthens the reliability of time synchronization by preventing malicious actors from injecting false time data or disrupting network operations, making it essential for critical systems that rely on precise and trustworthy timekeeping.

Summary

This chapter covered the implementation of IPv4 and IPv6 services. Dynamic addressing, name resolution, and time protocols are critical components of IT networking, enabling smooth communication and coordination among devices. Dynamic addressing simplifies network management by automating IP address allocation through methods such as DHCP and SLAAC while ensuring flexibility and scalability in network configurations. Name resolution, primarily through DNS, translates user-friendly domain names into IP addresses, with added security features such as DNSSEC and privacy-focused protocols such as DoH and DoT. Time protocols such as NTP and PTP ensure that devices maintain accurate and synchronized clocks, which is crucial for tasks such as secure communication, transaction logging, and system coordination. Together, these processes lay the groundwork for efficient, secure, and reliable network operations.

The knowledge gained in this chapter will prepare you to answer questions relating to exam objective 3.4 in your *CompTIA Network+ (N10-009)* exam.

Exam objective 3.4

Given a scenario, implement IPv4 and IPv6 network services.

Dynamic addressing: Automatic allocation of IP addresses

- **DHCP**: Method of dynamic IP address allocation:

    - **Reservations**: Pre-assign specific IPs to devices for consistency

    - **Scope**: Define ranges of assignable IP addresses

    - **Lease time**: Set the duration devices to retain assigned IPs

    - **Options**: Configure additional settings (e.g., DNS, gateway, etc.)

    - **Relay/IP helper**: Forward DHCP requests across network segments

    - **Exclusions**: Reserve specific IPs outside the DHCP range

- **Stateless address autoconfiguration (SLAAC)**: Enables IPv6 devices to auto-configure addresses without a server

Name resolution: Resolving names to IP addresses:

- **DNS**: Resolves hostnames to IP addresses

- **DNSSEC**: Encrypts DNS traffic to prevent tampering

- **DoH and DoT**: Encrypts DNS traffic to enhance privacy

- **DNS record types**:

    - **A**: Host records for IPv4 addresses

    - **AAAA**: Host records for IPv6 addresses

    - **CNAME**: Creates aliases for domain names

    - **MX**: DNS record for mail server

    - **TXT**: Stores metadata, often for verification purposes

    - **NS**: Specifies authoritative DNS servers for a domain

    - **PTR**: Reverse lookup record

- **Zone types:**

    - **Forward zones**: Resolve domain names to IP addresses for accessibility

    - **Reverse zones**: Resolve IP addresses to domain names for identification

  - **Authoritative**: Provides original DNS data directly from the source server

  - **Non-authoritative**: Provides cached DNS data from intermediate servers for faster response

  - **Primary**: Stores and manages the original DNS zone file data; writable

  - **Secondary**: Replicates DNS data from primary for redundancy and load balancing; read-only

  - **Recursive**: Finds DNS answers by querying other servers

- **The hosts file**: Local, manual mapping of IPs to domain names

Time protocols:

  - **NTP**: Synchronizes clocks across devices to ensure time accuracy

  - **Precision Time Protocol (PTP)**: Provides precise time sync for specialized applications

  - **Network Time Security (NTS)**: Protects time synchronization against attacks

Chapter review questions

Now that you've completed the chapter, you can check your knowledge using the practice questions provided in the online platform at `https://packt.link/N10-009ch16`. You can also use the QR code below. Accessing these questions requires you to unlock the accompanying online content first. Head over to Chapter 26 for detailed instructions.

17

Compare and Contrast Network Access and Management Methods

In many circumstances, you will need to have more than the standard access to your network. There are risks from eavesdroppers whenever there is communication across a network, but there are instances when security will be an absolute priority, even in remote communication. In this chapter, we will look at how **virtual private networks (VPNs)** create secure access to networks.

Understanding the differences between site-to-site and client-to-site VPNs, including variations such as clientless connections and the implications of split versus full tunnel configurations, is vital for ensuring secure and efficient remote access. Additionally, we will look at different connection methods, such as **SSH**, **GUI**, **API**, and console, highlighting how each serves different administrative needs and security requirements. This chapter introduces various methods and tools available for network access and management, each with distinct advantages and use cases.

This chapter covers the fifth objective in *Domain 3: 3.5, Compare and contrast network access and management methods.*

> **Note**
> A full breakdown of objective 3.5 will be given at the end of the chapter.

VPNs

Remote access, accessing a network from a geographically different location, has always been one of the advantages of the internet. It has grown exponentially in recent years as personal computing devices have become more portable, and globalization has spread across the globe. However, an increase in remote connections also means an increase in attack vectors for malicious actors, so the security of remote connections has become as important as reliability.

In *Chapter 4, Explain Common Networking Ports, Protocols, Services, and Traffic Types*, you encountered **Internet Protocol Security (IPSec)**, a suite of protocols that establish secure communication sessions called VPNs and IPSec tunnels between servers.

VPNs are important because they create a secure and private connection over the internet, protecting your data from being intercepted by hackers or eavesdroppers. They encrypt your online activities, making it difficult for anyone to see what you are doing, which is especially important when using public Wi-Fi networks. VPNs also allow you to access content that might be restricted in your region by masking your location, giving you greater freedom and security online. A VPN server resides within a company's network, and the client employs specific software to facilitate the connection, all of which takes place over the internet, reducing costs. This VPN setup allows for stringent control over incoming sessions, ensuring that only authorized users can gain access to the network.

Prior to using IPSec for VPNs, **Point-to-Point Tunneling Protocol (PPTP)** and **Secure Sockets Layer (SSL)** VPNs were popular choices, but they have since been surpassed by the more secure **Layer 2 Tunneling Protocol (L2TP)**/IPSec and user-friendly HTML5 VPNs.

HTML5 VPNs are simple, as they require only an HTML5-compatible browser such as Opera, Edge, Firefox, or Safari. However, they fall short in terms of security compared to the L2TP/IPSec VPN, which employs IPSec for enhanced protection. In this chapter, we will focus on L2TP/IPSec-based VPNs.

> **Note**
>
> You can revise concepts related to IPSec, including Diffie-Hellman groups, **authentication headers (AHs)** and encapsulated security payloads in *Chapter 4, Explain Common Networking Ports, Protocols, Services, and Traffic Types*, and *Chapter 2, Compare and Contrast Networking Appliances, Applications, and Functions*.

IPSec packet structure

L2TP/IPSec is the most common VPN tunnel, and the IPSec packet is comprised of the **authentication header (AH)**, which provides integrity, and the **encapsulated security payloads (ESPs)**, which provides encryption, authentication and anti-replay of the data.

Authenticated header (AH)	Encapsulated security payload (ESP)
SHA 1 MD5	DES – 56 bit 3DES – 168 bit AES – 256 bit

Figure 17.1: IPSec packet

IPSec modes of operation

There are three modes of operation for IPSec, which are shown in *Table 17.1*

IPSec modes	Technical description
Tunnel mode	In this mode, the user creates a VPN session from a remote location. During tunnel mode, the AHs and **ESPs** are both encrypted. Authentication methods include certificates, **Kerberos authentication**, and **pre-shared keys**.
Always-on mode	This mode is applied during the creation of a site-to-site VPN, the purpose of which is to build a point-to-point connection between two sites in possession of their own VPNs. The session is set to always-on to ensure the connection is available all the time. While a site-to-site VPN is active, both the AH and the ESP are encrypted.
Transport mode	This mode is used during the creation of an IPSec tunnel within an internal network using client/server-to-server communication. During transport mode, only the ESP is encrypted.

Table 17.1: IPSec modes of operation

The different modes of operation have both advantages and disadvantages, as we will cover now.

Site-to-site VPN

A **site-to-site VPN** enables secure communication between multiple private networks across different locations. Unlike remote access VPNs, which are typically initiated by individual clients to connect to a private network, a site-to-site VPN is designed to connect entire networks to one another. This allows organizations to maintain secure communication between their different branches or offices, even if they are geographically dispersed.

The core principle behind a site-to-site VPN is the establishment of a secure tunnel between the VPN gateways of the participating networks. It can replace a point-to-point connection or an expensive leased line. These gateways, which are usually routers or dedicated VPN appliances, handle the encryption and decryption of data as it travels across the VPN tunnel. This ensures that all communications between the connected sites remain private and secure from unauthorized access.

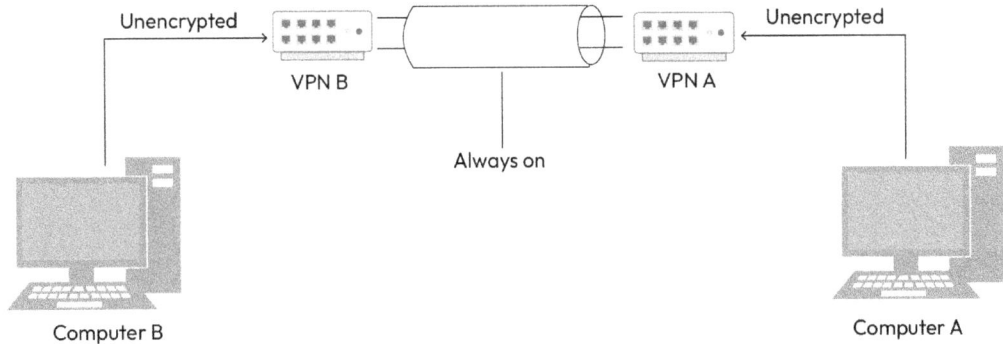

Figure 17.2: Site-to-site VPN

The connection process in a site-to-site VPN typically involves the following steps:

1. **Initiation:** Connection is initiated by a networking device, typically a router, firewall, or dedicated VPN appliance. This can happen either automatically or based on specific criteria such as the type of data being transmitted or the client's network configuration.

2. **Authentication:** Before the VPN tunnel is established, the gateways must authenticate each other. This is usually done using protocols such as IPSec or SSL/TLS. The authentication process ensures that the gateways are legitimate and can be trusted to establish a secure connection.

3. **Encryption:** Once authentication is successful, the data being transmitted between the sites is encrypted. This encryption process secures the data, making it unreadable to anyone who might intercept it during transmission.

4. **Routing:** The routing infrastructure at each site determines how data is sent through the VPN tunnel. In a site-to-site VPN, the routing can be static, where the connection is permanently in place, or dynamic, where the tunnel is established only when needed. Dynamic tunnels are particularly useful for optimizing network resources, as they reduce unnecessary traffic over the VPN.

5. **Data transmission:** After the VPN tunnel is established and the routing is configured, data can be securely transmitted between the sites. The VPN gateways decrypt the received data and pass it on to the appropriate devices within the network, ensuring seamless communication across the connected sites.

Types of site-to-site VPN tunnels

Site-to-site VPNs can be categorized into two types based on how the tunnels are established: **static tunnels** and **dynamic tunnels**. In a static tunnel configuration, the VPN connection is always active, regardless of whether there is data to transmit. This setup is ideal for organizations that require constant, uninterrupted communication between sites. Dynamic tunnels, also known as compulsory tunneling, are established based on specific triggers, such as the type of data being transmitted or the identity of the client initiating the connection. This approach can be more efficient, as it reduces unnecessary VPN traffic by creating tunnels only when needed.

Benefits of site-to-site VPNs

Having direct, constant connections between sites offers some real advantages. It allows collaboration and administrative efficiency across the organization. It also makes it easier to enforce consistent security measures across all connected sites. Implementing a site-to-site VPN offers further advantages over dedicated leased lines for organizations with multiple locations. By far the biggest benefit is enhanced security. By encrypting data transmitted between sites, site-to-site VPNs protect sensitive information from eavesdropping and unauthorized access. They are also far cheaper than leased lines, reducing the overall cost of maintaining secure communications between multiple locations. As an organization grows, additional sites can easily be integrated into the VPN without significant changes to the existing infrastructure, making them scalable and increasing security.

Setting up a site-to-site VPN can be complex, especially when multiple locations are involved. It requires configuring VPN appliances at each site, as well as securing and updating keys, authentication, and encryption protocols. Though they allow scalability when it comes to adding new sites, the administrative load makes it inefficient for shorter, individual connections, such as if a member of staff is working remotely from different sites, or if temporary access is needed for a remote contractor. For these instances, a **client-to-site VPN** might be more appropriate, as we will see now.

Client-to-site VPNs

The main structural difference between site-to-site and client-to-site VPNs is that a client-to-site VPN creates a temporary connection between an individual user's device and a central network, while a site-to-site VPN establishes a permanent connection between two networks. In a client-to-site VPN, the user initiates the connection using a VPN client installed on a personal device, such as a laptop, tablet, or phone. This tool creates a secure, encrypted connection to the organization's main network (e.g., a head office) using the same authentication and encryption protocols as a site-to-site VPN. Unlike site-to-site VPNs, which are maintained by gateway devices and allow entire networks to communicate, client-to-site VPNs are designed for individual remote users who need access to network resources. Client-to-site VPNs will normally require some kind of login information, which may even involve two-factor authentication.

As a manager or remote worker, you often need to stay connected to the office even when you're working from home. A client-to-site VPN is a tool that makes this possible, allowing you to securely access your office network and all its resources from wherever you are.

Client-to-site VPN example

Your office rings you while you are at home, and they need to review and approve a contract that's stored on your office's file server. Without a VPN, you'd have to either wait until you're back in the office or rely on someone else to send you the file. But with a client-to-site VPN, you can quickly and securely access the file server from home, review the contract, and approve it in real time, ensuring that your work continues smoothly and without delay.

Clientless VPNs

Even simpler than installing VPN software, a **clientless VPN** can be accessed in most standard web browsers using HTML5. It can be an easy way to access an organization's network without needing to install any software. Clientless VPNs typically use SSL or TLS encryption and often involve little more than opening a web page and logging in. Examples include **Cisco AnyConnect**, **Palo Alto Networks GlobalProtect**, and **Citrix Gateway**.

Clientless VPNs are ideal for users who require occasional or restricted access to internal network resources without the complexity of installing and managing VPN clients. They are widely used in scenarios where quick access is needed from a variety of devices or for third-party users, such as contractors or temporary workers, who may not be using company-provided equipment. For example, a graphic designer might need to access a company's visual assets, image banks, or other product information while working on an ad campaign. Using a browser, they simply log on and download some files from the company's server.

Clientless VPNs are easy to use but come with significant limitations, including restricted bandwidth and a lack of support for many applications. It may be difficult to connect to databases, for instance. They also introduce security concerns, inheriting vulnerabilities present in the browser, and without the ability to implement endpoint protection. Administrators are unable to enforce security policies, such as checking for anti-virus or the OS version.

They are also unable to implement special features, such as split tunneling, which you will read about now.

Example of a clientless VPN

An employee accesses the company's internal applications by logging into a secure web portal through a clientless VPN. Since no VPN software is installed on their device, they simply use a web browser to connect, allowing quick and secure access to resources from any device without needing a dedicated VPN client.

Split tunnel and full tunnel VPNs

A **split tunnel VPN** allows you to route some of your internet traffic through the secure VPN connection while the rest goes directly to the internet without encryption. This approach is beneficial when you want to access specific resources on a secure network, such as your office's internal files, while still using your regular internet connection for other activities, such as browsing or streaming. The main advantage of split tunneling is that it conserves bandwidth and improves performance for non-sensitive tasks since not all your traffic is encrypted and sent through the VPN.

Example of a split tunnel VPN

An employee working remotely connects to their company's VPN to access internal resources such as file servers and internal applications. With split tunneling enabled, only traffic destined for the corporate network goes through the VPN, while regular internet traffic – such as streaming video or browsing news sites – uses the employee's local internet connection. This reduces bandwidth load on the corporate VPN and improves performance for non-business traffic.

In contrast, a **full tunnel VPN** routes all your internet traffic from the start of the VPN connection to its final destination. This means every piece of data, whether it's accessing your office network or simply browsing the web, is encrypted and sent through the VPN server. This traffic is inspected thoroughly. Full tunneling offers the highest level of security since all your activities are protected, making it ideal for situations where security is the top priority. However, it can sometimes lead to slower internet speeds, as all traffic must pass through the VPN, which might not be necessary for all types of online activities.

Example of a full tunnel VPN

A remote worker connects to their company's full tunnel VPN, which routes all their internet traffic – both corporate and personal – through the company's network. This ensures that all data is encrypted and subject to the company's security policies, including web filtering and monitoring, providing maximum protection while working remotely.

Connection methods

Connection methods are the various ways administrators and users interact with and manage network devices and systems, each offering different levels of access, security, and ease of use. In the following section, we shall describe some of these.

SSH (Secure Shell)

SSH, or Secure Shell, is a cryptographic network protocol used to securely connect to remote devices, typically for **command-line interface** (**CLI**) access. It's widely used by network administrators to manage servers and network devices securely over an unsecured network such as the internet. It is lightweight and very fast. SSH encrypts the session, providing confidentiality and integrity, ensuring that commands sent to and data received from the remote device cannot be intercepted or tampered with by unauthorized parties. SSH is commonly used in scripts for automated tasks such as backups, deployments, or network configurations.

Graphical user interface (GUI)

A **graphical user interface** (**GUI**) provides a visual way to interact with systems, often using windows, icons, and menus. For those who prefer not to use CLIs, GUIs make it easier to perform tasks such as configuring settings, managing files, or monitoring system status. GUIs are user-friendly and accessible to people with varying levels of technical expertise, making them ideal for managing complex systems without needing to memorize commands.

APIs

APIs are widely used to enable communication between software systems and to automate tasks such as deploying network configurations or integrating services. In network and system management, APIs streamline operations by reducing manual effort and minimizing errors through automation. However, because most APIs are exposed to remote connections, they present a potential attack surface if not properly secured.

Strong authentication policies are essential to protect against unauthorized access. Avoid using admin accounts for routine tasks; instead, assign least-privilege accounts for automation. Programmatic access should be restricted to accounts with securely stored secret keys. Additionally, always use secure communication protocols such as HTTPS, and implement mutual authentication and strict access controls to ensure only authorized clients can issue API requests.

For example, a cloud administrator might use the AWS API to automatically launch and configure virtual servers, but must ensure secure access by storing secret keys safely and enforcing HTTPS connections to prevent unauthorized use.

Console

Unmanaged network devices, such as basic switches, function automatically without configuration, while managed appliances – including routers, firewalls, switches, and access points – offer advanced features that require user setup. These managed devices support various management interfaces, including the console and **auxiliary** (**AUX**) ports. The console interface provides direct, low-level access via a CLI and is commonly used for setup and troubleshooting. Connections are typically made through RS-232 serial ports, USB ports, or rollover RJ-45 to DB9 cables, which link the device to a computer's serial interface. The AUX port, similar to the console, is often used for out-of-band management, such as modem access for remote troubleshooting.

Jump box/host

A **jump box**, also known as a **jump host**, is a secure server that administrators use as an intermediary to access and manage devices on a protected network. Instead of directly accessing network devices, which may be behind firewalls or within sensitive environments, administrators first connect to the jump box. The jump box allows only secure connections such as SSH, and they are restricted to the IP address of the jump box. From there, they can securely manage the other devices. This setup helps isolate and secure the management plane, reducing the attack surface by limiting direct access to critical systems.

For example, a system administrator might use a jump box in a secure subnet to connect to internal servers in a private network. The jump box is the only machine exposed to the internet via SSH, and access to other servers is only allowed through it, reducing the attack surface and centralizing access control.

In-band vs. out-of-band (OOB) management

In-band management involves managing network devices over the same network that is used for regular data traffic. For example, using SSH over the internet to configure a router is an in-band management approach. While convenient, it shares bandwidth with regular network traffic and can be vulnerable if the network itself is compromised.

For example, a network administrator remotely configures a switch using SSH over the company's regular network connection. Since the admin accesses the device through the same network used for regular data traffic, this is an example of in-band management.

Out-of-band (OOB) management, on the other hand, uses a separate, dedicated management channel to access and manage network devices. If a system suffers a power failure or its normal remote access tools are unavailable, OOB management lets you connect through an alternative path. This could involve using a separate network connection, such as a serial port connected to a console server, or a dedicated management interface on a network device. OOB management is often used in critical environments where it's essential to maintain control over devices even if the primary network is down or compromised. It provides a more secure and reliable method for managing network infrastructure, especially in emergencies.

For example, a network admin might use an OOB management console connected via a dedicated serial port to access and troubleshoot a critical router when the main network is down. This separate management channel allows the admin to diagnose and fix issues even if the primary network connections are unavailable.

Summary

This chapter covered network access and management methods. These methods differ in how they provide secure access to IT resources. **Site-to-site VPNs** connect entire networks, while **client-to-site VPNs** allow individual users to connect securely, with options such as clientless access and split versus full tunnel configurations. Connection methods such as **SSH**, **GUI**, **API**, and console offer varying levels of control and ease of use. **Jump boxes** add an extra layer of security by acting as intermediaries, and **in-band** and **OOB** management provide different levels of security and reliability for managing network devices.

The knowledge gained in this chapter will prepare you to answer questions relating to exam objective 3.5 in your *CompTIA Network+ (N10-009)* exam.

Exam objective 3.5

Compare and contrast network access and management methods

Site-to-site VPN: Securely connects entire networks across different locations.

Client-to-site VPN: Enables secure access for individual users to a network.

- **Clientless VPN**: Access without dedicated VPN software, typically through a web browser.
- **Split tunnel**: Routes only specific traffic through the VPN, conserving bandwidth.
- **Full tunnel**: Routes all traffic through the VPN, enhancing security.

Connection methods

- **SSH**: Secure command-line access for remote management.

- **Graphical user interface (GUI)**: User-friendly interface for managing systems visually.

- **API**: Programmatic access for integrating and managing systems.

- **Console**: Direct control over hardware or virtual machines.

Jump box/host: An intermediary for secure access to network devices.

In-band management: Management within the same network as production traffic.

Out-of-band management: Management via a separate, dedicated, and secure network path.

Chapter review questions

Now that you've completed the chapter, you can check your knowledge using the practice questions provided in the online platform at `https://packt.link/N10-009ch17`. You can also use the QR code below. Accessing these questions requires you to unlock the accompanying online content first. Head over to Chapter 26 for detailed instructions.

Domain 4

Network Security

The fourth part of the book focuses on protecting network infrastructure. It covers logical and physical security concepts, identity and access management, compliance obligations, and segmentation techniques. Candidates will also study common attacks, including DDoS, ARP poisoning, rogue devices, and social engineering, along with defense techniques such as device hardening, NAC, ACLs, and zoning. This domain provides the essential skills to secure modern networks against diverse threats.

This part of the book includes the following chapters:

- *Chapter 18, Explain the Importance of Basic Network Security Concepts*
- *Chapter 19, Summarize Various Types of Attacks and Their Impact on the Network*
- *Chapter 20, Given a Scenario, Apply Network Security Features, Defense Techniques, and Solutions*

18

Explain the Importance of Basic Network Security Concepts

Securing your network is as important as designing, building, and maintaining a network. In fact, there are many concepts, such as firewalls or virtual private networks, covered in the first three domains of the CompTIA Network+ exam syllabus that are focused on securing your network. Network security is not separate from its architecture; however, as a network engineer, it is important to understand concepts that might normally be associated with cybersecurity roles.

This chapter covers **logical security**, which includes things such as **encryption, certificates,** and **identity and access management (IAM),** such as **multi-factor authentication (MFA)** and **role-based access.** It also covers **physical security** measures such as **cameras** and **locks,** and **deception technologies** such as honeypots and **regulatory compliance.**

Finally, this chapter covers **network segmentation,** which enhances security by isolating **IoT** devices, **industrial systems, guest networks, and personal devices.** Understanding these principles helps organizations prevent unauthorized access, mitigate risks, and ensure confidentiality, integrity, and availability.

This chapter covers the third objective in *Domain 4: 4.1, Explain the importance of basic network security concepts.*

> **Note**
>
> A full breakdown of objective 4.1 will be given at the end of the chapter.

Logical security

Very few organizations would leave their doors open, dispense with security guards, and allow access to all offices to anyone who asked. Physical security in most modern buildings will be a mix of barriers, locks, identity checks in the form of ID cards, and access controls, such as certain areas requiring special codes or passes. Likewise, the protection of digital assets should go beyond simply firewalls and include encryption and **identity and access management (IAM)**.

Security measures that involve software rather than physical infrastructure are commonly known as **logical security controls**. This section will cover **encryption** (designed to render data unreadable to those without permission), **certificates** (which verify the security of a website, server, or user), **IAM** (which controls who can access data), and geofencing (which controls access based on location).

Encryption

The process of transforming information so that only authorized parties can read it predates modern computing. This process protects both the secrecy and reliability of information, especially when it is transferred between parties. In networking, encryption is the transformation of the original data that is readable or usable, known as **plaintext**, into an encoded, unreadable, or unusable format, known as **ciphertext**, through a designated algorithm and cryptographic key.

While there are techniques to decrypt information, the complexity of the key determines how difficult it is to break. A key's complexity increases with its length because longer keys create more possible combinations, making brute-force attacks significantly more time-consuming. This means that the more bits a key has, the more computational power and time are required to break it.

If both the sender and receiver share the same key, this is known as **symmetric encryption**. In this method, a single key is used to encrypt and decrypt the data. Symmetric encryption often employs **block ciphers**, which process data in fixed-length blocks. If the data does not completely fill a block, **padding** is added to meet the required length. This approach is both secure and efficient.

Asymmetric encryption, on the other hand, has two keys, the private and the public keys, each of which has a unique role. The **private key** remains confidential and closely guarded by the entity to which the data belongs. The role of the private key is to decrypt data and generate digital signatures to help show the authenticity and integrity of the data, which is known as **non-repudiation**. In contrast, the **public key** is intended to be shared openly with anyone who wishes to communicate securely with the key holder. The role of the public key is to encrypt data and validate digital signatures.

When considering how data is encrypted, it's also important to think about whether it is being stored, sent, or used.

Data in transit refers to data on the move, traveling across networks or communication channels. This could be a credit card number being transported to a website during a purchase. The session in which the purchase is made is protected using a security protocol, such as **Transport Layer Security (TLS)**, **Secure Sockets Layer (SSL)**, which is an older version of TLS, or **HTTPS** (which is an abbreviation of **Hypertext Transfer Protocol Secure)**. A remote user might use a VPN that encrypts the data while in transit.

Data at rest is data that is not being used, such as documents, databases, backups, and archives, and is stored either on a hard drive, storage devices, files, or database servers. While it remains static until accessed, it is still susceptible to breaches if not adequately protected. Although it is not as exposed data in transit, it is still at risk of unauthorized access, by both physical and digital means.

By encrypting data at rest, you ensure that even if valuable or sensitive data is accessed, it can't be used. This is typically achieved using **full-disk encryption (FDE)**, file-level encryption, or database encryption, with encryption keys managed securely to prevent unauthorized decryption. The keys are stored in a **Trusted Platform Module (TPM)** chip on the motherboard.

Data in use is when you launch an application such as Word; you are not running the data for the application from the disk drive, but rather in **RAM** (which stands for **random access memory**). This is also known as **data in processing**, as the application is processing the data. Data running in RAM is volatile memory, meaning that should you power down the computer, the contents are erased.

Certificates

Encryption offers a way to ensure that when data is sent to another entity, such as a website or server, it can't be intercepted and read. However, how can we trust that the place we are sending the encrypted data to is trustworthy? This is where digital certificates come in.

Certificates are essential for protecting our online identities and enabling secure digital interactions. They bind a public key to an entity's identity, verified by a trusted issuer. The associated key pair enables security functions: the private key is used for creating digital signatures and decrypting data, while the public key is used for encrypting data verifying signatures.

PKI certificates, commonly known as **X.509 certificates**, can be issued by a **certification authority (CA)** using a **public key infrastructure (PKI)**, or they can be self-signed.

Self-signed

A **self-signed** certificate is a digital certificate that is generated and signed by the same entity to which it is issued. Unlike certificates issued by trusted third-party CAs, self-signed certificates are not verified by an external authority, which means that the entity creating the certificate is attesting to its own identity without any external validation. They are often used in internal structures such as private intranets, internal APIs, or internal services. They can also be used for personal projects or testing and development. Because they do not need a CA, they do not incur costs; however, they are often not trusted by browsers, and if not managed properly, can cause security vulnerabilities.

For example, if you are accessing email through a web browser such as Outlook on the web, and you get an error that the Microsoft Exchange server certificate is not trusted, then this is a self-signed certificate, and the administrators should replace it.

Public key infrastructure (PKI)

PKI is the infrastructure for issuing and managing asymmetric keys, where there are public and private keys. They consist of CAs, **certificate revocation lists** (**CRLs**), and **Online Certificate Status Protocol** (**OCSP**).

CAs validate digital identities using cryptographic keys, websites, and shared data are genuine. At the core of this process lies the **root key**, which is used to sign certificates. This process not only validates certificates but also links to the root key, creating an unbreakable trust chain.

CA type	Function
Online	Swiftly verify keys in real time
Offline	Prioritize security by working in isolated environments, away from online threats, but are slower
Private	Secure internal networks and communication
Public	Public CAs vouch for websites by issuing certificates that link a domain to its public key, proving the site is legitimate.

Table 18.1: CA types

Certificates are not immune to the passage of time or changes in security status. Certificate validity—a crucial aspect of maintaining a secure digital environment—is upheld through mechanisms such as **CRLs** and the **OCSP**:

- **CRLs**: These lists contain the serial numbers of certificates that have been revoked, compromised, or expired. CAs maintain CRLs and publish them regularly, and when a user encounters a digital certificate, they can cross-reference its serial number against the CRL to determine whether it has been revoked. If a certificate's serial number is on the list, it's deemed invalid. The CRL can be quite large and is downloaded from the CA.

- **OCSP**: The OCSP addresses some of the shortcomings of CRLs, one of which is speed. OCSP is comparatively much faster; it enables real-time certificate validation by allowing systems to query the CA's server directly.

Identity and access management (IAM)

Certificates are important because when you access websites or data, you need to be able to trust what you are accessing. The same is true the other way around; when people or other agents request access to your network, you need to be able to trust that they are who they say they are so that you can decide whether to grant the request. The process of **IAM** involves three main access controls: identification, authentication, and authorization. These are broken down next.

Identification

Identification in modern networks with IAM means that everyone has their own unique identity. This could be a password or a smart card linked to a user account. It's similar to everyone having their own bank account; the account is identified by the account details on the bank card. Identification in a secure environment may involve having a user account that is essentially the digital representation of a person, device, or software. All entities are given a unique **security identifier** (**SID**), which can be used to track them through a system.

Authentication

Once an identity has been established with a SID, there needs to be a way to authenticate the individual. The most obvious ones are passwords or **personal identification numbers** (**PINs**), but increasingly they include biometrics such as fingerprints or single-use codes sent to mobile devices. In many circumstances, an entity may be asked to supply more than one. This is known as MFA.

Authorization

Once a user has been authenticated, authorization is granted. During authorization, the correct level of access or permissions is applied. This is often based on a role or group membership. For example, a sales manager could access data from the sales group and then access data from the managers' group. Two of the main types of access control are as follows:

- **Least privilege**: The principle of least privilege is the idea that only the minimal permissions required to perform a specific job should be given to a user. For example, if an employee only needs to view and edit a subset of files in a shared directory, they should not be granted full administrative rights or access to other sensitive areas of the network.

  Least privilege is important because it minimizes the potential damage from accidents or malicious actions. By limiting access, organizations reduce the attack surface, helping prevent unauthorized access or the spread of malware. Additionally, it aids in compliance with regulatory requirements and simplifies auditing, as there are fewer high-level privileges that need to be monitored.

- **Role-based access control** (**RBAC**): RBAC is often employed within departments where specific roles require access to resources, helping to minimize the risk of unauthorized access to sensitive information. For example, there may be only two people within the finance department who are allowed to sign checks. Similarly, in the IT department, only two people may be allowed to administer the email server, as others may not have the skills.

Factors of authentication

Factors of authentication can be categorized into **something you know**, **something you have**, **something you are,** and even **somewhere you are**, as follows:

- **Something you know**: This involves knowledge-based information such as usernames, passwords, PINs, or dates of birth and functions as the initial layer of security in many systems.

- **Something you have**: This factor relates to the possession of physical objects, including secure tokens, key fobs, and smart cards. A hardware token, for example, generates a unique PIN periodically, and a proximity card grants access when in close range to the corresponding reader.

- **Something you are**: Biometric authentication falls under this category, using unique physiological or behavioral attributes of individuals for verification, such as fingerprint, vein, retina, or iris patterns, and voice.

- **Something you do:** This encompasses actions performed by users, such as swiping a card or dwell time while typing, and can include behavioral biometrics such as gait (which is the way you walk), keystroke dynamics, or signature analysis.

- **Somewhere you are:** Location-based factors consider the user's geographic location, adding another layer of contextual security and ensuring that users access systems from secure and approved locations.

A **factor of authentication** refers to which of the preceding groups a point of authentication belongs to. For example, both a password and a PIN are *something you know*, so they are the same factor. If, during authentication, you are asked for a username, PIN, password, or even date of birth, this is still **single-factor** authentication. Likewise, if you were asked for an iris scan and a fingerprint for authentication, it would also be a single factor (*something you are*).

If you are required to authenticate from two groups, such as combining a key card (*something you have*) with a PIN (*something you know*), this is known as **two-factor** or **dual-factor authentication (2FA)**.

Multi-factor authentication (MFA)

Your identity could be authenticated by a combination of three or more different factors, such as your gait being monitored and analyzed walking up to the entrance of a building (*something you do*), giving your fingerprint as part of getting the door to open (*something you are*), and completing the process with a PIN (*something you know*). This is considered **MFA** as the methods involved belong to three separate groups.

Passwords can be compromised, key cards can be stolen, and there are even ways to spoof fingerprints. However, adding a second or even third factor of authentication to a system can vastly increase security. If someone has actually managed to steal a key card, they will still need a PIN to access anything, so **MFA** is increasingly becoming commonplace. In some cases, such as when using Azure, it has become mandatory.

> **Note**
>
> Microsoft research states that MFA can reduce the risk of account compromise by more than 99 percent: https://packt.link/Wn3Qc.

The flipside to increased security through authentication is the increased account management complexity for the user. The number of services and platforms that people have to log on to in their professional or personal life has grown considerably in the last two decades, which means an increasing number of usernames and passwords to remember and even tokens to carry. Internal systems on servers, such as WAFs, VPNs, or switches, might also need to authenticate users and agents on a constant basis.

The solution is **federated identity management (FIM)**, which reduces the need for users to authenticate separately across different services by allowing a single identity to be used across multiple platforms. Combined with **FIDO** (which stands for **Fast IDentity Online** authentication standards), users can securely sign in without passwords using biometrics or hardware tokens, improving both convenience and security.

For the user, federated identities mean **single sign-on (SSO)**, which is an authentication process that allows users to access multiple applications or services with a single set of credentials. It is designed to simplify user experiences by reducing the number of times users must log in to relevant applications or devices to access various services—for example, a mail server. As there is no need to log in to every application separately, SSO significantly improves productivity and user satisfaction, while also reducing the time spent on password resets and support. However, it necessitates stringent security measures as any compromise of SSO credentials could potentially lead to unauthorized access to all linked services. Examples of authentication methods are Kerberos and federation services, which are covered in more detail later in this chapter.

> **Note**
>
> The time and administration efforts for password resets can be reduced by **self-service password reset (SSPR)**.

Just like users have SSO, there is also a way to help manage the authentication of remote users, such as the RADIUS protocol and **Terminal Access Controller Access Control System Plus (TACACS+)**.

Remote Authentication Dial-in User Service (RADIUS)

RADIUS is a network protocol and a server-client architecture widely used for centralizing **authentication, authorization, and accounting (AAA)** functions in corporate networks. It plays a key role in **IAM** by allowing organizations to manage user credentials and access policies from a central location.

Instead of storing user details on individual devices such as **wireless APs** or **VPN** servers, those devices send user authentication requests to a **RADIUS** server. This helps streamline security management and ensures consistent enforcement of access policies.

RADIUS is often used to manage wireless devices, such as enterprise **Wi-Fi** networks, by authenticating users who attempt to connect. For example, when a user connects to a secure wireless network, their credentials (e.g., username and password or certificate) are sent to the **RADIUS** server for verification.

After a user successfully authenticates, the **RADIUS** server handles authorization, determining what resources the user is allowed to access. This can be based on user attributes, group memberships, device type, or even location.

Once authenticated, the user moves on to **authorization**, which means **RADIUS** determines what resources the user can access and what restrictions apply based on factors such as user attributes, group membership, and location.

RADIUS's **accounting** feature maintains detailed logs of user activities, such as logging in and logging out of the system. This supports security incident detection and responses, post-incident analysis, and compliance. Clients are not end user devices, such as laptops, but servers in their own right, such as VPNs, wireless APs, and 802.1x authenticated switches, the last of which requires an endpoint certificate.

A **shared secret** (also known as a **shared key** or **shared password**) is used by the RADIUS client to communicate with a RADIUS server for authentication and authorization purposes, as shown in *Figure 18.1*.

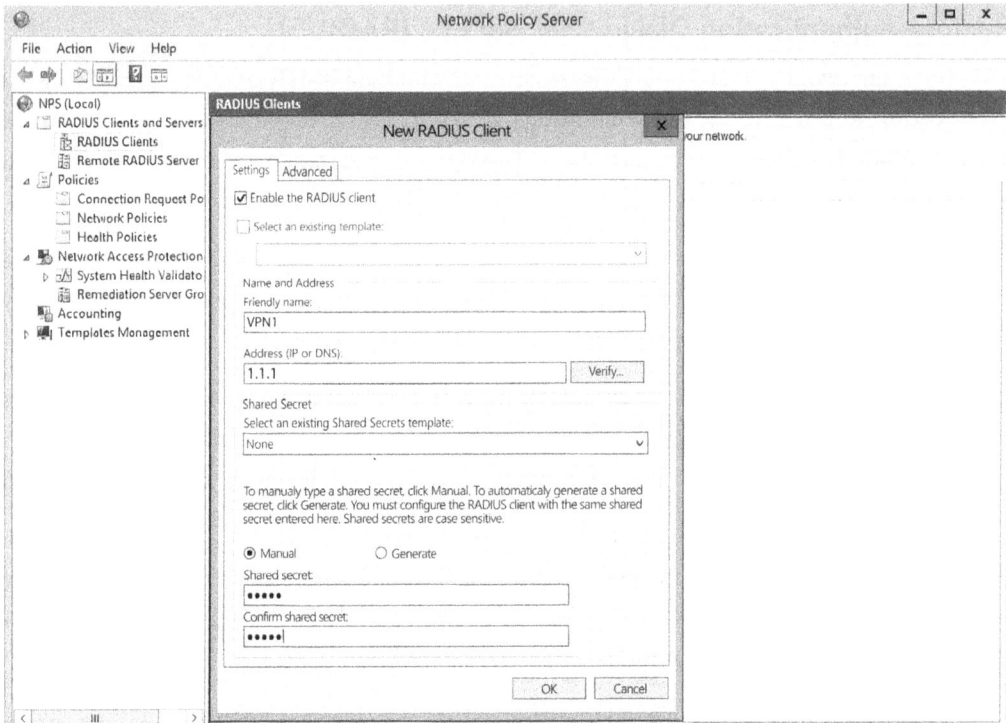

Figure 18.1: Creation of a RADIUS client

RADIUS servers often integrate with **LDAP**. In such a setup, **RADIUS** acts as an intermediary, receiving authentication requests from network clients (such as **VPNs**, **Wi-Fi**, or other network services) and querying an **LDAP** directory such as **Microsoft Active Directory** or **OpenLDAP** to verify user credentials.

This integration enables organizations to use a centralized directory service for both internal application access and network authentication, ensuring consistent identity management across systems.

Lightweight Directory Access Protocol (LDAP)

LDAP is commonly used as a directory service to store and manage user identities, authentication credentials, and attributes. It is used to query and modify directory services such as Microsoft **Active Directory** (**AD**). These directory services store information in a hierarchical structure based on the **X.500** standard defined by the **International Telecommunication Union** (**ITU**), though LDAP itself is a simplified version tailored for use over TCP/IP.

It manages AD by creating, updating, and querying objects that are stored in the X.500 format. These objects form what is called a **distinguished name** and are organized and stored by the LDAP. There are three key values in X.500 objects: **domain component (DC)**, **organizational unit (OU)**, and **common name (CN)**.

Figure 18.2 shows a domain called DomainA and an OU called Sales, where all the sales department users and computers reside:

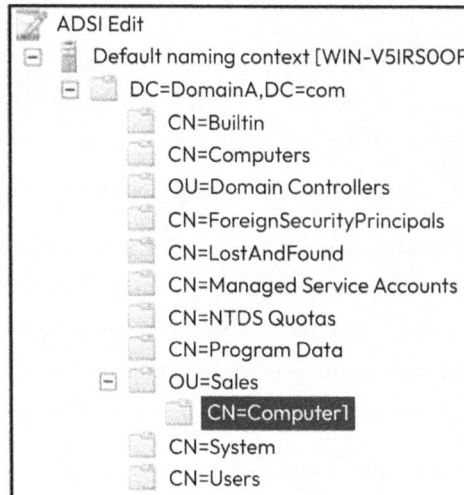

Figure 18.2: An example of an active directory

Figure 18.2 shows **ADSI Edit**, a tool used to manage and edit objects within AD. The domain name is DomainA; there are multiple CNs and OUs. OU=Sales contains the CN unit named Computer1. OUs can have group policies assigned, while CNs cannot.

Security Assertion Markup Language (SAML)

Federation services allow identity information to be shared across organizations and IT systems, normally for authentication purposes. The most common uses for federation services are joint ventures and cloud authentication, where third-party authentication is required. When two entities seek to do business on a joint project, rather than merge their entire IT infrastructures, they use federation services to authenticate the other third-party users for the purposes of the joint project.

When setting up federation services, the **Security Assertion Markup Language (SAML)** protocol is used to establish trust between different entities by allowing identity providers to issue authentication assertions to service providers. SAML is an XML-based standard for exchanging authentication and authorization data between parties, typically an **identity provider (IdP)** and a **service provider (SP)**.

An example would be a joint venture between *Company A* and *Company B*, each with three members of staff who need to access services and resources from each other, as seen in *Figure 18.3*.

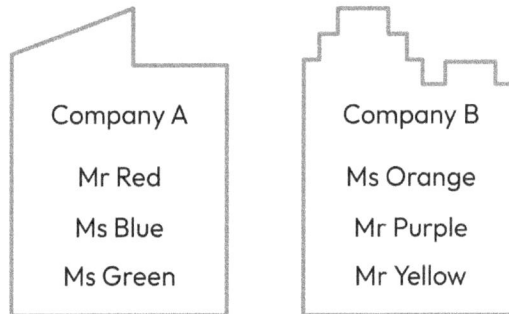

Figure 18.3: Company A and Company B

Figure 18.3 shows two entities, *Company A* and *Company B*. Each entity hosts distinct users in its own directory service. In a joint venture where each company maintains its own domain, a company can only authenticate users within its domain. For instance, Ms. Orange from *Company B* cannot be authenticated by *Company A*'s security administrator. The companies don't want to merge their IT management, so they need a third-party authentication model, and so they use federation.

In *Figure 18.3*, when Ms. Orange uses a service from *Company A* for which authentication is required, *Company A* uses SAML to pass Ms. Orange's credentials back to her IdP in *Company B* for validation. *Company A* is now known as the SP, as they are letting Ms. Orange access their resources. After the authentication has taken place, Ms. Orange will have a cookie placed on her device, allowing her to log in to other services in *Company A*.

Time-based authentication

Kerberos was designed by the **Massachusetts Institute of Technology (MIT)** in the 1980s as part of Project Athena to use strong cryptography to provide mutual authentication between clients and servers and prevent eavesdropping or replay attacks. The protocol has since been adopted and adapted widely, including its integration into Microsoft Windows domains as the default authentication protocol starting with Windows 2000.

In a Windows environment, especially within organizations that use AD, there are two main types of user accounts: **local accounts** and **domain accounts**. A local account is created and stored on a specific computer. It is only valid on that particular machine and is used for accessing local resources such as files or applications installed on that device. When logging in with a local account, users often prefix the username with .\ (for example, .\AdminUser). The dot tells Windows to authenticate using the local computer's user database instead of trying to use domain credentials.

On the other hand, a domain account is created and managed on a centralized server known as a **domain controller**; in a corporate environment, the domain account is used. The domain accounts are stored in the AD database.

Kerberos is a time-based authentication that uses a process called a **ticket-granting ticket (TGT)** session, in which the domain controller provides the user with a service ticket that is used to access resources such as the mail server. In a TGT session, a user sends their credentials (username and password, or smart card and PIN) to a domain controller that starts the authentication process and, when it has been confirmed, it will send back a service ticket with a 10-hour lifespan. This service ticket is encrypted and cannot be altered.

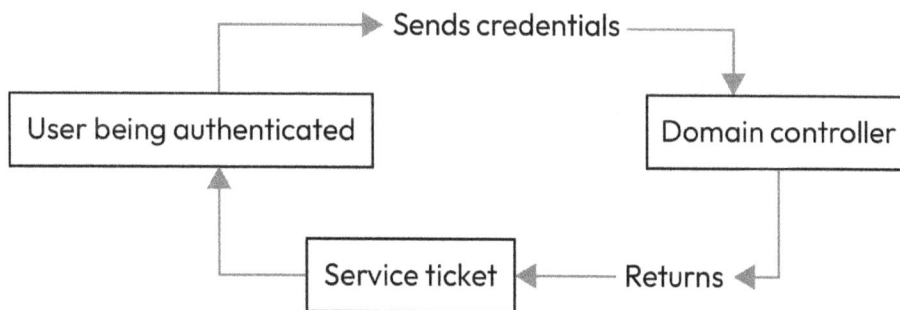

Figure 18.4: A Kerberos session

Figure 18.4 shows a user sending credentials to the domain controller, then the domain controller returning a TGT.

The computer clock times on all servers and computers must be within five minutes of each other. If Kerberos authentication fails, this is normally down to the user's computer or device time clock being out of sync with the domain controller by five minutes or more. A **Network Time Protocol (NTP)** server can be placed on your LAN to keep the domain computer and server clocks in sync with each other. If this is failing, check that the Windows Time service is running. If it is not running, the Windows machine will not be requesting time from the network.

Kerberos provides SSO authentication; the user presents the service ticket in a process called **mutual authentication,** where the user exchanges their service ticket with the resource, which then provides the user with a session ticket. It is called mutual authentication as both parties exchange tickets. *Figure 18.5* shows the user exchanging their service ticket in return for a session ticket for mutual authentication with a mail server.

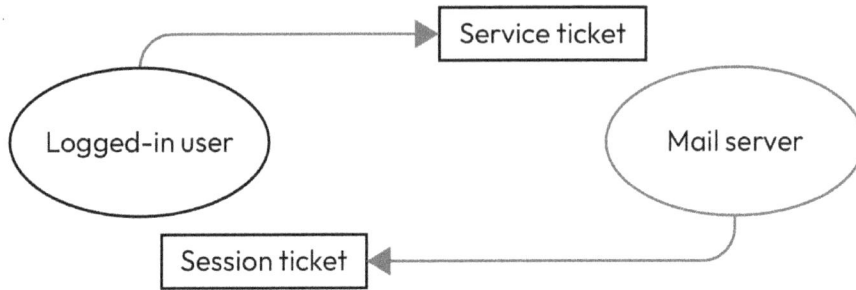

Figure 18.5: Mutual authentication

802.1x

802.1x is an overarching access control standard. It allows access to only authenticated users or devices and is therefore used by managed switches for port-based authentication. It needs a certificate installed on the endpoint (client or device), which is used for authentication. For wireless authentication, the switch needs to use a RADIUS server for enterprise networks.

TACACS+ is another AAA server created by CISCO. It is used to grant or deny access to network devices. TACACS+ clients often include routers, switches, and firewalls, or open source devices.

When creating user accounts In Linux, user account information is typically stored in two main locations: /etc/passwd, which contains basic information about user accounts, and /etc/shadow, which contains the password information. Only the administrator, or root, can access these two files. SSH key authentication in Linux uses cryptographic key pairs for secure, password-less remote access and authentication.

Geofencing

Geofencing, which leverages geolocation data to enforce location-based restrictions during the authentication process. By defining virtual geographic boundaries, systems can determine whether a login attempt originates from an approved area and respond accordingly. This adds an additional layer of security by ensuring that user access is not only tied to credentials, but also to where the user is physically located.

The **Global Positioning System (GPS)** is a satellite-based technology that provides precise location information by trilaterating signals from multiple satellites. This is known as **geolocation**. GPS is used by the satellite navigation system in cars to guide you to a destination, and GPS tracking uses these signals to determine the exact geographical coordinates of a device. While GPS itself relies on satellites, the device that receives GPS signals can transmit its location data over a cellular network or internet networks to enable remote tracking and location-based services.

Geolocation

Geolocation is a broader term that encompasses the process of determining a device's physical location using various methods. While GPS is one of the technologies commonly used for geolocation, it's not the only one.

Indoor positioning system (IPS) can also use Wi-Fi networks, cellular towers, Bluetooth beacons, and other location-based technologies to estimate a device's position.

Physical security

Although as a network engineer you will mostly be concerned with digital security, it's important to keep physical security in mind. Even the most sophisticated firewall will be unable to stop someone from walking into an office and stealing a hard drive. Physical defense includes a range of techniques from employing security firms, to creating barriers. This section will focus on the most important for the *Network+* exam, cameras and locks.

Camera

A **camera** is a detective control because it can film intruders, but they also a deterrent because if a would-be intruder sees a CCTV camera, they may be deterred from breaking in. Detection-based security adds an extra layer of protection when prevention methods fail. **Surveillance**, for instance, helps monitor and secure entry points. It ensures that any attempt to breach a barrier is detected, whether at the perimeter or inside a restricted area. Surveillance can be done through security personnel or cameras, with cameras being a more cost-effective option than stationing guards at every entrance.

Security cameras come in different types. For example, **fixed cameras** are ideal for capturing clear images of individuals at entry points. **Pan-tilt-zoom (PTZ)** cameras allow operators to scan large areas and focus on specific details, such as faces in a crowd. The right camera depends on the security needs of the location; a PTZ camera can move from side to side and up and down so that security personnel can follow someone approaching their company.

Locks

By securing individual rooms with servers and data centers, even if an intruder does get into the building, the most valuable data assets can still be protected. There are different types of locks, which are listed here:

- **Biometric locks:** Biometric locks use unique physical or behavioral characteristics, such as fingerprints, iris patterns, or facial recognition, to grant access. These locks scan and compare the biometric data with stored templates to verify the identity of the person attempting to gain entry.

- **RFID locks:** These locks use radio frequency signals to communicate between a card/tag and the lock. When the right RFID card/tag is near the lock, it unlocks automatically. No physical contact is needed, and there are commonly used for buildings, hotel rooms, and secure rooms/labs. They have no barrels and cannot be picked, although frequencies can be scanned with sophisticated equipment.

- **Badge reader locks:** These work like an RFID lock but typically require a swipe or tap of an ID badge. Some badge readers use magnetic stripes, while others use smart cards with chips. Badge reader locks can be integrated with employee access control systems. They are commonly used for corporate offices and government buildings. You can also track who enters the building.

- **Deadbolt locks:** Deadbolts are a stronger type of lock often used on exterior doors. Unlike spring locks, they don't automatically lock when closed, making them harder to pick or force open. **Single-cylinder deadbolt locks** use a key on the outside and a thumb turn on the inside. **Double-cylinder deadbolt locks** require a key on both sides, so they are good for glass doors. **Vertical deadbolt locks** are harder to pry open since the core moves up and down instead of in and out.

In addition to locks, **security cages** can create an extra barrier. They are metal mesh enclosures that surround one or multiple server racks or IT equipment. They can be full cages, which are floor-to-ceiling, or partial enclosures, which surround specific racks. Some use solid panels, while others have ventilated mesh to allow airflow. Security cages prevent unauthorized physical access to servers and protect against tampering and theft, and can help with compliance with regulations such as the **Health Insurance Portability and Accountability Act (HIPAA)**, PCI-DSS, and ISO 27001.

Deception technologies

While barrier protections, physical or logical, can help prevent access, there are other ways of protecting assets, one of which is to create digital decoys to fool intruders, transforming vulnerability into a strategic advantage. With digital decoys, you can learn more about intruders at the same time as safeguarding your resources, enabling you to build up a better understanding of your adversary. The three main techniques are the honeypot, honeynet, and honeyfile.

Honeypot, honeynets, and honeyfiles

When security teams are trying to find out the attack methods that hackers are using, they set up a website similar to a legitimate website with lower security, known as a **honeypot**, designed to encourage an attack. When the attack commences, the security team monitors the attack methods so that they can prevent future attacks. Another reason a honeypot is set up is as a decoy so that the real web server is not attacked. Honeypots are also known as decoy or non-production systems.

Honeynets are a group of honeypots that give the appearance of a network. These, too, are created as a decoy to draw attackers away from the actual network and can provide a testing ground through which cybersecurity professionals can study and analyze malicious activities. They act as a decoy through which cybersecurity professionals can study and understand malicious activities while safeguarding their actual networks from harm.

The **honeyfile** is bait that will catch an attacker who wants to steal your data. For example, it could be a file titled `password` that is saved on a desktop, designed to lure an attacker. Once accessed, it sets off alarms, marking the intrusion and triggering a proactive defense. This digital bait, seemingly innocuous, reveals an attacker's intent and direction, allowing defenders to anticipate their next move.

Common security terminology

Computer and network security is all about protecting data and keeping systems safe from cyber threats. This involves setting up rules, tools, and practices to prevent hackers, viruses, and other risks from causing harm. In this section, you will see some common terms used in computer security:

- **Risk** is the probability that a negative event will happen. In IT security, this means an event that results in loss or harm to an organization's assets, data, and/or reputation due to cyber threats or vulnerabilities. For instance, risk would measure the probability that your system could be hacked and data stolen.

- A **threat** is someone or something that wants to inflict loss on a company by exploiting vulnerabilities. For instance, it could be a virus carrying out a ransomware attack, or an inside threat stealing data for a competitor.

- A **vulnerability** is a weakness that helps an attacker exploit a system. This could be a weakness in a software package or a misconfiguration of a firewall.

- An **exploit** in cybersecurity is like a trick or a tool that hackers use to take advantage of a vulnerability in a computer system, software, or network. Exploits can be used to steal data, spread viruses, or take control of a system. Sometimes, hackers create special programs or codes called **exploit scripts** to automate the attack. Think of it like finding an unlocked door in a building—if someone knows about it and decides to sneak in, that's an exploit in action. Companies try to fix these weaknesses by releasing security updates, also known as **patches,** to close the "unlocked doors" before hackers can use them.

Risk tolerance is an organization's personalized threshold for embracing the unknown. It's a finely tuned balance that guides strategic decisions to combine financial strength with market dynamics and innovation pursuits.

For example, a mid-sized e-commerce company is assessing its cybersecurity strategy. The company handles customer data, including names, emails, and purchase history, but does not process payment information directly (payments are handled by a third-party provider such as Stripe or PayPal). The process would be as follows:

1. **Risk assessment outcome**: A security audit identifies that the company's current WAF provides only moderate protection against advanced bot attacks and zero-day exploits.

2. **Risk tolerance decision**: The leadership team decides that the likelihood and potential impact of a zero-day attack on their specific platform is low to moderate, and they determine that the cost of upgrading to a more advanced WAF (e.g., doubling the current security budget) is not justifiable at this time.

3. **Documented risk tolerance statement**: "*Based on our current threat model and asset sensitivity, the organization accepts a moderate level of risk related to advanced automated attacks. While improvements to our WAF could reduce this risk further, our current solution meets our acceptable risk threshold given our exposure, cost considerations, and existing incident response capabilities.*" This statement shows a conscious decision to accept some level of risk, which is a key component of defining risk tolerance.

Confidentiality, integrity, and availability triad

The **CIA** triad is a common concept across cybersecurity. It stands for **confidentiality, integrity, and availability**, which are the three pillars of digital security:

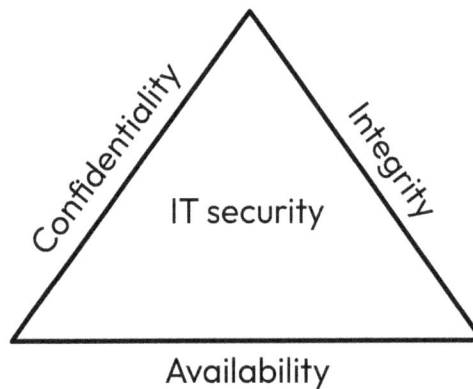

Figure 18.6: The CIA triad

- **Confidentiality** ensures that sensitive information remains shielded from prying eyes and that access is granted solely to those with the appropriate authorization. Confidentiality safeguards trade secrets, personal data, and any confidential information that requires a digital lock and key. It is achieved with encryption.

- **Integrity** ensures that your data remains unaltered and trustworthy. It prevents unauthorized changes or manipulations to your information, maintaining its accuracy and reliability. Hashing algorithms such as SHA1 or MD5 provide data integrity.

- **Availability** is the condition that your digital assets and services should be accessible when needed. Availability means that your systems are up and running, that your data can be accessed promptly, especially customer data, and that your online services remain accessible. This is achieved by ensuring your physical infrastructure is kept cool to prevent failure by using the correct **heating, ventilation, and air conditioning (HVAC)**. It is also achieved with redundancy, or a **redundant array of independent disks (RAID)**.

A RAID is a group of disks that act together as a set, so that if one disk fails, then the data is still available. There are different RAID levels, which describe configurations. The main ones are RAID 1, RAID 5, and RAID 6, as described here:

- **RAID 1**: This is also called a **mirror set**. It comprises two disks, and data is written to both disks simultaneously. If one disk fails, then the data is available on the other. It is sometimes used to mirror databases.

- **RAID 5**: This comprises 3–5 disks, striped with parity, meaning that the data is shared across the disks. If one disk fails, then the data is available, but if two disks fail, then the data is lost.

- **RAID 6**: This comprises 4–32 disks, striped with double parity. If two disks fail, then data is available, but if three disks fail, then data is lost.

Another form of availability is a **load balancer**, which balances the load across multiple identical hosts, where if one host fails, then the incoming requests are shared among the other hosts.

> **Note**
>
> Load balancers are covered in greater detail in *Chapter 2, Compare and Contrast Networking Appliances, Applications, and Functions.*

Audits and regulatory compliance

Various laws and standards dictate how data should be stored, processed, and protected, particularly when dealing with sensitive information such as financial or personal data. Compliance with these regulations is not just a legal necessity but also a critical component of maintaining trust with customers and partners.

Audits play a crucial role in regulatory compliance by systematically reviewing and verifying that organizations adhere to data locality laws, security standards, and privacy regulations, ensuring they meet legal requirements and avoid penalties. In the section below we will look at data locality and common regulations:

- **Data locality** ensures that data remains within the region where it was created and is subject to that region's laws. This concept is closely related to data sovereignty, which dictates that data is governed by the regulations of the country in which it originates. Many governments enforce strict rules to prevent data from being transferred across borders, even for legitimate purposes such as backup and disaster recovery.

  For example, multinational corporations and cloud service providers must carefully manage their data storage strategies to remain compliant with these laws. If an organization violates data locality requirements, it may face legal consequences, including fines and restrictions on operations. As businesses increasingly rely on cloud computing and global data exchanges, adhering to data locality principles becomes more important than ever.

- **Data sovereignty**: Any data that has been created is subject to the laws and regulations of the region in which it was created. It cannot be moved to another region even for a backup-related reason. This affects both cloud providers and multinational corporations, as they cannot simply move data where they want to.

They are some key regulatory frameworks that govern data security and privacy, including the PCI-DSS and the **General Data Protection Regulation** (**GDPR**). These standards help ensure that sensitive data is protected and that organizations remain compliant with evolving legal requirements. The next section covers them in greater detail.

Note

In 2023, Meta Platforms was fined 1.2 billion euros for transferring data from the EU to the US without adequate privacy protection. For more information, see `https://packt.link/BUM61`.

Payment Card Industry Data Security Standards (PCI DSS)

The **Payment Card Industry Security Standards Council (PCI DSS SSC)** was formed by five major credit card companies. PCI-DSS is a robust security standard designed to safeguard payment card data during transactions. Credit card data comprises the credit card number, the expiry data, and the CVC number next to the signature strip, using a PIN for authentication. It sets stringent requirements for organizations to protect sensitive financial information, ensuring secure commerce in an evolving digital landscape.

General Data Protection Regulation (GDPR)

The GDPR is a comprehensive data privacy law enacted by the EU to protect the personal data and privacy of individuals residing within the EU and the **European Economic Area (EEA)**. It governs how organizations collect, store, process, and share **personally identifiable information (PII)**.

GDPR is responsible for ensuring the security and protection of personal data within the EU. It applies not only to organizations based in the EU, but also to any organization—regardless of location—that offers goods or services to, or monitors the behavior of, EU citizens. This means that websites and companies outside the EU must also be GDPR-compliant if they process the personal data of individuals within the EU.

GDPR lays out the follow requirements:

- Organizations must obtain clear, informed consent before collecting or processing an individual's personal data
- Individuals (data subjects) have several rights, including the following:
    - The right to access their data
    - The right to rectify inaccurate data
    - The right to restrict or object to processing
    - The right to data portability
    - The right to erasure, commonly referred to as the right to be forgotten

The right to be forgotten allows an EU citizen to request that a company (the data controller) erase any personal data it holds about them. This must be done without undue delay, unless there is a legal basis to retain the data, such as compliance with a legal obligation or an ongoing criminal investigation.

Failure to comply with GDPR can result in substantial penalties, including fines of up to €20 million or 5% of global annual turnover, whichever is higher.

The 10 key GDPR requirements are as follows:

1. Lawful, fair, and transparent processing
2. Limitations of purpose, data, and storage
3. Data accuracy, integrity, and confidentiality
4. Data protection impact assessment
5. Privacy by design
6. Controller-processor contracts
7. Data subject rights
8. Data protection officer
9. International data transfers
10. Personal data breach reporting

In 2020, Google LLC was fined 7 million euros by the Swedish government. In the same year, they were fined 600,000 euros by the Belgian government. Both fines were for right-to-be-forgotten violations.

> **Note**
>
> For more details, please visit `https://www.edpb.europa.eu/news/national-news/2020/swedish-data-protection-authority-imposes-administrative-fine-google_en` and `https://lawrope.com/googles-failure-to-respect-the-right-to-be-forgotten-results-in-e600000-fine/`.

Network segmentation enforcement

A network has to be both secure and accessible. You need to allow the right visitors, customers, partners, and services to your network while protecting it from unwanted attackers. Having a single setup with the same level of security throughout could mean too much compromise either way, so modern networks are segmented to allow for different levels of security depending on the access needs.

The strategy of **network segmentation enforcement** means there are smaller, isolated segments that allow you to control traffic flow and limit access between different parts of the network. SDNs such as VLANs and subnets are both types of segments, and using firewalls and access control, different levels of security can be set depending on the needs of the segment and the sensitivity of its data. This is known as **local segmentation**.

For example, in a corporate environment, an organization may create separate VLANs for employees, guest Wi-Fi users, and critical business applications. Employee workstations can access internal resources, while guests are restricted to internet access only. Additionally, a highly sensitive database storing customer financial data could be placed in an isolated subnet with strict firewall rules, ensuring that only authorized servers or personnel can access it.

Network segmentation also happens at a much higher level. An organization's network is constantly moving data between the internet and individual end users, such as database servers or company computers. This movement goes through three distinct zones known as the WAN, the screened subnet, and the LAN. The **WAN** is the external public network covering a wide geographical area. This is considered untrusted as it includes the internet and other external networks where data can be intercepted, modified, or attacked by malicious actors.

A **screened subnet** is a boundary layer owned by a company whose purpose is to protect the company from external hackers. This is a neutral zone that hosts data accessible to people from both the trusted and untrusted zones. An example of this is a mail server, which has to communicate with both internal users and external senders. The screened subnet ensures that the mail server is accessible from the internet while preventing direct access to the internal network. This setup allows emails to be received and filtered for threats before being forwarded to the trusted internal network.

In addition to mail servers, other common examples of services hosted in a screened subnet include web servers, DNS servers, and VPN gateways.

The **LAN** is a network covering a small location such as a building or a company with staff working in close proximity, for example, an office building, a school campus, or a hospital. In a LAN, devices such as computers, printers, and servers are interconnected to enable efficient communication and resource sharing.

Note

VLANs, WANs, and subnets are explored in greater detail in the first part of this book, *Domain 1, Networking Concepts,* and the second part, *Domain 2, Network Implementation.*

Internet of Things (IoT) and Industrial Internet of Things (IIoT)

In addition to network devices and traditional endpoints, such as computers, increasing numbers of "smart" devices are being added to networks. Security cameras, thermostats, fridges, and evening lighting systems are now often internet-enabled as standard. **IoT** devices offer many advantages, such as remote access, monitoring, automation, and automatic firmware upgrading. At the same time, they increase the attack surface of your network.

Similar to IoT, the **Industrial Internet of Things** (IIoT) refers to smart, connected technologies used in industries such as manufacturing, energy, and logistics to improve efficiency, safety, and decision-making. These devices include sensors, cameras, and machines that collect real-time data and share it over the internet or private networks. By analyzing this data, companies can monitor equipment health, predict maintenance needs, automate processes, and reduce downtime. For example, IIoT sensors on factory machines can detect early signs of wear and alert technicians before a breakdown occurs.

However, as with IoT, the IIoT also increases the attack surface and increases the opportunity for industrial espionage, or even attacks on essential national infrastructure such as power generation plants.

Such devices can often be overlooked, and general security maintenance, such as changing default passwords and keeping security patches up to date, is essential. However, network segmentation can also play an important part in keeping both devices and networks secure.

IoT devices can be grouped into VLANs or subnets depending on functions, communication needs, and associated security risks. For instance, surveillance cameras, smart thermostats, and medical devices can each form distinct groups. This classification allows for tailored security policies and access controls for each segment.

The same is true for IIoT devices. In some circumstances, particularly sensitive machinery might be air gapped, that is, separated from the network entirely, perhaps in a separate LAN that isn't even connected to the internet.

Supervisory control and data acquisition, industrial control systems, and operational technology

Securing **industrial control systems (ICSs)** and **supervisory control and data acquisition (SCA-DA)** systems involves practices such as network segmentation, enhancing physical security measures, and regularly applying security updates to safeguard critical infrastructure.

Operational technology (OT) networks are specialized systems used to monitor and control industrial equipment, such as power plants, manufacturing machines, and transportation systems. Unlike traditional IT networks, which focus on data and communication, OT networks are designed for real-time control and reliability. These networks connect devices such as sensors, controllers, and industrial machines to ensure smooth operations and safety. OT needs to be segmented or isolated from parts of the network for security. For example, in a factory, an OT network allows machines to communicate with each other and with human operators to maintain production efficiency. As industries adopt more digital technologies, OT networks are increasingly integrated with IIoT and IT systems, improving automation and decision-making while also introducing new cybersecurity challenges. We need to keep them secure.

Guest networks and devices

In addition to the common, static devices in your network, such as PCs or other IoT devices, there will also be devices that do not belong to the network. These can be visitors coming into a premises for a short amount of time, or it might be members of staff who prefer to use their own personal laptops or tablets for work purposes. Because you might not have direct control over these devices, it's important to have secure policies. For example, a **guest network** is a separate Wi-Fi network that allows visitors to connect to the internet without accessing the main network, keeping personal or business data secure. Other policies include **bring your own device (BYOD)**, **choose your own device (CYOD)**, and **corporate-owned, personally enabled (COPE)**.

Bring your own device (BYOD)

BYOD policies allow employees to use their personal devices for work-related tasks. While this can boost productivity, it also presents a security risk as the nature of such policies means that company data and access are carried on a device that is regularly removed from business premises and otherwise employed for personal use. To mitigate these risks, organizations should implement containerization techniques to separate work and personal data and enforce strict security policies on the work-related portion of the device. The device must be compliant with security policies. The owner of the device cannot use the device for social purposes during working hours and must allow company-owned applications to be installed.

Choose your own device (CYOD)

CYOD is a policy in which the company provides employees with a selection of approved devices to choose from. These devices are owned and managed by the organization. This model allows for increased flexibility with company devices but still maintains security control.

Corporate-owned, personally enabled (COPE)

In COPE, organizations provide employees with corporate-owned devices that can be used for both business and personal use, but must comply with company policies. Full device encryption will be used on these devices to prevent data theft if the device is left unattended. It is important that mobile devices have strong passwords and screen locks to protect the data stored on the device.

Zones

In networking, when we move data between the internet and a company computer, we do so through three distinct zones: the WAN, the screened subnet, and the LAN.

A WAN is an external public network that covers a wide geographical area. This is considered an untrusted zone. A screened subnet is a boundary layer owned by a company whose purpose is to protect the company from external hackers. This is a neutral zone that hosts data accessible to people from both the trusted and untrusted zones. An example of this is a mail server.

For instance, *Company A* (a car manufacturer) has its office staff working from the LAN, but it also has mobile sales staff who travel externally. The company has placed the mail server in the screened subnet so that both office staff and remote users can access the company email using webmail.

The LAN is a network covering a small location, such as a building or a company with staff working in close proximity. This is seen as a trusted zone. This is where DC and SQL servers will reside, as they are deemed secure.

Logical segmentation

In a network setting, logical segmentation refers to dividing the network into smaller parts. This division is based on logical rather than physical boundaries. The crucial aspect of this process is the use of specific mechanisms to separate, secure, and manage data flow within a switch and across digital domains. Let's look at the main concepts:

- **Subnetting**: Subnetting is the process of breaking down a network into smaller networks called **subnets**. This can give you a higher level of security by reducing the broadcast domain, the area where devices can broadcast to each other. Imagine a fast-spreading virus. Using subnets can help contain the virus and prevent it from affecting too many devices.

- **Virtual local area network (VLAN)**: A VLAN is established through the software on a network switch. It allows you to group multiple network ports together, effectively creating a distinct and separate network within the larger network. This method of network division aids in controlling traffic flow and segregating communications for distinct functions or device groups. Each individual VLAN has an identification tag, which is readable by switches. Data packets include the VLAN identification tag so that when traffic arrives at the switch, the switch knows where to direct it.

Figure 18.7 shows a possible VLAN setup:

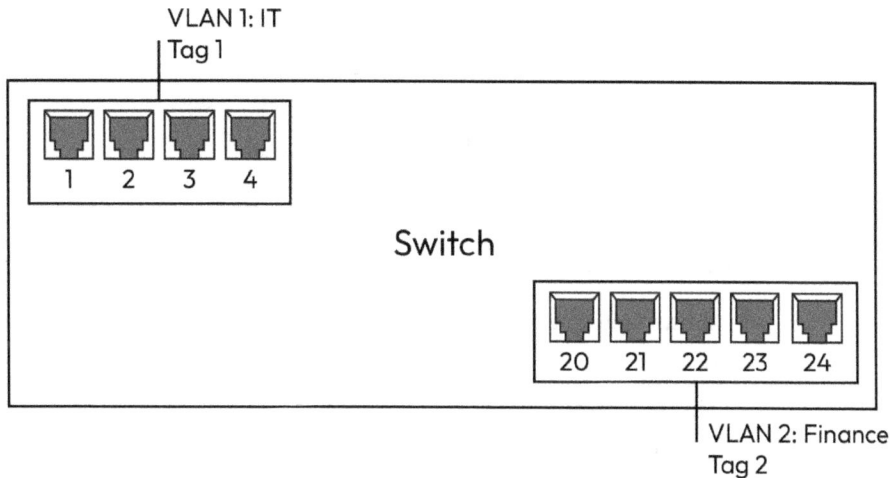

Figure 18.7: Two VLANs

In *Figure 18.7*, port numbers 1–4 have been used to create a VLAN for the IT department, and then ports 20–24 have been used to create another VLAN for the finance department.

Although both departments are on an internal device, creating the VLANs isolates them from other VLANs and the company's network.

Summary

In this chapter, you have learned that basic network security involves multiple layers, including logical security (encryption, access control, and certificates), physical security (cameras and locks), deception technologies (honeypots and honeynets), and compliance (PCI DSS and GDPR). Network segmentation helps protect IoT, industrial systems, and guest access. These measures work together to prevent cyber threats, protect data, and ensure secure access to systems.

The knowledge gained in this chapter will prepare you to answer questions relating to exam objective 4.1 in your *CompTIA Network+ (N10-009)* exam.

Exam objective 4.1

Explain the importance of basic network security concepts.

Logical security:

- **Encryption**: Changing plaintext data into ciphertext:

    - **Data in transit**: Encrypting data while being transmitted

    - **Data at rest**: Encrypting stored data for security

- **Certificates**: Digital credentials for secure communication:

    - **Public key infrastructure (PKI)**: Manages encryption keys and certificates

    - **Self-signed**: Certificates issued without an external authority

- **Identity and access management (IAM)**: Controls user identities and permissions:

    - **Authentication**: Verifies user identity before access:

        - **Multi-factor authentication (MFA)**: Requires multiple verification methods

        - **Single sign-on (SSO)**: One login grants access to multiple systems

        - **RADIUS**: Centralized authentication for network access

        - **LDAP**: Directory service for authentication and user management

        - **SAML**: Enables web-based single sign-on

        - **TACACS+**: Authentication protocol for network devices

        - **Time-based authentication**: Uses time-sensitive codes for verification

        - **Authorization**: Determines user permissions and access levels:

        - **Least privilege**: Grants minimal access necessary

        - **Role-based access control**: Assigns access based on user roles

- **Geofencing**: Restricts access based on location

Physical security: Protects physical assets from threats:

- **Camera**: Monitors and records activity for security

- **Locks**: Restrict physical access to secure areas

Deception technologies: Mislead attackers to detect threats

- **Honeypot**: Decoy system to attract attackers

- **Honeynet**: Network of honeypots for threat analysis

Common security terminology: Key concepts in cybersecurity

- **Risk**: Potential for loss or damage
- **Vulnerability**: Weakness that can be exploited
- **Exploit**: An attack taking advantage of vulnerabilities
- **Threat**: Potential danger to security
- **Confidentiality, integrity, and availability (CIA) triad**: Core security principles

Audits and regulatory compliance: Ensures adherence to security laws

- **Data locality**: Rules on where data is stored
- **PCI DSS**: Security standards for payment data
- **GDPR**: Regulations for data privacy in the EU

Network segmentation enforcement: Restricts access between network segments

- **IoT and IIoT**: Connects smart devices and industrial systems
- **SCADA, ICS, and OT**: Control and monitor industrial processes
- **Guest**: Isolated network access for visitors
- **Bring your own device (BYOD)**: Allows personal devices on corporate networks

Chapter review questions

Now that you've completed the chapter, you can check your knowledge using the practice questions provided in the online platform at `https://packt.link/N10-009ch18`. You can also use the QR code below. Accessing these questions requires you to unlock the accompanying online content first. Head over to *Chapter 26* for detailed instructions.

19

Summarize Various Types of Attacks and Their Impact on the Network

All IT networks are vulnerable to attacks, and as a network engineer, it is important to recognize the ways in which an attack might occur and how it will affect your network. Attacks can come in the form of malicious actors exploiting weaknesses in the network itself, such as **denial-of-service (DoS)** and **distributed denial-of-service (DDoS)** attacks, which disrupt services by overwhelming resources. Attacks could also come in the form of **social engineering**, which means targeting humans to gain access to a network. Examples of this include **phishing** and **shoulder surfing**.

In addition to the preceding, this chapter covers **VLAN hopping** and **MAC flooding**, which also exploit network vulnerabilities, ARP poisoning, **DNS poisoning**, and **DNS spoofing**, which redirect traffic to malicious sites. It also covers rogue devices, such as unauthorized **DHCP servers** and **access points**, along with **evil twins**, which further expose networks to on-path attacks, causing potential data breaches and service disruptions.

This chapter covers the second objective in *Domain 4, : 4.2, Explain the importance of basic network security concepts.*

> **Note**
>
> A full breakdown of objective 4.2 will be given at the end of the chapter.

Denial-of-service (DoS)/distributed denial-of-service (DDoS)

DoS and DDoS are types of cyberattacks aimed at making a network, service, or website unavailable for its users. In a **DoS attack**, a single attacker sends a flood of requests or data to overwhelm a target, such as a website or server. One way they do this is with a SYN flood attack, using lots of half-open connections. The target system expects an ACK packet, which is the third part of the TCP/IP handshake, but never receives it, which consumes resources and eventually leads to the system not being able to process legitimate requests. The target becomes so busy trying to handle all this fake traffic that it can't serve legitimate users, effectively causing the service to slow down or crash entirely.

A **DDoS attack** is similar but more powerful because it involves multiple computers, often thousands, working together to flood the target with traffic, as shown in *Figure 19.1*. These computers are usually part of a "botnet," which is a network of compromised devices controlled by the attacker. Since the attack comes from many different sources, it's much harder to block, making DDoS attacks particularly challenging to defend against.

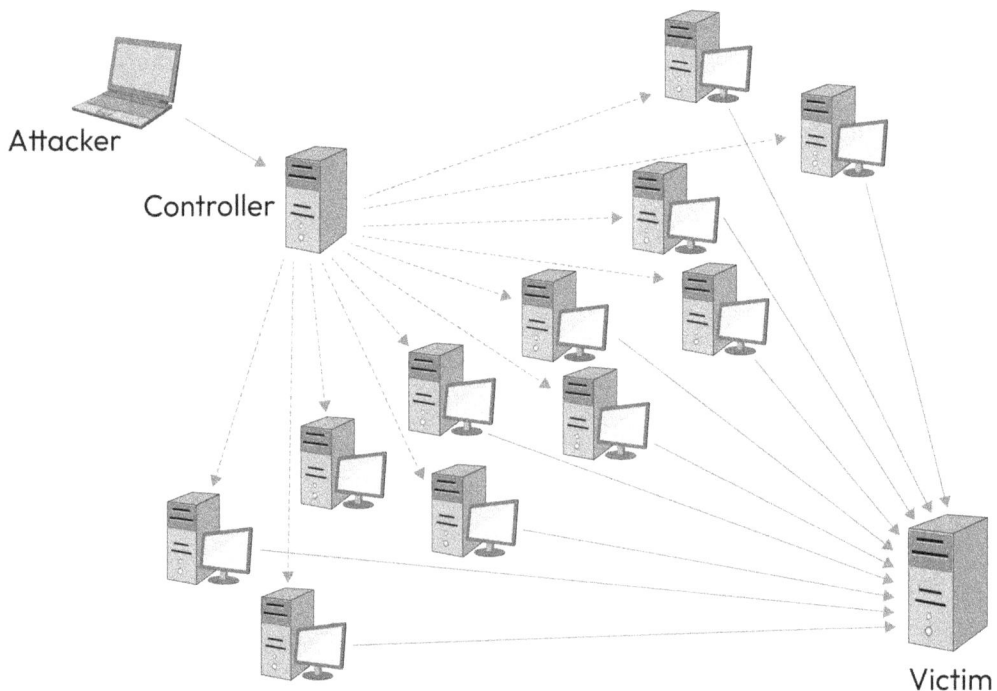

Figure 19.1: DDoS

The primary objective of a DDoS attack is to disrupt the availability of a service. This means making the targeted system slow to respond, intermittently unavailable, or completely inaccessible to legitimate users. For organizations, the consequences can be severe: downtime, financial losses, loss of customer trust, and reputational damage.

By exhausting server resources such as bandwidth, processing power, or application capacity, DDoS attacks directly violate the availability aspect of the **CIA triad**. Even when no data is stolen or modified, the mere unavailability of a service can cripple business operations or public services.

VLAN hopping

VLAN hopping is a network attack where an attacker exploits vulnerabilities in **VLAN** configurations to gain unauthorized access to traffic on VLANs other than their own. VLANs are designed to segment network traffic for security and performance by isolating broadcast domains.

In a VLAN hopping attack, the attacker crafts packets in a way that tricks a network switch into forwarding the packets to a different VLAN, bypassing the intended segmentation.

There are two common methods:

- **Switch spoofing**: The attacker configures their device to mimic a switch by tagging frames with multiple **VLAN IDs**, causing the target switch to treat it as a trunk port and forward traffic for multiple VLANs.
- **Double tagging**: The attacker sends packets with two VLAN tags. The first tag is stripped off by the first switch, and the second tag is interpreted on the next switch, forwarding the packet to a VLAN the attacker is not authorized to access.

Media access control flooding

In a **MAC** flooding attack, the threat actor rapidly sends a flood of Ethernet frames with spoofed, randomly generated source MAC addresses. This causes the **CAM** table to fill up with bogus entries. Once the CAM table reaches its capacity, the switch can no longer associate MAC addresses with specific ports. As a result, it enters a fail-open mode, in which it floods all incoming traffic out of all ports, similar to a hub. This behavior not only degrades network performance but also exposes network traffic to all connected devices, allowing the attacker to intercept sensitive data such as login credentials or session tokens by using packet-sniffing tools.

Poisoning

The **Address Resolution Protocol (ARP)** operates at **Layer 2** and **Layer 3** of the **OSI model**, mapping **IP addresses** to their corresponding MAC (hardware) addresses. In an **ARP poisoning attack**, an attacker sends forged AP replies across a **LAN**, tricking devices into associating the victims IP address with attacker's MAC address. As a result, traffic intended for the victim is redirected to the attacker. This attack can only occur within a local network and typically targets hosts such as routers or gateways, though any device on the LAN can be affected.

ARP spoofing

ARP spoofing is very similar to ARP poisoning. In ARP spoofing, the attacker sends fake messages to devices on a network, pretending to be someone else. They do this by making their device look like it has the same IP address as a real, trusted device on the network. This tricks other devices into sending their data to the attacker instead of the actual device. Once the attacker has the data, they can read it or even change it, making ARP spoofing a serious threat that can lead to data being stolen or unauthorized access to important information.

Domain name system (DNS) attacks

DNS is often referred to as the backbone of the internet because it is responsible for translating human-friendly domain names (such as `www.packtpub.com`) into numerical IP addresses (such as `192.0.2.1`) that computers use to identify each other on a network. This process, known as DNS resolution, allows users to access websites and online services without needing to remember complex IP addresses. DNS functions like a global address book or phone directory that ensures users are directed to the correct servers when visiting websites, sending emails, or using any domain-based service.

DNS name resolution

When someone types in the URL of a website – for example, www.packt.com – the DNS resolution process converts the hostname into its corresponding IP address. The name resolution process occurs in the following order:

1. The system first checks the **DNS cache**. This is stored on the local machine. To view the cache, you can type `ipconfig /displaydns` into the command prompt. Because the DNS cache is the first place visited for DNS resolution, it is a prime target for attackers.

2. If the URL is not in the DNS cache, the system then checks the **HOSTS** file. This is a text file on the local computer. It is located on Windows computers under `C:\Windows\System32\drivers\etc`.

3. If the URL is not in the cache or the **HOSTS** file, the local DNS server uses its `root hints` to contact the root servers, which then direct the query to the appropriate DNS servers on the internet.

DNS cache poisoning

DNS cache poisoning occurs when an attacker manipulates **DNS records** to redirect users to malicious websites. By poisoning the DNS cache with fake information, the attacker tricks users into believing they are visiting legitimate sites, all the while exposing them to fraudulent activities. In the **DNS resolution** process, the DNS cache is searched for the name of the website, but the attackers have poisoned the cache with fake entries to redirect the victim to a fake website that looks like the legitimate website being sought. The attackers could also place fake information in the **HOSTS** file, which is the second place searched during the DNS resolution process.

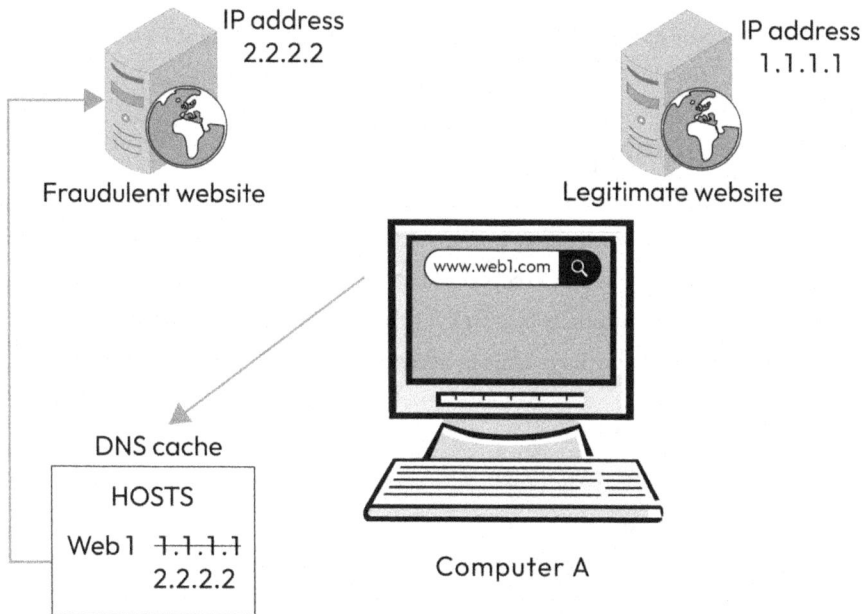

Figure 19.2: DNS cache poisoning

In *Figure 19.2*, you can see a DNS cache poisoning scenario. Here's a breakdown of what's happening. The legitimate website, **www.web1.com** has an IP address of 1.1.1.1, and the fraudulent website has an IP address of 2.2.2.2. The DNS resolver or local DNS cache has been manipulated so that **www.web1.com** resolves to the malicious IP address of 2.2.2.2, instead of the correct one, 1.1.1.1. When the user types www.web1.com, they will be sent to the spoofed website instead of the legitimate one.

DNS spoofing

DNS spoofing is similar to DNS poisoning, but instead of corrupting the DNS server's cache, the attacker directly sends false DNS responses to users trying to visit a website. When you type a website address into your browser, your computer sends a request to a DNS server to find out the IP address. In a DNS spoofing attack, the attacker intercepts this request and sends back a fake IP address that leads to a malicious website. This can trick users into thinking they are on a legitimate site, potentially leading to stolen data or other security issues.

Rogue devices and services

Rogue devices and services, such as unauthorized DHCP servers and **access points (APs)**, pose serious security risks by disrupting network operations and exposing sensitive data. These rogue elements can mislead users, redirect traffic to malicious sites, and allow attackers to intercept or gain unauthorized access to the network, making them a critical threat to network security. In the following section, we shall look at rogue DHCP servers and rogue APs.

Rogue access points

A **rogue AP** is an unauthorized wireless access point set up in a network. It might be installed by an attacker to trick users into connecting to it instead of the legitimate network. Once connected to the rogue AP, users' data can be intercepted, leading to stolen information or other malicious activities. Even if set up unintentionally by a well-meaning employee, a rogue AP can create security vulnerabilities, allowing unauthorized users to access the network and potentially cause harm.

Rogue DHCP servers

A DHCP server is responsible for assigning IP addresses to devices on a network, making sure each device has a unique address to communicate properly. A **rogue DHCP server** is an unauthorized or misconfigured DHCP service that can be introduced onto a network either deliberately – such as by an external attacker or a malicious insider – or inadvertently (for example, when a testing server is never decommissioned and later plugged into the corporate LAN). A rogue DHCP server could allocate duplicate IP addresses on your network, causing network connectivity problems.

When client devices broadcast their **DHCP requests**, they may receive IP addresses, **default gateway settings**, or **DNS server information** from this rogue server instead of the legitimate one. As a result, end users can experience network outages, be unable to reach the internet or internal resources, or be silently redirected to malicious websites. In the case of an insider attack, someone with legitimate network access could intentionally deploy a rogue DHCP server to intercept traffic, **man-in-the-middle (MITM)** attacks, or direct employees to counterfeit sites to harvest credentials.

Because a rogue DHCP server mimics normal DHCP behavior, detecting its presence often requires active network monitoring, such as DHCP snooping, **port security**, or DHCP server authorization controls, to ensure that only trusted servers issue addresses and configurations.

DHCP snooping is a security feature on network switches that helps prevent rogue DHCP servers from handing out unauthorized IP configurations. It works by classifying switch ports as either trusted (e.g., uplinks to legitimate DHCP servers) or untrusted (e.g., ports connected to client devices).

On trusted ports, all DHCP messages are allowed. On untrusted ports, only client requests (such as **DHCPDISCOVER**) are permitted. Any DHCP responses (such as **DHCPOFFER**) from untrusted ports are blocked, stopping rogue servers from assigning IP addresses.

As **DHCP traffic** flows, the switch builds a binding table that records each device's MAC address, assigned IP, port, and lease time. This table can be used to enforce additional protections, such as **IP Source Guard** or **dynamic ARP inspection**, which prevent spoofing and other attacks.

DHCP snooping protects against attacks such as the following:

- Rogue DHCP servers (often used in MITM attacks)
- DHCP starvation, where attackers exhaust available IP leases

By controlling which devices can act as DHCP servers, DHCP snooping ensures reliable and secure IP address assignment across the network.

DHCP starvation is a type of DoS attack that targets the DHCP on a network. In this attack, a malicious actor sends a large number of DHCP request packets using spoofed MAC addresses, rapidly consuming all available IP addresses in the DHCP server's pool.

As a result, legitimate devices attempting to join the network are unable to obtain an IP address, effectively blocking network access. In some cases, the attacker may follow up with a rogue DHCP server to assign malicious configurations to users, such as directing them to a malicious DNS server. DHCP starvation is commonly used as a setup for more advanced attacks and highlights the need for network defenses such as port security, DHCP snooping, and **MAC address filtering**.

Evil twin

An **evil twin** takes the concept of a rogue access point to another level. Not only does it impersonate a real network, but it also intercepts communications between users and the legitimate network. When you unwittingly connect to an evil twin, you are handing over your data to malicious actors who can eavesdrop on your online activities or launch attacks on your device.

To create an evil twin, the attackers create a duplicate network with a name (**SSID**) similar to a well-known network. For example, a café called "Café Brew" might have a Wi-Fi AP with the name *CafeBrew_FreeWifi*. A nearby attacker might create a network with the exact same name, *CafeBrew_FreeWifi*. Users are tricked into connecting, thinking they're accessing a trusted network.

Evil twins often manipulate encryption settings and authentication procedures, making it difficult for users to tell the difference. While connected to the evil twin network, you may notice that you cannot access certain resources – such as your company's private network or important websites you expect to connect to. This is because you are no longer on the legitimate network but on the rogue one. Essentially, while the attacker can monitor your activity and possibly steal data, they don't have access to the internal network resources that you would expect from the café's legitimate Wi-Fi.

If someone has copied your company's AP SSID, a tell-tale sign that you are on an evil twin is that you cannot access data on your company network. This is because you are on another network. An evil twin could help launch an on-path attack.

On-path attacks

On-path attacks, also known as **interception attacks**, involve an attacker positioning themselves within the communication path between two parties. This allows the attacker to secretly intercept, modify, or even block the communication without the knowledge of the original parties. The most common type of on-path attack is a **man-in-the-middle** attack, where the attacker acts as a relay or proxy, making the two parties believe they are directly communicating with each other when, in reality, the attacker controls the entire conversation.

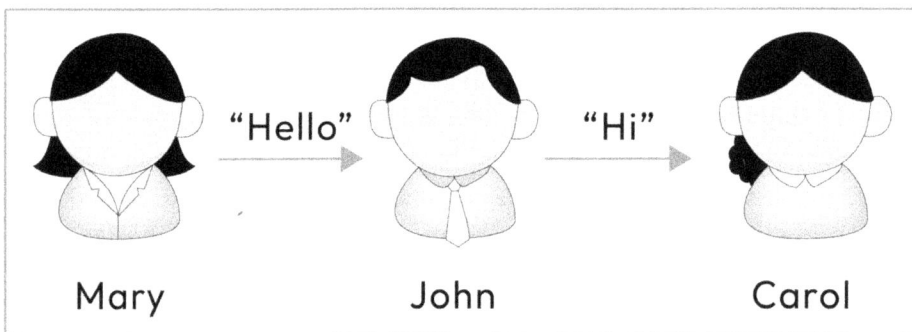

Figure 19.3: MITM attack

One major risk of MITM attacks is data interception. Attackers can eavesdrop on communications – especially on unencrypted or insecure networks – and capture sensitive information such as login credentials, financial data, or session cookies. Even when encryption is used, misconfigurations or weak protocols can be exploited. For example, users on public Wi-Fi may unknowingly expose personal data to attackers using packet sniffing tools.

In addition to observing data, attackers can also manipulate it. This includes altering transaction details or injecting malicious content into web pages. Such actions compromise the integrity of communications and can lead to further exploitation, such as malware infections or financial fraud.

MITM attacks also enable identity impersonation, where attackers pretend to be one of the parties in a communication. This can allow unauthorized access to systems or sensitive information and is particularly dangerous in environments that rely heavily on trust and authentication.

A further concern is that MITM attacks can undermine trust in secure protocols. Techniques such as SSL stripping downgrade **HTTPS** connections to **HTTP**, exposing users who believe they are protected. Attackers may also use forged digital certificates to pose as legitimate services.

> **Note**
>
> MITM attacks can also be known as "interception" or "person-in-the-middle" attacks.

Another variant of on-path attacks is the replay attack, where the attacker intercepts and records a legitimate communication or transaction, then reuses that information at a later time to deceive the system. For example, an attacker might capture and replay a legitimate login request to gain unauthorized access to a system. These attacks exploit weaknesses in the way data is transmitted and validated, making it crucial to implement strong encryption, secure authentication methods, and mechanisms to detect and prevent repeated transmissions of the same data. Kerberos, which uses updated sequence numbers and time stamps, prevents them.

Social engineering

Social engineering is where attackers exploit the vulnerabilities of human psychology to breach digital defenses. We could call this **hacking the human**, as the attacker tries to catch their victim off guard. The hacker exploits the victim's emotions—such as fear about security, desire for financial gain, or trust in a familiar person or company—in order to deceive them and gain unauthorized access or sensitive information. In the following section, we will look at examples of social engineering.

Phishing

Phishing is a cyberattack. Phishing is launched using an untargeted email attack in which attackers impersonate legitimate organizations or trusted individuals to trick recipients into revealing sensitive information such as login credentials, financial data, or personal details. These attacks appear convincing, often mimicking well-known brands, coworkers, or supervisors.

For example, an attacker might send a spoofed email that looks like it came from your bank, asking you to verify account details. In the workplace, phishing emails may appear to come from a manager asking you to purchase gift cards or provide internal access credentials. These messages often contain spoofed elements, such as email addresses or domain names with small differences – such as a misplaced dot or a letter swap – to deceive the recipient.

Phishing attacks typically create a sense of urgency, fear, or opportunity to encourage impulsive actions, such as clicking a malicious link or providing confidential information. Examples include fake warnings about account lockouts, messages about winning a prize, or requests to assist a colleague in an emergency.

To detect phishing attempts, users should check for minor discrepancies in the sender's address or domain, carefully inspect URLs by hovering over them to reveal the actual destination, and verify suspicious requests through a secondary channel. Clicking "Reply" and inspecting the email's return address is another way to catch spoofed emails.

Phishing doesn't just target end users – it can have serious implications for network engineers and IT staff. If a network engineer is tricked into revealing their credentials or clicking on a malicious link, attackers could gain elevated access to internal systems, network infrastructure, or administrative consoles. This can lead to the following:

- Unauthorized access to firewalls, switches, or routers
- Credential theft for VPNs or privileged accounts
- Deployment of malware or ransomware into the corporate network
- Data exfiltration or lateral movement across internal systems

Additionally, phishing attacks can cause service outages or network downtime if malicious payloads disrupt configurations or compromise network availability. Engineers must also handle the incident response, mitigation, and recovery process, which consumes time and resources.

Because of their elevated privileges, network engineers are often prime targets for phishing campaigns – sometimes as part of spear phishing attacks tailored specifically to them.

Dumpster diving

Dumpster diving is where an attacker will go through your trash cans looking for financial statements, such as for your bank or credit card. These risks can be reduced by using a cross-cut shredder or secure disposal services that will burn the documents. Digitally, they can scour deleted files, old emails, or discarded storage devices to recover confidential data.

Both types of dumpster diving pose serious risks to network security. Physical documents with passwords or network diagrams can give attackers easy access to systems. Digital data remnants can reveal credentials or system info, enabling hackers to breach networks, launch phishing attacks, or move laterally inside the organization.

To protect against dumpster diving, shred sensitive papers before disposal, and securely wipe or destroy digital storage devices. Training employees on safe data disposal is also essential to keep your network safe.

Shoulder surfing

A threat actor can figure out a password or PIN (or other secure information) by watching someone type it in. This is known as a shoulder surfing attack. The attacker doesn't necessarily have to be close to the person; they could be in the ATM queue behind you, filming your transaction with their smartphone, or even use CCTV to observe the target from a distance.

Tailgating

Tailgating and **piggybacking** are security risks where someone follows an authorized person into a secure area without permission; in tailgating, the unauthorized person slips in right behind the authorized person, while in piggybacking, they are often let in by the authorized person, either knowingly or unknowingly.

Malware

Malware in social engineering is when attackers trick people into downloading or opening harmful software on their devices. They often do this by pretending to be someone trustworthy, such as by sending an email that looks like it's from a friend or a company. When the victim clicks on a link or opens an attachment, the malware is installed on their device. This can lead to stealing personal information, spying on the victim, or even taking control of their device. Social engineering is dangerous because it relies on manipulating people rather than just breaking into systems.

Summary

This chapter covered various types of network attacks and how they can severely impact security and functionality. DoS and DDoS attacks overwhelm networks, causing disruptions. VLAN hopping and MAC flooding target network segmentation and device identification, compromising network integrity. ARP poisoning and spoofing, along with DNS poisoning and spoofing, mislead devices by altering address mappings, leading to data interception or redirection. Rogue devices, such as unauthorized DHCP servers or APs, create false networks, while evil twin attacks mimic legitimate networks to steal information. On-path attacks intercept communication, and social engineering tactics – such as phishing, dumpster diving, shoulder surfing, and tailgating – exploit human vulnerabilities. Finally, malware introduces malicious software that can disrupt, steal, or corrupt data.

The knowledge gained in this chapter will prepare you to answer questions relating to exam objective 4.2 in your *Comptia Network+ (N10-009)* exam.

Exam objective 4.2

Summarize various types of attacks and their impact on the network

Denial-of-service (DoS)/distributed denial-of-service (DDoS): Overloads network resources, causing service disruptions and downtime.

VLAN hopping: Exploits network segmentation to gain unauthorized access to other VLANs.

Media access control (MAC) flooding: Overwhelms a switch's CAM table, causing traffic to be broadcast.

Address resolution protocol (ARP) poisoning: Alters the ARP cache, redirecting traffic for man-in-the-middle attacks.

ARP spoofing: Fakes ARP messages to intercept or redirect network traffic.

DNS poisoning: Corrupts DNS data, redirecting users to malicious websites.

DNS spoofing: Falsifies DNS responses, leading users to fraudulent sites.

Rogue devices and services:

- **Rogue DHCP server**: Unauthorized DHCP server assigns incorrect IP configurations, disrupting network communication.
- **Rogue access point (AP)**: Unauthorized wireless access point compromising network security and privacy.

Evil twin: Mimics legitimate Wi-Fi to steal credentials and intercept communications.

On-path attack: Intercepts and potentially alters communication between two parties in real time.

Social engineering: Manipulating people to gain unauthorized access or information:

- **Phishing**: Deceptive emails or messages to steal personal information.
- **Dumpster diving**: Searching through trash to find sensitive information.
- **Shoulder surfing**: Watching someone enter sensitive information, such as a password.
- **Tailgating**: Following an authorized person into a secure area without permission.

Malware: Tricking people into accessing harmful software designed to damage, disrupt, or steal information.

Chapter review questions

Now that you've completed the chapter, you can check your knowledge using the practice questions provided in the online platform at `https://packt.link/N10-009ch19`. You can also use the QR code below. Accessing these questions requires you to unlock the accompanying online content first. Head over to Chapter 26 for detailed instructions.

20

Given a Scenario, Apply Network Security Features, Defense Techniques, and Solutions

In *Chapter 18, Explain the Importance of Basic Network Security Concepts*, and *Chapter 19, Summarize Various Types of Attacks and Their Impact to the Network*, you saw general security concepts and the risks you might face; now it's time to look at how to actually defend your network. Security is often discussed in terms of the CIA triad: confidentiality, integrity, and availability. This means ensuring that your organization's digital assets cannot be accessed or altered by malicious actors, while at the same time, making sure that they remain available for those who need them.

This chapter covers key strategies for enhancing network security, including device hardening, network access control, key management, and the implementation of security rules and zones. These measures, such as disabling unused ports, enforcing port security, and applying **access control lists (ACLs)**, work together to create a robust defense against potential threats, safeguarding the network from unauthorized access and malicious activities.

This chapter covers the third objective in *Domain 4: 4.3, Given a scenario, apply network security features, defense techniques, and solutions.*

Note

A full breakdown of objective 4.3 will be given at the end of the chapter.

Device hardening

The saying *prevention is better than the cure* is as true for IT networks as it is for anything. Though firewalls and virus scanners will add essential layers of protection to your entire system, you also need to think of the vulnerabilities of individual devices in your network. For example, poorly configured access management on a firewall could enable malicious actors to change settings, allowing them to create backdoors, disable security policies, or redirect traffic for malicious purposes. Similarly, routers with the latest security patches might allow unauthorized access if default credentials are not changed or if unnecessary services such as Telnet are left enabled, leading to potential vulnerabilities despite having the most up-to-date firmware.

Device hardening, simply put, means ensuring that devices are optimized to reduce vulnerabilities and minimize potential attack vectors. This process involves a series of actions designed to protect devices from unauthorized access and exploitation. It involves running security scans, checking access control and default credentials, and ensuring that unused services and ports are disabled.

Vulnerability scans help identify potential weaknesses by scanning the device for outdated software, misconfigurations, or known security flaws. For example, a scan might detect that a router is running an outdated firmware version that contains known security vulnerabilities, leaving it susceptible to remote code execution attacks. It could also flag weak encryption protocols such as SSL or TLS 1.0 being used for secure communication, which are no longer considered safe. Additionally, the scan may identify firewall misconfigurations, such as open ports that shouldn't be accessible from the internet, which could allow unauthorized access or attacks such as **distributed denial of service (DDoS)**. Once these issues are detected, the appropriate remediation steps, such as patching, reconfiguring the device, or upgrading encryption standards, can be taken to secure the system.

Unused ports

Another fundamental aspect of device hardening is **disabling unused ports**. Devices often come with numerous network ports, many of which may not be necessary for their operation. Each active port represents a potential entry point for attackers. By disabling ports that are not in use, you effectively reduce the number of opportunities for unauthorized access.

This step not only decreases the attack surface but also simplifies the security management of the device by limiting the number of elements that need ongoing monitoring. If a user tries to use a port that has been shut down, then the activity light on the network card will not flicker, indicating that there is no activity.

A **network switch** may have several open ports by default that are not needed for daily operations. If an attacker gains access to these unused ports, they could exploit vulnerabilities to intercept or reroute traffic, launch a **person-in-the-middle attack**, or gain unauthorized access to internal systems. Similarly, if a router has ports such as Telnet (TCP 23) or FTP (TCP 21) enabled, attackers could take advantage of these insecure, outdated protocols to steal credentials or remotely control the device. To reduce attack vectors, disable unnecessary ports and only allow essential ones, for example, SSH, for secure remote management. Fewer ports also mean security management is streamlined.

> **Note**
>
> Ports were covered in greater detail in *Chapter 4, Explain Common Networking Ports, Protocols, Services, and Traffic Types*.

Port security

When ports do have to be enabled, security is important, particularly at the level of network switches, which are usually open by default and allow easy access to the network if not protected. **Port security** controls and restricts which devices can connect to a network through specific switch ports. This is often done by limiting the number of devices allowed to connect to a single port or by enforcing access based on recognized MAC addresses. Port security ensures that only authorized devices can communicate within the network, adding an extra layer of protection against unauthorized access and potential intrusions.

Default passwords

Another essential step in device hardening is changing **default passwords**. Many network devices come with default usernames and passwords that are well known and easily accessible to attackers. If these credentials are not changed, they can be exploited to gain unauthorized access to the device. By setting strong, unique passwords, you ensure that even if a device is targeted, the likelihood of a successful breach is significantly reduced.

When installing a new device, either because the network is being scaled up or because devices are obsolete or broken, default passwords should be changed immediately. You should also consider how often passwords should be changed, carefully balancing the need for network administrators to know and share passwords and the ongoing security of the system.

Note

- You can find many default passwords at `https://cirt.net/passwords`.
- You will find the default passwords for most brands of security cameras at `https://securitycamcenter.com/default-username-password-cctv/`.

Device hardening is an ongoing concern and should be part of all security audits and updates. However, it is especially important when setting up new networks or scaling up existing networks. For example, a new corporate network has been set up and a firewall is being installed to protect against the usual threats. Once the network administrator has received the firewall, they should first change the default admin username and password and disable unnecessary ports and services. Before the firewall is placed into an active network, the latest firmware should be updated, even if it's a new device, which should include any new security patches. Final access control lists should be set up, and system logging should be turned on.

There are other circumstances that call for device hardening, such as after major software or firmware updates or when new vulnerabilities are discovered that could impact the device, for example, the emergence of a newly deployed virus.

Essentially, all devices need to be checked before being introduced to a network. However, if your network is constantly being updated, has wireless devices frequently connecting and disconnecting, or is incredibly large, managing access manually can be time-consuming and prone to human error. This is where **network access control** (**NAC**) comes in. NAC automates the process, ensuring that every device is properly authenticated, compliant, and secure before it gains access to the network, minimizing the risk of errors, as you will see in the next section.

Network access control (NAC)

NAC is a method to control who or what has access to the network. It is a set of procedures and automation tools that ensure that every remote device is fully patched, so they are not vulnerable to attacks. One of the core concepts is that of **health assessments**, which are checks for vulnerabilities such as outdated security patches and issues with a firewall. They are carried out by **agents** and the **health authority (HAuth)**.

Every device subject to NAC has an agent installed so that health assessments can be carried out by the HAuth. There are two types of agents—**permanent agents** and **dissolvable agents**. Permanent agents are installed on the host device, providing continuous monitoring and assessment, while dissolvable agents are also known as *temporary* or *agentless* agents. They are deployed for single-use health checks, allowing for flexibility in assessment without long-term installations.

Following user authentication, the HAuth diligently inspects the client device's registry to determine whether it is fully patched. A device that is up to date with all the necessary patches is labeled *compliant* and granted seamless access to the LAN. If a device has missing patches, it is categorized as *non-compliant* and redirected to what's often referred to as a boundary network or quarantine network, where it will encounter a remediation server.

The **remediation server** is positioned within the boundary or quarantine network and plays a pivotal role. When a non-compliant device is redirected to this network, it gains access to the missing updates and patches from the remediation server. Once the device achieves a fully patched status, it is then permitted to access the LAN without compromising security.

Port security

Port security is an NAC method that restricts which devices can connect to a switch port. By default, switches may allow any device connected to a wall jack to access the network, which can pose security risks. Port security addresses this by limiting the number of allowed MAC addresses per port or specifying which MAC addresses are permitted. If an unauthorized device (such as a switch) is connected and introduces additional MAC addresses, the port can be automatically blocked or disabled. This helps prevent unauthorized physical network extensions and protects the network from disruptions, all without relying on asset inventory systems.

There are different options to control access to the switch. You can use sticky MAC addresses, disable ports, use 802.1X authentication, and MAC filtering.

The first method mentioned, **sticky MAC addresses**, simplifies the port security process by storing the MAC addresses of authorized devices. When a device connects to a port, its MAC address is recorded and associated with that port. Subsequent connections from the same device are automatically permitted. If a different device attempts to connect to the same port, it is denied access as its MAC address does not match the recorded "sticky" MAC address.

A more proactive approach to network security is to regularly review port security settings and, when needed, disable ports. You can also remove patch panel cables that lead to unused areas of the building. This reduces risk by keeping access to a minimum.

802.1X

802.1X authentication uses a **RADIUS** server and occurs before a connection is established. This process involves the identity verification of the user or device seeking network access, employing the concepts of **supplicants** (devices seeking access), **authenticators** (network devices), and an **authentication server** (which verifies supplicant credentials).

Authentication is typically achieved through certificates, which ensure that only authorized devices can connect to the network. One key advantage of 802.1X is that it doesn't disable switch ports but, rather, selectively permits or denies access based on authentication status. This preserves the full functionality of the switch while maintaining robust security.

MAC filtering

A **MAC address** is a unique identifier assigned to a network interface on a device. It's used at the data link layer to ensure that data sent over a network reaches the correct hardware device.

Configuring **MAC filtering** on a wireless access point allows you to control which devices are allowed to connect to the wireless network based on their MAC addresses. Devices not on the approved list will be blocked from accessing the network.

On a managed network switch, a similar concept is applied through a feature called port security. This lets you specify which MAC addresses are allowed to connect to a specific physical port. If an unauthorized MAC address is detected, the switch can block traffic, disable the port, or send an alert, depending on how it's configured.

Key management

Key management refers to the processes and mechanisms used to generate, distribute, store, and destroy cryptographic keys. It is an essential component of any encryption system, as the security of encrypted data is directly tied to the security of the keys used. Poor key management can render even the most sophisticated encryption useless.

There are several types of keys used in cryptography, including symmetric keys, asymmetric keys (public and private keys), and session keys. Each type requires a different approach to management:

- **Symmetric keys** are single keys used for both encryption and decryption. Since both parties use the same key, securely distributing and storing this key is crucial.

- **Asymmetric keys** are a pair of keys—a public key, which can be shared openly, and a private key, which must remain confidential. The public key is used for encryption, while the private key is used for decryption.

- **Session keys** are temporary keys used for a specific session and then discarded. They are typically used in conjunction with asymmetric encryption to securely exchange the session key.

The lifecycle of a cryptographic key

The **key management lifecycle** can be broken down into several stages, each with its own set of best practices. The stages are generation, distribution, storage, usage, rotation, expiration and revocation, and finally, destruction. The cycle, in more detail, is as follows:

1. **Key generation**: This is the process of creating a new key. Keys should be generated using a secure and unpredictable method, such as a cryptographically secure random number generator. Weak key generation can lead to vulnerabilities, allowing attackers to predict or brute-force the key.

2. **Key distribution**: Once a key is generated, it must be securely distributed to the intended parties. For symmetric keys, this often involves using a secure channel or a key exchange protocol like Diffie-Hellman. In asymmetric cryptography, the public key can be distributed openly, but the private key must be securely delivered to the owner.

3. **Key storage**: Keys must be stored securely to prevent unauthorized access. A **key vault** is a secure storage solution designed to manage cryptographic keys, secrets, and certificates. It's typically a service or hardware-backed system that protects sensitive information from unauthorized access. **Key escrow** involves securely storing a copy of the private key with a trusted third party or within the organization itself. This allows for key recovery in case the original key is lost or inaccessible, although it also introduces the need for strict controls to prevent unauthorized access to the escrowed keys. This often involves encrypting the keys themselves and storing them in a key vault, such as a **hardware security module (HSM)** or a secure **key management system (KMS)**. Proper access controls should be in place to ensure that only authorized individuals or systems can access the keys.

4. **Key usage**: When a key is used for encryption or decryption, it should be handled in a secure environment to prevent exposure. Keys should never be hardcoded in application code or stored in plaintext in a filesystem.

5. **Key rotation**: Regularly rotating keys is a best practice to limit the exposure of any single key. This involves replacing the old key with a new one and re-encrypting the data with the new key. Key rotation helps mitigate the risk of key compromise.

6. **Key expiration and revocation**: Keys should have a defined lifespan, after which they are considered expired. If a key is compromised, it must be revoked immediately, rendering it invalid for future use. Key revocation mechanisms, such as CRLs or **OCSP**, are essential for managing expired or compromised keys.

7. **Key destruction**: When a key is no longer needed, it should be securely destroyed to prevent it from being recovered by unauthorized parties. This typically involves overwriting the key data with random information multiple times.

Security rules

So far, you have seen how individual devices should be hardened and how network tools can prevent non-compliant devices from accessing the network. However, it's equally important to ensure that traffic is monitored, with legitimate traffic flowing to the right places and potential malicious actors and viruses blocked. This is achieved by implementing the right security rules within your network.

Security rules are policies and configurations established to control and monitor network access, filter web traffic, and protect users from harmful content. These rules determine how data flows through the network and specify which types of connections, users, or content are allowed or blocked.

This is accomplished with ACLs, which control what resources an IP can access; URL filtering, which controls what websites can be accessed from the network; and content filtering, which examines the content of URLs for prohibited or harmful material.

Access control lists (ACLs)

ACLs are lists used by routers and firewall devices to grant or deny network traffic based on a set of rules, such as source and destination IP addresses, port numbers, protocols, or specific types of network traffic. For example, an ACL rule might allow traffic from a trusted internal IP range while blocking incoming requests from unknown or untrusted external addresses. By setting these rules, ACLs help control network access and improve security by filtering traffic based on established criteria.

A newly installed firewall or router will only contain one "deny all" rule, which means that all network traffic will be blocked by default, and to allow any access at all, you need to add exceptions to this rule. These exceptions are called **allow rules**, as can be seen in *Table 20.1*.

Firewall or router ACL			
Allow	HTTP	TCP port 80	Telnet
Allow	FTP	TCP port 21	TCP port 23
Allow	SSH	TCP port 22	
			No allow rule
Last rule	Deny all		Last rule applies called implicit deny

Table 20.1: Access control list

Should traffic attempt to cross the firewall or router, but there is no allow rule, then the last rule of *'deny all'* will apply; this is called **implicit deny**.

A second ACL is implemented in a file and data access environment to control who gets access to the different types of data and also restricts what level of access they get. For example, say there are two members of the sales team (Bill, the sales manager, and Ben, the sales administrator) and two folders on the file server, one for sales data and the other for marketing data. Since Bill and Ben both work in sales, they will both be given access to the sales data, but not the marketing data. This is their data type.

Proxy server

A **proxy server** is a server that acts as an intermediary between clients seeking resources on the internet or an external network. It serves as a go-between, making requests on behalf of clients while ensuring that external servers do not have direct knowledge of the requesting host. The proxy server maintains a log file of these requests to allow administrators to track users' internet usage. The flow of data through a proxy server typically moves from internal to external, which is why it's often referred to as a **forward proxy**. Its primary functions are URL filtering and content filtering.

URL filtering

A **URL filter** checks requested website addresses (URLs) against a predefined list (often referred to as a **blocklist**). For example, companies may restrict access to social media sites during working hours. If a user attempts to visit a blocked site, the request is denied, a warning or custom message may be displayed, and the attempt is typically logged for auditing or policy enforcement.

Content filtering

Content filtering involves the inspection of the actual content of the website that is being visited. It involves analyzing the actual content of web pages—not just their URLs—to determine whether access should be allowed or blocked. This typically involves inspecting text, images, scripts, or even metadata for specific keywords, categories, or patterns that violate predefined policies.

For example, if the keyword `gambling` is on the blocklist, a user trying to visit a site that contains content related to gambling may be blocked, even if the main domain is generally allowed. So, while a site such as `https://wikipedia.org` might be permitted overall, a specific page such as `https://wikipedia.org/wiki/Gambling_in_the_United_Kingdom` could be blocked because it contains restricted content.

Zones

One of the fundamental concepts in network security is the use of zones—segmented areas of a network with varying levels of trust, which help control and monitor traffic to prevent unauthorized access. This section explores the concepts of trusted versus untrusted zones and screened subnets, outlining their importance and the techniques used to secure them.

Trusted versus untrusted zones

Trusted zones are areas within a network where the systems, users, and devices are considered to have a certain level of trust. These zones typically house internal resources such as servers that hold internal company documents, databases for internal use, and applications that require protection from external threats. Because these zones contain critical assets, they are often heavily monitored and protected by strong security measures.

On the other hand, **untrusted zones** refer to areas where the level of trust is low, such as the internet or external networks. They may contain web servers that hold customer-facing websites or applications, email gateways, or public APIs. They might also host sandboxing or testing environments and systems that manage traffic, like load balancers.

These zones are considered high-risk because they are accessible by unknown or potentially malicious entities. To prevent unauthorized access to the trusted zones, strict controls such as firewalls and ACLs are enforced at the boundaries between trusted and untrusted zones, as will be discussed in the next section.

Defense techniques for trusted and untrusted zones

By categorizing different parts of a network into trusted and untrusted zones, organizations can better control and monitor the flow of traffic, thereby reducing the risk of unauthorized access and potential data breaches. To effectively manage these zones, a variety of defense techniques are employed. Each of these techniques serves to fortify the boundaries between trusted and untrusted zones, ensuring the integrity of the network:

- **Firewalls**: A critical component in separating trusted and untrusted zones, firewalls filter incoming and outgoing traffic based on predefined security rules. Firewalls can be configured to allow or deny traffic between zones based on IP addresses, ports, and protocols. Typically, these will be configured as a back-to-back firewall where we use a perimeter firewall and then an internal firewall between the trusted network and the screened subnet.

- **Intrusion detection and prevention systems (IDPSs)**: These systems monitor network traffic for suspicious activity. In trusted zones, they ensure that internal threats or compromised devices do not lead to data breaches. An IDS alerts administrators when suspicious activity is detected, while an IPS actively block or mitigates the threat in real time. In untrusted zones, IDPSs are commonly deployed at network boundaries, where they help detect and block external attacks before malicious traffic can penetrate deeper into the trusted network.

- **ACLs**: ACLs are used to define which users or devices are permitted to access specific resources within trusted zones. By implementing strict ACLs, organizations can ensure that only authorized personnel have access to sensitive data.

- **Encryption**: Data moving between trusted and untrusted zones should be encrypted to prevent interception by malicious actors. This is especially important for sensitive information such as passwords, financial data, and PINs.

- **Network segmentation**: Dividing a network into smaller segments with varying levels of trust helps limit the spread of attacks. If a breach occurs in an untrusted zone, segmentation ensures that the threat does not easily reach the trusted zones.

Screened subnet

A **screened subnet**, also known as a **demilitarized zone (DMZ)**, is a special type of zone that acts as a buffer between trusted and untrusted zones. It typically hosts publicly accessible services, such as web servers, mail servers, and DNS servers, while shielding the internal network from direct exposure to the internet. The screened subnet is designed to mitigate the risk of attacks on public-facing services, ensuring that even if these services are compromised, the internal network remains protected.

Defense techniques for screened subnets

To safeguard screened subnets, a series of defense techniques is employed to minimize the risk of attackers breaching the network and ensuring that internal networks remain secure. The following are some of the most effective strategies used to protect screened subnets:

- **Dual firewall architecture:** The most common implementation of a screened subnet involves two firewalls. The first firewall is the perimeter firewall that separates the untrusted zone (internet) from the screened subnet, filtering incoming traffic. The second firewall (internal) separates the screened subnet from the trusted zone, adding an additional layer of protection. This is also commonly known as a back-to-back configuration. It is shown in *Figure 20.1.*

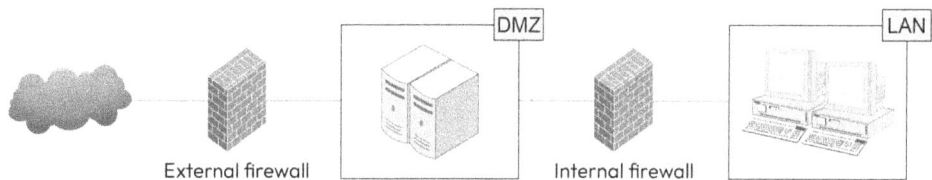

Figure 20.1: Dual firewall architecture

- **Reverse proxy servers:** In a screened subnet, reverse proxy servers are often used to forward requests from external clients to internal servers. By doing so, they prevent direct access to internal servers and can also cache content, reducing the load on internal resources. They typically carry out the functions of authentication and decrypting incoming data so that it can be investigated.
- **Security monitoring and logging:** All activities within the screened subnet should be closely monitored and logged. By analyzing these logs, organizations can detect unusual behavior or potential attacks and respond promptly to mitigate risks.

- **Network intrusion detection systems (NIDSs)**: Placing NIDS within the screened subnet allows for the real-time monitoring of traffic. This setup helps identify potential threats targeting public-facing services before they can cause harm.

- **Host-based security**: Servers and devices within the screened subnet should be hardened with security patches, antivirus software, and other defensive measures to minimize vulnerabilities.

Summary

This chapter outlined the implementation of network security features, encompassing device hardening, network access control, key management, and the establishment of security zones, to safeguard an organization's digital assets against unauthorized access and potential threats. These measures, including the deactivation of unused ports, enforcement of port security, adoption of robust password policies, and utilization of firewalls and encryption, collectively ensure the integrity, confidentiality, and availability of information, while providing a robust defense against both internal and external risks.

The knowledge gained in this chapter will prepare you to answer questions relating to exam objective 4.3 in your *Comptia Network+ (N10-009)* exam.

Exam objective 4.3

Given a scenario, apply network security features, defense techniques, and solutions.

Device hardening: Strengthen devices against attacks.

- **Disable unused ports and services**: Reduce attack surfaces

- **Change default passwords**: Prevent unauthorized access

Network access control (NAC): Regulate network access.

- **Port security**: Control access via switch ports

- **802.1X**: Authenticate devices before network access

- **MAC filtering**: Restrict connections by MAC addresses

Key management: Securely handle cryptographic keys

Security rules: Define access permissions and restrictions:

- **Access control list (ACL):** Manage network traffic access
- **Uniform Resource Locator (URL) filtering:** Block specific web addresses
- **Content filtering:** Restrict access to certain content

Zones: Segregate network areas based on trust.

- **Trusted network:** Internal zone with higher security and controlled access
- **Screened subnet:** Isolate public-facing services

Chapter review questions

Now that you've completed the chapter, you can check your knowledge using the practice questions provided in the online platform at `https://packt.link/N10-009ch20`. You can also use the QR code below. Accessing these questions requires you to unlock the accompanying online content first. Head over to Chapter 26 for detailed instructions.

Domain 5

Network Troubleshooting

The final part of the book develops the problem-solving skills required of a networking professional. It introduces a structured troubleshooting methodology, along with techniques for diagnosing cabling, interface, and hardware issues. Candidates will learn how to resolve common service and performance problems and how to apply the right tools—from protocol analyzers to CLI commands—to restore functionality and ensure stable network operations.

This part of the book includes the following chapters:

- *Chapter 21, Explain the Troubleshooting Methodology*
- *Chapter 22, Given a Scenario, Troubleshoot Common Cabling and Physical Interface Issues*
- *Chapter 23, Given a Scenario, Troubleshoot Common Issues with Network Services*
- *Chapter 24, Given a Scenario, Troubleshoot Common Performance Issues*
- *Chapter 25, Given a Scenario, Use the Appropriate Tool or Protocol to Solve Networking Issues*

21
Explain the Troubleshooting Methodology

There are as many ways for your network to go wrong as there are parts of your network. Attacks from malicious actors, equipment malfunctioning, and user errors are among the many things that can cause a range of problems, from a printer not working to a complete blackout of your entire system. When faced with a problem, it is seldom obvious what caused it, but as a network engineer, this is exactly what you need to do. It is your job to fix the problem. But to do that, you first need to find out what it is.

This is why effective troubleshooting is a critical skill within IT technical support. The troubleshooting methodology covered in this chapter is a structured approach to diagnosing and resolving issues that arise within systems and networks. This chapter covers how to identify, analyze, and solve problems in a logical and efficient manner. This process not only helps in pinpointing the root cause of an issue but also ensures that solutions are implemented effectively and sustainably.

This chapter covers the first objective in *Domain 5: 5.1, Explain the troubleshooting methodology*.

> **Note**
>
> A full breakdown of objective 5.1 will be given at the end of the chapter.

Identify the problem

When you have an issue in a network, whether it is a small issue, such as a printer not printing, or a large issue, such as not being able to connect to the internet, the first step to a resolution is identifying the problem. This is best done in a systematic approach of gathering information and engaging with users to get a complete picture of the issue, which will begin to narrow down potential causes. For example, if a printer is broken, by finding out whether only one user or all users are experiencing an issue, you can immediately start to discount causes. This early step forms the basis for effective problem resolution. The normal steps, in order, are as follows:

1. Gather information.

2. Question users.

3. Identify symptoms.

4. Determine whether anything has changed.

5. Duplicate the problem, if possible.

6. Approach multiple problems individually.

Each step is discussed in more detail in the following subsections.

> **Note**
>
> The exam will test your knowledge of these steps in order, and identifying each stage will be heavily tested.

Gather information

One way to start gathering information is by checking the data saved by the network and the devices in it. Modern networks leave a constant paper trail, recording everything from device connection histories to data flow patterns and system errors. By checking **log files**, **error reports**, **alerts**, and **configuration files**, you can uncover metrics, recent changes, and anomalies, such as spikes in network traffic or repeated login failures, which may indicate the root of an issue.

With configuration files, you can check metrics, recent changes, and anomalies.

Log management tools aggregate and analyze logs from various sources in real time. This helps in identifying patterns, detecting anomalies, and troubleshooting issues quickly by providing a centralized view of log data. Log files are a good source of information so that we can see what has been happening on a computer system. The three main logs are the following:

- **System logs**: Check system logs (e.g., /var/log on Unix/Linux systems) for error messages or unusual activity.

- **Application logs**: Review logs specific to the application in question. This might include web server logs, database logs, or application-specific logs.

- **Security logs**: Security logs record events relating to authentication, authorization, and access control. They include failed or repeated login attempts, firewall activity, intrusion detection/prevention alerts and suspicious patterns. Security logs are critical for identifying unauthorized access attempts, malware infections or other security-related anomalies that may be the root cause of a network or system issue. Reviewing these logs can help distinguish between operational problems (like misconfigurations) and security incidents (like brute-force attacks or intrusions).

Setting up **automated alerts** for critical metrics and error conditions ensures that you are notified immediately when issues arise. This allows for quick response and resolution. Reviewing detailed error reports generated by applications or monitoring tools can help pinpoint the exact cause of issues or narrow down the possibilities.

Regularly checking **configuration files** for any recent changes or misconfigurations can prevent issues from arising. It's crucial to ensure that the configurations are correct and up to date. Using version control tracks changes in configuration files and helps in identifying what changes were made and when. This is particularly useful in understanding the impact of recent changes and rolling back if necessary.

In some cases, it might be helpful to start questioning users first to avoid unnecessarily checking logs, but it's important to do so in a systematic way. This is detailed in the next section.

Question users

When troubleshooting, it's essential to ask questions in a way that gathers information effectively without assuming the person's knowledge is lower than your own. Knowing when to use open and closed questions can significantly enhance this process.

Open questions are best used to gather broad, detailed information, allowing the person to explain or describe something in their own words. These questions are valuable when exploring the context or background of a problem and encouraging the person to share their thoughts and feelings.

For example, asking, "Can you describe what happens when you try to start the program?" or "What changes have you made recently that might have affected this?" can provide comprehensive insights into the situation. These questions help identify patterns or common factors and ensure you gather all of the relevant information, although they can sometimes result in an overwhelming amount of data or be time-consuming.

On the other hand, closed questions are used to confirm details or narrow down possibilities. These questions are particularly useful when time is limited and precise answers are needed.

For example, asking, "Is the computer plugged in?" or "Did you receive any error messages?" helps to quickly narrow down the cause of a problem and confirm or eliminate potential issues. While closed questions provide clear, concise answers, they might miss out on important contextual information and can make the person feel interrogated if overused.

A balanced approach often works best in troubleshooting. Starting with open questions can help you gather a broad understanding of the problem, while closed questions can be used to home in on specific details.

For example, you might begin by asking, "Can you explain the issue you're experiencing?" to let the person describe the problem in their own words. Follow this with another open question, such as "What were you doing when you first noticed the issue?" to gather more context. Once you have a general understanding, you can use closed questions, such as "Did you receive any error messages?" or "Is this happening on all devices or just one?" to obtain specific information and narrow down the possibilities. Finally, returning to open questions such as "How often does this problem occur?" can help provide a sense of the frequency and consistency of the issue, while a closed question such as "Have you installed any new software recently?" can focus on recent changes that might have caused the issue.

Identify symptoms

Identifying symptoms involves carefully observing and documenting all the abnormal behaviors or errors associated with a problem. This step is crucial because the symptoms give clues about the underlying cause. Symptoms can manifest in various forms, such as error messages, slow performance, unexpected crashes, or unusual sounds (in hardware issues).

For example, suppose a user complains that their computer is "running slow." The symptom here is the sluggish performance, but you need to dig deeper:

- Does the slowness occur during specific tasks such as opening applications, browsing the internet, or playing videos?
- Are there any error messages appearing? If so, what do they say?

- Is the slowness consistent, or does it happen intermittently?
- Are there any unusual noises coming from the computer, such as a hard drive clicking?

These observations will help to further pinpoint the issue and give a good indication of the general area of the issue. If the slowness is caused only by heavy applications, this could point toward a RAM issue, while noises suggest a hardware issue.

Determine if anything has changed

Understanding recent changes to the system is vital because many problems are triggered by updates, new installations, or configuration changes. Identifying what has changed can help you trace the problem back to a specific event or modification, making it easier to resolve.

For example, imagine a printer that was working perfectly fine yesterday but is now unresponsive. Here are some steps you could take:

- Ask the user whether any new software or drivers have been installed recently
- Check whether there were any recent operating system updates or patches applied
- Determine whether any network changes have occurred, such as switching to a different router or modifying network settings
- Verify whether someone physically moved the printer or changed its connection type (e.g., from USB to network)

For instance, if a new driver was installed just before the printer stopped working, that could be the cause, and rolling back the driver might fix the problem.

Duplicate the problem, if possible

Replicating the issue is important because it helps you observe the problem in real time, understand its behavior, and test potential solutions. Duplicating the problem also confirms that the issue is not a one-off glitch but a consistent problem that needs addressing.

Suppose a user reports that their application crashes when they try to save a file. To duplicate the problem, do the following:

1. Open the same application and try saving a file in the same way the user described.
2. If the crash occurs again, you've successfully replicated the issue.
3. Note any specific conditions under which the crash happens (e.g., saving files with a certain name, size, or location).

If you can replicate the problem, you can then try different solutions, such as saving the file in a different format or location, which might help reveal an underlying problem. This also has the advantage of revealing any user errors.

Approach multiple problems individually

When dealing with multiple issues, it's essential to tackle each one separately. Addressing them individually prevents confusion, avoids overlooking details, and ensures that each problem is thoroughly investigated and resolved.

Imagine a scenario where a user is facing two issues: their email client is not sending messages and their internet connection is unstable. Instead of trying to fix both problems at once, approach them one by one. First, focus on the internet connection issue. Check the network settings, reset the router, or test the connection with another device. Once the internet is stable, move on to the email client issue. Check the outgoing mail server settings, verify the user's credentials, or test sending an email after reconfiguring the account.

By asking the right questions and checking the logs for salient information, trying to replicate the issue, checking for changes in the logs, and ensuring that you understand problems individually, you can start to build a good picture of what the issue actually is. In some cases, the solution might now become obvious; it could be a case of just replacing a cable or rebooting a device, or it could be complex with no obvious quick fix. Whatever the scale of the issue, the next step is to come up with an idea of why the problem is happening.

Establish a theory of probable cause

To solve a problem, you must understand what is causing the problem, so the next step is to establish a theory of probable cause. This involves forming an educated guess using your knowledge of the network, previous experiences, and logic. At this stage, you might duplicate the problem.

However, this stage can be overwhelming, so it helps to break it down into steps to avoid falling into common pitfalls, such as assuming the causes are more complex than they are. The following points can help in this stage.

Question the obvious

This technique involves checking for the most straightforward and common issues first before moving on to more complex possibilities. Often, problems can be caused by something simple that is easily overlooked. If your computer won't turn on, then check whether the computer is plugged into a power source. Ensure the power outlet is working by plugging in another device. You might find out that the power strip the computer was plugged into was turned off. Turning it back on solves the problem. In this case, questioning the obvious (checking the power connection) led to a quick resolution without needing to explore more complex causes such as hardware failure.

Consider multiple approaches

When you face a more complex problem, it's helpful to approach troubleshooting from different angles. Two common approaches are the **top-to-bottom/bottom-to-top OSI model** method and the **divide-and-conquer** method.

In the top-to-bottom approach, you start troubleshooting from the application layer (Layer 7) down to the physical layer (Layer 1). In the bottom-to-top approach, you start from the physical layer (Layer 1) and work up to the application layer (Layer 7).

> **Note**
>
> You can revise the layer names and functions by referring to *Chapter 1, Explain Concepts Related to the Open System Interconnection (OSI) Reference Model.*

For example, take the issue that a user is unable to access a website. You can start at the top layer, which is the **application layer (Layer 7)**. Check whether the web browser is working properly. Clear the browser cache or try a different browser. Then, move to the **transport layer (Layer 4)**, and check whether the **TCP/IP** connection is functioning properly by using the ping command to test connectivity to the website's server. This is followed by the **network layer (Layer 3)**, where we ensure that the correct **IP address** is being used and that there are no issues with routing. You could use the tracert tool to test connectivity from the computer to the final destination. You could also use a tool called pathping that shows latency and packet loss. Finally, we go to the **physical layer (Layer 1)** to check the network cables and the network card to ensure they are properly connected and functioning. You might discover that the issue is at the transport layer (Layer 4), where the TCP port needed to access the website is being blocked by a firewall. Configuring the firewall rules resolves the issue.

The divide-and-conquer technique involves breaking down the system into smaller components or segments and testing each one individually to isolate the source of the problem.

Take, for example, a network printer that doesn't print documents from any computer in the office. If we choose to divide and conquer, we check from the printer side and then from the computer side.

First, we verify that the printer is powered on and has paper and ink. We print a test page directly from the printer. If that works, we check the network connectivity by testing whether the printer is connected to the network by pinging its IP address from a computer.

Then, from the computer, we check the computer configuration to ensure that the computers are properly configured to send print jobs to the correct printer and not set to **Print to PDF**, for instance. If the printer and computers are configured correctly, check whether the issue lies in the network, such as a faulty switch, router, or cable.

You might find that the printer's IP address had changed due to DHCP reallocation, and the computers were trying to print to the old IP address. Updating the printer's IP address in the computer settings resolves the problem.

Test the theory to determine the cause

When you're troubleshooting an issue, you develop a theory based on the symptoms and possible causes. The next step is to test this theory to confirm whether it correctly identifies the root of the problem. This often involves performing specific diagnostic steps, running tests, or observing behavior under controlled conditions to see whether the theory holds true. There are two things that can happen when you test your theory: one is that it's correct and the other is that it's incorrect. We will look at those two scenarios here.

If the theory is confirmed, determine next steps to resolve the problem

If your testing validates the theory, meaning you've identified the root cause of the issue, the next step is to determine how to resolve it. This involves planning the fix, implementation, verification, and documentation.

Planning the fix could involve making a decision to replace faulty hardware, update software, reconfigure settings, or perform other corrective actions. When implementing the plan, ensure that all necessary precautions are taken to avoid further issues. This might include scheduling downtime, backing up data, informing stakeholders, or other change management steps. After implementing the fix, verify that the problem is resolved by retesting the system. This ensures that the corrective action was successful and did not introduce new problems.

It's also important to document the issue, the steps taken to resolve it, and any relevant information that could help in future troubleshooting. This record can be valuable for future reference or for other team members who might encounter similar problems. This is covered in more detail later in the chapter.

If the theory is not confirmed, establish a new theory or escalate

If the testing disproves your initial theory, it indicates that the actual cause of the problem has not yet been identified. In this case, you have two main options, which are to establish a new theory or escalate the issue.

Based on the results of your tests, reconsider the symptoms and possible causes, and formulate a new hypothesis. This could involve considering other components, systems, or external factors that might be contributing to the issue. Once a new theory is developed, repeat the process of testing to determine whether it is correct.

If you're unable to establish a new theory, or if the problem is beyond your expertise, it may be necessary to escalate the issue to higher-level support. This could involve bringing in more experienced technicians, consulting specialized resources, or contacting external support teams, such as vendors or service providers. When escalating, ensure you provide a detailed account of the steps already taken and the results of your tests, so the next level of support has a clear understanding of the situation.

Additional considerations

Each troubleshooting experience, whether successful or not, provides valuable lessons. Use these experiences to improve your understanding of the systems you work with and refine your problem-solving skills.

Sometimes, discussing the problem with colleagues or brainstorming as a team can lead to insights that might not emerge when working alone. Collaboration can be especially useful when establishing new theories or when escalation is needed.

Make use of diagnostic tools, system logs, and documentation to aid in testing your theories. Proper use of these resources can make troubleshooting more efficient and effective.

Establish a plan of action to resolve the problem and identify potential effects

As mentioned, once you've identified the root cause of a problem, the next step is to establish a plan of action to resolve it. For larger issues, you might have to get approval for your plan of action by implementing change management and sending your plan to the **change advisory board (CAB)** for approval. For small issues, this might only take a few seconds, for instance, plugging in a cable or rebooting a device. However, more complex issues might take more time and resources, and it's important to be transparent and methodical in this part of the process, including all key stakeholders. Going straight into a fix without careful planning could cause unexpected downtime for other users, tie up resources that are needed elsewhere, or even create new issues.

As mentioned, start by outlining the specific steps required to fix the issue. This could involve replacing components, updating software, reconfiguring settings, or applying patches. This will then enable you to determine what resources (tools, personnel, time, etc.) will be needed.

Identify and assess any potential side effects or risks associated with the solution. For example, will applying a fix cause downtime? Could it affect other systems or users? Could a hardware fix go wrong and take out a vital network device? You also need to develop a backup plan in case the initial solution doesn't work as expected. This might involve having an alternative fix ready or a rollback plan to restore the system to its previous state if something goes wrong.

Implement the solution or escalate as necessary

Once the plan is established, it's time to carefully execute it. This could involve executing commands, changing configurations, replacing parts, or other technical actions. It's important to implement the solution methodically, ensuring each step is completed correctly. As you implement the solution, monitor the system closely to ensure it behaves as expected. Watch for any signs that the problem is resolved, as well as any unexpected issues that might arise.

If, during implementation, it becomes apparent that the solution is not effective, or if complications arise that are beyond your expertise, you should escalate the issue. Escalation might involve bringing in more experienced personnel, consulting specialized teams, or seeking external support. When escalating, provide a clear summary of what has been done so far, including any findings and challenges encountered.

Verify full system functionality and implement preventive measures if applicable

It's essential to make sure a fix works once it's in place, as well as thinking about any changes that can be made to prevent the issue from occurring again in the future. Conduct thorough tests to ensure the problem has been resolved and that the system is functioning as expected. This includes checking that all related components or processes are working correctly, starting at Layer 1 and working up through the layers from bottom to top, and that no new issues have been introduced. If the problem affected end users, seek their feedback to confirm that the issue is resolved from their perspective as well.

If applicable, take steps to prevent the problem from recurring. This could involve updating documentation, applying patches, changing configurations, or improving monitoring systems to detect similar issues earlier in the future. Preventive measures help to strengthen the system's resilience and reduce the likelihood of future issues.

Document findings, actions, outcomes, and lessons learned throughout the process

Once the issue is solved, it's a good idea to keep a record of the incident. This can help to identify patterns that might indicate preventative measures that can be taken. For instance, if there are regular device failures because of user errors. Some training could help prevent this. It might also help other people troubleshoot similar issues in the future.

Document all steps taken during the troubleshooting process, including the initial symptoms, theories tested, actions implemented, and the final resolution. This creates a clear record that can be referred to in the future if similar issues arise. Note whether the problem was successfully resolved or whether further action is needed. Include any preventive measures implemented and their expected impact.

Reflect on the troubleshooting process and document any lessons learned. This could include insights into what worked well, what could have been done differently, and any new knowledge gained, including details about the incident report process itself.

Share the documentation with relevant stakeholders, such as team members, managers, or clients. This ensures that everyone involved is informed about what happened and how it was resolved, and it contributes to the overall knowledge base of the organization.

Summary

This chapter covered the troubleshooting methodology. It begins by identifying the problem through gathering information, questioning users, identifying symptoms, and noting any recent changes, while attempting to duplicate the issue and addressing each problem individually. Next, establish a theory of probable cause by questioning obvious factors and considering various approaches, such as top-to-bottom or bottom-to-top analysis of the OSI model, or dividing and conquering the problem. Once a theory is formed, test it to determine the cause; if confirmed, proceed with resolving the issue, or if not, establish a new theory and repeat the process.

The knowledge gained in this chapter will prepare you to answer questions relating to exam objective 5.1 in your *CompTIA Network+ (N10-009)* exam.

Exam objective 5.1

Explain the troubleshooting methodology

Identify the problem:

- Gather information
- Question users
- Identify symptoms
- Determine whether anything has changed
- Duplicate the problem, if possible
- Approach multiple problems individually

Establish a theory of probable cause:

- Question the obvious
- Consider multiple approaches:

    - Top-to-bottom/bottom-to-top OSI model
    - Divide and conquer

Test the theory to determine the cause:

- If the theory is confirmed, determine the next steps to resolve the problem
- If the theory is not confirmed, establish a new theory or escalate

Establish a plan of action to resolve the problem and identify potential effects

Implement the solution or escalate as necessary

Verify full system functionality and implement preventive measures if applicable

Document findings, actions, outcomes, and lessons learned throughout the process

Chapter review questions

Now that you've completed the chapter, you can check your knowledge using the practice questions provided in the online platform at `https://packt.link/N10-009ch21`. You can also use the QR code below. Accessing these questions requires you to unlock the accompanying online content first. Head over to Chapter 26 for detailed instructions.

22

Given a Scenario, Troubleshoot Common Cabling and Physical Interface Issues

Chapter 21 gave you a full overview of the general troubleshooting methodology, and now, in the final four chapters of this book, we'll cover problem solving for more specific circumstances. This chapter focuses on the physical backbone of your network, namely cabling and interfaces.

Understanding how to troubleshoot common cabling and physical interface issues is essential for the *Network+* exam, as it directly relates to maintaining reliable network performance. Network professionals must be able to identify and resolve problems such as **incorrect cable types**, **signal degradation**, and **improper terminations**, all of which can cause connectivity failures. Additionally, recognizing interface issues such as **CRC errors**, **packet drops**, and **port status** problems ensures smooth data transmission. Hardware-related concerns, including **PoE** limitations and transceiver mismatches, also play a critical role in network troubleshooting. Mastering these concepts will not only help in passing the exam but also in real-world networking scenarios.

This chapter covers the second objective in *Domain 5: 5.2, Given a scenario, troubleshoot common cabling and physical interface issues.*

> **Note**
>
> A full breakdown of *objective 5.2* will be given at the end of the chapter.

Cable issues

When we deal with cable issues, we are looking at the physical layer of the OSI reference model, and we should work our way up through the different layers to resolve issues.

When dealing with cable issues, it's important to understand that different types of cables serve different purposes. Using the wrong cable can lead to slow speeds, poor connectivity, or complete network failure. Following is a breakdown of the common cable types and their specific issues. An incorrect pinout on the patch cable could prevent network connectivity due to being mismatched.

Incorrect cable

If you use the wrong type of cable in a network, it can cause problems such as slow internet, dropped connections, data errors, or being unable to reach any servers. Not all cables are the same; some are made for fast speeds over short distances, while others are better for longer distances or areas with a lot of electrical interference. For example, a **Cat 5** cable is not designed to handle very high speeds such as **10 gigabit Ethernet**, so using it for that purpose will not work well. Also, if a cable does not have shielding and it is used in a place with lots of electrical noise, the signal can get messed up. To avoid these issues, always check the label printed on the cable to make sure it's the right type for your setup.

Single-mode vs. multimode

Single-mode fiber (**SMF**) is designed for long-distance communication (up to 100 km) using a single beam, and its wavelength is 1,310 **nanometers** (**nm**) / 1,550 nm. **Multi-mode fiber** (**MMF**) is used for shorter distances (up to a few hundred meters) and allows multiple light signals that bounce off the core's cladding as they travel down the fiber to travel at the same time, which can cause more signal dispersion (blurring). Its wavelength is 850 nm/1,300 nm. When using fiber optic cables, ensuring compatibility and proper maintenance is crucial.

Issues with SMF and MMF

Different scenarios cause different issues. For example, a mismatch between SMF and MMF can cause communication failure or severe signal loss because they are designed to work with different types of light signals and fiber cores. One common issue is that the **transmit** (**TX**) and **receive** (**RX**) fibers might be reversed.

If you are using an SMF transceiver with an MMF cable, the single-mode transceiver emits a narrow, focused light signal that is not optimized for MMF's larger core. This leads to signal dispersion, data loss, and unreliable communication.

If you are using an MMF transceiver with an SMF cable, the multimode transceiver sends multiple light signals that do not properly transmit through SMF's narrow core, causing total signal failure. A proper fiber patch cord and matching transceivers are required to avoid this issue.

If a fiber optic cable breaks completely, data transmission stops because the light signal cannot pass through. Unlike copper cables, which may still function partially when damaged, fiber optics require an unbroken optical path. Breaks can be caused by overbending, physical damage, or excessive tension. While minor damage may cause signal degradation or intermittent issues, a full break results in total signal loss. Repairs typically involve splicing the fiber ends together or replacing the damaged section.

Dirty or clogged fiber connectors can also cause issues. Fiber optic connectors need to be clean and free of dust, dirt, or oil for proper signal transmission. Even microscopic particles can weaken or block the light signal. This can be caused by dust, fingerprints, or debris clogging the connector end-face. This will result in increased signal loss (attenuation), poor performance, or intermittent connectivity. To remedy this situation, use fiber cleaning tools such as lint-free wipes, isopropyl alcohol, or specialized cleaning pens to clean connectors before plugging them in. Proper fiber maintenance, correct cable selection, and careful handling can prevent these issues and ensure reliable network performance. Creating fiber cables is a specialist role; not everyone can perform it.

Category 5/6/7/8

Understanding the differences between various categories of Ethernet cables is essential for selecting the right one for your networking needs. Let us look at each of them in turn:

- **Category 5e (Cat5e):** This is an older category than the others and supports data transfer rates up to 1 Gbps. Its optimal performance is up to 100 meters (328 feet). It is commonly used in residential and small office networks.

- **Category 6 (Cat6):** Cat6 is capable of up to 10 Gbps speed, but only up to 55 meters (180 feet); for distances up to 100 meters, speeds are up to 1 Gbps. It is commonly used for high-speed applications in office environments.

- **Category 6a (Cat6a):** Cat6a consistently supports 10 Gbps data rates over distances up to 100 meters (328 feet). It's ideal for data centers and networks requiring high bandwidth over longer distances.

- **Category 7 (Cat7)**: Cat7 cable supports data transfer speeds of up to 10 Gbps over distances of up to 100 meters (328 feet). It is designed for high-speed networking environments such as data centers and large enterprise networks. Unlike earlier Ethernet cables (such as Cat5e or Cat6), Cat7 always uses **shielded twisted pair (STP)** or **screened foiled twisted pair (S/FTP)**, which helps reduce interference and crosstalk.

  To fully comply with the Cat7 standard, it must be terminated with specialized connectors, such as **GG45** or **TERA**, instead of the common **RJ45** connectors. These connectors support higher frequencies (up to 600 MHz for Cat7) and offer better shielding performance than other categories, which is important for maintaining signal quality at high speeds.

  GG45 is a special connector for Cat7/Cat7A cables. It looks like an **RJ45** but includes extra contacts for higher speeds. It can accept regular RJ45 plugs but performs best with GG45 plugs. It is fully shielded.

- **TERA** is another high-performance connector for Cat7/Cat7A, offering very high bandwidth and shielding. It is not compatible with RJ45 and uses a unique design, mainly for advanced data and video applications.

- **Category 8 (Cat8)**: Cat8 cables support extremely high data transfer rates of 25 to 40 Gbps, but only over short distances, up to 30 meters (98 feet). They are primarily used in data centers, where short, high-speed connections are needed, such as switch-to-switch or server-to-server links, typically in **top-of-rack (ToR)** setups. A ToR setup is a way to organize network equipment in a data center. In this setup, a small network switch is placed at the top of each rack. All the servers in that rack connect to this switch using short cables.

- There are two variants of Cat8, as defined by the **ISO**:

  - **Cat 8.1 (Class I)**: Equivalent to the **TIA/EIA** Cat8 standard and uses standard RJ45 connectors, making it compatible with existing Ethernet equipment

  - **Cat 8.2 (Class II)**: Requires shielded or screened cabling and must use GG45 or TERA connectors, which offer better shielding and higher performance for specialized environments

Cat8 cables are always shielded to reduce interference and support the high frequencies needed for such fast data rates. Cat8 cabling requires precise termination practices to ensure signal integrity and reduce interference. One common requirement is to wrap the end connections in copper tape to maintain shielding and reduce electromagnetic interference. Crosstalk can often be caused by improper termination of cables.

Shielded twisted pair (STP) versus unshielded twisted pair (UTP)

Selecting whether to use **STP** or **UTP** is crucial. STP has extra shielding to protect against interference from electrical devices and requires grounding to be effective. This makes it useful in industrial areas or places with a lot of electronic equipment. However, it is more expensive and harder to install than UTP.

UTP lacks shielding, making it more vulnerable to interference, but it is cheaper and easier to install. Most home and office networks use UTP cables.

Plenum-grade cables

From a safety perspective, it is important to use the correct type of cable jacket for the area where the cable is installed:

- **Plenum-rated cables** must be used in plenum spaces. These are areas used for air circulation in buildings (such as the space above a drop ceiling or below a raised floor). These cables are made with materials that are fire-resistant and produce non-toxic fumes with very little smoke if they catch fire.

- In riser spaces (vertical shafts between floors), you can use riser-rated or plenum-rated cables, but not the other way around; riser-rated cables are not safe for use in plenum spaces. Riser cables are tested to slow vertical flame spread, which is why they are safe for use inside walls or riser shafts, but not in open-air spaces. When burned, the PVC outer cover can give off dense black smoke and toxic gases such as hydrogen chloride. This is dangerous, especially in areas where air circulates freely.

Signal degradation

Signal degradation refers to the loss of quality or strength of a signal as it travels through a medium or system. There are three main types of signal degradation: crosstalk, interference, and attenuation, which we will look at here.

Crosstalk

Crosstalk refers to the unwanted transfer of signals between communication channels, leading to interference and potential data errors. This occurs when the electromagnetic fields of signals in one wire induce undesired currents in adjacent wires. Imagine trying to have a conversation in a room where another discussion is happening nearby; the overlapping voices could make it challenging to hear clearly. Similarly, in cabling, crosstalk can disrupt the clarity and integrity of data transmission.

There are two types of crosstalk, **near-end crosstalk (NEXT)** and **far-end crosstalk (FEXT)**. NEXT occurs when interference is measured at the same end of the cable where the signal originates. It's like speaking into a phone and hearing an echo of another conversation right in your earpiece. FEXT happens when interference is measured at the opposite end from where the signal was sent. It's akin to your friend on the other end of the line hearing parts of someone else's conversation.

Interference can corrupt the data being transmitted, leading to errors that require retransmission. To combat errors, systems might slow down data transfer rates, leading to slower network performance. Excessive crosstalk can weaken signals, causing devices to lose connection temporarily or permanently.

There are ways of minimizing crosstalk. For instance, twisting the wires together helps cancel out electromagnetic interference, reducing crosstalk. This is why Ethernet cables have pairs of wires twisted around each other. Ensuring cables are not bent sharply, are adequately spaced, and are correctly terminated can prevent crosstalk. Using cables with additional shielding can block external interference, further reducing the chance of crosstalk.

Interference

Interference refers to the disruption of signals as they travel through cables or wirelessly. This disruption can cause slower network speeds, poor connection quality, or even complete signal loss. Interference happens when external signals or electronic devices disrupt the intended data transmission, making it difficult for devices to communicate properly. One of the most common types of interference occurs in Wi-Fi networks, where co-channel interference happens when too many Wi-Fi networks use the same frequency (channel). Imagine a crowded room where everyone is talking at the same time – it becomes hard to hear.

For example, if you live in an apartment building and all your neighbors' Wi-Fi routers use the same 2.4 GHz channel, your internet may slow down. Switching to a less crowded channel (or using 5 GHz Wi-Fi) can help.

Wireless signals travel through the air, and other electronic devices – such as microwaves, cordless phones, and Bluetooth devices – can interfere with them. If you've ever noticed your Wi-Fi slowing down when using a microwave, that's because both operate on the 2.4 GHz frequency, causing interference. Similarly, having too many Wi-Fi networks in the same area, such as in an apartment building, can lead to congestion and poor performance.

Interference also affects wired networks, where electrical cables, fluorescent lights, and large machinery can create **electromagnetic interference** (EMI), which disrupts network signals in nearby Ethernet cables. This is especially a problem for unshielded twisted pair cables, which don't have protection against external interference, and may require more thought when designing routes for cables. Crosstalk is another type of interference that occurs when signals from one network cable "leak" into another, which can cause data errors and slow speeds.

Another common type of interference occurs in fiber optic networks, though fiber optics are generally more resistant than copper cables. However, physical factors such as bending the cable too much or exposing it to extreme temperatures can still cause signal disruption.

To reduce interference, it's important to use STP instead of UTP in environments with high electrical noise. Keeping network cables away from power lines and using proper grounding techniques can also help. For Wi-Fi, using the 5 GHz frequency instead of 2.4 GHz can reduce interference from household devices. Additionally, placing the router in an open, central location and avoiding obstacles such as thick walls can improve signal strength.

Attenuation

Attenuation refers to the gradual weakening of a signal as it travels through a medium, such as a network cable, fiber optic line, or even Wi-Fi signals in the air. As signals travel longer distances, they lose strength, which can lead to slower data speeds, poor communication quality, or even complete signal loss. One common example of attenuation occurs in wired network cables, such as Ethernet cables. If an Ethernet cable is too long, typically beyond 100 meters, the signal can degrade before reaching its destination. This can cause data loss or slower speeds. Similarly, Wi-Fi signals also experience attenuation. If you are close to your Wi-Fi router, the signal is strong, but as you move further away, especially through walls or floors, the signal weakens. This is why Wi-Fi performance may be poor in some areas of a home or office.

Attenuation is also a concern in fiber optic communication, although fiber optics generally experience less signal loss than traditional copper cables. However, when transmitting data over extremely long distances, such as between cities or under the ocean, attenuation can still occur. To solve this, network providers install signal boosters or repeaters along the way to strengthen the signal and maintain communication quality.

Aside from internet and network cables, attenuation can also impact audio and video signals. For example, if you use a very long **HDMI** cable to connect a computer to a TV, the video quality may degrade, leading to flickering or lower resolution. Similarly, in phone calls or online meetings, a weak microphone or poor internet connection can result in a faint or distorted voice, which is another form of attenuation.

To reduce attenuation, it's important to use high-quality cables that are properly shielded, avoid excessive cable lengths, and place network devices strategically. For Wi-Fi, placing the router in a central location and reducing interference from other electronic devices can help maintain a strong signal. In professional networking setups, technicians use repeaters, amplifiers, or fiber optics to minimize signal loss over long distances.

Understanding attenuation is essential for anyone working with networks, as it directly affects performance and reliability. By recognizing the causes of signal loss and applying the right solutions, you can ensure a stronger and more efficient network connection.

Improper termination

Improper termination occurs when a cable or connection is not correctly finished, leading to signal reflections, network errors, and poor performance. This issue is especially critical in older network types such as coaxial cable networks, where termination resistors must be placed at the end of the cable to prevent data signals from bouncing back. Without proper termination, signals can reflect and interfere with new transmissions, causing slow or unreliable connections. In coax networks, improper termination can cause the entire network to fail almost immediately.

Improper termination can also affect fiber optic networks. If the ends of fiber cables are not properly polished or aligned, light signals may scatter, resulting in data loss and weak communication. Likewise, in twisted-pair Ethernet cables, improper termination – such as leaving cable ends unconnected or failing to follow wiring standards – can degrade network performance.

To avoid improper termination, it's important to use the correct terminators, connectors, and cabling standards for each network type. For modern Ethernet, this means using properly crimped RJ45 connectors and following wiring schemes such as **T568A** or **T568B** to ensure reliable connections. In fiber optics, clean and well-seated connectors are essential to prevent data loss.

Transmitter (TX) transposed

The **TX** is the part of a device that sends data signals. **TX transposed** occurs when the TX wires are accidentally swapped or misconnected, preventing proper communication between devices. This mistake can happen when setting up network cables, fiber optics, or serial connections. When the

TX is transposed, the data being sent does not reach the correct destination, leading to connection failures or poor performance. To avoid **TX transposition**, it's important to follow proper cable wiring standards, such as T568A or T568B for Ethernet cables, and to use cable testers to verify connections before finalizing a setup. In fiber optics, ensuring the correct alignment of TX and RX ports helps maintain smooth communication. Fixing a transposed TX connection is usually simple – just identifying and correcting the mis-wired connections ensures data can flow correctly.

Receiver (RX) transposed

The **RX** is the part of a device that receives data signals. **RX transposed** happens when the receiving RX wires are incorrectly connected or swapped, preventing proper data reception. This issue can occur in Ethernet cables, fiber optics, or serial connections, leading to failed communication or unstable network performance. To prevent RX transposition, it's important to follow proper wiring standards and use network testing tools to verify connections. In fiber optic networks, ensuring that the RX and TX ports are correctly aligned prevents data loss. If RX is transposed, fixing it is as simple as correcting the cable placement, ensuring the device receives the data it's supposed to.

Cable testing tools

When you are troubleshooting, it's useful to use some of the most common cable testing tools. These include **tone generators, cable testers, visual fault locators (VFLs)**, **optical power meters (OPMs)**, and **optical time-domain reflectometers (OTDRs)**.

A **tone generator** and **probe** help locate and trace cables in a network. The tone generator sends a signal through a cable, and the probe detects the signal, making it easier to identify cables hidden in walls or bundled with others. This tool is useful for troubleshooting cable connections and identifying misrouted or disconnected cables. This is also known as a **fox and hound**. Popular options include **Fluke Networks Pro3000** and **Klein Tools VDV500-820**.

A cable tester checks whether an Ethernet or fiber optic cable is properly wired and functioning. It verifies continuity, identifies broken wires, and detects incorrect wiring (such as crossed or split pairs). Using a cable tester helps ensure cables are correctly installed and free from damage that could cause network issues. Good options include **Fluke Networks MicroScanner2** for professionals and **Klein Tools VDV526-200** for basic testing.

A VFL is a handheld tool that sends a bright red laser through the fiber cable to check for breaks, bends, or poor splices. If the fiber is damaged, the light will escape at the fault location, making it visible. This tool is great for quick troubleshooting of short fiber runs. Good examples are the Fluke Networks VisiFault, which is durable and reliable for locating breaks in fiber. The Klein Tools VDV526-055 is compact and affordable for quick troubleshooting.

An **OPM** measures the signal strength (dBm) in a fiber optic cable. It helps determine whether a cable is transmitting at the correct power level or whether there is excessive signal loss. It's commonly used with a light source for more accurate testing. The EXFO PON Power Meter is ideal for testing fiber in **passive optical networks** (**PONs**).

An **OTDR** is used for advanced fiber testing. It sends pulses of light into the fiber and measures reflections to detect faults, breaks, splice losses, and overall cable length. This tool is essential for diagnosing long-distance fiber issues. The Fluke Networks OptiFiber Pro OTDR is great for enterprise networks, whereas the EXFO MaxTester 730C is compact and user-friendly for field technicians.

Interface issues

Interface status commands can help identify network issues, including collisions, which happen when data signals interfere with each other. Collisions may occur if the duplex settings between a switch port and a connected device do not match or if an older hub or **NIC** is used. Other issues can arise due to physical layer problems, such as faulty cables or signal interference. Interface issues affect network ports on devices such as routers and switches, leading to slow speeds, connection failures, or error messages. In the following sections, we will explore the common interface problems and how to troubleshoot them.

Increasing interface counters

Interface counters track network activity on devices and provide insights into performance and potential issues. Key counters include link stats, resets, and drops. Link stats measure the overall status of a network connection, including speed, errors, and uptime. Resets occur when an interface is restarted or a connection is reestablished due to issues such as link failures or configuration changes. Drops indicate packets that were discarded due to congestion, misconfiguration, or network errors. Increases in these counters can result from normal network activity, high utilization, or issues such as congestion, hardware faults, misconfigurations, or security threats. Monitoring tools such as show interfaces, **SNMP**-based software, and packet analyzers help diagnose anomalies.

Cyclic redundancy check (CRC)

CRC errors occur when data packets transmitted across a network or storage medium become corrupted. These errors indicate that the checksum calculated by the receiving device does not match the checksum appended to the data by the sender, suggesting possible data corruption due to interference, faulty cables, or hardware issues. High CRC error rates can lead to network performance degradation, packet loss, and retransmissions, which negatively impact efficiency. Common causes include **EMI**, damaged or low-quality cables, and misconfigurations in network devices. Diagnosing CRC errors involves checking physical connections, replacing defective cables, and ensuring proper network configurations.

Runt

A **runt** is a network packet that is smaller than the minimum required size for a valid Ethernet frame, which is 64 bytes. When a packet is too short, it is considered a runt and is typically discarded by network devices. Runts can be caused by collisions in half-duplex networks, faulty hardware, or misconfigurations. A high number of runts may indicate network congestion, poor cabling, or duplex mismatches between devices. Troubleshooting involves checking for proper duplex settings, ensuring high-quality cables, and reducing network congestion through proper network design.

Giant

A **giant** is a network packet that exceeds the maximum allowed size for transmission. Ethernet frames, for example, have a standard maximum size of 1,518 bytes (or 1,522 bytes with VLAN tagging). If a packet surpasses this limit, it may be classified as a giant and discarded by network devices, leading to performance issues. Giants can result from misconfigured network settings, faulty hardware, or software bugs. Diagnosing **giant frames** involves checking **MTU** settings and ensuring that all network devices follow consistent configurations.

Drops

A **drop** occurs when a network device, such as a switch or router, discards a packet due to congestion, buffer overflow, or errors. Drops can degrade network performance, causing slow speeds, lag, or incomplete data transmission. Common causes include excessive network traffic, overloaded devices, and hardware faults. To reduce packet drops, network administrators optimize bandwidth usage, implement **QoS** policies, and upgrade hardware to handle higher data loads effectively.

Port status

The status of a port on a switch or router determines whether it can send and receive data. If a port is inactive or experiencing issues, it can disrupt communication between devices. Understanding different port statuses is essential for troubleshooting and maintaining a stable network. The following are some common port status conditions.

Error-disabled

A port in an **error-disabled** state has been automatically shut down by the switch due to a detected issue, such as excessive errors, security violations, or STP inconsistencies. This status helps prevent network problems but requires manual intervention to restore functionality. Common fixes include identifying the root cause, resolving the issue (e.g., replacing faulty cables or adjusting configurations), and re-enabling the port.

For example, if someone plugs in a bad cable, the switch might disable the port to prevent network issues. A network admin must manually fix and re-enable the port.

Administratively down

A port marked as **administratively down** has been manually disabled by a network administrator using commands such as shutdown on Cisco devices. This is often done for security reasons, to control access, or during maintenance.

Suspended

A **suspended** port is temporarily disabled by the switch, often due to a configuration issue or a mismatch in features such as EtherChannel settings. Unlike an error-disabled port, a suspended port may automatically recover if the configuration issue is resolved. Common causes include mismatched port settings, VLAN inconsistencies, or issues with link aggregation.

Hardware issues

Hardware issues can impact network performance, causing connectivity problems and device failures. In the following section, we break down common hardware issues caused by problems with **PoE** and **transceivers**.

Power over Ethernet (PoE)

PoE allows network cables to deliver both data and electrical power to devices such as IP cameras, wireless access points, and **VoIP** phones. However, PoE-related issues can disrupt network operations.

Power budget exceeded

One issue is **power budget exceeded**. **PoE** switches have a limited power supply that they distribute across connected devices. If too many high-power devices are connected, the switch may not have enough power to support them all, causing some devices to lose power or function intermittently. To fix this, network administrators should check the power budget of the switch and redistribute devices or upgrade to a higher-capacity PoE switch.

Incorrect standard

Incorrect standards can also cause issues. PoE comes in different standards, such as **802.3af (PoE)**, **802.3at (PoE+)**, and **802.3bt (PoE++)**, each with different power levels. If a device requires more power than the switch can provide, it may not function correctly. Ensuring that both the switch and the device support the same PoE standard prevents compatibility issues.

Transceiver issues

Transceivers are small modules used to send and receive data over fiber optic, Ethernet connections, and Wi-Fi in the case of Wi-Fi transceivers. Problems with transceivers can lead to poor signal quality or failed network connections.

Transceivers must be compatible with both the switch and the cable type in use. A **mismatch** is when you use an incorrect transceiver. For example, mixing single-mode and multi-mode fiber transceivers. Mismatches can cause connection failures. Always check manufacturer recommendations to ensure compatibility.

Signal strength is also important. Fiber optic transceivers rely on strong signal transmission to function properly. If the signal is too weak or too strong, it can cause errors or a complete loss of communication. Factors such as dirty or damaged fiber cables, long-distance connections, or incorrect transceiver types can affect signal strength. Cleaning fiber connectors and using the correct transceivers helps maintain a stable connection.

Summary

In this chapter, you have seen how to identify and troubleshoot common cabling and physical interface issues that impact network performance. You have learned how to recognize incorrect cable types, address signal degradation factors such as crosstalk and attenuation, and resolve termination errors. Additionally, you will now be able to diagnose interface issues such as CRC errors, runts, giants, and packet drops, and manage port status problems such as error-disabled or administratively down ports. Finally, you will understand hardware-related concerns, including PoE limitations, transceiver mismatches, and signal strength issues. These troubleshooting skills will be invaluable for both the Network+ exam and real-world networking environments.

The knowledge gained in this chapter will prepare you to answer questions relating to Exam objective 5.2 in the *CompTIA Network+ (N10-009)* exam.

Exam objectives 5.2

Troubleshoot common cabling and physical interface issues

Cable issues:

Incorrect cable: Using the wrong type affects performance and connectivity.

- **Single mode:** Supports long distances but needs compatible transceivers.
- **Multimode:** Shorter distances, more signal dispersion than single mode.

    - **Category 5:** Limited speed and distance, outdated for high-speed networks.
    - **Category 6 issues:** Better than Cat5 but sensitive to interference.
    - **Category 7 issues:** Shielding reduces noise, but compatibility can be problematic.
    - **Category 8 issues:** Designed for high-speed data but requires proper shielding.
    - **Shielded twisted pair (STP) issues:** Reduces interference, but harder to install.
    - **Unshielded twisted pair (UTP) issues:** Easier to install but vulnerable to noise.

- **Signal Degradation:**

    - **Crosstalk:** Signal leakage between wires causes data corruption.
    - **Interference:** External signals disrupt network communication.
    - **Attenuation:** Signal weakens over long distances.

- **Other Cable Issues:**

    - **Improper termination:** Loose or incorrect connections cause data loss.
    - **Transmitter (TX) transposed:** TX wires swapped, preventing proper transmission.
    - **Receiver (RX) transposed:** RX wires swapped, causing reception failure.

- **Interface Issues:**

    - **Increasing interface counters:** High error counts indicate network problems.

        - **Cyclic redundancy check (CRC):** Data corruption due to noise or faulty cables.
        - **Runts:** Packets smaller than the minimum size, often due to collisions.
        - **Giants:** Oversized packets exceeding the allowed frame size.
        - **Drops:** Packets discarded due to congestion or errors.

- **Port Status:**

    - **Error disabled**: Port shuts down due to errors or security violations.

    - **Administratively down**: Port disabled manually by an administrator.

    - **Suspended**: Port inactive due to configuration or network issues.

Hardware Issues:

Power over Ethernet (PoE): Delivers power and data over network cables.

    - **Power budget exceeded**: Too many devices, drawing more power than available.

    - **Incorrect standard**: Using incompatible PoE standards prevents proper power delivery.

Transceivers:

Mismatch: Incompatible transceivers cause connection failures.

    - **Signal strength**: Weak signal leads to poor performance or disconnections.

Chapter review questions

Now that you've completed the chapter, you can check your knowledge using the practice questions provided in the online platform at `https://packt.link/N10-009ch22`. You can also use the QR code below. Accessing these questions requires you to unlock the accompanying online content first. Head over to Chapter 26 for detailed instructions.

23

Given a Scenario, Troubleshoot Common Issues with Network Services

Having looked at troubleshooting physical issues, such as cabling and interface issues, in *Chapter 22*, it's time to turn your attention to network services. As data packets find their way around networks, complex operations such as routing, VLAN assignment, and address resolution take place. Even in the best, most efficient systems, issues can arise with networking services. As a network engineer, it is important for you to understand the most common problems and how to troubleshoot them.

This chapter covers practical approaches to troubleshooting common issues such as switching problems caused by network loops, incorrect VLAN assignments, and **access control list (ACL)** misconfigurations. It also includes how routing mishaps, such as incorrect default gateways or errors in route selection, can impede communication between devices. Additionally, it covers address-related issues, such as duplicate IPs and subnet mask mismatches, as well as the consequences of running out of available IP addresses. In the following section, we start off by looking at common switching issues.

This chapter covers the third objective in *Domain 5: 5.3, Given a scenario, troubleshoot common issues with network services.*

> **Note**
>
> A full breakdown of objective 5.3 will be given at the end of the chapter.

Troubleshooting

When troubleshooting network issues, start by checking whether the problem affects just one user or multiple users—if multiple people are affected, find out which switch or network device they are all connected to. It's important to check whether they are all on the same switch, and whether users who still have access are connected to a different switch or network segment.

We then look for hardware connections and power supply—before looking into more complex network or software issues. Troubleshooting begins at **Layer 1**—the **physical layer**—and continues upward through the OSI model layers. Network equipment needs a reliable power source to work properly. Problems such as power surges, voltage drops, or sudden outages can damage equipment, cause it to restart, or stop working entirely.

Many businesses use backup systems such as **UPSs** to keep devices running for a short time during a power issue. This allows time to safely shut down systems or switch to backup power, such as a generator. If the problem is serious or affects the whole building, it may need to be handled by an electrician or the power provider.

Switching issues

A **switch** is a network device that connects users and devices within a building or organization. Sometimes, users may not have network access, and an IT technician needs to troubleshoot the issue. We would check the switch first, then the router.

One of the first steps in troubleshooting is checking the small lights near the network cable ports on the computer and the switch. These lights are called **light-emitting diodes (LEDs)** and act as status indicators to help show whether the network connection is working properly.

Here is what the LED lights usually mean:

- **No light:** There may be no connection, the cable might be unplugged, or the port could be disabled
- **Solid green:** The connection is established, but no data is currently being transferred
- **Blinking green:** The connection is active and data is being sent or received. Faster blinking can indicate higher speed

- **Solid amber:** The port is blocked by the **Spanning Tree Protocol (STP)** to prevent network loops
- **Blinking amber:** A problem has been detected, such as a settings mismatch or communication errors

By checking these lights, IT technicians can quickly gather clues about what might be wrong before moving on to deeper troubleshooting.

We might need to check the status of the switch ports. Switch ports use different status indicators to show how the connection is behaving. These are shown in the following list:

- **Down/down:**
    - The port is not connected or turned off
    - Could be due to an unplugged cable or a disabled port
- **Administrative down/down:**
    - The port has been manually disabled by an administrator
- **Down/error:**
    - The port is experiencing errors, preventing it from working properly
- **Up/up:**
    - The port is connected and working normally
- **Up/down (suspended):**
    - The port is part of a link aggregation group, but the connection hasn't been properly set up
    - Check that both sides have matching speed, duplex, port count, and link type
    - With **LACP**, at least one side must be "active" to negotiate the connection

The following are some troubleshooting tips:

- If the port shows down/down, verify the speed and duplex settings
- A common problem happens when one side is manually set (fixed speed/duplex) and the other side is set to auto-negotiate
- For example, if the host is fixed at 100 Mbps/full duplex but the switch is auto-negotiating, the link may fail
- To avoid issues, set both sides to auto-negotiate

- Remember the following:
- A speed mismatch usually causes the link to fail completely
- A duplex mismatch causes slower speeds, packet loss, and errors

When managing or troubleshooting a Cisco network device such as a switch or router, `show` commands are essential tools. They provide real-time information about the device's configuration, status, and performance. Here are some common `show` commands:

- `show config`: Shows the device's overall configuration (similar to `running-config`). It is useful for a quick overview
- `show startup-config`: Displays the saved configuration that loads at device startup. It helps with checking whether recent changes were saved
- `show running-config`: Shows the current active configuration in use. It is useful to see real-time settings and spot differences from `startup-config`
- `show interface`: Provides detailed info about interfaces (ports), including status, speed, errors, and traffic. It helps with identifying physical or connection issues

By running various `show` commands, you can see which interfaces are up or down, how traffic is flowing, what security measures are in place, and whether the device's configuration matches what it should be. This helps pinpoint problems faster and ensures the network runs smoothly.

A triangular topology refers to a network layout where three switches are connected in a triangle-like shape. Each switch is connected to the other two, creating three redundant paths between them, as shown in *Figure 23.1*.

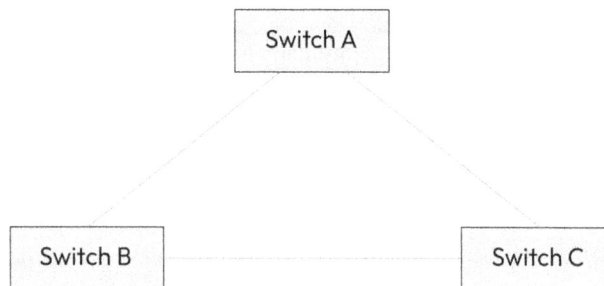

Figure 23.1: Triangular topology

The main purpose of this network setup is to provide redundancy and fault tolerance. If one connection fails, traffic can still be routed through the remaining switches, allowing the network to stay operational. Each switch has multiple devices connected. When a device on switch A sends an ARP request to find another device's MAC address, the request is broadcast within the local VLAN.

Switch A forwards the ARP broadcast to switches B and C. Without a loop prevention protocol such as STP, switches B and C may forward the broadcast to each other and back to switch A, causing a broadcast storm. This type of storm generates excessive traffic, consumes bandwidth, and can cripple the network in seconds.

Other common switching issues include incorrect VLAN configurations, which can isolate devices, and misconfigured ACLs, which may block or permit unintended traffic. Table 23.1 shows some possible switching issues:

Issue	Cause	Effect	Resolution
Broadcast storm	Switching loop without STP	Network congestion or failure	Resolve by using STP or RSTP
Incorrect VLANs	Misconfigured VLAN tagging	Inaccessible devices	Resolve by VLAN auditing
Faulty ACLs	Improper ACL rules	Disrupted traffic flow	Resolve by ACL validation

Table 23.1: Switching issues

Spanning Tree Protocol (STP)

As you have just seen, when a network uses multiple switches, there is a danger that broadcast storms can be created or looping happens between switches, where traffic just flows in a circular motion, slowing down the network. STP prevents this from happening by logically blocking loops.

Network loops

A **network loop** occurs when data packets continuously circulate through the network without reaching their destination. This usually happens because broadcast traffic sent by switches is forwarded out of all ports (except the one it came in on).

If there are redundant links—multiple connections between switches—these broadcasts can loop endlessly between switches. As the loop continues, the switches become confused about where devices (MAC addresses) are located, often associating the same MAC address with different ports. This causes them to clear their MAC address tables and flood all unicast traffic (which should be directed to a single device) out of every port, creating severe congestion and potentially crashing the network.

To prevent this, STP is used. STP detects loops and automatically disables one of the redundant ports to break the loop. If STP has shut down a port, this isolates the problem to a specific segment.

Here's what to check:

- Inspect the disabled ports on the switch. These may point to the source of the loop.
- At the patch panel, make sure no cable connects two ports on the same switch.
- On the office floor, ensure there's no patch cable connecting two wall ports.
- Check the switch logs for MAC address flapping, which indicates a MAC address is rapidly appearing on different ports—a strong sign of a loop. MAC flapping can be stopped by enabling STP, which prevents network loops by blocking redundant paths.

Root bridge selection

When setting up STP, one switch is selected as the root bridge, serving as the central reference point for the network's topology.

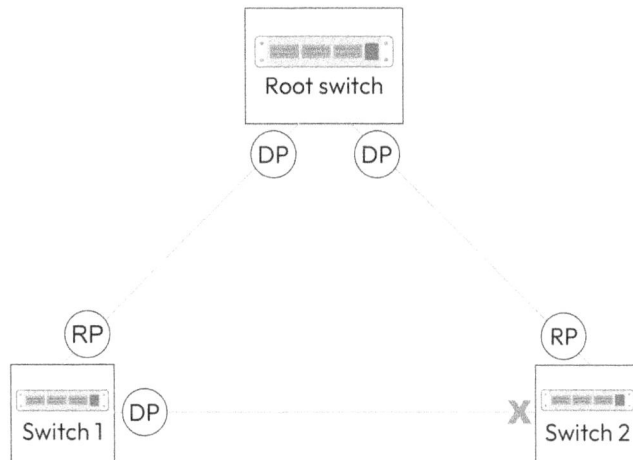

Figure 23.2: Spanning Tree Protocol

Figure 23.2 shows STP in action. It prevents network loops by selectively blocking redundant links. The **root switch** is designated as the **root bridge**. All other switches calculate the best path to the root switch, using this as the reference point. This is done by having ports fulfil different roles to direct the traffic. These roles are **designated ports** (labeled **DP** in the diagram), **root ports** (labeled **RP** in the diagram), and **blocked ports** (labeled with an **X** in the diagram).

Each switch, except the root switch, identifies one port with the shortest path to the root switch. This is the RP, and the switch uses it to forward traffic to the root switch. DPs forward traffic to the root switch or onto the active network segment. A designated port is responsible for forwarding traffic to and from a specific network segment. It is the port on the switch with the lowest path cost to the root switch for that particular segment.

The blocked port blocks traffic to prevent looping. STP identifies redundant links (extra connections that could cause loops) and places one of the ports into a blocking state.

Port states

STP has different types of port settings:

- **Blocking**: The port does not forward or receive traffic (used to prevent loops)
- **Listening**: The port listens for STP messages but does not forward traffic
- **Learning**: The port learns MAC addresses but doesn't forward data packets yet
- **Forwarding**: The port forwards traffic and participates in the network
- **Disabled**: The port is administratively turned off and doesn't participate in STP

Spanning Tree Protocol (STP) vulnerabilities

STP is critical for preventing network loops in Ethernet LANs. While it's designed to maintain a stable topology, STP can sometimes introduce problems or become a target for attacks if not properly configured. A switch sends a **bridge protocol data unit** (**BPDU**), which is a special type of network message used by switches to exchange information in networks that use STP. It's like saying to other switches, "I am here."

STP can be manipulated by an attacker who introduces a rogue switch with a lower bridge priority than the legitimate root bridge. Since STP always selects the switch with the lowest priority as the root, this rogue switch could become the new root bridge—rerouting traffic and potentially intercepting sensitive data. To protect against this, we need to do the following:

- **Enable the root guard on access ports**: This feature blocks ports from accepting superior BPDUs that try to change the root bridge
- **Enable the BPDU guard on ports that should never receive BPDUs (e.g., end user devices)**: If a BPDU is received, the port is shut down automatically to protect the topology

Slow convergence

After a topology change (such as a switch reboot), STP can take 30–50 seconds to converge under the original 802.1D standard. This results in temporary loss of connectivity and dropped packets. We can fix this by using **RSTP** defined in 802.1w, which converges in just a few seconds, or we can enable PortFast on access ports that connect to end devices. PortFast is a Cisco STP feature that is used to immediately transition a switch port into the forwarding state, bypassing the usual STP listening and learning states.

Access control lists

ACLs use port numbers, IP addresses, and protocols to control traffic flow. When setting up a firewall or router, it often begins with no specific allow rules. In such cases, an implicit deny rule, the default behavior of denying any traffic not explicitly allowed, is enforced.

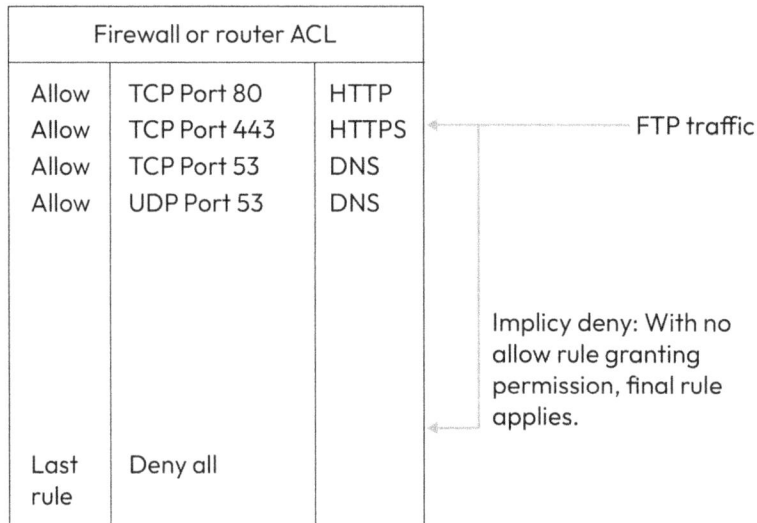

Firewall or router ACL		
Allow	TCP Port 80	HTTP
Allow	TCP Port 443	HTTPS
Allow	TCP Port 53	DNS
Allow	UDP Port 53	DNS
Last rule	Deny all	

FTP traffic

Implicy deny: With no allow rule granting permission, final rule applies.

Figure 23.3: ACL

For example, John recently purchased an e-book online. His browser initially used HTTP (TCP port 80) to access the website, then switched to HTTPS (TCP port 443) for the payment transaction. However, when attempting to download the e-book, the request is blocked.

This happens because the firewall's ACL permits ports 80 and 443, but not the ports required for FTP, such as port 21 for control and port 20 (or a range of passive-mode ports) for data transfer. Without an allow rule for those ports, the firewall defaults to the implicit deny, blocking the download. While this example uses a firewall, similar ACL behavior applies to routers.

ACLs are used to control network traffic, but if they're not set up correctly, they can cause problems. One common issue is accidentally blocking important connections, such as remote access for administrators. This can lock people out of the system. ACLs also include an implicit deny rule, which means any traffic not specifically allowed will be blocked by default. If you forget to add the right allow rules, even normal traffic can be stopped.

Problems can also happen if the rules are too broad or in the wrong order. For example, if a general allow all rule comes before a more specific rule, the specific rule might never be used. On some devices, ACLs don't automatically allow reply traffic, so you need to manually allow both directions. Mistakes such as applying a rule to the wrong interface, not updating rules as the network changes, or not documenting why a rule exists can all lead to confusion or security risks.

Finally, relying only on ACLs for security is risky. They should be just one part of a full security setup that includes firewalls and other protections. Reviewing ACLs regularly helps keep the network secure and running smoothly.

Incorrect VLAN assignment

Imagine you have the IT, finance, and HR teams all on separate VLANs. They all require isolation, but also need to communicate with each other. Someone on the finance team reports that they are trying to access some HR records but are unable to connect; they are getting the error "Network path not found." You have checked that all connections are working properly, and that the user isn't making errors when trying to connect. The next thing to check is that the VLANs are properly assigned.

You may recall from *Chapter 10, Given a Scenario, Configure Switching Technologies and Features*, that VLANs are created by configuring the switch with a unique VLAN ID and assigning switch ports to that VLAN. VLANs often correspond to subnets. Each VLAN typically has its own subnet IP address range, and all devices in the VLAN will share the same subnet mask. The default gateway is used for communication between VLANs or external networks. If the subnet mask is incorrect, devices may fail to communicate due to routing issues. Devices in the same VLAN can communicate with each other without needing the default gateway, but to reach devices outside the VLAN, the gateway is required. If a device cannot communicate within its VLAN, check that the switch port is assigned to the correct VLAN, as being on a port belonging to a different VLAN will isolate it from the intended VLAN.

In the *CompTIA Network+* exam, the switches normally operate at Layer 2 of the OSI and use MAC addresses, but it is possible on a modern network to create the VLAN on a Layer 3 switch that uses IP addresses. If a Layer 3 switch is used for VLAN implementation, the default gateway is typically set as an SVI, such as interface VLAN 10. The show commands on the switch can be used to confirm the configuration and VLAN port assignments. With these commands, you can troubleshoot assignment issues, as shown in the following examples.

Example 1

You can show the VLAN configuration using the following command:

```
show vlan brief
```

The output would look something like this:

```
VLAN Name Status Ports
---- -------------------------------- --------- --------------------------
1 default active Gi1/0/1, Gi1/0/2
10 VLAN10 active Gi1/0/3, Gi1/0/4
```

From this, we can see that VLAN 1 (the default VLAN) is active, and ports Gi1/0/1 and Gi1/0/2 are assigned to this VLAN.

Example 2

You can show the SVI configuration by running the following command:

```
show ip interface brief
```

The output would look something like this:

```
interface IP-Address OK?  Method Status Protocol
vlan1 192.168.1.1 YES     manual up up
vlan10 192.168.16.1 YES manual up up
```

From this, you can see that both vlan1 and vlan10 are up and operational. The interfaces are active, and the IP addresses assigned to them (192.168.1.1 for vlan1 and 192.168.16.1 for vlan10) are manually configured and valid.

For example, a switch is configured with three VLANs:

- VLAN 10 – HR
- VLAN 20 – Finance
- VLAN 30 – IT

Each VLAN contains the devices (with their IP addresses) that belong to that department. If a finance computer is accidentally connected to a switch port assigned to VLAN 30 (IT), it won't be able to communicate with the finance VLAN devices. A red "X" in the monitoring software would show that communication has failed. To fix this, the network administrator must reassign that finance device to the correct VLAN (VLAN 20).

Route selection

When data needs to travel from one host to another, a route must be selected using a routing table. It is like using a map to choose one of the routes to travel to see a friend in another town. This is known as route selection. In the following section, we will describe routing tables and the default route.

Routing table

The routing table is used to make the route selection. If you have a missing or incorrect route, then traffic might not get to its final destination.

Figure 23.4 shows a Windows routing table:

```
IPv4 Route Table
===========================================================================
Active Routes:
Network Destination        Netmask          Gateway       Interface  Metric
          0.0.0.0          0.0.0.0      192.168.0.1    192.168.0.173      25
        127.0.0.0        255.0.0.0         On-link        127.0.0.1     331
        127.0.0.1  255.255.255.255         On-link        127.0.0.1     331
  127.255.255.255  255.255.255.255         On-link        127.0.0.1     331
      192.168.0.0    255.255.255.0         On-link    192.168.0.173     281
    192.168.0.173  255.255.255.255         On-link    192.168.0.173     281
    192.168.0.255  255.255.255.255         On-link    192.168.0.173     281
        224.0.0.0        240.0.0.0         On-link        127.0.0.1     331
        224.0.0.0        240.0.0.0         On-link    192.168.0.173     281
  255.255.255.255  255.255.255.255         On-link        127.0.0.1     331
  255.255.255.255  255.255.255.255         On-link    192.168.0.173     281
===========================================================================
Persistent Routes:
  None
```

Figure 23.4: Windows routing table

The IPv4 route table in *Figure 23.4* shows the following:

`Network Destination`: The destination network or host that the route applies to. The network destination of `0.0.0.0/0` is the default route. If the route is not matched to the routing table, the packet is sent through the route that normally goes to your ISP. `127.0.0.1` (localhost) is the loopback route, which is used for internal communication within your own device. For example, `127.0.0.1` is commonly called "localhost." This tells you that the TCP/IP stack is initiated. `224.0.0.0` is the multicast address that allows a single device to send data to multiple devices simultaneously (e.g., video streaming or routing updates). The broadcast address is `255.255.255.255`, which sends data to all devices in the local network. All IP addresses ending in 255 are the local broadcast addresses, and those ending in 0 are the network IDs.

Netmask: The **subnet mask** is used to determine the size of the destination network (how many devices it includes). Take the following examples:

- 255.255.255.255 means a single device (a host route)
- 255.255.255.0 means a network that can contain up to 256 devices (e.g., 192.168.0.0/24)

Gateway: The gateway is the next-hop IP address or device that traffic will go through to reach the destination. This is the router on your network. On-link means the destination is directly reachable without using a gateway.

Interface: This is the local network interface used to send the traffic (e.g., an IP address on your device).

Metric: This is a cost value that determines the priority of the route. Lower metrics are preferred for routing traffic.

Persistent Routes: Any static route that has been added will be listed under Persistent Routes. There are none at present.

Default routes

If a route cannot be found on a routing table, then 0.0.0.0/0 is selected. This is known as the default route and will normally go to your ISP. This can be seen in the top entry in *Figure 23.4*. In a Cisco environment, the default route is known as Gateway of last resort. This is shown in the following excerpt from a Cisco routing table:

```
Gateway of last resort is 192.168.1.1 to network 0.0.0.0
192.168.1.0/24 is variably subnetted, 2 subnets, 2 masks
C 192.168.1.0/24 is directly connected, GigabitEthernet0/1
L 192.168.1.1/32 is directly connected, GigabitEthernet0/1
S 0.0.0.0/0 [1/0] via 192.168.1.1
```

In this excerpt, C = connected, L = local, and S = static route.

Address pool exhaustion

A DHCP server dynamically assigns an IP address when a client joins the network by booting up their machine. The process starts with the client sending a broadcast packet, using the IP address 255.255.255.255 to find a DHCP server. Normally, each network has its own DHCP server. If a DHCP server is on another network, then the router joining the network needs to be **RFC 1542** compliant, allowing the router to act as DHCP/BOOTP relay agents, meaning they can forward

DHCP requests from one subnet to a DHCP server on another subnet. An alternative is to install a DHCP relay agent whose job is to forward the requests to the DHCP server. The router can use the IP helper address, which can be set up as a DHCP relay agent, where the broadcasts can be converted to unicast traffic and forward the requests to the DHCP server.

For example, on a Cisco router, you can run the following command to enable the IP helper address:

```
ip helper-address <DHCP server IP>
```

An alternative is to configure one of your servers as a DHCP relay agent to forward the requests to the DHCP server. If a computer cannot contact a DHCP server or the server has run out of IP addresses to allocate, and the IP address is in the range 169.254.0.1 to 169.254.255.254, this is known as an **automatic private IP address (APIPA)**, used for troubleshooting by the network administrator.

> **Note**
>
> Running out of IP addresses is also known as exhaustion.

Incorrect default gateway

When you are troubleshooting network problems, you can ping a host on your local network. If you get a reply, then you know that the subnet mask is correct. The next step is to ping the default gateway, which is the router's IP address on the local network. If you get a destination host unreachable reply, there is a configuration error, such as having an incorrect IP address for the gateway. It could also be caused by incorrect entries in the routing table, or the router is offline. The symptoms of an incorrect default gateway could be one of the following:

- Inability to browse the internet or access external resources
- "Request timed out" errors when pinging external IPs
- Local network communication works but not external communication

Incorrect IP address

A host on a network or subnet will need to have an IP address in the same range as the other hosts. They need to have the same subnet mask and default gateway; otherwise, they will not be able to communicate with or ping any other host. To find out this information, you can run the ipconfig /all command. This will let you know whether the host's IP address is configured manually or allocated by DHCP.

Duplicate IP addresses

Each device on a network must have a unique IP address within the same subnet. However, duplicate IP addresses can occur due to misconfiguration, such as assigning the same static IP to multiple devices or a DHCP server assigning an IP already in use. When a duplicate IP exists, systems may behave differently: Windows typically shows a warning and disables the IP, while Linux may log a warning and keep the interface active (though behavior varies by distribution).

In a duplicate IP scenario, network traffic may unpredictably go to one device or the other, causing intermittent connectivity issues. To diagnose the problem, tools such as arping -D on Linux can detect duplicate replies. Once identified, you should reassign unique IP addresses to affected devices.

Duplicate MAC addresses

Though rare, duplicate MAC addresses can also cause network issues. These usually occur when locally administered MAC addresses are set manually or by virtualization platforms. When this happens, both devices may respond to ARP requests, leading to inconsistent or broken communication. You can inspect the ARP cache using the arp -a command to identify which IP addresses are associated with which MAC addresses and locate the conflict.

Incorrect subnet mask

A **subnet mask** is used to define which portion of an IP address represents the network and which part represents the host. If the subnet mask is incorrect, a device may misinterpret its own network boundaries. This can result in communication failures, for example, a device may mistakenly believe that another device on the same local network is on a different subnet and attempt to send traffic to it via the default gateway instead of directly.

- Common symptoms of an incorrect subnet mask include the following:
- Inability to reach nearby devices that should be on the same network
- Unnecessary routing of local traffic through a gateway
- General network connectivity issues despite correct IP and gateway settings

Ensuring that all devices on the same subnet have the correct and consistent subnet mask is critical for proper network communication.

Summary

This chapter focused on how to troubleshoot network service issues and address common problems such as switching errors, including network loops, incorrect root bridge selection, port roles/states in STP, and incorrect VLAN assignments. You learned how to check ACL configurations, routing tables, and default routes for route selection issues. You also learned how to resolve address-related problems such as IP address conflicts, subnet mask errors, address pool exhaustion, and misconfigured default gateways.

The knowledge gained in this chapter will prepare you to answer questions relating to exam objective 5.3 in your *CompTIA Network+ (N10-009)* exam.

Exam objective 5.3

Given a scenario, troubleshoot common issues with network services.

Switching issues: Problems affecting data transmission between devices via network switches:

- **STP:**

    - **Network loops**: Unchecked loops can overload switches and disrupt networks
    - **Root bridge selection**: Chooses the primary switch to control traffic in STP
    - **Port roles**: Defines each port's function, such as forwarding or blocking
    - **Port states**: Determines whether a port is active, learning, or idle in STP

Incorrect VLAN assignment: Leads to miscommunication between devices in separate network segments.

ACLs: Regulates network access by controlling traffic through defined rules.

Route selection: Ensures data follows the best path to its destination:

- **Routing table**: Lists known paths for directing network traffic
- **Default routes**: Provides a backup path for undefined destinations

Address pool exhaustion: Depletes available IP addresses for connected devices.

Incorrect default gateway: Prevents devices from accessing external networks.

Incorrect IP address: Misconfigured or duplicate IPs disrupt device connectivity.

Incorrect subnet mask: Impedes communication by misidentifying network boundaries.

Chapter review questions

Now that you've completed the chapter, you can check your knowledge using the practice questions provided in the online platform at `https://packt.link/N10-009ch23`. You can also use the QR code below. Accessing these questions requires you to unlock the accompanying online content first. Head over to *Chapter 26* for detailed instructions.

24

Given a Scenario, Troubleshoot Common Performance Issues

Network services issues, as discussed in *Chapter 23*, affect the availability, functionality, or accessibility of key services such as **DNS**, **DHCP**, and **VPNs**. However, even when services are running, networks often experience problems with speed, stability, and connection quality. Understanding how to troubleshoot these performance issues is a crucial skill for network engineers.

In this chapter, we'll explore common problems such as network congestion, bandwidth bottlenecks, wireless interference, and signal loss. We'll also explain important performance factors such as bandwidth, latency, packet loss, jitter, and wireless-specific challenges such as channel overlap and client disassociation.

By mastering these concepts, you will be equipped to identify and resolve performance bottleneck effectively in various scenarios.

This chapter covers the fourth objective in *Domain 5: 5.4, Given a scenario, troubleshoot common performance issues.*

> **Note**
>
> A full breakdown of *objective 5.4* will be given at the end of the chapter.

Congestion/contention

One of the most common complaints you might get from users on your network is that it is "too slow." Of course, "too slow" is an entirely subjective measure. It is too slow compared to what? You can check the basics. The user's machine might just need upgrading, or there may be faulty cabling. However, once you have established that it's a network problem, then you need to start troubleshooting what the issue is.

One common problem could be **congestion**, which occurs when more data is sent than the network can handle. Think of a highway at rush hour—too many cars lead to a slowdown for everyone. The same is true for networks: if demand exceeds available bandwidth, performance drops. For example, a 100 Mbps link can quickly become saturated if employees all stream 4K video during lunch, or if multiple machines run large file backups to a server at the same time. Even simply connecting too many devices to one network can create congestion.

Contention happens when multiple devices compete for the same limited network resources. A good analogy is water pressure in an apartment building—when someone turns on the kitchen tap, the shower may lose pressure. Similarly, in shared networks like public Wi-Fi or home internet with many users, contention doesn't always create congestion but can slow down performance.

To troubleshoot contention, you can use monitoring tools such as **ping** to measure latency and packet loss. The most direct fix is upgrading the network, but when that's not feasible, administrators can apply policies to restrict bandwidth-heavy activities, for example, 4K streaming or peer-to-peer file sharing. Other effective strategies include load balancing to distribute traffic evenly and VLAN segmentation to reduce competition between users or departments.

> **Note**
>
> Tools for solving network issues will be covered in the next chapter, *Chapter 25, Given a Scenario, Use the Appropriate Tool or Protocol to Solve Networking Issues.*

Bottlenecking

Congestion refers to a network as a whole not being able to handle traffic. However, sometimes the issue might not be with the whole network but only a specific part, sometimes centered around a single component. For example, your company's internal network has multiple departments, each using high-speed applications such as VoIP, video conferencing, and cloud storage. You add three new 10 Gbps connections, but the main network switch connecting all departments only has a 1 Gbps uplink. The switch is unable to handle multiple departments sending data simultaneously, choking the network and causing performance issues. This is called a **bottleneck.**

Bottlenecking happens when one device or link in the network path slows down the entire data flow because it can't handle the speed or volume of traffic that other devices can. Think of it like traffic trying to go from a four-lane highway into a one-lane tunnel – the tunnel is the bottleneck that slows everything down.

It's often caused by the following:

- Underpowered hardware (such as a slow switch, router, or IPS)
- Misconfigured network devices
- Incompatible speed settings

For example, after upgrading a company's core router, users begin to report slower network speeds. A network technician is called in to investigate and runs speed tests from different points in the network:

Location	Download speed	Upload speed
Server room (Router)	940 Mbps	930 Mbps
Office PC (Wired)	87 Mbps	90 Mbps
Laptop (Wireless)	85 Mbps	88 Mbps

The technician reviews the network path and identifies that, between the core router and the office network, sits a legacy **IPS** rated for only 100 Mbps throughput. The router shows near-gigabit speeds (940/930 Mbps), indicating the internet connection is fast.

Both wired and wireless clients are getting around 85–90 Mbps – much lower than the router's speed. Since both wired and wireless speeds are capped around the same limit, it suggests a common point of limitation.

The legacy IPS can only handle 100 Mbps of throughput – making it the bottleneck.

Software misconfigurations can also be a cause of bottlenecks. If network rules have been improperly set, they can lead to uneven traffic distribution. A load balancer might be misconfigured to send 90% of the traffic to one server. **QoS** policies can also lead to uneven traffic distribution. Software bugs may also create inefficiencies in how data is transmitted and received, such as if a router used for inter-VLAN communication is incorrectly set to route traffic through a 100 Mbps interface, even though the switches and devices are capable of gigabit speeds.

Similar to congestion, if activities on a particular VLAN consume too much bandwidth – such as video streams, applications sending large amounts of data, or the use of outdated, inefficient protocols – it can overload a router, potentially creating a bottleneck.

External factors such as interference in wireless networks or bandwidth throttling by ISPs can also contribute to bottlenecks. In growing networks, scalability issues arise when the infrastructure cannot support an increasing number of users or devices.

Bottlenecks can be solved first by ensuring equipment is fit for purpose, up to date, and can provide enough throughput for its intended use. Checking software and network policies can also help. In cases where the traffic in a network has grown suddenly – for example, if a new data-heavy application is being used – new network policies can be set, or further network segmentation can be carried out. For example, a sales department that conducts a lot of video calls could be put on a different VLAN to a data inputting department, with the sales department getting higher bandwidth and better QoS policies for the video calls.

Bandwidth

When we talk about bandwidth, we are referring to the ideal or theoretical capacity of a device or network. It's important to consider because a device is never going to be able to handle more than its bandwidth, so the maximum bandwidth in a signal chain is the lowest bandwidth of any single device. If you have a router, switch, and computer all with a bandwidth of 1 Gbps, but a server card of 100 Mbps, then the data transmission speed is restricted to 100 Mbps. Therefore, when checking for bottlenecks, start with a device with the lowest bandwidth.

Throughput capacity

Throughput capacity is the *actual* amount of data that can successfully move through a network in a given amount of time. The figure measures how much data is actually being transmitted, not just the potential maximum (which is bandwidth). If your throughput capacity is too low, tasks such as streaming, downloading, or video calls will slow down or not work properly.

Network congestion has a negative impact on throughput for a number of reasons. Firstly, if too many devices are using the network at the same time, then the throughput for individual devices is greatly reduced. Network congestion can also cause packet loss, which will be explained later in the chapter. When packets are lost, protocols such as TCP detect the loss and request retransmission, consuming additional bandwidth and reducing overall throughput capacity. Similarly, **latency**, which you will read about next, can also reduce throughput by delaying packet transmission, thus reducing the overall amount of data traversing the system.

Latency

Latency refers to the delay in data transfer between two points on a network. It is measured in milliseconds (ms) and represents how long it takes for an action – such as clicking a link – to receive a response. In real-time applications such as video calls or online gaming, high latency can cause noticeable delays, such as hearing someone's voice a second late or experiencing gameplay lag.

Several factors contribute to latency. Physical distance is a major one – data traveling long distances, such as between continents, takes more time. Other causes include network congestion, outdated equipment, and wireless interference.

Low latency is essential for a smooth experience, particularly in real-time communication and gaming. Ideally, latency should remain below 50 ms, while anything over 200 ms can result in disruptive delays.

To minimize latency, you should use wired connections instead of wireless, such as Wi-Fi or **Bluetooth**. Outdated network equipment can also introduce latency, for example, if **CPUs** are too slow to handle high-speed data inspection or don't support protocols. You should also optimize your internet service for low-latency activities by preferring fiber optic connections.

Packet loss

Packet loss occurs when data packets traveling across a network fail to reach their destination, resulting in incomplete or delayed communication. They can create latency, cause disconnection from remote servers such as VPNs or virtual desktops, or cause corruption in downloaded files. They can also cause or contribute to latency and bandwidth issues, and cause low-quality voice and video calls, interrupted and slow downloads, and poor online gaming connections.

For example, several employees at a company report issues during video conferencing. They describe symptoms such as frozen video, choppy audio, and occasional disconnections, especially when multiple participants are on the call. These problems appear intermittently but are more frequent during peak business hours. These are common symptoms of packet loss.

To troubleshoot, the network administrator uses Wireshark to monitor traffic on the network. The capture shows a high rate of **TCP** retransmissions and duplicate **ACKs** for several types of traffic, not just video. These retransmissions indicate that packets are not being successfully delivered on the first attempt and are being resent. Additionally, some **ICMP** ping tests to external sites show variable response times and occasional dropped packets (e.g., 10–15% packet loss).

Other applications that rely on reliable delivery, such as file transfers, may slow down but recover, whereas video and voice suffer more visibly.

Many of the tools mentioned in the next chapter can help to narrow issues down to packet loss and pinpoint where it is happening. Knowing where the packet loss is – your network, your ISP, or the destination server – will help in troubleshooting. For example, if you pinpoint packet loss to your Wi-Fi, it might be down to a weak signal or a faulty wireless transmitter. Physical objects and electronic devices can also disrupt transmission. If the packet loss is on a specific device, then check for software bugs or misconfigurations that interfere with traffic flow.

Packet loss is particularly disruptive for real-time applications such as **VoIP** calls and online gaming, leading to choppy video, distorted audio, and lag. While occasional packet loss is normal, consistent or high packet loss signals a problem that needs attention.

To combat packet loss, you can upgrade outdated routers, switches, or network cables. Ensure correct network configurations and use a wired connection for better stability.

Jitter

Jitter is the variation in how long it takes data packets to travel across a network. Ideally, packets should arrive in a consistent, orderly manner. However, when some packets arrive faster, slower, or out of order, jitter occurs, disrupting real-time activities such as video calls, online gaming, and VoIP. It can be caused by network congestion and peak usage times increasing traffic inconsistency. Wireless devices with weak signals, obstacles, or competing devices that affect transmission can also cause jitter, as can outdated or faulty hardware. Poor-quality routers and network switches can also contribute to jitter.

Measuring Jitter

One way to diagnose jitter is to use the **mean opinion score** (**MOS**), which is a subjective metric used to assess the quality of voice or video communication in a network. It provides a numerical rating (1 to 5) based on user experience and thus should reflect latency, packet loss, jitter, and **codec** performance.

> **Note**
>
> A codec (short for coder-decoder) is a technology used to compress and decompress audio or video data. It allows efficient transmission, storage, and playback of media over networks or devices.

MOS score	Quality description
5 (Excellent)	Clear and distortion-free
4 (Good)	Minor issues, but acceptable quality
3 (Fair)	Noticeable problems, but intelligible
2 (Poor)	Significant issues, difficult communication
1 (Bad)	Unintelligible or unusable

A MOS score above 4.0 is considered good for video conferencing and VoIP calls, while a lower score indicates degraded quality.

Reducing jitter

Strategies for reducing jitter include prioritizing real-time traffic such as VoIP and video conferencing and using QoS settings, using wired connections for improved stability, and upgrading network hardware to reduce processing delays. For example, the Zoom conferencing tool recommends wired connections only. **Voice-over IP (VoIP)** bandwidth requirements for voice calls can vary, but allowing 100 kbps per call upstream and downstream should be sufficient in most cases. Creating dedicated VLANs for video conferencing isolates traffic and improves performance.

Monitoring tools such as **SolarWinds's VoIP and Network Quality Manager** can continuously track VoIP call quality and provide insights for troubleshooting network issues.

Wireless

Wireless networks often face performance issues that disrupt connectivity. Problems such as interference from overlapping channels or competing signals can lead to slow speeds and disconnections. Signal degradation from physical barriers or distance weakens connections, while insufficient coverage creates "dead zones." Additional issues, such as client disassociation (unexpected device disconnections) and roaming misconfiguration (preventing seamless transitions between access points), further impact network reliability. Proper planning, optimization, and regular monitoring are essential to address these challenges and maintain stable wireless performance. Next, we'll explore some of these aspects in detail.

Interference

Wireless interference occurs when external factors disrupt the performance of a wireless network, leading to reduced speed, connectivity issues, and inconsistent user experiences. This interference can arise from various sources, including overlapping Wi-Fi channels, environmental factors causing signal degradation or loss, and gaps in wireless coverage. Additionally, client disassociation issues, where devices disconnect unexpectedly, and improper configuration of roaming settings in multi-AP setups can further exacerbate these problems. Addressing these challenges requires careful network design, proper configuration, and regular monitoring to ensure reliable and efficient wireless performance.

Example 1

An office recently rearranged its workspace, including relocating the 2.4 GHz **wireless AP** to a new position closer to the employee break area. Soon after, the IT department began receiving tickets complaining about intermittent Wi-Fi dropouts and slow speeds – but only during lunchtime hours, typically between 12:00 P.M. and 1:00 P.M.

Users report that their laptops lose connection or become extremely slow during video calls or while accessing cloud applications. However, everything works fine the rest of the day.

To investigate, a network technician runs a wireless spectrum analyzer around the affected area during the reported time window. The scan shows high levels of **radio frequency** (**RF**) interference in the 2.4 GHz band, particularly around channel 6, where the wireless AP is operating. The interference is not constant throughout the day – it spikes sharply during lunchtime.

Upon further inspection, the technician observes multiple employees using microwave ovens to heat their lunches. The break room, now closer to the relocated wireless AP, has two commercial-grade microwaves running simultaneously during peak hours.

Channel overlap

Channel overlap refers to the interference caused when multiple wireless APs operate on overlapping or identical frequencies within range of one another. This can negatively affect network performance. There are two primary types of channel interference **co-channel interference** (**CCI**) and **adjacent channel interference** (**ACI**).

CCI is when multiple devices share the same Wi-Fi channel, leading to congestion. Each Wi-Fi channel is treated as a "collision domain," where devices take turns transmitting data. Devices use a system called **carrier-sense multiple access with collision avoidance** (**CSMA/CA**) to detect and wait for an opportunity to transmit. However, too many devices competing on the same channel increases delays. CCI can be measured by monitoring channel utilization using tools such as a Wi-Fi analyzer or directly from the access point's settings. As a design goal, a channel should ideally not exceed 50% utilization to maintain good performance.

ACI happens when APs operate on overlapping but different channels, such as channels 1 and 3 in the 2.4 GHz band. **Overlapping channels** increase noise and make it harder for devices to communicate efficiently, slowing down the transmission process. To prevent ACI, aim for a spacing of at least 25 MHz between channels in the 2.4 GHz band.

To optimize performance in environments with multiple access points, you can use the following strategies:

- **Use non-overlapping channels**: In the 2.4 GHz band, only three channels (1, 6, and 11) are completely non-overlapping. For example, assign channel 1 to AP1, channel 6 to AP2, and channel 11 to AP3.

- **Leverage the 5 GHz band**: The 5 GHz band provides more non-overlapping channels than 2.4 GHz, making it a better choice for larger or denser networks.

- **Control power levels**: Adjusting the transmit power of APs can prevent them from overlapping too much with nearby APs. Using maximum power may cause interference in adjacent areas and result in situations where a device can "hear" the AP but lacks sufficient power to respond effectively.

By carefully planning channels and power levels, you can minimize interference and ensure smooth network performance, even in complex environments.

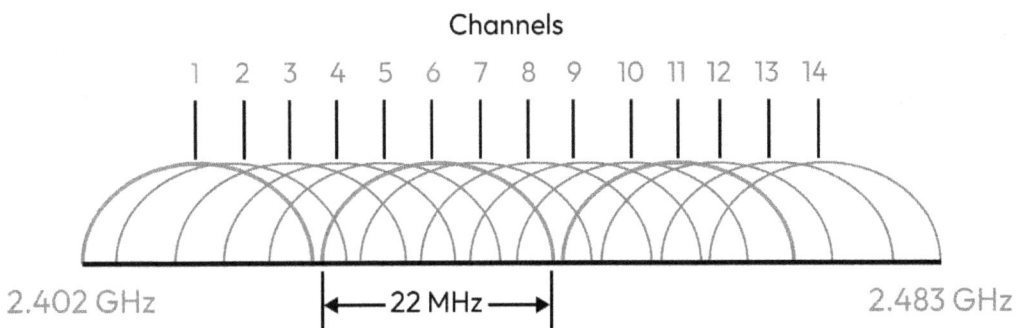

Figure 24.1: Overlapping channels

Figure 24.1 shows how different Wi-Fi channels in the 2.4 GHz range can interfere with each other. Think of each channel like a radio station – if two stations are too close in frequency, their signals overlap and cause static. Wi-Fi works the same way. Even though there are 11 available channels in this band, each one is about 22 MHz wide, meaning it takes up space on either side of its center frequency.

But the channels themselves are only 5 MHz apart, so most of them overlap with their neighbors. This overlap causes interference, making Wi-Fi slower and less reliable. That's why network professionals usually only use channels 1, 6, and 11 – they're the only ones spaced far enough apart that their 22 MHz-wide signals don't interfere with each other. Using just those three helps keep the network fast and stable.

Example 2

After a company upgraded its wireless network with new APs, users began reporting a strange issue: when sitting still at their desks, their Wi-Fi connection would randomly drop and reconnect every 20 to 30 seconds. This happened throughout the office and affected both laptops and mobile devices.

To troubleshoot, the network administrator reviewed the access point logs and noticed that the APs were frequently switching channels. This behavior indicated that the APs were using automatic channel selection, a feature that scans for interference and changes channels to avoid it. However, each time an AP changed channels, users connected to that AP experienced a brief disconnection.

The root cause turned out to be channel interference from nearby devices and possibly neighboring Wi-Fi networks. Since the APs detected this interference, they kept trying to avoid it by switching to new channels – but in doing so, they caused frequent disruptions to user connections.

Signal degradation or loss

When you use a wireless network (such as Wi-Fi or mobile data), your device connects to a router or cell tower using radio waves. These waves carry information, such as the websites you visit, the videos you stream, or the emails you send. However, these radio waves don't always travel perfectly from the source (such as a router) to your device. Sometimes, the signal becomes weak, distorted, or gets lost entirely. This is called signal degradation or loss. Think of it like having a conversation with someone across a big, noisy room. If the room is quiet and you're close to each other, you can hear them clearly. But if there is loud music, people talking, or you're far apart, it becomes harder to hear. Wireless signals work the same way – they can be affected by obstacles, interference, and distance. The following are the most common causes of signal degradation or loss.

Distance from the source

The farther you are from the AP, the weaker the signal gets. Wireless signals lose strength over distance because the energy in the radio waves spreads out. The actual amount of degradation is an inverse square of the distance, meaning the signal's power decreases as a square of the distance.

Obstacles in the way

Walls, furniture, and other physical objects can block or weaken wireless signals. For example, if your AP is in one room and you're trying to use Wi-Fi in another room, the signal has to pass through walls, which can reduce its strength. Materials such as concrete, brick, and metal are particularly bad for wireless signals. Wireless signals share space with many other devices that use radio waves, such as microwaves, cordless phones, and baby monitors, causing **radio frequency interference (RFI)**. For example, microwaves emit RFI on the 2.4 GHz band, which could overlap with wireless devices on a 2.4 GHz channel, and this could cause signal interference or termination.

Where possible, use different channels from other equipment; in this case, a 5 GHz channel would avoid microwave interference.

Signal reflection and refraction

Wireless signals can bounce off surfaces such as mirrors, glass, or water, which may distort or weaken them. Sometimes, signals also bend (**refract**) as they pass through materials, causing a weaker signal to reach your device. Refraction is where glass or water can cause radio waves to bend and take a different path to the receiver. This can also cause the data rate to drop. Absorption happens when a wireless signal (radio wave) loses energy as it travels through materials such as walls, windows, or even people. This energy isn't destroyed; instead, it's converted into heat inside the material.

Weather conditions

Outdoors, things such as rain, fog, and snow can affect wireless signals, especially for long-distance communication such as satellite or cellular networks. These weather conditions can absorb or scatter the radio waves, causing signal loss.

Network congestion

When too many devices are connected to the same network, the available bandwidth gets split among them. This is called **network congestion**. This can make your connection slower or less stable, even if your signal strength is good.

To troubleshoot weak connections, you can try some of the following tactics:

- Move closer to the router or signal source
- Place your router in a central, open location to minimize obstacles
- Reduce interference by keeping your router away from other electronics
- Use signal boosters or range extenders to amplify weak signals

- Switch to a less crowded channel on your router if interference is an issue
- Upgrade your equipment, such as your router or antennas, for better performance

Insufficient wireless coverage

Insufficient wireless coverage happens when certain areas in a building have little or no Wi-Fi signal, making it difficult or impossible for devices to connect to the network. This can occur due to physical obstacles, such as walls or furniture, or because the APs are too far away to provide a strong signal. Tools such as heat maps can be used to identify these weak spots. Heat maps visually represent signal strength across the building, making it easier to pinpoint problem areas. If the signal cannot be improved by reducing interference, the solution is often to install another device, such as an additional AP. If running cables for the new AP isn't possible, you can use a wireless bridge or a range extender to fill the coverage gap.

> **Note**
>
> Heat maps are covered in further detail in *Chapter 13, Explain the Purpose of Organizational Processes and Procedures.*

Client disassociation issues

When a client (device, user, or system) is suddenly disconnected from the network, this is known as **client disassociation**. As mentioned, this could be due to a weak signal caused by congestion, interference, or the client being in an area not covered by the Wi-Fi signal. It can also be caused by roaming issues – for example, if the client has moved between APs or security and authentication key mismatches.

Clients and access points use management frames to establish, maintain, or end connections, and disassociation and deauthentication frames signal a connection's termination. Frequent disconnections, also known as **flapping**, or unexpected deauthentication issues, can often be traced by reviewing the AP or controller logs to identify the root cause.

Example 3

A user working on their laptop in an office near the edge of the Wi-Fi coverage suddenly loses connection because the signal is weak and interference from nearby Bluetooth devices disrupts communication; the AP sends a disassociation frame, causing the laptop to disconnect unexpectedly. This issue is worsened by the office Wi-Fi being overloaded with many devices, and the laptop's outdated wireless driver struggles to maintain a stable connection, resulting in frequent disassociations that interrupt the user's work.

Roaming misconfiguration

As mentioned in the previous section, wireless roaming allows devices to switch between APs as you move, ensuring a stable connection. However, misconfigurations in the setup can cause problems such as dropped connections, slow performance, or devices sticking to a weak AP instead of switching to a stronger one. Common misconfiguration issues include using different network names or SSIDs, meaning devices can't roam seamlessly. APs on the same or overlapping channels can also cause interference and reduce performance.

If these issues happen, you should check that advanced features such as **802.11r**, also known as **fast roaming**, or 802.11k/v have been enabled. Without them, transitions between APs can be slow.

To resolve the issues caused by roaming misconfiguration, you can use the same SSID and password for all APs, assign non-overlapping channels for better performance, and enable roaming features for smooth and efficient switching.

Summary

This chapter covered how to troubleshoot common performance issues in both wired and wireless networks. Key topics included congestion, bottlenecking, and bandwidth limitations, along with wireless-specific challenges such as interference, insufficient coverage, and roaming misconfigurations. You also explored the impacts of latency, packet loss, jitter, and signal degradation on overall network performance. By applying these troubleshooting strategies, you can identify and address performance bottlenecks, ensuring a more efficient and reliable network experience.

The knowledge gained in this chapter will prepare you to answer questions relating to Exam objective 5.4 in your *CompTIA Network+ (N10-009)* exam.

Exam objective 5.4

Given a scenario, troubleshoot common performance issues

Congestion/contention: High network traffic causing delays or reduced performance.

Bottlenecking: Resource limits slowing data flow at a specific point.

Bandwidth: The maximum data transfer rate of a network connection.

- **Throughput capacity**: Actual data successfully transferred over a network.

Latency: Delay in data transmission across the network.

Packet loss: Dropped data packets reducing connection reliability.

Jitter: Variations in data delivery time causing disruptions.

Wireless:

- **Interference**: External signals disrupting wireless communication.

    - **Channel overlap**: Multiple devices using the same frequency, causing interference.

- **Signal degradation or loss**: Weakening of a wireless signal over distance or obstacles.

- **Insufficient wireless coverage**: Inadequate signal strength in specific areas.

- **Client disassociation issues**: Devices disconnecting unexpectedly from the network.

- **Roaming misconfiguration**: Poor transitions between access points during movement.

Chapter review questions

Now that you've completed the chapter, you can check your knowledge using the practice questions provided in the online platform at `https://packt.link/N10-009ch24`. You can also use the QR code below. Accessing these questions requires you to unlock the accompanying online content first. Head over to Chapter 26 for detailed instructions.

25

Given a Scenario, Use the Appropriate Tool or Protocol to Solve Networking Issues

Effective troubleshooting is the key to maintaining a stable and high-performing network. This final domain, *5.0 Network Troubleshooting*, has so far covered the troubleshooting methodology, troubleshooting physical issues, services, and performance. This last chapter will focus on the various tools and protocols that are available for diagnosing and resolving issues. Understanding how to use these tools will enable you, as a network professional, to efficiently troubleshoot and maintain stable network environments.

This chapter introduces key software, such as protocol analyzers and command-line functions, as well as hardware tools that assist in identifying and solving networking problems. Protocol analyzers and command-line utilities such as ping, traceroute, and nslookup help diagnose connectivity and performance issues. Similarly, hardware tools such as cable testers and Wi-Fi analyzers are critical for pinpointing physical layer problems.

This chapter covers the fifth and final objective in *Domain 5, 5.5, Given a scenario, use the appropriate tool or protocol to solve networking issues.*

> **Note**
>
> A full breakdown of objective 5.5 will be given at the end of the chapter.

Software tools

As we have seen in the previous chapters of *Domain 5, Networking Troubleshooting*, diagnosing and fixing network issues is more complex than simply looking at components in isolation. A router might be working perfectly, while data is still not being delivered due to a misconfiguration. For this reason, a lot of troubleshooting for complex systems will begin by analyzing network traffic rather than individual components. Analyzing data packets directly enables network engineers to get granular information on how traffic is flowing, and there are many command-line tools that can be installed to do different checks on the network. You can also use protocol analyzers, which are diagnostic software tools that allow administrators to capture and analyze packet data from network interfaces and then carry out filtering and analysis. Both **command-line tools** and **protocol analyzers** will be covered in this section.

Protocol analyzer

Imagine, for instance, the internal users in your building are experiencing slow access to a critical web application hosted within the corporate network. Standard troubleshooting steps, such as checking server load and network bandwidth, have not helped, so you need to look further. You want to be able to capture data packets and filter them by HTTP/HTTPS to ensure you are looking at web traffic. This is where the protocol analyzer comes in.

By capturing packets, cybersecurity administrators can analyze network activity on the organization's network. This process, often called **packet sniffing**, is typically done with protocol analyzers such as **Wireshark** or the Linux-based **tcpdump**. **Packet captures** (**PCAPs**) are often saved for later analysis, allowing administrators to trace specific network events.

For example, packet capturing can help troubleshoot issues such as a user not receiving an IP address from the DHCP server, which is responsible for automating IP address allocation. In a successful DHCP exchange, four packets are exchanged. If the cybersecurity administrator observes only the first packet without a response, it indicates a problem with IP address renewal or allocation. This issue could mean the DHCP server has run out of IP addresses to allocate. In this case, the system might generate an **automatic private IP addressing** (**APIPA**) address in the range of 169.254.0.1 to 169.254.255.254, with a default subnet mask of 255.255.0.0, but there is no default gateway address; therefore, it is limited to the local network. It cannot communicate with other devices unless they also have an APIPA address.

Note

For more details on Wireshark and `tcpdump`, you can check their websites at `https://www.wireshark.org/` and `https://www.tcpdump.org/`, respectively.

Figure 25.1 shows an example Wireshark trace. A manager might ask the network administrator to monitor internet usage while investigating efficiency. The Wireshark session has captured visits to the official NFL website. On analyzing the trace, we can see that the request is using the HTTP GET verb. This is the request for a page on `www.nfl.com`, specifically `https://www.nfl.com/news/josh-dobbs-mike-glennon-drawing-trade-interest-0ap3000000952209`.

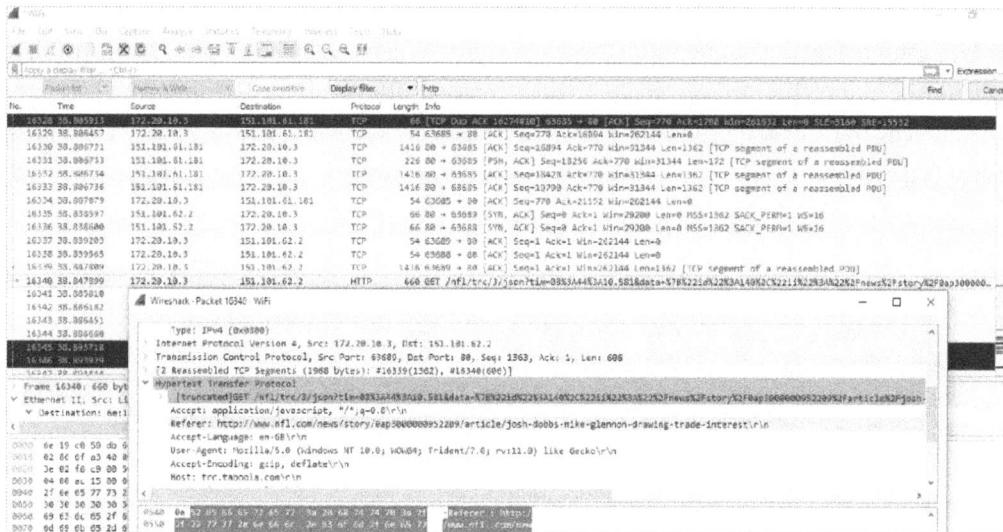

Figure 25.1: Wireshark trace

Protocol analyzers offer deep granular information and also allow users to filter through large numbers of packets. However, sometimes you might need to do quicker checks on specific aspects of the network, and to do that, you can use command-line tools.

Command-line tools

Before using more complex and time-consuming protocol analyzers, it's a good idea to do simpler checks to rule out more basic issues or pinpoint the area that you should be looking at. Command-line tools help you gather information about network connectivity, configuration, and performance, often providing quick insights into potential issues. They can also be used to manage and automate parts of your network. This section will describe some of the most useful command-line tools for the diagnosis of network issues, starting with the simple ping.

Packet Internet Groper (ping)

One of the first things you might wish to check in a network is whether a device is online. Using ping, you can check the reachability of a device by sending **Internet Control Message Protocol (ICMP)** echo requests and measuring response times. When a ping command is successful, it will provide four replies, as in *Figure 25.2*, which is based on a Windows environment. In a Linux environment, by default, the ping command sends ICMP packets continuously until you manually stop it (e.g., with *Ctrl + C*). Most of the networking in the *Network+* exam is based on Windows.

```
C:\Windows\System32>ping www.nfl.com

Pinging global.nfl.map.fastly.net [151.101.1.153] with 32 bytes of data
Reply from 151.101.1.153: bytes=32 time=84ms TTL=61
Reply from 151.101.1.153: bytes=32 time=85ms TTL=61
Reply from 151.101.1.153: bytes=32 time=92ms TTL=61
Reply from 151.101.1.153: bytes=32 time=87ms TTL=61

Ping statistics for 151.101.1.153:
    Packets: Sent = 4, Received = 4, Lost = 0 (0% loss),
Approximate round trip times in milli-seconds:
    Minimum = 84ms, Maximum = 92ms, Average = 87ms
```

Figure 25.2: A successful ping packet

Figure 25.2 shows a CLI window system being used to *ping* the NFL website using the command followed by the web address, as in this example:

```
ping www.nfl.com
```

The CLI then confirms that four replies have been received from the site's IP address, 151.101.1.153. The statistics confirm that 4 packets were sent, and 4 received with an average round trip of 87 ms. Similarly, if you wanted to check whether a router was online, you could use the ping command to check the IP address of the router; any missing replies or longer than expected round-trips would indicate the need to check for further issues.

The loopback address (127.0.0.1) is used to test a host's local **TCP/IP** stack, ensuring that the networking components of the operating system are functioning properly. By using the ping command with 127.0.0.1, you can verify that the TCP/IP stack is working correctly without sending data over the network.

traceroute/tracert

If you think that you are having connectivity problems between two hosts, you can use traceroute on Linux or macOS or tracert on a Windows device. The tool measures the time it takes for data to travel between each intermediary router (hop) along the way. The result is a list showing each hop between you and the destination. For each hop, it shows the time it takes in milliseconds. If there's a delay or a problem, you can see exactly which hop is causing it. This is demonstrated in *Figure 25.3*:

```
C:\Windows\System32>tracert www.bbc.co.uk

Tracing route to gtm-live.pri.bbc.co.uk [212.58.236.129]
over a maximum of 30 hops:

  1     *        *        *       Request timed out.
  2   106 ms    94 ms    94 ms   5-101-139-193.as42831.net [5.101.139.193]
  3   125 ms    98 ms    94 ms   bbc-linx.pr01.thdow.bbc.co.uk [195.66.224.103]
  4    93 ms    94 ms   100 ms   132.185.249.84
  5    93 ms    90 ms    94 ms   212.58.236.129

Trace complete.
```

Figure 25.3: tracert to www.bbc.co.uk

Looking at the output in *Figure 25.3*, we can see the following:

- **Hop 1**: Request timed out. The first hop shows Request timed out. This is common and usually means the router closest to you (often your local router or ISP gateway) is configured not to respond to ICMP tracert probes. This does not necessarily indicate a problem; the packets are likely still being forwarded normally.

- **Hops 2 to 5**: Successful responses. The subsequent hops return response times in milliseconds, showing round-trip times for each probe (three times per hop). These hops identify the routers along the path, including domain names and IP addresses when available, such as 5-101-139-193.as42831.net and bbc-linx.pr01.thdow.bbc.co.uk.

- **Final hop (hop 5)**: Destination reached. The fifth hop shows the IP address of the destination website, confirming that the trace was successful.

nslookup

Name server lookup (nslookup) is a simple command-line tool used to find the IP address associated with a domain name or to find the domain name associated with an IP address. It's like looking up someone's phone number in a directory or finding out who a phone number belongs to. You can see this in the following example:

```
nslookup
set type=mx
```

In this example, nslookup starts the query tool, and set type=mx sets the query type to look specifically for **mail exchanger (MX)** records, which are used to find the mail servers responsible for a domain.

The output would look something like the following:

```
microsoft.com MX preference = 10, mail exchanger = mail1.microsoft.com
microsoft.com MX preference = 10, mail exchanger = mail2.microsoft.com
microsoft.com MX preference = 10, mail exchanger = mail3.microsoft.com
microsoft.com MX preference = 10, mail exchanger = mail4.microsoft.com
microsoft.com MX preference = 10, mail exchanger = mail5.microsoft.com
mail1.microsoft.com internet address = 131.107.3.125
```

This output shows that microsoft.com has five mail servers (mail1 through mail5.microsoft.com), all with the same priority of 10, which provides redundancy and load balancing for handling incoming email. The IP address 131.107.3.125 is listed for mail1.microsoft.com, which could be used directly by email systems if needed.

nslookup is also useful for checking IP addresses in your network. For example, to check the IP address of a device called PC1, you would simply run nslookup PC1.

tcpdump

tcpdump is used to capture and analyze network traffic. It saves the capture as a .pcap file, which contains similar details to the output of Wireshark. It is useful for troubleshooting network issues, checking security, and understanding how data travels between devices. When network problems arise, such as slow performance or unexpected connections, tcpdump can help pinpoint the issue by showing details of each data packet sent or received, and can reveal connectivity problems, unauthorized access, and help to debug applications that rely on network communication.

For example, if you want to check all traffic on your network to a specific IP address, `192.168.1.10`, you would open the command line and run the following:

```
tcpdump host 192.168.1.10
```

This command starts capturing all packets to and from that IP address, showing information such as the source, destination, and type of each packet. This information can then help you figure out whether the traffic is normal or whether there's unusual activity that needs attention.

dig

Domain information groper (dig) is a powerful command-line tool, primarily used on Linux or Unix systems to query name servers directly and retrieve DNS records. It is commonly used to troubleshoot DNS issues, verify DNS settings, and ensure that domains are properly configured.

When you run a `dig` command, it sends a DNS query to a DNS server, requesting specific information about a domain name. The server responds with DNS records such as the IP address (an A record), mail server details (an MX record), or other relevant data.

A basic `dig` command to find the IP address used by Google's website would be as follows:

```
dig google.com
```

When you run this command, you'll see an output similar to the following:

```
; <<>> DiG 9.10.6 <<>> google.com
;; global options: +cmd
;; Got answer:
;; ->>HEADER<<- opcode: QUERY, status: NOERROR, id: 12345
;; flags: qr rd ra; QUERY: 1, ANSWER: 1, AUTHORITY: 0, ADDITIONAL: 1

;; QUESTION SECTION:
;google.com.                    IN      A

;; ANSWER SECTION:
google.com.             300     IN      A       142.250.190.78

;; Query time: 24 msec
;; SERVER: 8.8.8.8#53(8.8.8.8)
;; WHEN: Mon Nov 06 14:23:47 UTC 2023
;; MSG SIZE  rcvd: 55
```

Underneath `ANSWER SECTION:` is the IP address of google.com, in this case, 142.250.190.78.

When you run the `dig` command, it shows the information right on the screen. But sometimes, you might want to keep that information in a file so you can look at it later or share it with someone.

To do that, you just add the > symbol after the command, followed by the name of the file where you want to save the results. This is shown in the following example:

```
dig google.com > mydnsinfo.txt
```

This code runs the `dig google.com` command, but instead of showing the result on the screen, it saves everything into a file called mydnsinfo.txt. You can then open this file with any text editor to see the results. If you want to add more results to the same file (without deleting what's already there), use two > symbols (i.e., >>), as follows:

```
dig google.com >> mydnsinfo.txt
```

This adds the new output to the end of the file.

netstat

Network statistics (netstat) is a command-line tool used to display network connections, routing tables, interface statistics, and other network-related information. It's helpful for troubleshooting network problems and monitoring network activity. It can show which computers you're connected to, what ports are being used, and whether data is being sent or received.

There are some common `netstat` options, also called **switches**, which are detailed as follows:

- `netstat -a`: Shows all active connections and listening ports.
- `netstat -n`: Displays addresses and port numbers in numerical form, instead of trying to resolve hostnames.
- `netstat -r`: Displays the routing table, showing how data travels through the network.
- `netstat -e`: Shows detailed network interface statistics, such as the number of packets sent and received.
- `netstat -o`: Shows active connections and the **process ID (PID)** that owns each connection. Useful for identifying which application is using a particular connection.
- `netstat -s`: Displays statistics for each protocol, such as **TCP** or **UDP**.

For example, if you want to see all the active connections on your computer, you can use the following:

```
netstat -a
```

The output will look something like this:

```
Proto  Local Address        Foreign Address       State
TCP    192.168.1.5:50000    93.184.216.34:80      ESTABLISHED
TCP    192.168.1.5:50001    172.217.11.174:443    CLOSE_WAIT
```

In the preceding output, Proto is the protocol used, which, in this case, is TCP. Local Address is your computer's IP and port number, Foreign Address is the IP and port of the remote computer you're connected to, and State is the status of the connection. State could be ESTABLISHED, which means an active connection, or CLOSE_WAIT, which means your computer has received a request to close the connection from the remote host and is waiting to close its side.

netstat is useful for checking whether your computer is connected to the internet or other devices, finding services that are running, discovering which ports are open, and listening for connections. It is useful in troubleshooting because you can check whether connections are being established correctly.

ip/ifconfig/ipconfig

These are all commands used on various systems to configure network devices. The ip command is used on Linux, ifconfig is an older command for Linux and Unix systems such as macOS, and ipconfig is specific to Windows operating systems.

The ip command is used on Linux to configure network interfaces and routes, and to display network settings. It's more modern and commonly used than ifconfig.

There are some common ip switches, as follows:

- ip addr show: Displays all network interfaces and their IP addresses
- ip link show: Shows details about the network interfaces (such as Ethernet and Wi-Fi)
- ip route show: Displays the routing table, showing how data is directed through the network
- ip addr add [IP address] dev [interface]: Assigns a new IP address to a network interface
- ip link set [interface] up / ip link set [interface] down: Enables (up) or disables (down) a network interface

ifconfig

ifconfig is a command-line tool traditionally used on Unix and Linux systems to display and configure network interfaces. It shows details such as IP address, subnet mask, **media access control (MAC)** address, and interface status.

However, on many modern Linux distributions, ifconfig has been largely replaced by the more powerful and flexible ip command from the iproute2 suite. An example of ifconfig is as follows:

```
ifconfig eth0
```

This command displays the network configuration for the interface named eth0, including its IP address, subnet mask, broadcast address, and other details such as packet statistics.

ipconfig is used on Windows to display and manage network interface settings. It's similar to ifconfig and ip but specifically for Windows.

The common ipconfig command switches are shown here:

- ipconfig: Shows the basic network configuration, including IP addresses and default gateways
- ipconfig /all: Displays detailed network configuration information for all interfaces, including DNS servers, MAC addresses, and so on
- ipconfig /release: Releases the current IP address obtained from a DHCP server, making it available for other devices
- ipconfig /renew: Requests a new IP address from the DHCP server
- ipconfig /displaydns: Shows the contents of the DNS resolver cache, listing recently resolved domain names and their corresponding IP addresses
- ipconfig /flushdns: Clears the DNS resolver cache, which can help solve DNS-related issues

For example, if you wanted to check the connections of a LAN adapter, you would use ipconfig /all and then check the output for the section that says WLAN adapter, as shown in *Figure 25.4*.

```
Wireless LAN adapter WiFi:

    Connection-specific DNS Suffix  . :
    Description . . . . . . . . . . . : Realtek RTL8852BE WiFi 6 802.11ax PCIe Adapter
    Physical Address. . . . . . . . . : 20-0B-74-16-10-1E
    DHCP Enabled. . . . . . . . . . . : Yes
    Autoconfiguration Enabled . . . . : Yes
    Link-local IPv6 Address . . . . . : fe80::4ee5:d78f:ddbf:bcfc%16(Preferred)
    IPv4 Address. . . . . . . . . . . : 10.1.3.34(Preferred)
    Subnet Mask . . . . . . . . . . . : 255.255.254.0
    Lease Obtained. . . . . . . . . . : 15 October 2024 06:46:28
    Lease Expires . . . . . . . . . . : 22 October 2024 11:49:32
    Default Gateway . . . . . . . . . : 10.1.3.254
    DHCP Server . . . . . . . . . . . : 10.1.3.254
    DHCPv6 IAID . . . . . . . . . . . : 169872244
    DHCPv6 Client DUID. . . . . . . . : 00-01-00-01-2C-FC-5C-32-0C-37-96-40-F9-3D
    DNS Servers . . . . . . . . . . . : 8.8.8.8
                                        8.8.4.4
    NetBIOS over Tcpip. . . . . . . . : Enabled
```

Figure 25.4: The partial output of ipconfig /all

`ipconfig /release` and `ipconfig /renew` work together for refreshing DHCP settings and resolving IP conflicts.

ARP

Address Resolution Protocol (**ARP**) is a communication protocol used to map an IP address to a MAC address. ARP operates at the **data link layer** of the OSI model (Layer 2) and is primarily used in LANs to enable communication between devices.

For example, you want to print a document from your laptop using the Wi-Fi printer. For your laptop to send the print job to the printer, it needs the printer's MAC address but only has its IP address, which is 192.168.1.20. The computer sends a request basically asking "who has this IP address?" to all devices in the network. The printer will see the request and send a response that includes its own MAC address, BB:BB:BB:BB. Your laptop will store this information for future use in an ARP table similar to the following:

IP address	MAC address
192.168.1.20	BB:BB:BB:BB:BB
192.168.1.18	CC:CC:CC:CC:CC

When a device needs to communicate with another device on the same local network, it needs the recipient's MAC address. Since it only has the IP address, it uses ARP to find the MAC address associated with that IP.

ARP is crucial for communication on local networks because it allows devices to find each other using IP addresses and send data to the correct hardware addresses.

The arp command is used to view and manage the ARP cache on your computer. Here are some common switches:

- `arp -a` displays the current ARP cache, showing all the IP addresses and their corresponding MAC addresses that the computer knows about.
- `arp -d [IP address]` deletes a specific entry from the ARP cache, forcing the computer to do a new ARP request for that IP address next time it needs it. This is useful if an IP address has been changed or a piece of equipment has been replaced.
- `arp -s [IP address] [MAC address]` manually adds a static entry to the ARP cache, associating a specific IP address with a specific MAC address. This is less common but can be used for troubleshooting, testing, or the prevention of ARP poisoning.

For example, to see the current ARP cache on your computer, run the following:

```
arp -a
```

You would get an output similar to the following:

```
Internet Address      Physical Address    Type
192.168.1.1           00-14-22-01-23-45   dynamic
192.168.1.50          00-16-34-56-78-90   dynamic
```

In this output, `Internet Address` is the IP address of other devices on the network. `Physical Address` is the corresponding MAC address of those devices, and `Type` indicates whether the entry was learned dynamically. With an ARP request, it is `static`, as it is set with the `arp -s` command. The dynamic entry was automatically learned through an ARP request when your computer needed to find the MAC address for an IP address. If the entry was `static`, it means the entry is manually added using the `arp -s` command and does not expire or get updated automatically.

Here is an example of Wireshark capturing ARP traffic:

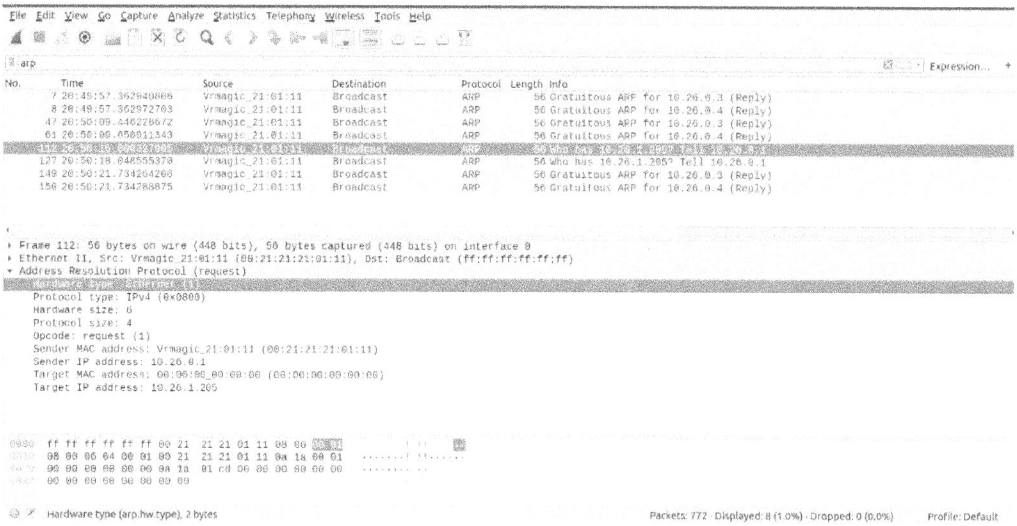

Figure 25.5: Wireshark capturing ARP traffic

Note

Figure 25.5 is presented courtesy of the **Syddansk Universitet** website: `https://imada.sdu.dk/u/jamik/dm557-19/wireshark/wireshark-arp.html`.

This Wireshark trace shows the following:

- A device on 10.26.0.1 broadcasting an ARP request to find the MAC address for 10.26.1.205
- Several gratuitous ARP replies (devices announcing their own IP and MAC address to the network)

Network mapper (nmap)

nmap is used to scan networks and computers to find out important information about devices connected to a network. It outputs information on the devices connected to the network, the services running on those devices, which ports are open or closed, and what operating systems the devices are using.

The nmap command can map out the whole network and then can be used to map out the details of any host on the network, so it is useful for network inventory and security auditing troubleshooting. For example, you can find out all devices on a network, or check for open ports that hackers might exploit.

A basic command would look like the following:

```
nmap 192.168.1.0/24
```

This command tells nmap to scan all devices on the 192.168.1.0/24 network, which is a typical local network range, to see what's connected.

Link Layer Discovery Protocol (LLDP)

LLDP is a tool used mainly in Windows to help devices on a network find and understand each other. It allows Windows computers and other **Link Layer Topology Discovery** (**LLTD**)-enabled devices to map out the network and show how everything is connected. It helps in identifying the connected switch and the specific port to which a device is connected. LLTD creates a visual map of your network, showing things such as computers, printers, and routers. This makes it easier to see how devices are connected and understand the network structure. If you're having trouble connecting a device, LLTD can help by showing where the issue might be, such as a broken connection or a device that's not responding. For example, when you add a new device (such as a printer or another computer), LLTD can automatically detect it and show it on the map. This makes sure the device is connected and working properly.

Cisco Discovery Protocol (CDP)

CDP is a Layer 2 network protocol used by Cisco devices to communicate and gather information about directly connected Cisco equipment. It is useful for network administrators who need to quickly get information about devices on the same network segment, even if they haven't configured them manually.

CDP enables device discovery by allowing devices to share information about their interfaces, IP addresses, software versions, and device types. It can help map out network topology by providing data on directly connected devices and identifying misconfigured or incorrect connections in the network.

CDP uses the following basic commands:

- `show cdp neighbors` displays information about directly connected Cisco devices, such as the device ID, local interface, hold time, and port ID
- `show cdp neighbors detail` provides detailed information, including the IP address, model number, and software version of the connected devices
- `cdp enable` enables CDP on a specific interface

For example, if you run the `show cdp neighbors` command, then you can verify what devices are directly connected to a Cisco switch or router. This is helpful if you need to troubleshoot connectivity or understand device roles without logging in to each device individually.

CDP only works within a Cisco environment, so it won't provide information about non-Cisco devices.

```
RouterA#show cdp neighbors detail
-----------
Device ID: RouterB.lab.local
Entry address(es):
IP address: 10.10.10.2
Platform: Cisco 2691,  Capabilities: Router Switch IGMP
Interface: Serial0/0,  Port ID (outgoing port): Serial0/0
Holdtime : 126 sec
Version :
Cisco IOS Software, 2600 Software (C2691-ADVENTERPRISEK9-M),
Version 12.4(25d), RELEASE SOFTWARE (fc1)
Technical Support: http://www.cisco.com/techsupport
Copyright (c) 1986-2010 by Cisco Systems, Inc.
Compiled Wed 18-Aug-10 05:35 by prod_rel_team
advertisement version: 2
VTP Management Domain: "
```

Figure 25.6: CDP neighbors detail output

When you run show cdp neighbors detail, the output shows all of the details of one particular device—this time, RouterB, as seen by RouterA. As well as the platform and capabilities, which were shown by the summary version, it also shows the network layer address(es) (this time, an IP address, 10.10.10.2) and a glimpse of the show version command of the neighbor device. It shows just a few lines, but it is enough to tell you about the version of the operating system, the feature set, and copyright information.

Speed testers

Speed testers are tools or commands used to measure the speed and quality of network connections, such as download and upload speeds, latency, and packet loss. Speed testing is essential to diagnose issues such as slow connections or bandwidth limitations.

iPerf3 and **iPerf2** are both tools used for testing network speeds. They help measure things such as how fast data moves across a network and how stable the connection is. iPerf3 (released in 2014) is the newer version and is usually what people mean when they mention *iPerf*. iPerf3 works well for testing general network performance, such as the speed between two devices on a wired or wireless network. iPerf2 is the older version but is still widely used, especially for testing Wi-Fi speeds. Some people prefer it for Wi-Fi because it can be more accurate in measuring how fast data moves over wireless connections.

Both iPerf2 and iPerf3 can run similar tests, and either one can give you a good sense of network speed and quality. iPerf requires both a client and server setup to measure connection speeds between two endpoints.

Some important commands are as follows:

- iperf -s starts the server mode on one endpoint
- iperf -c [IP address] runs the client to connect to a server, providing a report on throughput and latency

For example, you might be testing the connection between two devices to check actual speeds over your internal network. For basic latency testing, you would use ping to see how fast data is reaching a specific host, which is especially useful for diagnosing connectivity issues in real time.

The ping command can help us test latency by sending packets to a specified IP and measuring the time it takes for them to return. The ping -c 4 [hostname] command will send four packets and provide an average response time, indicating latency.

The traceroute command (or tracert on Windows) will map the path data takes across the network, identifying potential delays along the route. The traceroute [hostname] command shows each hop along the route and the time it takes to reach them, useful for identifying where bottlenecks occur.

Hardware tools

In IT networking, certain tools help with setting up, checking, and fixing network cables and connections. In the following sections, we describe some of the common tools.

Toner and probe tool

A **toner and probe tool**, also known as a **tone generator and probe** or **fox and hound**, is used to trace and identify individual cables within a bundle or to locate the termination points of cables in wiring closets, patch panels, or wall plates. The **toner** (or **fox**) sends an electrical signal through the cable, and the **probe** (or **hound**) detects the signal—usually as an audible tone or visual indicator—allowing technicians to quickly and accurately identify cables.

This tool is especially useful in complex or crowded environments such as server rooms or **intermediate distribution frames** (**IDFs**), where tracing cables by sight alone is difficult.

For example, a client has moved into a new office and notices that some wall jacks are not working or are not properly labeled. The best tool to identify the proper wiring in the IDF would be a toner and probe. It helps pinpoint which wall jack corresponds to which cable run, making it easier to organize, label, and troubleshoot the network infrastructure.

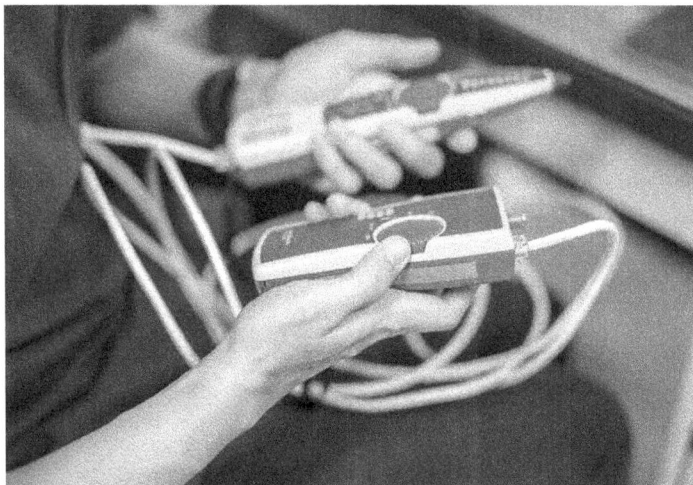

Figure 25.7: A toner and probe

A **cable tester** is used to check whether a network cable is functioning properly. It can detect common physical issues such as breaks, shorts, or improper terminations that can disrupt data transmission. This tool helps ensure that the cable is correctly wired and won't cause connectivity problems. It is especially useful in troubleshooting issues that may prevent devices, such as access points, from connecting to the internet.

Figure 25.8: Network cable tester

A network **test access point (TAP)** is a hardware device used to monitor network traffic. It creates a passive copy of all data passing through a specific point in the network. TAPs ensure uninterrupted monitoring without affecting the network's performance or introducing latency. They're often used in high-security environments.

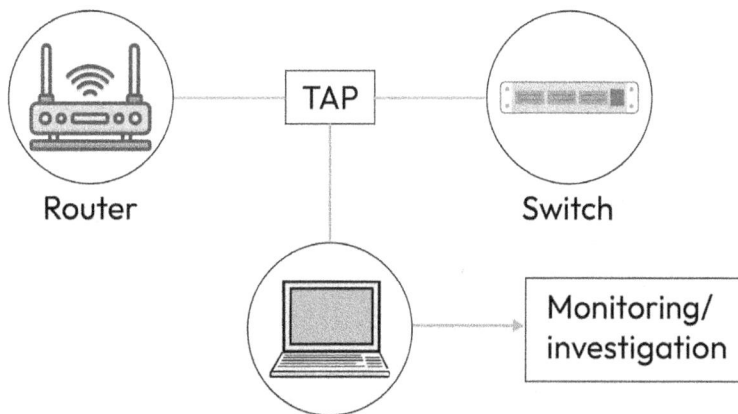

Figure 25.9: Network TAP

Think of it like a window into the network, where you can see what's happening without stopping the data flow. TAPs are useful for checking the health and security of a network, as they help IT staff see any potential issues or threats in real time. In *Figure 25.9*, a network administrator is capturing data between the router and switch for analysis without impeding the network traffic.

A **Wi-Fi analyzer** helps troubleshoot and improve Wi-Fi networks. It checks things such as signal strength and interference from other networks or devices. This information is helpful for figuring out why a Wi-Fi connection might be slow or unreliable and making changes to improve it.

A **visual fault locator** (**VFL**) is used with fiber optic cables, which are special cables that send data as light signals. If there's a problem in the cable, such as a break or bend, the VFL sends a bright light through the cable so you can see where the issue is. This tool helps locate and fix problems quickly, so the cable can work properly.

Figure 25.10: Fiber optic VFL

Basic networking device commands

So far, you have seen some software and hardware tools that can be used to check different parts of your network. The software tools are applications or utilities used to perform various network diagnostics, analysis, and monitoring tasks; however, there are also commands that are specific for individual devices that gather information and make configuration changes at the hardware level. These commands are often accessible with commands such as access using **secure shell** (**SSH**) or a console. While the software tools mentioned earlier focus on analyzing your network and devices in a broader context, the commands discussed next are suited for concentrating on or configuring specific network devices.

show mac-address-table

show mac-address-table displays the MAC address table of a network device, typically a switch. It's helpful for tracking devices across the network and identifying where specific devices are physically located, and which ports they are using.

> **Note**
>
> SSH is covered in *Chapter 4, Explain Common Networking Ports, Protocols, Services, and Traffic Types.*

For example, to check the devices on a switch, you would first connect using SSH and then use the following command:

```
Switch# show mac-address-table
```

The output would look something like the following:

```
Mac Address Table
-------------------------------------------------
Vlan    Mac Address      Type       Ports
1       001a.2b3c.4d5e   DYNAMIC    Fa0/1
1       005f.6a7b.8c9d   STATIC     Fa0/2
```

This shows the VLAN that the switch is part of, in this case, *VLAN 1*, which is normally the default. Mac Address is the unique address for each connected device. Type tells you how that MAC address was learned; in this case, one is dynamic, meaning the switch discovered this MAC address on its own by listening to network traffic, rather than being told about it manually. Ports lists the specific ports that the devices are connected to, in this case, Fa0/1 (FastEthernet 0/1) and Fa0/2 (FastEthernet 0/2).

show route

show route displays the routing table on routers and Layer 3 switches, helping to diagnose routing issues or verify that routes are set up correctly.

After connecting to the device, use the following command:

```
show route
```

An example output would be as follows:

```
Codes: C - connected, S - static, R - RIP, B=BGP, O - OSPF
Gateway of last resort is 192.168.1.1 to network 0.0.0.0
C    192.168.1.0/24 is directly connected, FastEthernet0/0
S    10.0.0.0/8 [1/0] via 192.168.1.1
```

In the preceding output, C is the network directly connected to the router; 192.168.1.0/24 means the network address with a subnet mask of /24 (255.255.255.0), which covers IPs from 192.168.1.0 to 192.168.1.255.

S is the static route, so it was manually configured. 10.0.0.0/8 is the destination network with a subnet mask of /8 (255.0.0.0), which includes IPs from 10.0.0.0 to 10.255.255.255. [1/0] means that the administrative distance is 1 and the metric is 0. via 192.168.1.1 means the next hop for this route is 192.168.1.1, so traffic destined for the 10.0.0.0/8 network will be sent to this IP.

> **Note**
>
> Administrative distance and metric are covered in *Chapter 9, Explain Characteristics of Routing Technologies*.

If a device can't reach a certain network, you can check the routing table to verify that the route to that network exists. The gateway of last resort is known as the default route, which is used when a required route is not in the routing table.

show interface

The show interface command provides details about each interface on the device, including status, IP address, and error counts. This command can be used to check whether an interface is up and running and to view its health metrics, such as bandwidth usage and errors. If you wanted to check the FastEthernet 0/0 interface, you would use the following command:

```
show interface FastEthernet0/0
```

The output would be something like this:

```
FastEthernet0/0 is up, line protocol is up
Hardware is Fast Ethernet, address is 00e0.bb0d.5f01
Internet address is 192.168.1.1/24
MTU 1500 bytes, BW 100000 Kbit
```

The following explains the output.

- **Interface status**: FastEthernet0/0 is up and fully operational
- **Hardware type**: Indicates a 100 Mbps Ethernet interface
- **MAC address**: 00e0.bb0d.5f01
- **IP address**: 192.168.1.1/24 with a subnet mask of 255.255.255.0
- **MTU**: 1,500 bytes, the default size for an Ethernet network
- **BW**: The **bandwidth**, in this case, 100,000 Kbit, equivalent to 100 Mbps, typical for fast Ethernet

If an interface appears down, this command can reveal whether it's administratively disabled or has a physical connectivity problem:

Interface state	Description	Possible causes
Up/up	Interface is fully operational at both the physical (Layer 1) and protocol (Layer 2) levels	Normal working state; link is active and passing traffic
Down/down	Interface is physically and logically down	Cable unplugged, hardware failure, or no signal detected
Administratively down/down	Interface has been manually disabled by an administrator	Shutdown command applied in interface configuration
Up/down	Physical layer is up, but protocol layer is down	VLAN mismatch, no keepalive, duplex mismatch, or STP blocking
down/err-disabled	Interface is error-disabled due to a security or protocol violation	Port security violation, BPDU guard, or unidirectional link detection
up (suspended)/ down (suspended)	Interface is suspended by the system (often part of an EtherChannel)	Inconsistent EtherChannel config, incompatible port settings, and so on

Table 25.1: Connectivity problems

show config

show config shows the current configuration of a device, including IP addresses, VLANs, and security settings. This is particularly useful when setting up new devices or auditing device settings, as it's important to check for accuracy. The show config command could give the following output:

```
Current configuration:
!
hostname Router1
```

```
enable password cisco
!
interface FastEthernet0/0
ip address 192.168.1.1 255.255.255.0
```

This shows the current running configuration of the router, Router1. The enable password cisco command is used to enter privileged EXEC mode on the device, which allows for configuration and management of the device. It also shows the interface, FastEthernet0/0, which has the IP address of 192.168.1.1 and subnet mask of 255.255.255.0.

> **Note**
>
> show config may not work on all devices. On Cisco devices, the command is usually show running-config or show startup-config.

show arp

The show arp command displays the ARP table, which was covered earlier in the chapter, and is the IP-to-MAC address mappings on a device. This is normally run on routers (CISCO IOS) or Layer 3 switches. This is useful for understanding how devices communicate at the data link layer using MAC addresses while using IP addresses at the network layer. The output might look something like the following:

```
Protocol   Address      Age(min)   Hardware Addr   Type   Interface
Internet   192.168.1.2     2        00a0.c9f7.abc3  ARPA   FastEthernet0/0
```

This output tells us the following:

Protocol: Internet refers to the IP protocol, indicating that the entry corresponds to an IP address.

Address: The IP address of the device, in this case, 192.168.1.2.

Age (min): Indicates how long ago (in minutes) the ARP entry was learned or refreshed. In this case, the entry is 2 minutes old, so it's relatively recent.

Hardware Addr: The MAC address associated with the IP address, 00a0.c9f7.abc3.

Type: Typically ARPA, which denotes the encapsulation method used—in this case, Ethernet (standard Ethernet II framing).

`Interface`: The local interface through which the device with this IP is reachable—here, `FastEthernet0/0`.

Figure 25.11 shows a screenshot of the ARP cache in a Windows computer. You can run either the `arp -a` or `arp -g` command to view this.

```
C:\Users\Administrator.WIN-HB5RLG5VD60>ARP -A

Interface: 192.168.0.173 --- 0x6
  Internet Address      Physical Address      Type
  192.168.0.1           ac-f8-cc-8c-f9-80     dynamic
  192.168.0.93          22-a3-f6-cb-3b-3a     dynamic
  192.168.0.129         92-01-0c-48-f1-11     dynamic
  192.168.0.165         74-40-be-fa-a1-ba     dynamic
  192.168.0.255         ff-ff-ff-ff-ff-ff     static
  224.0.0.22            01-00-5e-00-00-16     static
  224.0.0.251           01-00-5e-00-00-fb     static
  224.0.0.252           01-00-5e-00-00-fc     static
  239.255.255.250       01-00-5e-7f-ff-fa     static
  255.255.255.255       ff-ff-ff-ff-ff-ff     static
```

Figure 25.11: Windows ARP cache

show vlan

`show vlan` lists the VLANs configured on a switch. This command is used to verify which VLANs are active on a switch and to check port assignments. It is essential for managing network segmentation.

The `show vlan` command would give the following output:

```
VLAN Name                   Status    Ports
---- ---------------------- --------- ----------------
1    default                active    Fa0/1, Fa0/2
10   Finance                active    Fa0/3, Fa0/4
```

This tells us there are two VLANs on this device, `VLAN 1` and `VLAN 10`. `VLAN 1` is the default VLAN, is active, and is assigned to ports `Fa0/1` and `Fa0/2`. `VLAN 10` is for the finance team, is active, and is assigned to ports `Fa0/3` and `Fa0/4`.

show power

`show power` displays power-related information, such as PoE status for connected devices. We use this command to check the power consumption of each port. This is particularly useful if devices such as IP phones or cameras are not powering on.

For example, to check a Cisco device, you would use the following command:

```
show power inline
```

The output could be something like this:

```
Interface      Power           Device
-----------    ------------    --------------------
Fa0/1          15.4 Watts      IP Phone
Fa0/2          7.0 Watts       Security Camera
```

This tells us that PoE is being used to supply power to two devices: IP Phone on the Fa0/1 interface and Security Camera on the Fa0/2 interface. The IP phone requires 15.4 watts, which is the maximum power available for a standard IEEE 802.3af PoE device, and the security camera is drawing 7.0 watts of power.

If a PoE device isn't turning on, this command can confirm whether the device is receiving power from the network switch.

Summary

The chapter covered a wide range of networking tools and protocols, providing a foundational guide to resolving common networking issues. Key software tools such as tcpdump, nmap, and netstat enable professionals to analyze traffic and manage network configurations, while hardware tools such as toners and TAPs assist with diagnosing physical connections. Additionally, tools such as LLDP/CDP aid in discovering devices within a network, and speed testers ensure that network performance meets expectations. Whether it's software or hardware, understanding when and how to use these tools is crucial for effective network management and troubleshooting.

The knowledge gained in this chapter will prepare you to answer questions relating to exam objective 5.5 in the *CompTIA Network+ (N10-009)* exam.

Exam objective 5.5

Given a scenario, use the appropriate tool or protocol to solve networking issues.

Software tools:

- **Protocol analyzer:** Captures and analyzes network traffic data
- **Command line:** Provides text-based network diagnostics:
    - `ping`: Tests network connectivity between devices
    - `traceroute`/`tracert`: Traces the path packets take across a network
    - `nslookup`: Queries DNS to obtain domain or IP information
    - `tcpdump`: Captures and analyzes network packets
    - `dig`: Performs DNS lookups and troubleshooting
    - `netstat`: Displays network connections and protocol statistics
    - `ip`/`ifconfig`/`ipconfig`: Configures and displays network interfaces
    - `arp`: Resolves IP addresses to MAC addresses on a local network
    - `nmap`: Scans networks for open ports and vulnerabilities
- **LLDP/CDP:** Identifies connected network devices
- **Speed tester:** Measures internet connection speed

Hardware tools:

- **Toner:** Traces and identifies cables
- **Cable tester:** Tests and verifies network cable integrity
- **TAPs:** Monitors network traffic passively
- **Wi-Fi analyzer:** Analyzes and optimizes wireless networks
- **Visual fault locator:** Identifies fiber optic cable faults with visible light

Basic networking device commands:

- `show mac-address-table`: Displays MAC addresses associated with network ports
- `show route`: Shows the routing table and network paths
- `show interface`: Displays interface status and statistics
- `show config`: Displays current device configuration
- `show arp`: Shows ARP table mapping IP addresses to MAC addresses

- `show vlan`: Displays VLAN configuration and status
- `show power`: Shows device power usage and status

Chapter review questions

Now that you've completed the chapter, you can check your knowledge using the practice questions provided in the online platform at `https://packt.link/N10-009ch25`. You can also use the QR code below. Accessing these questions requires you to unlock the accompanying online content first. Head over to Chapter 26 for detailed instructions.

26

Accessing the Online Practice Resources

Your copy of *CompTIA® Network+® N10-009 Certification Guide,* comes with free online practice resources. Use these to hone your exam readiness even further by attempting practice questions on the companion website. The website is user-friendly and can be accessed from mobile, desktop, and tablet devices. It also includes interactive timers for an exam-like experience.

How to Access These Materials

Here's how you can start accessing these resources depending on your source of purchase.

Purchased from Packt Store (packtpub.com)

If you've bought the book from the Packt store (packtpub.com) eBook or Print, head to https://packt.link/N10-009unlock. There, log in using the same Packt account you created or used to purchase the book.

If you face any issues accessing your free resources, contact us at customercare@packt.com.

Purchased from Amazon and Other Sources

If you've purchased from sources other than the ones mentioned above (like *Amazon*), you'll need to unlock the resources first by entering your unique sign-up code provided in this section. **Unlocking takes less than 10 minutes, can be done from any device, and needs to be done only once.** Follow these five easy steps to complete the process:

STEP 1

Open the link `https://packt.link/N10-009unlock` OR scan the following **QR code** (*Figure 26.1*):

Figure 26.1: QR code for the page that lets you unlock this book's free online content

Either of those links will lead to the following page as shown in *Figure 26.2*:

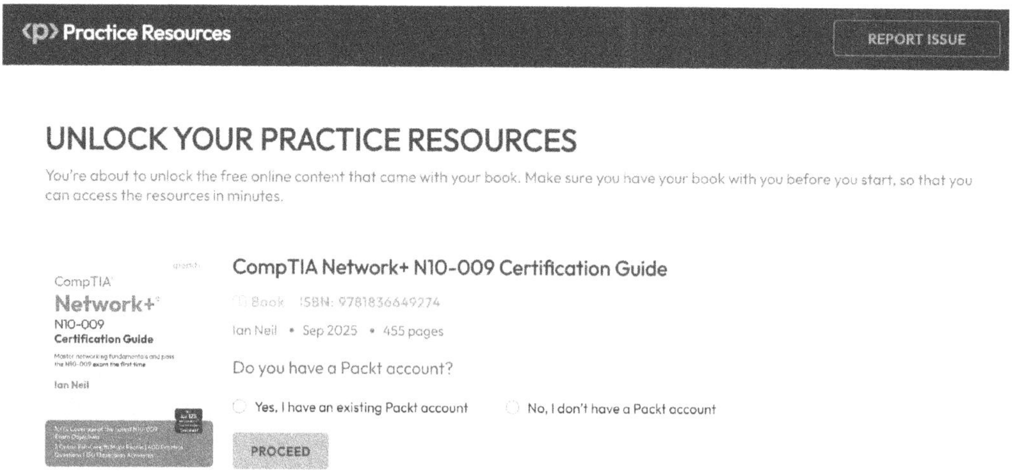

Figure 26.2: Unlock page for the online practice resources

STEP 2

If you already have a Packt account, select the option **Yes, I have an existing Packt account**. If not, select the option **No, I don't have a Packt account**.

If you don't have a Packt account, you'll be prompted to create a new account on the next page. It's free and only takes a minute to create.

Click **Proceed** after selecting one of those options.

STEP 3

After you've created your account or logged in to an existing one, you'll be directed to the following page as shown in *Figure 26.3*.

Make a note of your unique unlock code:

LIY2432

Type in or copy this code into the text box labeled **Enter Unique Code:**

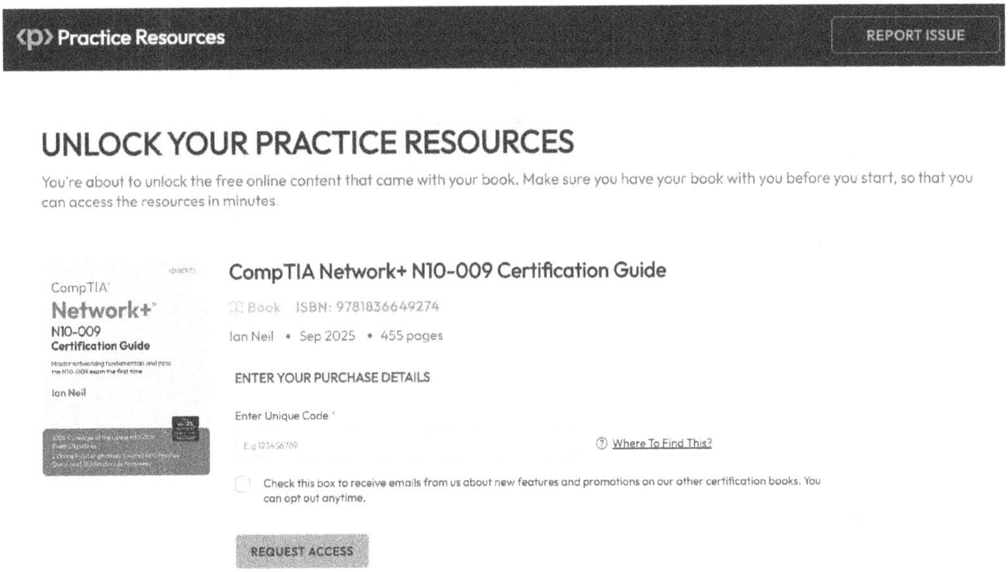

Figure 26.3: Enter your unique sign-up code to unlock the resources

Troubleshooting tip

After creating an account, if your connection drops off or you accidentally close the page, you can reopen the page shown in *Figure 26.2* and select **Yes, I have an existing account**. Then, sign in with the account you had created before you closed the page. You'll be redirected to the screen shown in *Figure 26.3*.

STEP 4

Note

You may choose to opt into emails regarding feature updates and offers on our other certification books. We don't spam, and it's easy to opt out at any time.

Click **Request Access**.

STEP 5

If the code you entered is correct, you'll see a button that says **OPEN PRACTICE RESOURCES**, as shown in *Figure 26.4*:

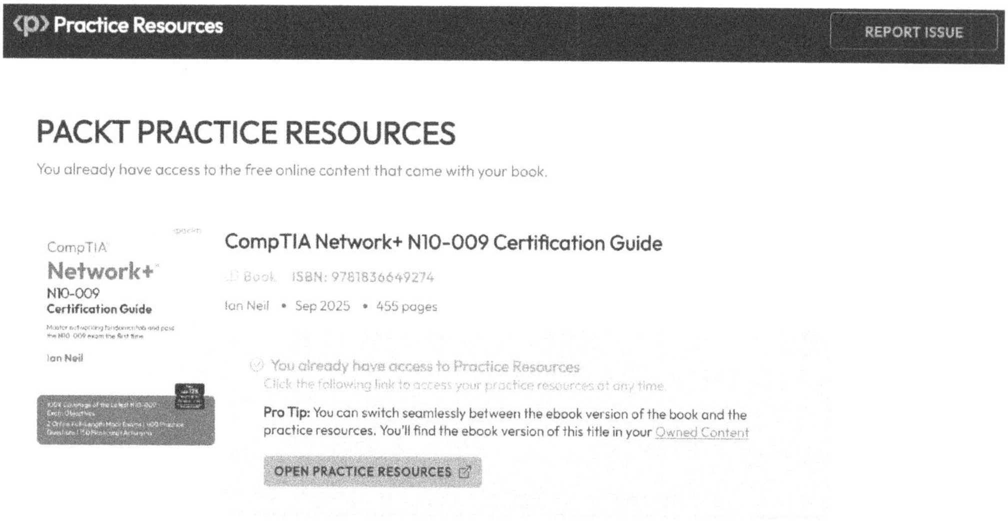

Figure 26.4: Page that shows up after a successful unlock

Click the **OPEN PRACTICE RESOURCES** link to start using your free online content. You'll be redirected to the Dashboard shown in *Figure 26.5*:

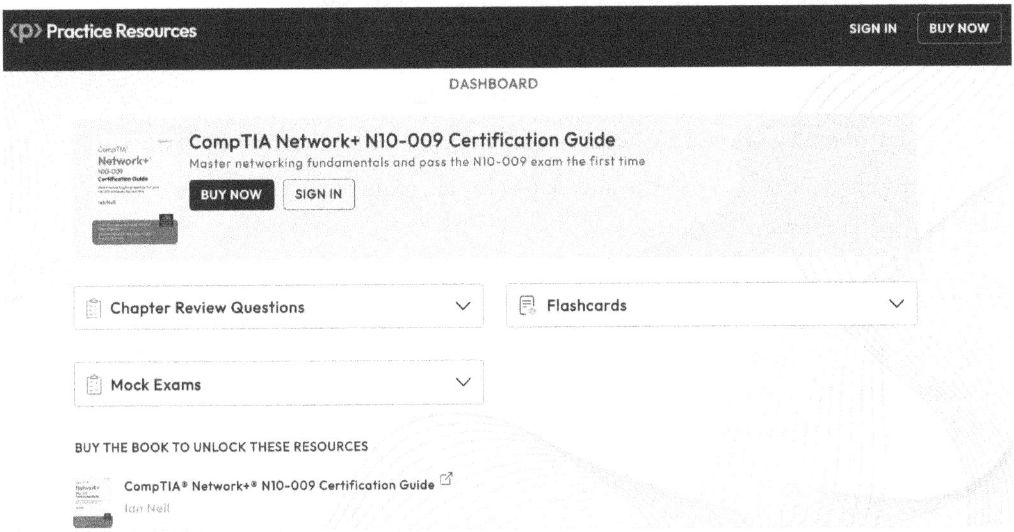

Figure 26.5: Dashboard page for Network+ N10-009 practice resources

Bookmark this link

Now that you've unlocked the resources, you can come back to them anytime by visiting https://packt.link/N10-009 or scanning the following QR code provided in *Figure 26.6*:

Figure 26.6: QR code to bookmark practice resources website

Troubleshooting Tips

If you're facing issues unlocking, here are three things you can do:

- Double-check your unique code. All unique codes in our books are case-sensitive and your code needs to match exactly as it is shown in *STEP 3*.
- If that doesn't work, use the **Report Issue** button located at the top-right corner of the page.
- If you're not able to open the unlock page at all, write to customercare@packt.com and mention the name of the book.

Share Feedback

If you find any issues with the platform, the book, or any of the practice materials, you can click the **Share Feedback** button from any page and reach out to us. If you have any suggestions for improvement, you can share those as well.

> **Note**
>
> Certain elements of the website might change over time and thus may end up looking different from how they are represented in the screenshots of this book

‹packt›

packtpub.com

Subscribe to our online digital library for full access to over 7,000 books and videos, as well as industry leading tools to help you plan your personal development and advance your career. For more information, please visit our website.

Why subscribe?

- Spend less time learning and more time coding with practical eBooks and Videos from over 4,000 industry professionals
- Improve your learning with Skill Plans built especially for you
- Get a free eBook or video every month
- Fully searchable for easy access to vital information
- Copy and paste, print, and bookmark content

At www.packt.com, you can also read a collection of free technical articles, sign up for a range of free newsletters, and receive exclusive discounts and offers on Packt books and eBooks.

Other Books You May Enjoy

If you enjoyed this book, you may be interested in these other books by Packt:

CompTIA® Security+® SY0-701 Certification Guide, Third Edition

Ian Neil

ISBN: 978-1-83546-153-2

- Differentiate between various security control types
- Apply mitigation techniques for enterprise security
- Evaluate security implications of architecture models
- Protect data by leveraging strategies and concepts
- Implement resilience and recovery in security
- Automate and orchestrate for running secure operations
- Execute processes for third-party risk assessment and management
- Conduct various audits and assessments with specific purposes

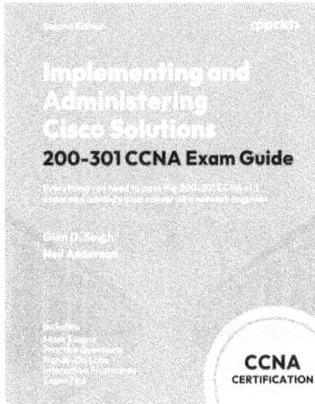

Implementing and Administering Cisco Solutions 200-301 CCNA Exam Guide, Second Edition

Glen D. Singh and Neil Anderson

ISBN: 978-1-83588-748-6

- Understand how switching, routing, and IP addressing work in network environments
- Create VLANs and configure static and dynamic routing using Cisco CLI commands
- Set up IP services including DHCP, NAT, DNS, and NTP across network devices
- Apply wireless settings, security features, and access control to secure networks
- Use Cisco Packet Tracer to build, test, and troubleshoot network configurations
- Solve realistic practice questions that mirror the actual CCNA 200-301 v1.1 exam format

Packt is searching for authors like you

If you're interested in becoming an author for Packt, please visit authors.packtpub.com and apply today. We have worked with thousands of developers and tech professionals, just like you, to help them share their insight with the global tech community. You can make a general application, apply for a specific hot topic that we are recruiting an author for, or submit your own idea.

Share your thoughts

Now you've finished *CompTIA® Network+® N10-009 Certification Guide*, we'd love to hear your thoughts! Scan the QR code below to go straight to the Amazon review page for this book and share your feedback or leave a review on the site that you purchased it from.

https://packt.link/r/1836649274

Your review is important to us and the tech community and will help us make sure we're delivering excellent quality content.

Index

Z

Coupon Code for CompTIA Network+ N10-009 Exam Vouchers

Coupon Code for 12% Off on CompTIA Network+ N10-009 Exam Vouchers

Take advantage of the 12% discount by following the below instructions:

1. Go to `https://www.testforless.store/discounts`.
2. Click the **Buy Now** button.
3. Add the **exam voucher** to your cart.
4. From your cart, verify your credentials and product details. Then, proceed to **check out**.
5. The **12% discount** is already applied. No promo code is required.

Note

This is a global voucher and is available for tests anywhere in the world.

www.ingramcontent.com/pod-product-compliance
Lightning Source LLC
Chambersburg PA
CBHW081218220326
41598CB00037B/6816